INTANGIBLE HERITAGE

**EXPEDITIONS, OBSERVATIONS AND
LECTURES BY ROBERTO BURLE MARX
AND COLLABORATORS**

María A. Villalobos H. and Carla Urbina

with the participation of:
Jacques Leenhardt
José Tabacow
Isabela de Carvalho Ono
Lúcia Maria Sá Antunes Costa
Oscar Bressane
Sítio Roberto Burle Marx
Instituto Burle Marx
Botanical City

INTANGIBLE HERITAGE

EXPEDITIONS, OBSERVATIONS AND LECTURES BY ROBERTO BURLE MARX AND COLLABORATORS

María A. Villalobos H. and Carla Urbina

with the participation of:
Jacques Leenhardt
José Tabacow
Isabela de Carvalho Ono
Lúcia Maria Sá Antunes Costa
Oscar Bressane
Sítio Roberto Burle Marx
Instituto Burle Marx
Botanical City

Illinois Institute of Technology
Arquine

Intangible Heritage: Expeditions, Observations and Lectures by Roberto Burle Marx and Collaborators
First edition, 2022
ISBN 978-607-8880-09-6

© Arquine, S. A. de C. V.
Ámsterdam 163 A
Hipódromo, 06100
Mexico City
arquine.com

© IIT Architecture Press
College of Architecture
3360 South State Street
Chicago, IL 60616-3793
United States
arch.iit.edu

Illinois Institute of Technology

Dean
Reed Kroloff
IIT College of Architecture

Coordination
Sasha Zanko
MCHAP Program Coordinator

Amber Lochner
Academic Administrative
Assistant

Research, writing, translation and editing
María A. Villalobos H. and Carla Urbina

Titles of original texts in Portuguese
Burle Marx, R. (1984). *Expedição Burle Marx a Amazônia* – 1983. *Rio de Janeiro*: CNPq

Leenhardt, J. (2016). *Nos jardins de Burle Marx*. *São Paulo*: Editora Perspectiva

Burle Marx, R. Tabacow, J. (1987). *Arte e Paisagem. São Paulo*: Livraria Nobel S. A.

Tabacow, J. (2004). *Arte e Paisagem. São Paulo*: Editorial Livros Studio Nobel Ltda.

Title of the original text in French
Leenhardt, J. (1994). *Dans les jardins de Roberto Burle Marx*. Le Crestet: Actes Sud

Foreword
Lúcia Maria Sá Antunes Costa

Prologues
Isabela de Carvalho Ono

Revision of the translations of original texts
Jacques Leenhardt
José Tabacow
Oscar Bressane

Revision of botanical terms
Caetano Troncoso

Cladogram
María A. Villalobos H. and Benjamin Jensen

Maps
María A. Villalobos H. and Gu Yuxuan

Conceptualization and graphic design
María A. Villalobos H. and Carla Urbina

Design of figures and graphic editing
Natalia Castillo

English translation of Patrimonio Inmaterial
Angela Kay Bunning

English translation of Botanical Tables
Jorge Mayorga

Arquine

Director
Miquel Adrià

Editorial coordination
Andrea Griborio
Brenda Soto Suárez

Digital layout
Estudio la fe ciega
Domingo N. Martínez
Yolanda Garibay

ACKNOWLEDGMENTS

Illinois Institute of Technology
College of Architecture, Chicago, United States
Raj Echambadi, President
Alicia Bunton, Assistant Vice President Community Affairs
Ron Henderson, Professor, Master of Landscape Architecture + Urbanism

Sítio Roberto Burle Marx SRBM, Rio de Janeiro, Brazil
Claudia Storino, Director
Marlon da Costa Sousa, Technical Director
Caetano Troncoso, Technical Division
Jéssica Santana, Executive Secretary

Escritório Burle Marx Ltda. e Instituto Burle Marx,
Rio de Janeiro, Brazil
Isabela de Carvalho Ono, Director
Tatiana Leiner, Coordinator

Universidade Federal do Rio de Janeiro, UFRJ. PROURB
Lúcia Maria Sá Antunes Costa, Professor

Jardim Botânico do Rio de Janeiro, Rio de Janeiro, Brazil
Rafaela Campostrini Forzza, Herbarium
Maria Da Penha Fernandes Ferreira, Library

Instituto Moreira Salles, Rio de Janeiro, Brazil
Vera Lucia F. Silva Nascimento, Deputy Executive Coordinator

École nationale supérieure de paysage, Versailles, France
Catherine Chomarat-Ruiz and Pierre Donadieu

Fundación Jardín Botánico de Maracaibo

Universidad Rafael Urdaneta, URU, Maracaibo, Venezuela

Universidad del Zulia, LUZ, Maracaibo, Venezuela

University of Pennsylvania, Philadelphia, United States

Botanical City

A special acknowledgment to the Phyllis Lambert Endowment Funds

The authors would like to extend special thanks to the people and institutions that helped support the principles expressed in this publication, with particular importance placed on the photographic work by: Adrián Capelo Cruz, Adriano Gambarini, Andry Jons, Bernard Picton, Caetano Troncoso, Carlo Rodríguez, Clauss Meier, Danilo Alvarenga Zavatin, Eduardo Izaguirre, Enrique Ascanio, Felipe Werneck, José Tabacow, Koiti Mori, Leonardo Leiva, Ligia Ararat, Luiz Alberto Gomes Cancio, Marcella Del Signore, Marcos Santos, Marcos V. A. Villalobos H., Marlon de Souza, Matt Lavin, Oscar Bressane, Pedro Romero, Robert T. Wahlen, Rodolph Delfino and Trisgel Labrador.

The publisher has made every effort to ensure that the URLs for all external references in this book were correct at the time of printing. The publisher is not responsible for the websites and cannot guarantees that the sites will remain active or that the content will remain available. All efforts have been made to recognize copyrights. If any have not been reflected, or have been cited incorrectly, the publisher commits to making the necessary revisions in any future reprints and new editions.

CONTENTS

8   **Foreword**
Lúcia Maria Sá Antunes Costa

12   **Prologue**
Isabela de Carvalho Ono

20   **Introduction**
María A. Villalobos H. and Carla Urbina

31   **I. Burle Marx's Expedition to the Amazon — 1983**
Roberto Burle Marx

96   Landscape Architecture and Devastation, 1983

107   **II. Landscape, Botany and Ecology: Interviews with Roberto Burle Marx
from the book *Dans les jardins de Roberto Burle Marx* — 1994**
Jacques Leenhardt

163   **III. Selected Lectures from the book *Arte & Paisagem: Conferências escolhidas* — 1954-1983**
Roberto Burle Marx. José Tabacow (org.)

167   Landscape Design in Large Areas, 1962
189   Considerations on Brazilian Art, 1966
211   Garden and Ecology, 1967
241   Landscape Architecture and Brazilian Flora, 1975
267   Landscape Resources of Brazil, 1976
291   Statement to the Federal Senate, 1976
313   Problems with Nature Conservation, 1976
321   The Involvement of Botanists in My Professional Training, 1983
335   Landscape Design in the Urban Structure, 1983

348   **Nature as a Source**
José Tabacow

352   **Suggested bibliography and chronology
of urban landscape designs by Roberto Burle Marx
and collaborators included in this book**

354   **Bibliography**

FOREWORD
LÚCIA MARIA SÁ ANTUNES COSTA[1]

Roberto Burle Marx, one of the most important Brazilians of the 20th century, introduced an innovative language to modern landscape architecture that had a lasting influence, not only in Brazil but also beyond its borders. His work continues to be disseminated and discussed nationally and internationally, which stands as a testimony to the fertile and fruitful terrain of his work as a whole.

Intangible Heritage: Expeditions, Observations and Lectures by Roberto Burle Marx and Collaborators offers the English-language reader a selection of texts and interviews relevant to the understanding of his work and his legacy in the construction of modern landscape design. The selection of these texts, their translation into Spanish and English, and their publication, are the result of research by María A. Villalobos H. and Carla Urbina – two landscape architects and tireless researchers dedicated to the protection and dissemination of the work of Burle Marx.

We came into contact for the first time as a result of their passionate defense of the Maracaibo Botanical Garden (MBG) in Venezuela, designed by Burle Marx in collaboration with the Venezuelan botanist Leandro Aristeguieta. The garden was in a state of decline and in serious risk of irreparable damage. The comprehensive rehabilitation plan for the MBG, which Villalobos and Urbina developed and managed, was presented for the first time to the scientific community at the IFLA[2] World Congress in *Rio de Janeiro* in 2009 and served as a fundamental element in the garden's protection. This restoration work (see Urbina and Villalobos 2014) earned Carla and María the National Architecture Award at the XII Caracas Architecture Biennial in 2017, an important recognition of their efforts to preserve the botanical garden, which, together with the *Parque del Este*, constitutes a large part of Burle Marx's landscape legacy in Venezuela.

For this book, María Villalobos and Carla Urbina formulated a proposal that goes beyond the simple translation of Burle Marx's writings. Here, his discourse is expanded with a careful selection of photographs, engravings, designs and other images that enter into a dialogue with his texts and help readers better understand his landscape universe, while also offering contextualization for his way of thinking and working. The images are not merely illustrative, they are part of the initial purpose behind the book: the dissemination and intensification of the understanding of a significant portion of Burle Marx's work. This research adds an incredibly original quality to the book, and it takes a create approach to conveying important aspects of the legacy left behind by Brazil's most important landscape architect.

Among other relevant aspects of Burle Marx's legacy, this book highlights one of the fundamental interdisciplinary practices in his career, which influenced the practices of Brazilian landscape designers for years: his joint work with botanists. In several of his texts and lectures, he recognizes the importance, impact, and repercussions of his associations with botanists, and this question is also widely discussed in the national and international literature on his work (e.g., Tabacow 2011, Adams 1991, among many others).

Beginning w th Burle Marx, the practice of associating with botanists was incorporated by many of the important Brazilian landscape architects who came after, including Rosa Kliass in *São Paulo* and Fernando Chacel in *Rio de Janeiro*, who, in turn, expanded these interdisciplinary collaborations into other fields of knowledge based on their design interests.

It should be noted that this influence was not one-sided. It wasn't just the botanists who had a strong influence on Burle Marx. In his turn, he influenced many botanists, broadening their visions of the plant world beyond taxonomy and other aspects specific to the discipline, and highlighting the potential of plants in the construction of new landscapes. In that sense, Burle Marx's contribution to the field of botany, and beyond the field of landscape architecture, is indisputable.

Intangible Heritage: Expeditions, Observations and Lectures by Roberto Burle Marx and Collaborators offers one of the lectures he gave to the Sociedade Botânica do Brasil after his expedition to the Amazon. In it, he talks passionately about being dazzled by the local vegetation and expresses his indignation at the loss of Brazilian plant heritage because of public policies permitting deforestation.

This aspect of collaboration was always emphasized by the botanist Luiz Emygdio de Mello Filho who, in addition to undertaking significant work in *Rio de Janeiro* as the director of the Department of Parks and Gardens, worked with Burle Marx on important public projects in that region, such as the *Plaza Salgado Filho* in front of the *Santos Dumont Airport* and the *Parque do Flamengo*, among many others. In addition, the two colleagues went on var ous botanical expeditions together to collect plant species (see Tabacow 2011). Luiz Emygdio used to say that Burle Marx was the closest thing to a botanist among landscape architects, and Burle Marx would say that Luiz Emygdio was the closest thing to a landscape architect among botanists. Their mutual respect was evident not only in their words, but in their discoveries of certain new plant species, which they each named for the other – such as *Heliconia aemygdiana*, first described by Burle Marx, or *Heliconia burle-marxii*, described by Luiz Emygdio and named in honor of his colleague.

This book offers a broad visual synthesis of the species associated with Burle Marx and invites the reader to further pursue this avenue of investigation.

Lúcia Maria Sá Antunes Costa is coordinator of the Landscape Architecture Research Group (PAISA) for the postgraduate program in Urbanism (PROURB) at the School of Architecture and Urbanism (FAU) at the Universidade Federal do Rio de Janeiro and founder of the first and only Master's program in landscape architecture in Brazil: the Professional Master's Degree in Landscape Architecture. She earned a degree in architecture from the Universidade Santa Úrsula in 1980 and a PhD in Landscape Architecture from University College London in 1992. Her dissertation *"Popular Values for Urban Parks. A Case Study of the Changing Meanings of Parque do Flamengo in Rio de Janeiro"* (1992) discusses the role of Burle Marx's landscape designs in the construction of the urban landscape. Her most recent publication, organized together with Maria Cecilia Barbieri Gorski, *"O livro da Rosa – vivência e paisagens"*, presents the personal and professional experiences of the landscape architect Rosa Grena Kliass. The publication received the 2021 prize from the Institute of Architects of Brazil.

[2] International Federation of Landscape Architects (IFLA).

Although Burle Marx worked masterfully with other materials from the universe of landscape design – stones, water, soil, among many others – there was an undeniable compositional predominance of plant life in his designs. Adams (1991, p. 25) highlights the importance of the knowledge of plants in Burle Marx's professional activity: *"Because of his sophisticated horticultural knowledge, Burle Marx was taking a direction far different from anything proposed by contemporary architects or by garden designers in Europe."*

He argues that the advances in architecture based on the international experiences of modernism did not have a corollary in the field of landscape design until the emergence of Burle Marx's innovative proposals. This is evident in his recognition as *"the creator of the modern garden"* by the *American Institute of Architects*, as highlighted by Sima (1991). Burle Marx's profound knowledge of plants came both from his relationship with botanists and from a long training process that involved participation in a variety of other activities. Among the ones that appear in the texts selected for this book, it is worth highlighting two in particular: the construction of his plant collection and the realization of botanical expeditions through Brazil.

Few landscape architects built a space of the magnitude and relevance of the former *Sítio Santo Antônio da Bica* – now called the *Sítio Roberto Burle Marx* – to house their plant collections and to support studies and experiments in the fields of botany and landscape design. This slow process, which began at the end of the 1940s, was essential to the construction of Burle Marx's vision of landscape design as an experimental field. While some areas of the *Sítio* were structured, essentially definitive landscape interventions, others were sites for experimentation and new discoveries, landscapes into which Burle Marx introduced constant changes. He liked to say that the *Sítio* was his *cadinho* [melting pot][3] – a place where he deliberately tried out new combinations and associations, experimenting with the interdisciplinarities that are so characteristic of his work. Burle Marx was not just a plant collector, he was also a scholar with an adventurous spirit. A professional who was observant and curious about the plant world, he initially began studying plants for their beauty and sculptural possibilities, and later because he realized that understanding botanical and ecological questions would enable him to work more effectively with their associations. With that in mind, he began his travels. Over the course of several years, Burle Marx organized various expeditions to different Brazilian biomes to collect plant species and to learn about their associations in their natural habitats.

Intangible Heritage: Expeditions, Observations and Lectures by Roberto Burle Marx and Collaborators includes the English version of the report from one of his most important expeditions: to the Brazilian Amazon, carried out in 1983, when Burle Marx was more than 70 years old. This expedition stands out from the rest for a number of reasons. First, because, among other sources of funding, it received support from the CNPq,[4] one of the most important public research development agencies in Brazil. This demonstrates the Brazilian scientific community's recognition of the research nature of this expedition, as well as its relevance in terms of knowledge production. The texts included in this book also highlighted that a large number of the species the team collected were pressed locally and sent to research institutions in Brazil. Live plants, in turn, were sent directly to the *Sítio*, where Burle Marx did his studies on the propagation and use of species in landscape design, together with his botanist colleagues.

In addition, the expedition to the Amazon took place at a time when the integrity of the forests was being threatened. This book also highlights Burle Marx's role as one of the voices condemning the intense destruction of the Brazilian Amazon as early as the 1980s. He took a firm and courageous stance: even during the period of the Brazilian dictatorship, he spoke out publicly and with indignation against what he referred to as a crime, a devastation, a disaster, and an environmental tragedy. Burle Marx repeatedly stood up against the public policies of the Brazilian dictatorial government that endangered the landscapes of the expansive Brazilian biomes, mainly the Amazon.

Burle Marx was a bold and passionate activist, unafraid to make a strong stand (see also Nordenson 2018). He openly criticized the policy of deforestation and occupation of the forest that failed to consider environmental standards, during a period when Brazil was still living under the rule of the military dictatorship, albeit in its final years. For these and many other elements, *Intangible Heritage: Expeditions, Observations and Lectures by Roberto Burle Marx and Collaborators* offers English-language readers the possibility for new analyses of a multi-faceted scholarly legacy that will no doubt broaden the understanding of Burle Marx's immense contributions, in his role – in the words of Mello Filho (1994, p. 18) – as the *"landscape architect whose presence and work dignified the 20th century"*.

[3] See the documentary "Eu, Roberto Burle Marx", 1989, video by Tamara Leftel and Soraia Cals.

[4] National Council for Scientific and Technological Development.

Works Cited:
Adams, William H. (1991). *Roberto Burle Marx: The Unnatural Art of the Garden*. New York: The Museum of Modern Art.
Nordenson, Catherine S. (2018). *Depositions: Roberto Burle Marx and Public Landscapes under Dictatorship*. Austin: University of Texas Press.
Mello Filho, Luiz Emygdio de. (1998). *"Botânica e Arquitetura – ou, segundo a ordem alfabética, Arquitetura e Botânica"*. In Costa, L.M.S.A (ed.) *Anais do I Encontro de Ensino de Paisagismo em Escolas de Arquitetura*. Rio de Janeiro: PROURB, pp. 15-18.
Motta, Flavio (1984). *Roberto Burle Marx e a nova visão da paisagem*. São Paulo: Nobel. Tabacow, José. (2011). *"La Science de la perception"*. In Cavalcanti, L.; El-Dahdah, F. and Rambert, F. (eds.) *Roberto Burle Marx: La modernité du paysage*. Paris: Cité de l'Architecture/Actar, pp. 63-67.
Sima, Eliovson. (1991). *The Gardens of Roberto Burle Marx*. London: Thames and Hudson.
Urbina, Carla and Villalobos, María (2014) *"Rehabilitación integral del Jardín Botánico de Maracaibo. Recuperación del paisaje cultural como patrimonio, obra de Roberto Burle Marx"*. Last accessed April 15, 2021 at: http://trienal.fau.ucvve/2014/cd/PDF/hyp/HP-19.pdf.

PROLOGUE
ISABELA DE CARVALHO ONO[5]

Figure 1. Haruyoshi Ono and Roberto Burle Marx in the garden at the *Escritório de Paisagismo Burle Marx*. *Laranjeiras*, Street *Cardoso Júnior, Rio de Janeiro,* Brazil. Photograph: Claus Meyer, date unknown. Archive of the *Instituto Burle Marx*.

During his childhood, in the context of his own family, Roberto Burle Marx faced the challenges of understanding and combining very different cultural experiences: his parents came from a materially advanced Europe and from a South America where there was still much progress to be made. Born in the city of *São Paulo* in 1909, he was the fourth of six children born to Wilhelm Marx, a German from Stuttgart, and Cecília Burle, a Brazilian from Recife. He grew up in a cultured and well-off family, who valued the arts as an important part of a child's education. Encouraged by his mother and his nanny, Anna Piaseck, he was fascinated by the world of plants from an early age. In 1913, the family moved to *Rio de Janeiro*, then the federal capital of Brazil, and settled in the Leme neighborhood.

At the beginning of 1928, Burle Marx and his family spent an extended period in Berlin. It was then that he was able to make his first visits to major international museums, and he came into contact with works by the central figures in European modern art, from Van Gogh to Kandinsky. He also visited the tropical greenhouses of the Dahlem Botanical Garden, where he had his first contact with the richness and diversity of the Brazilian biomes. Returning to *Rio de Janeiro* in October 1929, Burle Marx reenrolled at the School of Fine Arts, on the suggestion of Lucio Costa, his neighbor and oldest friend, to study painting. An enormously important figure in the career of the young Burle Marx, Lucio Costa was responsible for helping him secure his first two projects in landscape design: the gardens of the residences of Alfredo Schwartz (1932) and Ronan Borges (1933), both n *Rio de Janeiro*. Costa also provided fundamental support by introducing Burle Marx into the social circles of modern writers, artists and architects in Rio and around the country, which quickly brought about new job opportunities. That is how Burle Marx arrived in Recife to take over the direction of the Municipal Department of Parks and Gardens in the period from 1935 to 1937.

In the growing city of Recife, which was looking to update its urban development, the 26-year-old landscaper launched an experimental program for the renovation of existing squares and parks, which also proposed creating new spaces. But what was the initiative's goal? It consisted of introducing tropical Brazilian plants that had been absent or used very infrequently in Brazilian urban areas up to that point. Two projects are particularly noteworthy in this regard: the *Cactário da Madalena* and the *Jardín de Casa Forte*. Now called the *Praça Euclides da*

[5] **Isabela de Carvalho Ono** has been the director of the *Escritório de Paisagismo Burle Marx since 2017* and director of the *Instituto Burle Marx* since 2019. She earned her degree from the Faculty of Architecture and Urbanism at the Federal University of Rio de Janeiro in 1997 and completed her Master's Degree in Landscape Architecture at the PROURB-UFRJ in 2004. She joined the *Escritório de Paisagismo Burle Marx* in 1992 as an architecture student, on invitation from her father, Haruyoshi Ono. Starting in 2004, she became a partner at the company, acting as co-author in the conception and development of various national and international landscaping projects, including the *Tropical Island* (Berlin), the renovation of the *Parque do Flamengo* (*Rio de Janeiro*) and the *Praça da Revolução* (*Acre*). From 2004 to 2006 she was a professor of landscape architecture for the Faculty of Architecture and Urbanism at the Pontifical Catholic University of Rio de Janeiro (PUC-RJ).

Cunha, the *Cactário da Madalena* focused on typical species from the *caatinga* biome, showcasing plants collected in area around Recife, in an unprecedented initiative to support their use in public gardens there and in other cities around the country. The *Jardim Casa Forte* introduced another protocol that was no less exciting and pioneering at the time: using species mainly from the Amazon biome, including everything from aquatic plants to marshland flora and trees.

Unflagging, visionary, and unique, Roberto Burle Marx was an artist with a multifaceted spirit and a humanistic education, who introduced concepts from architecture, ecology, botany, landscaping, design, and science into his work. He understood landscape design as a living art form to be experienced and explored through the creation of new spaces and unexpected perspectives with the power to spark curiosity and reveal the qualities of the landscape. From the beginning of his career, he sought to transcend the limits between the fields of landscape design, art and architecture, while questioning how we live in cities. His landscape designs responded to his pursuit of aesthetic expression, taking on a transitory and changeable character that can be transformed by the dynamics of the natural elements and by the experiences, involvement and use on the part of the community. In his organic or geometric compositions, he planned out an organized nature, using principles adopted from the arts such as form, texture, volume, color contrasts and shadows to transform the space. Much of his work carried a sense of timelessness and perfection.

With an admiration and undeniable respect for nature, early in his career Burle Marx learned to observe the natural landscapes of Brazil and to draw profound lessons from them, which he applied in the creation of new gardens, recognizing and giving new meaning to the exuberance of Brazilian flora. Throughout his life, he demonstrated a true fascination for natural landscapes, the complex plant associations they include, and the dynamics that exist in the relationships between natural elements (vegetation, water, rock formations, air, wind), which always inspired him in the creation of new gardens, parks and works of art.

Also noteworthy are the purpose of his public discourse and his environmental activism, touching on issues that are still at the center of global debates, such as environmental conservation and the fight against the devastation of biomes and the extinction of species, adopting a perspective that is fully aligned with today's global agenda and the Sustainable Development Goals for 2030. Beyond the arguments he laid out in his public speeches, he put his environmental activism into practice through a powerful, everyday aesthetic experience that can be felt in his landscape designs, and through the planning and implementation of projects to make cities greener and healthier. Burle Marx connected different areas of knowledge such as art, landscape, botany, architecture, and the environment so that they could be applied to people's daily lives in cities. He was one of the pioneers in the fight for the preservation of Brazilian biomes and his agenda included discussions about the environment and sustainability from the very beginning of his career, and with more intensity starting in 1960. At the same time, he drew on the formal concepts from the visual arts, he never lost sight of the issues and human experiences inherent in the process of creating green spaces and new built landscapes.

With the aim of broadening the debate, exchanging knowledge, and reflecting on the contributions of Roberto Burle Marx and his collaborators through the preservation and dissemination of their landscape tradition, the *Instituto Burle Marx* was founded in 2019, housing more than 120,000 items in different formats related to the trajectory of the Brazilian designer and his team. Headquartered in the city of *Rio de Janeiro*, it is a non-profit civil organization, created for the purpose of disseminating the importance of the collective contributions of Roberto Burle Marx and his collaborators to the world, as well as inspiring new initiatives and celebrating their art.

At the end of 2019, in addition to receiving its first international support through the *Leon Levy Foundation* and private donors from Brazil, the *Instituto Burle Marx* signed a technical association agreement with the *Instituto Moreira Salles* to safeguard and preserve more than 70,000 unpublished drawings from the "Haruyoshi Ono Collection" documenting the day-to-day of Burle Marx's work — landscape designs, expeditions, works of art and botanical species. Haruyoshi Ono was Burle Marx's creative partner for almost three decades and was appointed by Burle Marx himself to take over the design studio and protect its material legacy, contained in the studio's documentary collection.

In 2020, as the inventory and cataloging process began, Burle Marx's ongoing desire to recognize and expand knowledge on Brazilian natural biomes showed through clearly in the material from the archive. In addition to the environmental questions, many articles from the archive at the *Instituto*, some of which were translated for this book, demonstrate the broad universe of topics of interest that Roberto Burle Marx reflected on: art, culture, and the history of Brazil; forms, uses and access to urban space; citizens' rights, public policy, socio-environmental transformation, development models and impact on the quality of life of local populations. This public discourse throughout his career is recorded in newspapers, letters, articles, and lectures.

In reading through the archive of landscaping projects, it is interesting to try to understand how the creative process took place and the decisions that were made over the course of the creation of each project, through the observation of the sketches and initial designs through to their completion and execution. In landscape design, the artistic and humanist dimensions are obvious, expressed by the clear intent of creating spaces for coexistence and social gatherings, pleasure, leisure, and rest in cities. Spaces focused on integrating urban and natural landscapes, and encouraging greater connection between inhabitants, while remaining sensitive to their individual and collective experiences; topics that are incredibly timely and present in the reflections on livability in cities adapted to the global context.

Over six decades, the projects show a wide thematic diversity, a broad scope across the national territory, and contributions on the international scene, both in the private and public spheres.

It is also worth highlighting the development of projects for public facilities related to health, education, and leisure, indicating a strong commitment to positive social transformations. In his time, Burle Marx contributed to building the future, and today he continues to inspire us to think about the possibilities of forging new paths for the country and for humanity, based on his powerful and creative aesthetic experience, fueled by the art of landscape design.

The *Instituto Burle Marx* believes in promoting this legacy as a social contribution, at a time when possible, reinterpretations of the relationships between people and the environment are increasingly necessary.

The aim is, based on the contributions of Burle Marx and his collaborators – as represented by the examples of projects and documents from the archive – to support knowledge exchange and reflections on the experience in cities from a positive, inclusive, and collaborative perspective. The work of the organization includes cataloging, preserving and eventually digitizing the archive, in addition to other initiatives and actions in the areas of education, culture and the environment.

This book is meaningful in placing value on the immaterial legacy of Burle Marx and his collaborators, broadening the discussion and promoting access, dialogue, diversity, and inclusion. Disseminating Burle Marx's immaterial legacy to the English-speaking public means bolstering and offering new meaning to his narrative and his career, building new bridges, and fostering knowledge exchange.

The *Instituto Burle Marx* applauds the efforts and the selection of work contained in this book, aimed at advocating Burle Marx's thought, and bringing it into the current debate, with special recognition for the researchers, authors, institutions, and professionals who made the dissemination and publication of this book possible in English, thus celebrating a collective legacy.

In his time, Burle Marx imagined and designed democratic and generous spaces for everyone. Now it is up to us to take up the responsibility for communicating that legacy and promoting its values every day, which demonstrate ways of thinking about possible, more positive futures in community, at a time when the healthy relationship between humankind and nature is increasingly fundamental.

Haruyoshi Ono: The Discreet and Dedicated Artist, more than a Disciple

"...living elements that are essential to me, to my work..., cultivating plants, treating each other well, watering, pruning, all those things..., the response to that, that relationship, is the beauty that they give you, visually, rousing your feelings."

– Haruyoshi Ono

The son of Japanese parents who emigrated to the interior of *São Paulo*, Haruyoshi Ono was born in *Rio de Janeiro* in 1943 and spent his childhood in the north of Rio. From an early age, Ono liked plants and considered studying agricultural science, but he ultimately opted for the Faculty of Architecture because of his love and vocation for design. In 1965, visiting the *Parque do Flamengo* with his friend from college, José Tabacow, they saw the *Escritório Burle Marx* listed on a site information panel and decided to get in touch. It was not an easy task, but they persevered and, to the surprise of both, Roberto Burle Marx himself met with them. After a brief conversation, Burle Marx accepted them both as interns, which marked the beginning of a working relationship and friendship that lasted almost 30 years. That creative association between the three men resulted in globally iconic projects such as, for example, in the 70s, the promenade on the *Av. Atlântica* and the designs for *Brasília:* the National Theater, the *Parque da Cidade* and the projects for the *Palácio Itamaraty, Palácio da Justiça* and the *Praça Triangular do Exército*. In the case of the *Praça do Exército*, it is worth repeating one of Ono's anecdotes. Burle Marx had given him the challenge of creating an artistic composition inspired by the crystal formations from the central region of Brazil. Ono worked in silence and surprised Burle Marx with his creation. Burle Marx liked it so much that he kept the sculptures in the project, and, to this day, they are still the central elements of the reflecting pool.

Another project from early in Ono's career is the sculpture garden at the Museum of Modern Art in *Rio de Janeiro* (MAM-RJ):

"One time I was really proud, because Roberto put me in charge of installing some stone sculptures at the MAM. He left me there with Magú[6] and a crane. I hadn't even finished my degree in landscape design yet. I was a student at the time. So, I had to install all those stones, making sure he would be pleased when he got back from his trip. I think it went well."

– Haruyoshi Ono

In the 1980s, after Tabacow's departure from the *Escritório*, Ono continued his creative association with Burle Marx on national and international projects like Biscayne Boulevard in Miami and the project for Rosa Luxemburg Platz in Berlin. In the early 1990s, Burle Marx made the first site visits for the development of a public park in Kuala Lumpur, Malaysia.

[6] *"Magú"* is the nickname of the architect María Augusta Leão da Costa Ribeiro.

He was able to complete the initial sketches, but unfortunately did not live long enough to develop the landscape concept. Ono picked up the basic concepts and was responsible for the final project for the Kuala Lumpur City Centre Park, one of his first public gardens at the head of the *Escritório Burle Marx*.

"For me, inspiration comes from the challenge of developing any project. The greater the complexity of the program, combined with the possibility of creating something different that can appeal to a diverse community, the more it serves as a source of inspiration."

– Haruyoshi Ono

Ono shared a workspace with Burle Marx for almost 30 years and was his most lasting and important creative partner. Burle Marx left him with the responsibility of carrying on his legacy, taking over the *Escritório de Paisagismo Burle Marx*, safeguarding its projects and its archive. After Burle Marx's death, Ono remained at the head of the *Escritório* as the author of new projects for another 20 years. He dedicated his life to the task, always with respect and loyalty for the principles Burle Marx had taught him, using his energy to support and preserve this material and immaterial legacy, which helped to disseminate and perpetuate the name of Burle Marx. Ono actively participated in all the exhibitions, enquiries, publications, auctions, and institutional tributes that sought to disseminate Burle Marx's art in Brazil and across the world. He also carried out the restoration and revitalization of many of the gardens Burle Marx developed.

Ono was a unique and discreet person who exuded charisma and calm, and who maintained a tireless strength. Like Burle Marx, he did not see his profession as work. Beneath his Asian features and his Zen attitude, he was a dedicated, generous and vibrant artist. His creative energy flowed naturally from his drafting table into colorful and well-crafted sketches.

His hands gave birth to the designs for squares, gardens, terraces, artistic panels, sculptures, and floor patterns with their own imprint, such as the

Kuala Lumpur City Centre Park (Malaysia), the *Praça da Revolução* (Acre), the Tropical Islands (Berlin) and the *Museu do Amanhã* (*Rio de Janeiro*). Other notable projects include the *Teleporto* (*Rio de Janeiro*) for private residences and his last large landscape design project, the *Parque da Vila dos Atletas*, developed to create a public park where athletes had been housed for the Rio 2016 Olympics.

In addition to his important role in the documentary preservation of the landscape legacy of Roberto Burle Marx and his collaborators, Ono played a fundamental role as a source for the newly created *Instituto Burle Marx*, having served as one of the main sources of material for the international exchange of knowledge on the subject, through his personal photographic collection, which captured a large part of the history of the *Escritório*. Haruyoshi Ono deserves to be recognized for his talent as an artist, a landscape designer, and a creator. Over the years, he built a harmonious creative partnership with Burle Marx, which gave him the opportunity to contribute with his drawings and his ideas to the creation and development of various important projects. As director of the *Escritório Burle Marx*, he developed new designs for artistic panels, gardens, sculptures, and pavements with a unique artistic aesthetic, but above all he was able to keep alive the generosity of his mentor, not only maintaining the essence of the organic and geometric forms Roberto Burle Marx taught him, but also the humanitarianism and passion for the profession.

"Every time i come back to this beautiful garden, it makes me realize that it was worth it, and it makes me want to build more gardens..."

– Haruyoshi Ono
Casa Brasileira Férias, in GNT, 2016

Biographical note: *Instituto Burle Marx*, 2021.

INTRODUCTION
MARÍA A. VILLALOBOS H. AND CARLA URBINA

Figure 2. Maracaibo Botanical Garden, Maracaibo, Venezuela. Photograph: Ligia Ararat, 2014.

"I still have the possibility of making people aware of this disaster, with all the strength I have left. I still have the opportunity to convince someone with decision-making power listen to me. And, mainly, I still have the hope that people will realize that they are not the masters of an inexhaustible nature. Just the opposite, people are dependent on it for balance and for our own survival."

– Roberto Burle Marx,
São Paulo, November 26, 1983.

Intangible Heritage: Expeditions, Observations and Lectures by Roberto Burle Marx and Collaborators & *Patrimonio inmaterial: Expediciones, Observaciones y Conferencias de Roberto Burle Marx y colaboradores, offers, in two parallel editions in English and Spanish,* offer the thoughts and actions of the greatest representative of tropical landscape design and the most prolific landscape architect of the 20th century. Here, the invisible pedagogical structures take center stage and invite us to discover the most intricate details of the construction of the tropical urban landscape. This book delves into Roberto Burle Marx's interest in understanding the past and living material and immaterial values for the purpose of:

"Fight for the preservation of creative expression in all fields of knowledge and human activity, seeking out a language of our own that reflects our desires for a better, more balanced life where we can all grow together, while encapsulating the feeling of contemporaneity, which lends value to art as a contribution to universal culture." (p. 207)

That is the mission disseminated by Burle Marx and presented in this book, as an interdisciplinary and multicultural, living ancestral substrate of his legacy.

Pedagogy *Burle-Marxii*

To articulate the different educational mechanisms, present in the work of Burle Marx, *Intangible Heritage* was envisioned as a *"symphony"*[7] – that is, as a space for *"all sounds"* to come together. Here, photographs taken by the designers and collaborators, expedition briefs, maps, diagrams, comments in footnotes, biographies and lectures are presented in both implicit and explicit forms. Geological and biological formations, native and non-native plants, architectural and sculptural monuments, as well as diverse cultural practices in construction and the arts invite the reader to discover the invisible principles that make up a possible *Pedagogy Burle-marxii*. This gives rise to a reflection on the work of a landscape architect, artist and botanist who embodied a constant search for balance between everyday life and exception, between scientific knowledge and the arts, permanence, and instability, praxis, and education, among many other facets of the paradoxical relationship between opposites inherent in landscape architecture as a discipline.

---

[7] The word *"symphony"* comes from the Greek συμφωνία and means *"concordant in sound"*. Burle Marx used this concept often to conceptualize and communicate his landscapes.

This is the key to the first principle that defines the graphic approach used to communicate an immaterial and precise legacy, like the classical music that Burle Marx studied a length and practiced with love. Centered on the idea of a staff, the approach the authors developed for this book is based on a minimal linear, regular, and reticular structure. Its simplicity fosters clarity and a mixture of the heterogeneous expressions of living things and life over time, just like Burle Marx's gardens – inhabited by hybrid principles that are free of academic rules.

A Symphony in Three Movements

Intangible Heritage presents three movements or chapters that introduce the reader to relevant principles, experiences and working methods associated with Roberto Burle Marx and his collaborators. Each section evokes the authors' reflections when it came to making editorial decisions drawing on what they learned during the process of writing and compiling this book. In that sense, *Intangible Heritage* is simultaneously a system for communicating experiences in time, as well as for translating words and methods.

The following pages offer an introduction to the content and aims of each chapter, as well as the principles governing the relationship between the key teachings contained in the texts and the authors' editorial, compositional and communication-related decisions.

The first movement, *Burle Marx's Expedition to the Amazon – 1983* and the lecture *"Landscape Architecture and Devastation – 1983"*, offers the English text of the official report of the expedition to the public for the first time. *The aim is to explore how botanical-artistic expeditions play a role in the process of landscape construction. Expeditions of this kind were important tools in Roberto Burle Marx's thought and practice, since they are the expressions of collaborations that take place in, through and about the landscape. In Burle Marx's own words:*

"With the aim of expanding the vocabulary of landscape design through the discovery of new plants, and faithful to the principle of acknowledging and appreciating the Brazilian flora, we took this trip, mantaining the appropiate proportions, imbued by the spirit of the European travelers who visited us last in the previous century."[8] (p. 35)

The text offers an intimate view of the operations, routes, schedules and materials, and the diverse backgrounds of the working team, together with historical and unpublished photographs, compiled thanks to the support and generosity of José Tabacow, Oscar Bressane, Koti Mori, and Luiz Cancio. Subsequently, the same section includes the lecture *"Landscape Architecture and Devastation"*, delivered in *São Paulo*, Brazil, on November 26, 1983.

[8] The third chapter, dedicated to Burle-Marx's lectures, offers further information about European travelers, their methods, observations, and contributions, especially regarding the understanding of Brazilian phytogeography and flora.

This oral testimony reaffirms the relevance of *"expose city-dwellers to the knowledge of our natural riches while helping, in some way, to bolster species threatened with extinction."* (p. 97)

A first principle refers to *the relevance of preserving native heritage*. In this sense, the text respects the sounds and rhythms of the Portuguese language in the names of cities, rivers, mountains, lakes, plants, animals, and cultural and religious practices. All these words are left in the original language to preserve their diversity and richness; visually they are marked with italics occasionally, and explanations are offered through photographs and bibliographic references. Words like *araras*, *borboletas*, *quaresmeiras*, which were initially unfamiliar to the Spanish-speaking authors, became a language of their own, intimate, and shared memories, and plans conjured by this book.

A second principle recognizes *the importance of interdisciplinarity and teamwork*. In that vein, extensive biographical notes are provided for the members of the artistic and scientific orchestra who, together with Burle Marx, performed and planted the tropical landscape over the years. In *Intangible Heritage*, the visual presence of the works and contributions of Burle Marx's collaborators, both his contemporaries and others, invites reflection on how every work is the result of an extensive process of decantation and transformation over time, outside the realm of coincidence, and in a constant celebration of generations past and those to come. Thus, Burle Marx reminds us that the responsibility of the landscape designer, and any citizen who loves living things, encompasses all the arts and sciences in a universe of essential reciprocities, no matter how invisible they may seem.

The third principle is related to *the value of social criticism and the active defense of living heritage as an inherent part of the practice of landscape design*. The absence of project blueprints and illustrations, the photographic selection and treatment of color, the relationships and sequencing between texts and images, and the selection of bibliographic references, are all an invitation to reflect on and experience the gardens of Burle Marx not as static works in time, but as living beings that are subject to the continuous practices of devastation and preservation of natural and built landscapes. Thus, the work of Burle Marx teaches us that preserving local richness, interdisciplinarity, and the defense of living heritage all demand the urgent reexamination and reformulation of academic standards that ignore local considerations in favor of design, construction and communication strategies that place value on the living essence of what makes a place special, and at full force.

The second movement offers the reader a conversation between friends about Roberto Burle Marx's satisfactions, challenges and hopes, touching on how an artist should represent his homeland and his era. This is the first English translation of the interview *Landscape, Botany and Ecology*, carried out between Jacques Leenhardt and Roberto Burle Marx in 1992. It is based on the Spanish version of this book, which drew on the French and Portuguese texts, published respectively in: Leenhardt, J. (2016). *Dans les jardins de Roberto Burle Marx*, Actes Sud, Paris, pp. 65-87, and

Leenhardt, J. (2010). *Nos jardins de Burle Marx*, Perspectiva, *São Paulo*, pp. 47-67. The conversation moves through historical landscapes, theological, compositional and botanical notions, as well as feverish descriptions of diverse experiences with the landscape. The interview highlights the structural, and not incidental, role of aesthetic criteria in the articulation of the built landscape. Burle Marx makes an appeal:

"Beyond the implications derived from economic demands (transportation, agriculture, culture, housing, manufacturing, etc.), let us not forget that the landscape is also defined by an aesthetic demand, which is not a luxury or a prodigality, but an absolute necessity for human life and without which civilization itself would be emptied of its purpose." (p. 113)

The scope of this reflection stretches beyond the scale of the garden and out towards the metropolitan scale, where the transformation of the relationship between man, animals, plants, and all living things depends on education in cities. Burle Marx calls attention to the presence of a living urban heritage:

"Little by little they are being destroyed by the local population, who fail to understand that it is a treasure, and by European immigrants, who are transplanted without adapting, who have maintained the criteria for beauty from the countries of origin." (p. 135)

Additionally, in this interview Burle Marx offers a vision of the persistence of the ethical implications of shaping the landscape:

"During certain historical periods and in certain countries, the balance of the social order is projected in the art of shaping the landscape. We can say without exaggeration that the history of the garden (that is, the built landscape) ties in with the history of the ethical and aesthetic ideas of each era." (p. 138)

New editorial principles also come into bloom in this second chapter. In *Intangible Heritage*, the chromatic sequences of images of living things conjure the authors' experiences in the landscapes planted and evoked by Burle Marx. These decisions were inspired by the *principle of expanding the structural role of aesthetic demands in the construction of the landscape*. In that sense, for example, for the authors, ascending the *Serra dos Órgãos* becomes an exercise in observing best practices in road construction, in enjoying the violet and gold blooms amid the dark Atlantic green, a lead-up to visiting the gardens designed by Burle Marx and his collaborators, and the opportunity to share Burle Marx's teachings with fellow travelers. Roberto Burle Marx's legacy is alive on the paths that lead up to the experiences of his gardens, his plants, and all the habitats that he learned from, celebrated, and demanded we protect. The selection of images in *Intangible Heritage* invites readers to discover those paths for themselves and to uncover new ones.

Secondly, *the principle regarding the key role of ethical relations in devising the program that animates the urban landscape* is behind the decision to publish the historical photographs in black and white. This resource in the photographic treatment is meant to highlight details associated with the role of the spaces as aesthetic compositions. At the same time, the use of color for the photographs that show the current state of Burle Marx's gardens is intended to communicate the different living ecological capacities inherent in landscape projects that *"are finished by time"*.[9]

Thirdly, *the principle related to the explicit educational mission in the construction of public and urban space* shines through in the editorial style with the choice of images that exclusively depict public parks intended for the enjoyment of all citizens. As Burle Marx put it:

"I tried to understand the garden as applied to our nature, by that I mean human nature, and above all to the needs of Brazilians. Because I don't want to design gardens just for millionaires' houses. I would like to build gardens that everyone can share."[10]

The third chapter, and the final movement, of this work offers the English translation of a selection of Burle Marx's lectures, compiled, organized, edited, and commented by José Tabacow. These lectures were originally published in Portuguese in: Burle Marx, Roberto, and Tabacow, José. *Arte e Paisagem. São Paulo*: Editorial Livros Studio Nobel Ltda. 1987. The publication was part of the *Ciudad Abierta* collection. Two of these lectures, *"Gardens and Ecology"* and *"Landscape Projects for Large Areas"* were published by Lars Müller in 2020, in a different translation, in the book Roberto Burle Marx Lectures: Landscape as Art and Urbanism, edited by Gareth Doherty. Tabacow's selection includes 11 lectures, 10 of which appear in this translation. The lecture *"Concepts in Landscape Composition"* (1954) was not included, because the authors determined that many of the concepts it contains are already present in Chapter II of this book. The lecture *"Landscape Architecture and Devastation"* (1983) has been included in Chapter I, due to its connection with the original report on the expedition to the Amazon.

What follows is a summary of the pedagogical objectives of each lecture.

Landscape Design in Large Areas, 1962. In this lecture, Burle Marx talks about the need for balanced growth between nature and the urban landscape. The importance of territorial and urban planning is also described as a way to guarantee the coexistence of geological, ecological and historical-cultural timelines. For Burle Marx, gardens, squares, parks, orchards and, especially, botanical gardens, are essential educational spaces for all generations:

---

[9] *Finished by Time: Burle Marx, Classic and Unpublished Works* or *O tempo completa: Burle Marx, clássicos e inéditos* is the name of the exhibition that opened in November 2021 in Rio de Janeiro, Brazil. The exhibition was organized by the *Instituto Burle Marx* and the *Instituto Casa Roberto Marinho* and was curated by Lauro Cavalcanti and Isabella Ono.

[10] Text translated from the video created for the exhibition *Finished by Time: Burle Marx, Classic and Unpublished Works* or *O tempo completa: Burle Marx, clássicos e inéditos*, held in Rio de Janeiro, Brazil, 2021.

"The functions of a botanical garden, which is, in essence, a scientific institution, include research and dissemination, systematic and unsystematic teaching, the undertaking of botanical explorations, the curation of collections of living plants and herborized materials, the exchange of plants, seedlings and seeds, the organization of regular exhibitions, courses, etc. A garden of that kind is perfect for you can display plants, whether on their own or in combinations. It is a place where you can compare plants from the same family and understand their ability to adapt to extremely diverse environments and living conditions." (p. 177)

Considerations on Brazilian Art, 1966. In this text, Burle Marx offers a synthetic description of the evolution of artistic traditions in Brazil, from Baroque architecture to the present. The process is described as a rich mixing of different races, the origin of which lies in the violence of colonization. According to Burle Marx, artistic creation *"does not mean simply borrowing certain elements from folklore, believing that it will result in art with a national expression."* (p. 205) He continues his defense of invention, synthesis and mixture by asserting that if we fail to account for the local details and the many historical layers, then *"that would offer just an 'appearance', because the content would be divorced from the worldview. Instead, we need to look at the foundations of popular culture, in order to use that vocabulary to recreate a new syntax, a new language."* (p. 205) This lecture clearly shows how Burle Marx employs musical metaphors, like *adágio* and *allegro vivace*, to describe the landscape making use of sentimental expressions related to sweetness, passion, and darkness. Finally, Burle Marx recalls:

"Anyone wishing to practice conscious and profound landscape design must take advantage of the immense heritage of the exuberant Brazilian flora, which has been so poorly understood by landscape architects and garden lovers." (p. 218)

Garden and Ecology, 1967. In this lecture, Burle Marx focuses on describing his perspective on the relationship between humans and plants and the associations with other living beings. He talks about flora reserves as true natural gardens, whose mission should be to preserve the communities and endemic species of the different botanical provinces. As he sees it, *"The social mission of a landscape architect has the educational aspect of communicating the feeling of admiration and the understanding of the value of the nature to the public through contact with gardens and parks."* (p. 238) And he offers a message for landscape design in the tropics:

"Today the richness of the flora of the tropical zones is such that, speaking from my own experience, I can say that I never made an excursion in which I failed to find or collect plants unknown both to me and to science" (p. 216). [...] *Still, the work does not end there. We have to fight against greed and the desire for immediate profit, to preserve the flora, the vegetation – in short, what remains of the magnificent heritage that we should be leaving as a legacy to the coming generations."* (p. 207)

Landscape Design and Brazilian Flora, 1975. This lecture examines the process of natural devastation that has been recorded in the work of naturalist explorers, beginning with Saint Hilaire and Martius in the 17th century and continuing into the 20th century. In the face of that devastation, Burle Marx lays out his goal:

"Saving at least a part of our decimated flora, collecting specimens from nature, discovering their potential for landscape design, reproducing species to be able to use them properly in gardens, showing their immense value (when used correctly) in harmony with their surroundings." (p. 245)

In the lecture, Burle Marx also talks about the idea for a plant nursery that would work towards those goals. Today, that nursery is known as the *Sítio Roberto Burle Marx*, and in July 2021 it was declared a UNESCO World Heritage Site. The different collections held at the *Sítio* were made possible thanks to botanists such as Mello Barreto, from whom Burle Marx learned that *"plants do not live in isolation, but in associations; they have their own logic and their own beauty. I learned that it is important to understand their natural habitat before trying to use them in gardens."* (p. 249)

Landscape Resources of Brazil, 1976. This lecture establishes a series of criteria for understanding the landscape and conscious human intervention, to *"guarantee a sequence of landscapes through the territory, which can maintain a basic quality or balance, despite being diversified and subject to a wide variety of uses and regimes, whether natural or humanized."* (p. 276)

In this sense, Burle Marx proposes criteria for *"landscape zoning"* including the study of the geographical environment, the biogeography, the flora and fauna, and the evolution of the landscape for the construction of professional maps of landscape areas. In the text, Burle Marx highlights the importance of the cultural and educational mission of national parks, as well as the need for ease of access considering the significance of roads. This is how he explains it:

"Moving through the landscape will show the attentive traveler the rhythm of the formations, the interrelations between their various aspects. Forests, fields, farmhouses, plantations, mountains, rivers, waterways follow one another in their own sequences, characteristic of each region, since, as they are interdependent elements, their distribution obeys its own laws." (p. 282)

Statement to the Federal Senate, 1976. In this statement, Burle Marx denounces the ever-increasing devastation of nature. He clarifies the difference between reforestation and environmental preservation, as well as the importance of preserving mixed forests for the natural regeneration of living things. The grievances he voices refer explicitly to problems of environmental devastation in the Brazilian territory. However, the issues he cites are present in other countries: deforestation, devastation (whether due to mechanical intervention, burning, or the indiscriminate use of weed killers), replacing native forests with species that threaten the ecological balance in the regions where they are planted, among many other aggressions tied to inadequate policies for conservation, management, administration and control. Burle Marx is committed to raising awareness as a necessary means to achieve a balanced coexistence.

Problems with Nature Conservation, 1976. This text argues that, while individual action *"is the result of a profound understanding of the man-nature connection, destruction is impersonal. Destruction is dictated by the* economic interests of groups, regions and, sometimes, the entire country." (p. 315) In that sense, working on preservation means working collectively, through raising awareness and reforging the human connection with the earth, to defend living things and life.

The Involvement of Botanists in My Professional Training, 1983. When being named an honorary member of the Brazilian Botanical Society in 1983, Burle Marx delivered this speech. It is a testimony to his work experience and friendship with plant scientists and how those exchanges enriched his life as a landscape architect. According to Burle Marx, his interactions with botanists helped him to understand and value the flora, the environmental needs of each species, and the associations between plants.

Landscape Design in the Urban Structure, 1983. This final lecture is of special importance in understand the vision of the urban landscape's mission in the processes of defending, conserving, and communicating the values offered by nature. Here, Burle Marx talks about the need for a balance of growth between nature and the urban landscape, to support all living beings and in the interest of preserving our living heritage, especially plant life. In Burle Marx's words:

"All that richness is within our reach. But we need to really understand and interiorize the importance of parks. Every city, every municipality, should have enough parkland to serve its population. And each State should have its own nurseries, where species that are valuable to the region can be grown intensively to make it possible to distribute them to the different districts and to individuals, so that they can be used in gardens, on streets, in squares, and in parks. These nurseries should also support experiments in the field of applied botany, selecting species, studying the possible unique functions of trees, shrubs, and understory vegetation." (p. 346)

This journey through the discourse of Burle Marx can be distilled into a tangible editing principle: *the preservation of traces throughout the long process of building the landscape of cities and building our own paths as landscape architects, educators, and writers.* This book contains different living markers on a path, both collective and personal, through the gardens of Burle Marx, spanning almost 13 years. Seeds, petals, notes, travel lists, photographic secrets, exceptional human encounters, they all are all present in the lectures, statements, and reflections, and they offer the reader not only the translations of the words, but a philosophy and a way of life in the construction, conservation, and dissemination of the tropical landscape.

Living Ambitions

Intangible Heritage presents the reader with experiences and ongoing lessons, maps, and mosaics of images of the landscape that celebrate the ongoing relevance of the message offered to us by Roberto Burle Marx, who, with boundless generosity, a teacher's patience, and an undying curiosity laid out the paths toward the understanding, preservation, and propagation of cultural diversity and tropical nature. The decision to write this book emerged organically from the modest goals of teachers who were hoping to make specific texts accessible to young people studying to become architects, urban planners, and landscape architects.

The authors had the opportunity to learn, from their families and from an early age, the botanical-ecological-cultural values that appear in the landscapes of Burle Marx. The book project first took root at the Maracaibo Botanical Garden (MBG) in Venezuela, the authors' country of birth, as a part of the efforts to restore the landscape and reopen the garden after more than 20 years of neglect.

This exemplary botanical garden was designed by Burle Marx and collaborators, in 1983, intended as a school for the preservation of the tropical dry forest. At the end of the 1970s, the famous Venezuelan botanist Leandro Aristeguieta invited his friend Burle Marx to work on the project, along with his collaborators in landscape design: Haruyoshi Ono, José Waldemar Tabacow, Maria Isabel Braga Câmara, Sérgio Martins Treitler, F. Jorge, Luiz Alberto Gomes Cancio, Maria de Fátima Gomes de Souza. The team also included architects such as: Ángela de Parodi, Carlos Millot, and Ricardo Faccini. The renowned Venezuelan botanist Ernesto Foldats Andins was also a participant. All the team members contributed to the conceptualization, design, and construction of the project, while participating in teaching activities at the same time.

The authors first gained access to the MBG in 2009, 26 years after it first opened to public and 22 years after its doors were closed. Flowering bushes obscured all the paths. The play areas had been overgrown by all kinds of vegetation, and the brick and concrete structures had crumbled. The leisure areas had been demolished. The spaces reserved for exhibiting the botanical collections, designed according to a carefully structured phylogenetic classifications, had been occupied by commercial plantations. There was no time for laments or sadness. The exuberant life of the tropical dry forest protected by Roberto, Leandro and their collaborators assuaged any doubts and made it clear that keeping the garden alive would require reviving the push for education. In that sense, the first action toward rehabilitating the MBG was immaterial – or perhaps it had a different kind of materiality. It was a system of large-scale educational measures, drawn up with scientific precision, a passion for landscape design, and incorporating the most relevant global inputs in the fields of landscape architecture, philosophy, and history, among others. Academic and practical work came together in the implementation of a broad educational campaign using traditional academic channels, social networks, digital messaging groups, television, radio, fashion magazines and any media interested in listening. Through this process of communicating and educating, it became clear that the essential legacy of Burle Marx's work is invisible to the eye and that its beating heart is the educational power of his work and, therefore, its level of epistemological invention.

Beginning at that moment in 2009, the authors began extensive travels through Burle Marx's gardens in Venezuela, Brazil, Argentina, and France, in addition to engaging in intellectual experiences through archives, lectures, interviews, videos and every kind of available record. The escalation of artistic, scientific, and political efforts toward more effective protection and expansion made it possible to reopen the MBG in 2013, together with a broad team of collaborators. Currently, the MBG is once again serving a metropolitan population of three million citizens.

Today, that same urgency and emotion that we felt when traveling through tropical Latin America underpins the publication of this collection of Roberto Burle Marx's oral and written testimony to the English-speaking public.

I. BURLE MARX'S EXPEDITION TO THE AMAZON
1983

Figure 3. Back cover with an original signature by Roberto Burle Marx and the date (in blue ink) on the copy of *Expedição Burle Marx a Amazônia* that belongs to the library of the *Sítio Roberto Burle Marx*. "Despite humanity, there is still time." Thiago de Mello.

This journey begins with a part of Roberto Burle Marx's wealth of knowledge from one of his many botanical expeditions: the expedition to the Amazon, which took place in 1983.

The text *Expedição Burle Marx a Amazônia – 1983* was compiled in *Rio de Janeiro* in 1984. The report was submitted to the National Council for Scientific and Technological Development (CNPq). *Intangible Heritage* offers this report to the general public for the first time; this is also the first time it has been published in English. The text narrates the expedition through the Brazilian Amazon carried out by Roberto Burle Marx and an interdisciplinary team, with financing from the CNPq and logistical support and consulting from Varig, Petrobras and a long list of people and institutions. The report was designed, produced and executed by José Tabacow, María de Fátima de Souza Menezes, Cíntia Aparecida Costa Chamas and Luiz Alberto Gomes Cancio.

The expedition report contains an introductory text by Roberto Burle Marx. Next it offers a list of participants and equipment, the historical account, the map of the route, the chronology, the list of materials collected (live plants, botanized plants, field annotations), a personal statement from Luis Carlos Gurken, the expedition results, the conclusions and, as a closing, the lecture *"Landscape Architecture and Devastation"*, given by Burle Marx in *São Paulo* upon his return from the expedition.

In addition to collections, the expedition produced a series of documents: articles for the media, extension courses and practical courses on landscape design for professionals, technical sessions, presentations for public entities and associations for environmental protection, among others.

Botanical expeditions are one of the tools Burle Marx used to broaden the knowledge of nature, the relationships between living beings, and the biological associations in the landscapes he explored.

Expedição Burle Marx a Amazônia – 1983 contributes to the knowledge about a significant number of herborized plants and about the plant collection of the *Sítio Roberto Burle Marx*'s (plants that were later used in various parks and gardens). Additionally, the document contributes to the understanding of the immaterial aspect of Burle Marx's legacy by illustrating the teaching mechanisms that bring to life a working method that is both inductive and deductive, which operates and reflects *in situ* and *ex situ*, combining both practice and research at the same time. This coexistence of scientific and emotional knowledge in the work of Burle Marx offers clues for the creation of contemporary mechanisms to address the evident vulnerability of living things, and to engage in protest, defense and action.

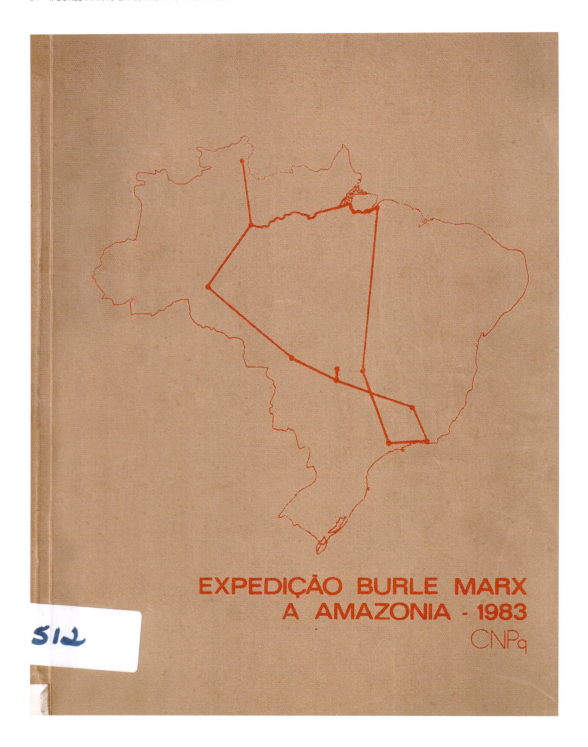

Figure 4. Cover of the original publication: Burle Marx, Roberto. *Expedição Burle Marx a Amazônia – 1983*. Conselho Nacional de Desenvolvimento Científico e Tecnológico (CNPq). Rio de Janeiro: 1984.

Foreword. Roberto Burle Marx, 1984

A trip to the Amazon came 20 years too late. At my age, there is a disconnect between the physical reality and the emotional side of things, and I have to content myself with collecting samples near the roads, letting the rest of the team handle the strain of going deeper into the mountains or climbing the hills.

Two decades ago, the situation would have been reversed. Although we did venture deeper in, it was hardly even necessary. The natural formations reached right up to the edges of the roads, and because the technical power of destruction was more limited then, the road construction respected the topography and vegetation much more.

Our expedition showed that, today, those roads, rather than offering a simple connection between two cities, are a ferocious battlefield of destruction. In some points the forest is set back tens of kilometers from the edge of the road and walking to the point of interest takes up valuable hours that could otherwise be dedicated to collecting. On the other hand, the time at our disposal was too limited for such a long journey. While we brought back 400 plants of ornamental interest, we could have achieved a much more significant result if the time had not been so short and, mainly, if there had not been so much destruction concentrated along the roads and rivers.

With the aim of expanding the vocabulary of gardening through the discovery of new plants, and faithful to the principle of acknowledging and appreciating the Brazilian flora, we took this trip, maintaining the appropriate proportions, imbued with the spirit of the European travelers who visited us in the previous century. The 19th century was essential to broadening the horizons of botanical knowledge. The desire to see little-explored territories, combined with the development of navigation techniques, meant that the cream of European scientists and naturalists all made their way here, including Von Martius, Saint-Hilaire, Gardner, and many others.

These scientists, as well as many gardeners and horticulturists financed by commercial plant sellers, introduced large numbers of species to European cultures that were later used commercially and eventually returned as novelties imported from Europe. This is the case of *Bougainvilleas*[11] and *Gloxinias*,[12] for example. Now, our flora includes some tens of thousands of species. We don't need to import exotic plants, often alien to our climate conditions and our landscapes. First and foremost we need to understand our natural values, discover their potential, and define what is usable.

---

[11] *Bougainvillea Comm.* ex Juss. Botanical genus of the family Nyctaginaceae Juss. For more information, see: Hassler, Michel, 2004-2021. *Bougainvillea Comm.* ex Juss. *World Plants. Synonymic Checklist and Distribution of the World Flora* (Hassler M., Bougainvillea Comm. ex Juss, 2021).

[12] *Gloxinia L'Hér.* Botanical genus of the family Gesneriaceae Rich. & Juss. For more information, see: Hassler, Michel, 2004-2021. *Gloxinia L'Hér. World Plants. Synonymic Checklist and Distribution of the World Flora* (Hassler M., Gloxinia L'Hér, 2021).

Meanwhile, throughout the trip, as we passed through cities, we witnessed how the regional flora is dismissed as *monte* (scrub) and rejected in favor of species imported from *Rio* or *São Paulo*, since those cities are perceived by those in the country's interior as paradigms of perfection, as ideal urban solutions.

But the native flora has an unimaginable richness. It should be recognized and valued for the regional heritage that it represents.

That was the spirit of our trip. Although the results were not as expected, the experience that remained was worth it. We came away with a cursory view of 11,000 km of roads. The most interesting points could not be explored in detail as we might have liked. However, the team that came together for the trip had the opportunity to observe the landscapes, the ecosystems, the phytophysiognomies. We collected the plants that we deemed interesting, and we did it with the scientific support of William Rodrigues, Paul Hutchinson, and Luis Antônio Mathes. Thus, we were able to further strengthen the relationship, which I consider symbiotic, between botanists and landscape designers.

Beginning from the natural landscape, we were able to glean fundamental information for the composition of man-made landscapes. And, if any of the plants we brought back – even just one – eventually appear in our gardens, propagated and preserved, even for commercial purposes, then I can consider the trip's aim has been achieved.

Roberto Burle Marx

Figure 5. [Top left] Itinerary of the trip taken by Martius and Spix in Brazil. Von Martius, Carl Friederich Phillip; Von Spix, Johann Baptist. *Tabula geographica Brasiliae et terrarium adjacentium, exhibens itinera botanicorum.* Digital version available at: Martius & Spix, 1794-1868. **Figure 6.** [Top right] Map published in *Voyage à Rio Grande do Sul* (Brazil) by Auguste de Saint-Hilaire (published posthumously in 1887). Digital version available at: Saint Hilaire, 1887. **Figure 7.** [Center] Devastation from the construction of roads and lack of protection for roadside areas seen during the trip to the Amazon, *Manaus-Boa Vista*, Brazil. Photograph: Oscar Bressane, Koiti Mori and José Tabacow, 1983. **Figure 8.** [Bottom left] *Mauritias* in the *Praça dos Cristais, Brasilia*, Brazil, according to a design by Roberto Burle Marx and collaborators. Photograph: María Villalobos, 2021. **Figure 9.** [Bottom right] Burle Marx sitting on a piece of furniture made from the petioles of the leaves of the *Buriti* palm tree or moriche palm (*Mauritia flexuosa*, syn. *Mauritia vinifera*). Expedition to the State of Bahia. Photograph: Oscar Bressane, 1982.

Figure 10. Plant collection during the expedition to the Amazon, Brazil. Photograph: Luiz Cancio, 1983.

Participants in the expedition to the Amazon:

1. Roberto Burle Marx. Landscape architect. General supervisor.
2. José Tabacow. Landscape architect. Coordination, photography and text.
3. Maria de Fátima Gomes de Souza Menezes. Landscape architect. Record-keeping and field documentation.
4. Luiz Carlos Gurken. Researcher. Collection of live plants.
5. Koiti Mori. Landscape architect. Photography.
6. Oscar Bressane. Landscape architect. Photography and collection of live plants.
7. Luiz Alberto Gomes Cancio. Student of landscape architecture. Collection of living plants, coordination of campsites and meals.
8. Cíntia Aparecida Costa Chamas. Landscape architect. Photographer's assistant.
9. Jorge Crichyno Pinto. Landscape architect. Collection of living plants and packaging.
10. Rosangela Cunha Rocha. Landscape architect. Record-keeping and field documentation.
11. Hugo Biagi Filho. Assistant. Collection of living plants and bookkeeping.

Guests:

12. Dr. William Rodrigues. Botanist at the INPA-*Manaus*. Collection of plant specimens for herbaria.
13. Dr. Paul Hutchinson. Botanist from the Tropic World Foundation, California. Collection of plant specimens for herbaria and field drying.
14. Luiz Antônio Ferraz Mathes. Agronomist and ecologist from the IAC, *Campinas*. Collection of plant specimens for herbaria and collection of live plants.

Equipment list:

1. Vehicles:
Kombi Volkswagen YR-7096 - RJ.
Kombi Volkswagen TZ-9846 - RJ.
Toyota Bandeirante NV-4797 - RJ.
Hahn TW-1634 cargo trailer - RJ
(Capacity: 1.6 m^3).
Turiscar trailer, camper model AY-0558-
Petrópolis.

The first three vehicles were outfitted with the following equipment:

Manual cable winch with a steel box (20 m).
Independent brakes,
on the rear wheels.*
Trailer tow hook.
Roof rack.
Off-road tires.
Premium wideset tires.*

*Except Toyota.

2. Collection material:
Spade.
Shovel.
Pick.
Hoe.
Trimmer.
Axe.
Machete.
Pruning shears.
Presses.
Camp stove (gas).
Paper boxes, plastic bags, and other materials for packaging and airmail shipping.

3. Photographic equipment:
Two Nikon F cameras.
Nikkormat camera.
Nikkor 43/86 mm zoom lens.
Nikkor 200 mm lens.
Micro-Nikkor 105 mm lens.
Two Nikkor 50 mm lenses.
Two Vivitar 285 flashes.
Gossen Luna-Pro light meter.
Minolta Flashmeter III.
Various rings and filters.
Camera tripod.
Two light stands.

The photographic equipment was transported in a special aluminum dry box.

4. Camping equipment:
2-person tent.
Eight jungle hammocks.
3 x 5 m plastic awning.
Cooking equipment.

Figure 11. Preparations for boarding river transport on the *Iguapo-Açu River, Manaus-Porto Velho*, Brazil. Photograph: Oscar Bressane, Koiti Mori and José Tabacow, 1983.

Objectives:

Focusing on the use of autochthonous flora in landscape design, the main objective of the expedition was the collection of live plants that might potentially be usable in landscaping projects due to their ornamental value.

To support their subsequent identification, three collections were put together for the herbaria of the University of Campinas (UNICAMP), the Rio de Janeiro Botanical Garden, and the National Institute of Amazonian Research (INPA). To round out the information, some 1,500 photographs (35 mm slides) were taken to document the plants that were collected, their habitats, associations and phytosociological importance, etc. In addition to the objectives described above, it is worth highlighting the purposes of the *in situ* studies and observations, especially in terms of the phytogeographical aspects, including ongoing observations of the main phytophysiognomies, their contact areas and enclaves.

The team was attuned to the particularities of human interference, especially with regard to the predatory use of land and natural resources, as well as the techniques used in road construction.

Roberto Burle Marx's Expedition to the Amazon. Historical Account:

The itinerary included the exploration of two areas outside the Amazon: the *Serra do Caiapó*, in *Goiás* and the *Chapada dos Guimarães*, in *Mato Grosso*. Their inclusion stipulated only a broad view of these areas, an initial contact, with an eye to future more specific expeditions. We stayed in the Serra do Caiapó for three days (see chronology), exploring the formations along the *Jataí-Caiapônia* road, the area surrounding the city of *Caiapônia*, and a section between *Caiapônia* and *Piranhas*.

The team decided to cancel the trip to the Chapada dos Guimarães, given that we were already behind schedule (initial calendar) and, mainly, due to information obtained in Cuiabá regarding the conditions of the Cuiabá-Porto Velho road. This information, often contradictory, suggested we might have difficulties that would surely add a few more days of delay to the trip.

In Cuiabá, we sent off the first shipment of material we had collected. Both the live plants, duly conditioned, and the exsicatas, the dried herbarium specimens, dried in a field stove overnight, were sent to Rio de Janeiro, accompanied by the respective field data.

This shipment, and all the others during the trip, were carried out with the support of Varig, which provided us with free air shipping. The live plants,

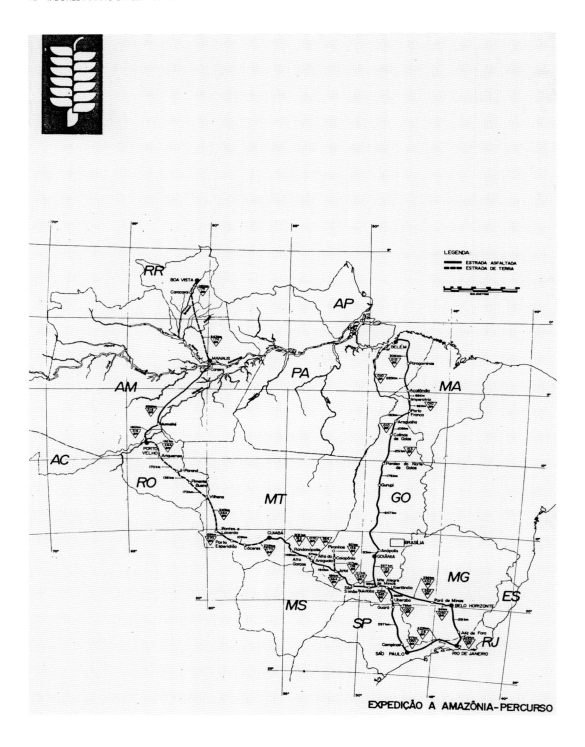

Figure 12. Route map of the expedition to the Amazon. Roberto Burle Marx, 1983 (Burle Marx R., 1984, p. 8).

upon their arrival in *Rio de Janeiro*, were immediately planted in nurseries at the *Sítio Santo Antônio da Bica*[13] owned by Roberto Burle Marx. The dry material was stored in a suitable location, awaiting the return of the team for subsequent distribution.

In general, the collection throughout the trip followed a routine that began at a stopping point, identified in response to an interest from one of the participants. An area or formation was explored, usually at the edge of the road, and the selected plants were photographed. Then, a number of live individuals (seedlings, cuttings, or seeds) were collected, in addition to material for the three herbaria collections. The live plants were then wrapped in plastic bags, with the roots enveloped in damp moss. The material for the herbaria was immediately placed in presses to be dried in the field stove later, usually overnight. In parallel to the collection, field annotations were made relating to the material and the location of the collection point.

These activities continued each day until sunset, when the team then drove on to the nearest fueling point without stopping. There, the team made camp and the field stove was set up to dry the plants.

The routine of camping near gas stations proved to be extremely comfortable, since there were facilities available, such as toilets, kitchens, etc.

The camp activities mainly involved drying plants for the herbaria and wrapping up the live plants in their final packaging for shipping. The samples were dried in a specially constructed gas-fired field oven. The samples remained under the heat throughout the night and sometimes part of the morning. This way, the plants could be sent to Rio already dry, and thus they could be stored until the team's return. After our return, the samples were organized into a collection. Each specimen received a definitive collection number. The respective field data was typed up and the material was sent to UNICAMP.

In the camps, two ridge tents were set up, and jungle hammocks were hung between the vehicles, tied to the roof racks.

As for the financial aspects, the trip was carried out in a regime of the utmost frugality. Staying in hotels and even pensions was avoided.

---

[13] *The Sítio Santo Antônio da Bica* is known as the *Sítio Roberto Burle Marx* (SRBM) or simply *the Sítio*. It was Roberto Burle Marx's home and was donated to IPHAN in 1985; that same year, it was listed as Brazilian cultural heritage (IPHAN, 2014). The *Sítio Roberto Burle Marx* was declared a World Heritage Site by UNESCO in 2021.

1º caderno □ sexta-feira, 16/12/83

Coluna do Castello

Burle Marx vê tragédia ambiental

Brasília — De Roberto Burle Marx, paisagista e pintor que dispensa adjetivos, recebi a seguinte carta:

"Prezado Senhor,

Tendo retornado recentemente de uma expedição à Amazônia, com o objetivo de colher plantas potencialmente utilizáveis em projetos de paisagismo, bem como o de observar habitats, associações e vínculos ecológicos dessas mesmas plantas, sinto-me na obrigação de denunciar, por todos os meios possíveis, a verdadeira tragédia ambiental que, ao longo de 2.000 km de rodovia, presenciei, tomado de um sentimento de frustração e impotência.

Acostumado a viajar pelo interior de nosso país, parti do Rio já preparado para constatar a devastação imediatista, a cupidez com que nossos recursos naturais são vilipendiados. Entretanto, confesso que errei em minha avaliação. E, lamentavelmente, meu erro foi o de não dimensionar a extensão dessa catástrofe. Onde está o homem, está a destruição. Pretender tratar, com palavras, um desastre de tais proporções é tarefa impossível. Após essa viagem, vi confirmadas algumas afirmações e conceitos meus que, tendo sido publicados, foram taxados de românticos, de verborréia fácil e outras qualificações depreciativas. Entretanto, depreciar um conceito, criticando a forma, sem contra-argumentos em relação ao conteúdo, é prática costumeira dos que, sentados em seus gabinetes refrigerados de Brasília, pretendem ditar as leis de intervenção na natureza, sem o menor conhecimento da realidade amazônica. E o que é mais grave, sem ouvir habitantes da região, que têm a experiência de toda a vida e os cientistas especializados no estudo daquele ecossistema.

Admitir uma legislação genérica para uma formação natural com uma infinidade de matizes e circunstâncias tão específicas, é, no mínimo, ingênuo ou tendencioso. Permitir aos donos da terra que derrubem a metade da floresta em sua propriedade (Código Florestal), independentemente das potencialidades do solo, das condições topográficas, das possibilidades de escoamento da produção e de uma infinidade de outros aspectos nos levará irreversivelmente à perda do patrimônio. Incentivar a remoção da capa vegetal, baixando os impostos por considerar a eliminação da floresta como benfeitoria, é crime de lesa-pátria.

Pode parecer estranho enviar esta carta a um jornalista especializado no comentário e na análise dos fatos políticos. Justifico meu proceder na crença que tenho de que só será possível um uso consciente dos nossos recursos naturais a partir de uma legislação baseada no conhecimento científico dos problemas. Enquanto a discussão desses problemas estiver restrita aos gabinetes do poder decisório, teremos verdadeiros abortos sob a forma de leis inadequadas e mesmo ridículas, porque emanadas da vaidade, da ignorância e, o que é pior, da necessidade do faturamento político eficiente no angariar prestígio, porém gerando dispositivos legais estéreis, como, por exemplo, a lei que proíbe a derrubada da castanheira do Pará (ao ser removida a floresta, a árvore fica isolada em meio ao pasto, não sendo, por isso, visitada pelo inseto polinizador, jamais voltando a frutificar).

Meu propósito, ao fazer esta denúncia, não é o de que frutifiquem apenas as castanheiras, mas também leis que, nascidas de conhecimento real dos problemas, possam, a curto prazo, deter o processo suicida de eliminação sumária de um patrimônio muito maior do que a nossa dívida externa, do que nosso pluripartidarismo, do que as eleições diretas para Presidente, problemas importantes apenas enquanto houver um Brasil pelo qual ainda valha a pena lutar.

Atenciosamente,

A) Roberto Burle Marx."

The vast majority of days we ate just one formal meal (dinner), and this daily meal was supplemented with breakfast and a light lunch during the day. Thus, we saved time and avoided interrupting our activities during working hours. Despite all the frugality, the budget available for the trip was insufficient. This scarcity of resources was due to several factors, including:

1. The time that elapsed (over a year) between the request for funds and their release by the National Council for Scientific and Technological Development (CNPq), with the budget correction coming in lower than the inflation for the period.

2. The preparation of the vehicles was more expensive than expected.

3. Fuel prices increased during the trip.

4. The price of river transport was much higher than what was reported.

5. The engine in one of the two vehicles was irreparably damaged and had to be replaced.

6. Endless car repairs were necessary, especially welding and reinforcement, on all the vehicles, including the caravan and trailer, given the poor condition of the roads, especially in the section between *Cuiabá and Porto Velho*.

Anticipating these difficulties, the team jumped into action a few days before departure and secured additional financial support from Petrobras and free air transportation for the material from Varig. Additionally, minor material support was obtained, including packaging from Piraquê, film from Kurt and a few other contributions.

Figure 13. Article: *"Burle Marx Describes an Environmental Tragedy"*, in *Columna do Castelo* (16/12/1983). The article describes the letter Burle Marx sent to a political journalist, in which he denounces the environmental tragedy he saw during his expedition covering 11,000 km. In the closing, he writes: *"My goal in denouncing this situation is not only to protect the castanheiras [Brazil nut trees], but also to promote laws that are based on a real knowledge of the problems, that can rapidly stop the suicidal march toward destroying a heritage that is more significant than our foreign debt, or than direct elections for president – problems that can only matter if there is still a Brazil left worth fighting for."*

46 I. BURLE MARX'S EXPEDITION TO THE AMAZON

Figure 14. Camps set up at the gas stations, taking advantage of the existing service infrastructure, *Humaitá-Manaus*, Brazil. Photography: Oscar Bressane, Koiti Mori and José Tabacow, 1983.

Chronology

Date	Traveled Distance	Km
September		
27	Rio de Janeiro - Pará from Minas	534
28	Pará from Minas - São Simão	721
29	São Simão - Caiapônia	440
30	Caiapônia - Serra from Caiapó - Caiapônia	113
October		
1	Caiapônia - Jataí	160
2	Jataí - Alto Araguaia	215
3	Alto Araguaia - Cuaibá	439
4	Cuaibá	1
5	Cuaibá – Oasis Station	160
6	Oasis Station - Porto Esperidião	188
7	Porto Esperidião – Sapê Farm	194
8	Sapê Farm - Road near Comodoro Station	147
9	Road near Comodoro Station - Vilhena	139
10	Vilhena - Pimenta Bueno	236
11	Pimenta Bueno - Ji-Paraná	155
12	Ji-Paraná - Porto Velho	456
13	Porto Velho	-
14	Porto Velho	-
15	Porto Velho - Humaitá	211
16	Humaitá – Gaudérios Station	179
17	Gaudérios Station – Petroselva Station	260
18	Petroselva Station - Manaus	274
19	Manaus	98
20	Manaus - INPA Reserve	67
21	INPA - Santo Antônio do Abonari	163
22	S. Antônio do Abonari - Rio dos Peixes	196
23	Rio dos Peixes - Caracaraí	240
24	Caracaraí - Boa Vista	143
25	Boa Vista - Caracaraí	156
26	Caracaraí - Rio dos Peixes	300
27	Rio dos Peixes - Igarapé das Lajes	286
28	Igarapé das Lajes - Manaus	143
29	Manaus	-
30	Manaus	-
31	Manaus	-
November		
1	Raft on dock	-
2	Raft on dock	-
3	Raft on dock	-
4	Rio Amazonas	-
5	Rio Amazonas	-
6	Rio Amazonas	-
7	Rio Amazonas	-
8	Belém	-
9	Belém	100
10	Belém - Imperatriz	601
11	Imperatriz – Mil Station (Colinas de Goiás)	356
12	Mil Station - São Jorge Station (Gurupi)	369
13	São Jorge Station – Espigão Station	476
14	Espigão Station - Goiania	276
15	Goiania - Guará	597
16	Guará - São Pablo	418
17	São Pablo - Rio de Janeiro	467
	TOTAL ROUTE	**10674 km**

141 — Monstera (Araceæ) — 241 km de Porto Esperidião, direção Porto Velho, BR-364/MT
142 — Philodendron (Araceæ) — Folha pequena, trepador. 334 km de Porto Esperidião, direção Porto Velho, BR-364/MT
143 — Philodendron (brasiliensis?) (Araceæ) — Pleno sol. 408 km de Porto Esperidião, direção Porto Velho, BR-364/MT
144 — Passiflora (Passifloraceæ) — Flores vermelhas, frutos ovais verdes. 201 km de Porto Esperidião, direção Porto Velho, BR-364/MT (PCH 8597)
145 — Philodendron (Araceæ) — Trepador, folhas sagitadas, reptante, meia sombra. 23 km de Vilhena, direção Porto Velho, BR-364/RO (PCH 8614)
146 — Philodendron (Araceæ) — Parece PCH 8610. Erecto, folhas sagitadas, mais estreitas que 8614. 23 km de Vilhena, direção Porto Velho, BR-364/RO (PCH 8615)
147 — Epiphyllum phyllanthus (Cactaceæ) — Parece Rhipsalis, ca. 640 msm. 38 km de Vilhena, direção Porto Velho, BR-364/RO (PCH 8616)
148 — Heliconia (Musaceæ) — Semi umbrófila, lugar alagadiço, 2,00m de altura, folhas dísticas, face dorsal pruinosa, flores ligeiramente hirsutas, cor verde, inflorescência dística, ocasionalmente polística. Coletada na cidade de Pimenta Bueno, RO.
149 — Philodendron (Araceæ) — Sementes, igual a 143. Pimenta Bueno - RO
150 — Heliconia (Musaceæ) — Jovem, borda vermelha, altura 0,40m. Pimenta Bueno, R
151 — Philodendron maximum (Araceæ) — Tronco, folha 1,00 x 0,50m. Entre Pimenta Bueno e Ji-Paraná, RO.
152 — Orchidaceæ — Pequenos bulbos estriados, folhas finas. Entre Pimenta Bueno e Ji-Paraná, RO.
153 — Aechmea fernandæ (Bromeliaceæ) — Folha grande com espinhos. Entre Pimenta Bueno e Ji-Paraná, RO.
154 — Monstera (Araceæ) — Estacas e sementes. Entre Pimenta Bueno e Ji-Paraná, RO
155 — Syngonium (Araceæ) — Entre Pimenta Bueno e Ji-Paraná, RO

Figure 15. Original publication page with illustrations representing morphological characteristics of the collected plants.

Collected Live Plants

List of Collected Live Plants.*
Field annotations and drawings: Fátima from Souza Menezes

#	Name	Family	Notes	Localization
1	*Philodendron*	Aracaceae	Riparian forest, *Cerrado* altered, half shade.	5 km from *Caiapônia*, to *Piranhas*, BR-158/GO (*Serra do Caiapó*).
2	*Costus*	Zingiberaceae	Riparian forest, *Cerrado* altered, partial shade.	5 km from *Caiapônia*, to *Piranhas*, BR-158/GO (*Serra do Caiapó*).
3	*Clusia*	Guttiferae	White flower, oval fruit, 2.50 m tall, seedlings and seeds, sun.	5 km from *Caiapônia*, to *Piranhas*, BR-158/GO (*Serra do Caiapó*).
4	*Vanilla*	-	-	40 km from *Caiapônia*, to *Piranhas*, BR-158/GO (*Serra do Caiapó*).
5	*Renealmia*	Iridaceae	2 m tall, similar leaf to clusia.	60 km from *Caiapônia*, to *Piranhas*, BR-158/GO (*Serra do Caiapó*).
6	*Anthurium*	Araceae	Clay soil with stones.	65 km from *Caiapônia*, to *Piranhas*, BR-158/GO (*Serra do Caiapó*).
7	*Philodendron*	Araceae	Partial shade.	65 km from *Caiapônia*, to *Piranhas*, BR-158/GO (*Serra do Caiapó*).
8	*Norantea*	Marcgraviaceae	Flower wine in bunches.	65 km from *Caiapônia*, to *Piranhas*, BR-158/GO (*Serra do Caiapó*).
9	*Clusia*	Guttiferae	Round fruit.	65 km from *Caiapônia*, to *Piranhas*, BR-158/GO (*Serra do Caiapó*).
10	*Vellozia*	Velloziaceae	Collected by Roberto Burle Marx.	65 km from *Caiapônia*, to *Piranhas*, BR-158/GO (*Serra do Caiapó*).
11	*Dyckia*	Bromeliaceae	-	65 km from *Caiapônia*, to *Piranhas*, BR-158/GO (*Serra do Caiapó*).
12	-	Bromeliaceae	Roadside, muddy soil with gravel, altered *Cerrado*.	65 km from *Caiapônia*, to *Piranhas*, BR-158/GO (*Serra do Caiapó*).
13	*Dyckia*	Bromeliaceae	-	47 km from *Caiapônia*, to *Jatal*, BR-158/GO (*Serra do Caiapó*).
14	*Cyrtopodium*	Orchidaceae	-	47 km from *Caiapônia*, to *Jatal*, BR-158/GO (*Serra do Caiapó*).
15	*Pseudobombax*	Bombacaceae	-	47 km from *Caiapônia*, to *Jatal*, BR-158/GO (*Serra do Caiapó*).
16	*Dyckia*	Bromeliaceae	-	49 km from *Caiapônia*, to *Jatal*, BR-158/GO (*Serra do Caiapó*).
17	*Manihot*	Euphorbiaceae	-	49 km from *Caiapônia*, to *Jatal*, BR-158/GO (*Serra do Caiapó*).
18	*Costus*	Zingiberaceae	Hairy leaf, 0.30 m tall.	49 km from *Caiapônia*, to *Jatal*, BR-158/GO (*Serra do Caiapó*).
19	*Cephaelis*	Rubiaceae	Opposite leaves, yellow flower, red bracts and blue fruits (feeding birds), 1.80 m high, shade, flooded place. PCH 8532.	47 km, from *Jatal* to *Rondonópolis*, BR-364/GO.
20	*Clusia*	Guttiferae	-	47 km from *Jatal* to *Rondonópolis*, BR-364/GO.

* Table elaborated cataloging information according to: number, name, family, notes, location and images. Spaces without information are marked with a hyphen (-). Question marks (?) are typical of the original.

21	*Costus*	Zingiberaceae	Leaves 0.10 x 0.25 m, 2 m tall, marsh. PCH 8533.	47 km from *Jataí*, to *Rondonópolis*, BR-364/GO.
22	*Manihot*	Euphorbiaceae	-	47 km from *Jataí*, to *Rondonópolis*, BR-364/GO.
23	*Dyckia*	Bromeliaceae	-	47 km from *Jataí*, to *Rondonópolis*, BR-364/GO.
24	*Vellozia*	Velloziaceae	PCH 8543.	47 km from *Jataí*, to *Rondonópolis*, BR-364/GO.
25	*Vellozia*	Velloziaceae	Large leaves, lilac flower. PCH 8541.	47 km from *Jataí*, to *Rondonópolis*, BR-364/GO
26	-	Iridaceae	White flower, green leaf, thin, 1.5 cm wide, 0.50 m tall, bulbs. PCH 8527.	47 km from *Jataí*, to *Rondonópolis*, BR-364/GO.
27	-	Bromeliaceae	Pink inflorescence with 0.60 m, clay-sandy soil, sun, *Cerrado* altered, 840 m.a.s.l. approx. PCH 8556.	42 km from *Alto Araguaia*, to *Rondonópolis*, BR-364/MT.
28	*Manihot*	Euphorbiaceae	Large leaves, shrub. 1.50 m tall, 2.50 m in diameter (seeds collected). PCH 8546.	42 km from *Alto Araguaia*, to *Rondonópolis*, BR-364/MT.
29	*Manihot*	Euphorbiaceae	Thin leaf, 0.50 m tall, sun. PCH 8547, WR 10392.	42 km from *Alto Araguaia*, to *Rondonópolis*, BR-364/MT.
30	*Dyckia*	Bromeliaceae	0.30 m tall, inflorescence 1 m high, sun. PCH 8552.	*Serra da Petrovina.* 133 km from *Alto Araguaia*, to *Rondonópolis*, BR-364/MT.
31	*Hippeastrum*	Amarillidaceae	Greenish yellow (flower), sun. PCH 8551.	*Serra da Petrovina.* 133 km from *Alto Araguaia*, to *Rondonópolis*, BR-364/MT.
32	*Philodendron*	Araceae	Partial shade, grotto with vegetation, with soil with gravel. PCH 8557.	*Serra da Petrovina.* 135 km from *Alto Araguaia*, to *Rondonópolis*, BR-364/MT.
33	*Anthurium*	Araceae	Partial shade, grotto with vegetation, with white sole with gravel. PCH 8553.	*Serra da Petrovina.* 135 km from *Alto Araguaia*, to *Rondonópolis*, BR-364/MT.
34	-	Bromeliaceae	Partial shade. Terrestrial.	*Serra da Petrovina.*
35	*Pavonia*	Malvaceae	Lemon yellow, 1,50 m tall, roadside. WR 10398.	*Serra da Petrovina.* 79 km from *Alto Araguaia*, to *Rondonópolis*, BR-364/MT.
36	*Vellozia*	Velloziaceae	580 m.a.s.l. approx.	133 km from *Alto Araguaia*, to *Rondonópolis*, BR-364/MT. *Serra da Petrovina.*
37	*Vellozia*	Velloziaceae	Roadside, *Cerrado*, soil muddy with stones.	*Serra da Petrovina*, 133 km from *Alto Araguaia*, to *Rondonópolis*, BR-364 /MT.
38	*Astrocaryum*	Palmaceae	Altered *Cerrado*.	9 km from *Caiapônia*, to *Piranhas*, BR-158/GO. *Serra do Caiapó.*
39	*Scheelea*	Palmaceae	-	35 km from *Caiapônia*, to *Piranhas*, BR-158/GO.
40	*Attalea acaule*	Palmaceae	Infrutescence in the form of scorpion.	43 km from *Caiapônia*, to *Piranhas*, BR-158/GO. *Serra do Caiapó.*
41	*Acrocomia*	Palmaceae	-	65 km from *Caiapônia*, to *Piranhas*, BR-158/GO.
42	*Orbygnia* (?)	Palmaceae	-	35 km from *Caiapônia*, to *Piranhas*, BR-158/GO.
43	*Philodendron mellobarretoanum*	Araceae	-	*Collected in the city of Caiapônia.*
44	*Doliocarpus*	Dilleniaceae	Woody climber.	*Serra do Caiapó.*
45	*Eriotheca*	Bombacaceae	-	27 km from *Caiapônia*, to *Piranhas*, BR-158/GO.

46	*Dillenia*	Dilleniaceae	-	20 km from *Caiapônia*, to *Jataí*, BR-158/GO.
47	*Dyckia*	Bromeliaceae	-	65 km from *Caiapônia*, to *Jataí*, BR-158/GO.
48	*Jacaranda*	Bignoniaceae	Seeds.	University of *Cuiabá*.
49	*Butia*	Palmaceae	Large plant.	*Jataí* Station.
50	*Hymenaea*	Leguminosae	Dark standing fruits, 8 m tall, 0.25 m trunk diameter. WR 10377.	*Serra do Caiapó.*
51	*Cryptanthus*	Bromeliaceae	Saxícola, heliófila, 1300 m.a.s.l. approx. PCH 8478.	*Serra da Moeda*. 40 km to the south of *Belo Horizonte*, BR-040/MG.
52	*Heliconia hirsuta*	Musaceae	Heliophyte, 2 m tall, border of road, very flowery. PCH 8498.	*Ribeiro*/MG.
53	-	Bromeliaceae	1190 m.a.s.l. approx., terrestrial, heliophyte. PCH 8488.	*Alto Paraíba*/MG.
54	*Bromelia* sp.	Bromeliaceae	Small formations along the road, fragile, not sun, red bracts, 830 m.a.s.l. approx. PCH 8501.	*Municipality Jataí*/GO.
55	-	Bromeliaceae	Terrestrial, heliophyte, small formation, total red bracts in full bloom, pink flowers, 920 m.a.s.l. approx. PCH 8502.	*Estancia*/G.
56	*Hippeastrum*	Amaryllidaceae	Terrestrial, heliophyte, 1040 m.a.s.l. approx. PCH 8503.	*Caiapônia.*
57	-	Bromeliaceae	Species of great size, umbrophyll or semi-heliophyte, relatively common, low central inflorescence, dark green leaf sheet when in bloom, red sheets, hairiness next to maroon flowers and at the base of the leaves, 1040 m.a.s.l. approx. PCH 8504.	*Caiapônia.*
58	*Anthurium*	Araceae	*Rupicolous*, semi-umbrophyll. PCH 8548.	Separated 1 km from the road, Municipality *Pedra Preta*/MT, 84 km from Alto Araguaia, to Rondonópolis, BR-364/MT.
59	*Catasetum o Cyrtopodium* (?)	Orchidaceae	Terrestrial, heliophyte.	Municipality *Pedra Preta*/MT, 84 km from *Alto Araguaia*, to *Rondonópolis*, BR-364/MT.
60	-	Velloziaceae	Terrestrial, heliophyte. PCH 8549.	Municipality from *Pedra Preta*/MT, 84 km from *Alto Araguaia*, to *Rondonópolis*, BR-364/MT.
61	*Heliconia*	Musaceae	Growing in a flood zone, heliophyte, 3 m tall, 300 m.a.s.l. approx. PCH 8555.	84 km from *Alto Araguaia*, to *Rondonópolis*, BR-364/MT.
62	*Bactris o Acrocomia*	Palmaceae	Large plant, 750 m.a.s.l. approx.	27 km from *Luz*/MG, BR-262.
63	*Philodendron*	Araceae	Partial shade.	Estancia, Municipality of *Caiapônia*/GO.
64	*Dyckia pummila*	Bromeliaceae	Heliophyte, rupcula, organge flowers, 920 m.a.s.l. approx. PCH 8515.	*Serra do Caiapó*/GO - *Caiapônia.*
65	*Anthurium*	Araceae	Given by José Guilherme.	*Cuiabá*/MT.
66	*Anthurium*	Araceae	720 m.a.s.l. approx. PCH 8505.	*Caiapônia.*
67	*Cattleya nobilis* (?)	Orchidaceae	Given by Ofromrlig Marium de Abreu (Forest Engineer).	*Cuiabá*/MT.
68	*Philodendron*	Araceae	Large leaf, going up in *Scheelea*, low vegetation, *Cerrado* half burned. PCH 8560.	120 km from *Cuiabá*, to *Cáceres*, BR-364/MT.

69	Bactris	Palmaceae	Low, 0.90 m tall, leaves sawn, thorns on the central nerve. PCH 8559	120 km from *Cuiabá*, to *Cáceres*, BR-364/MT.
70	Triplaris	Polygonaceae	Live red flowers and other plants light pink, 5 m tall, 1.50 m diameter.	Serra da Caixa Furada, Ouricuri, 122 km from *Cuiabá*, to *Cáceres*, BR-364/MT.
71	Guazuma ulmifolia	Sterculiaceae	12 m tall, 6 m diameter, seeds. PCH 8562.	160 km from *Cuiabá* (Oasis Station), to *Cáceres*, BR-364/MT.
72	Bixa (Urucum)	-	Shrub, 3 m tall, 1.50 m diameter, seeds, sun, wet clay.	160 km from *Cuiabá* (Oasis Station), to *Cáceres*, BR-364/MT.
73	Zephyranthes	Amaryllidaceae	White flower, yellow stamens, green leaf, narrow, 0.30 m tall.	160 km from *Cuiabá* (Oasis Station), to *Cáceres*, BR-364/MT.
74	-	Bromeliaceae	Nest. Low inflorescence, red plant and green outras, clay soil, low forest, sun. PCH 8568.	182 km from *Cuiabá*, to *Cáceres*, BR-364/MT.
75	Zamia	Cycadaceae	Bolivian? Thin leaf, 0.60 m tall, shrub without stem, with rhizome, light yellow fruit when young, brown when ripe. PCH 8565.	182 km from *Cuiabá*, to *Cáceres*, BR-364/MT.
76	Dyckia	Bromeliaceae	Large, clay soil.	182 km from *Cuiabá*, to *Cáceres*, BR-364/MT.
77	Hippeastrum	Amaryllidaceae	Lemon cream flower, leaf 2 cm. Matte green. PCH 8569.	182 km from *Cuiabá*, to *Cáceres*, BR-364/MT.
78	-	Orchidaceae	Terrestrial, leaf 0.07 m wide 0.02 cm, small bulbs. PCH 8570.	182 km from *Cuiabá*, to *Cáceres*, BR-364/MT.
79	Cochlospermum	Malvaceae	1.50 m tall, big flower, showy, sun.	182 km from *Cuiabá*, to *Cáceres*, BR-364/MT.
80	Philodendron	Araceae	Maybe the same 68. Large leaf, climbing in tree, sun.	187 km from *Cuiabá*, to *Cáceres*, BR-364/MT.
81	Heliconia episcopalis	Musaceae	Large shape, 3 m tall, elongated leaf, shade, river edge. 280 m.a.s.l. approx. PCH 8571.	185 km from *Cuiabá*, to *Cáceres*, BR-364/MT.
82	Vanilla	Orchidaceae	In palm tree trunk.	Serra do Boi Morto, BR-364/MT.
83	Anthurium	Araceae	Large leaves, stone, clay soil. PCH 8574.	203 km from *Cuiabá*, to *Cáceres*, BR-364/MT.
84	Mediocactus?	Cactaceae	Triangular, epiphyte, sun. PCH 8573.	203 km from *Cuiabá*, to *Cáceres*, BR-364/MT.
85	Erythrina	Leguminosae papilionoidea	Stakes.	203 km from *Cuiabá*, to *Cáceres*, BR-364/MT.
86	-	Bromeliaceae	Long leaves, nest type, light green. PCH 8575.	203 km from *Cuiabá*, to *Cáceres*, BR-364/MT.
87	Dyckia	Bromeliaceae	Light green. PCH 8572.	203 km from *Cuiabá*, to *Cáceres*, BR-364/MT.
88	-	Bignoniaceae	Seed. PCH 8576.	206 km from *Cuiabá*, to *Cáceres*, BR-364/MT.
89	Philodendron	Araceae	Growing on palm tree.	207 km from *Cuiabá*, to *Cáceres*, BR-364/MT.
90	-	Bromeliaceae	Red and white inflorescence, 0.50 m tall, 0.70 m diameter. PCH 8566.	182 km from *Cuiabá*, to *Cáceres*, BR-364/MT.
91	Acrocomia	Palmae	Small, round fruits.	233 km from *Cuiabá*, to *Cáceres*, BR-364/MT.
92	Pithecellobium	Leguminosae	10 m tall, seeds.	167 km from *Cuiabá*, to *Cáceres*, BR-364/MT.
93	Acrocomia	Palmae	Seeds. PCH 8581.	Porto Esperidião. 109 km from *Cáceres*, to Vilhena, BR-364/MT.

78

81

94	*Lueheopsis*	Tiliaceae	-	*Cáceres* Road/*Porto Esperidião.*
95	*Tabebuia*	Bignoniaceae	Pink-white flower, seeds. PCH 8582.	6 km from *Porto Esperidião,* to *Vilhena,* BR-364/MT.
96	-	-	-	-
97	-	-	-	-
98	*Clusia*	Guttiferae	Clay-sandy soil, roadside, 1 m tall. PCH 8588.	53 km from *Porto Esperidião,* to *Porto Velho,* BR-364/MT.
99	*Philodendron or Syngonium* (?)	Araceae	Climber. PCH 8585.	53 km from *Porto Esperidião,* to *Porto Velho,* BR-364/MT.
100	*Philodendron*	Araceae	Leaf 0.40 x 0.25 m, clay soil-sandy, climbing, new shape with dark green leaf. PCH 8583.	53 km from *Porto Esperidião,* to *Porto Velho,* BR-364/MT.
101	-	Orchidaceae	On dry branch on the edge of the road. PCH 8586.	53 km from *Porto Esperidião,* to *Porto Velho,* BR-364/MT.
102	*Mauritiella aculeata*	Palmaceae	4 m high, 4 m diameter, oval fruits with 2 x 3 cm with scales. PCH 8590.	57 km from *Porto Esperidião,* to *Porto Velho,* BR-364/MT.
103	*Cyrtopodium*	Orchidaceae	Epiphyte, shade, humid forest.	57 km from *Porto Esperidião,* to *Porto Velho,* BR-364/MT.
104	*Attalea*	Palmaceae	Oval fruits, 5 x 7 cm, when ripe, 2 m tall. PCH 8589.	57 km from *Porto Esperidião,* to *Porto Velho,* BR-364/MT.
105	*Caladium*	Araceae	*Striatipes?* Leaf 11 x 30 cm, green with light green stretch marks, swamp.	57 km from *Porto Esperidião,* to *Porto Velho,* BR-364/MT.
106	*Costus*	Zingiberaceae	-	57 km from *Porto Esperidião,* to *Porto Velho,* BR-364/MT.
107	*Hippeastrum*	Amaryllidaceae	Orange flower, with light center.	67 km from *Porto Esperidião,* to *Porto Velho,* BR-364/MT (PCH 8591).
108	*Cyrtopodium*	Orchidaceae	Terrestrial.	78 km from *Porto Esperidião,* to *Porto Velho,* BR-364/MT.
109	*Philodendron*	Araceae	Climber, giant leaves, growing on *Orbygnia*	97 km from *Porto Esperidião,* to *Porto Velho,* BR-364/MT (PCH 8593).
110	*Astrocaryum?*	Palmaceae	Orange fruits, seeds, pre elongated trunk, 4 m tall, with thorns, scrub.	192 km from *Porto Esperidião,* to *Porto Velho,* BR-364/MT (PCH 8594). *Sapê* farm.
111	*Bactris*	Palmaceae	Small purple fruits, small inflorescence, trunk and leaves with thorns, 2 to 3 m tall.	192 km from *Porto Esperidião,* to *Porto Velho,* BR-364/MT (PCH 8595). *Sapê* farm.
112	*Hymenaea*	Leguminosae	Seeds, sun.	194 km from *Porto Esperidião,* to *Porto Velho,* BR-364/MT.
113	-	Bromeliaceae	Seeds, sun.	194 km from *Porto Esperidião,* to *Porto Velho,* BR-364/MT.
114	*Heliconia*	Musaceae	Very delicate.	194 km from *Porto Esperidião,* to *Porto Velho,* BR-364/MT.
115	*Syagrus*	Palmaceae	Fine palm tree, green fruits, black seeds, 7 m tall. PCH 8598.	203 km from *Porto Esperidião,* to *Porto Velho,* BR-364/MT.
116	*Heliconia*	Musaceae	-	194 km from *Porto Esperidião,* to *Porto Velho,* BR-364/MT.
117	*Syagrus*	Palmaceae	Marsh, shade.	235 km from *Porto Esperidião,* to *Porto Velho,* BR-364/MT.
118	*Ceiba*	Bombacaceae	Enormous.	246 km from *Porto Esperidião,* to *Porto Velho,* BR-364/MT.

54 I. BURLE MARX'S EXPEDITION TO THE AMAZON

119	*Acrocomia*	Palmaceae	Orange pulp.	Purchased in *Cuiabá*.
	Acrocomia	Palmaceae	Green pulp.	Purchased in *Cuiabá*.
120	*Sapium* sp.	Euphorbiaceae	-	-
121	*Scheelea* sp.	Palmaceae	3/4 m tall. PCH 8600.	208 km from *Porto Esperidião*, to *Porto Velho*, BR-364/MT.
122	*Iriartea exorrhiza*	Palmaceae	Orange-yellow fruit, brown seed, 15 m tall. PCH 8599.	204 km from *Porto Esperidião*, to *Porto Velho*, BR-364/MT.
123	*Philodendron speciosum* (or *brasiliensis*?)	Araceae	3 m tall, multiple and erect petioles. PCH 8611.	438 km from *Porto Esperidião*, to *Porto Velho*, BR-364/ RO.
124	*Rodriguesia*	Orchidaceae	-	286 km from *Porto Esperidião*, to *Porto Velho*, BR-364/MT.
125	*Epidendron*	Orchidaceae	-	286 km from *Porto Esperidião*, to *Porto Velho*, BR-364/MT.
126	*Tillandsia*	Bromeliaceae	Small leaves.	334 km from *Porto Esperidião*, to *Porto Velho*, BR-364/MT.
127	*Tillandsia*	Bromeliaceae	Large leaves.	334 km from *Porto Esperidião*, to *Porto Velho*, BR-364/MT.
128	*Erythrina*	Leguminosae papilionoidea	Seedling.	263 km from *Porto Esperidião*, to *Porto Velho*, BR-364/MT.
129	*Guzmania brasiliensis*	Bromeliaceae	Green leaves with green light spots	263 km from *Porto Esperidião*, to *Porto Velho*, BR-364/MT.
130	*Anthurium*	Araceae	Large leaf, tree, shade.	263 km from *Porto Esperidião*, to *Porto Velho*, BR-364/MT.
131	*Heliconia*	Musaceae	-	334 km from *Porto Esperidião*, to *Porto Velho*, BR-364/MT.
132	*Asplenium*	Polypodiaceae	-	334 km from *Porto Esperidião*, to *Porto Velho*, BR-364/MT.
133	*Philodendron*	Araceae	Reddish back, with stretch marks.	402 km from *Porto Esperidião*, to *Porto Velho*, BR-364/MT.
134	-	Bromeliaceae	-	286 km from *Porto Esperidião*, to *Porto Velho*, BR-364/MT.
135	*Ischnosiphon*	Marantaceae	Bluish green leaf.	442 km from *Porto Esperidião*, to *Porto Velho*, BR-364/MT.
136	*Philodendron*	Araceae	Full sun, climber.	408 km from *Porto Esperidião*, to *Porto Velho*, BR-364/MT.
137	*Philodendron*	Araceae	-	402 km from *Porto Esperidião*, to *Porto Velho*, BR-364/MT.
138	*Philodendron*	Araceae	Climber, partial shade. PCH 8600.	208 km from *Porto Esperidião*, to *Porto Velho*, BR-364/MT.
139	*Monstera*	Araceae	Climber.	208 km from *Porto Esperidião*, to *Porto Velho*, BR-364/MT.
140	*Monstera?*	Araceae	Small leaf.	286 km from *Porto Esperidião*, *Porto Velho*, BR-364/MT.
141	*Monstera*	Araceae	-	241 km from *Porto Esperidião*, to *Porto Velho*, BR-364/MT.

142	*Philodendron*	Araceae	Small leaf, climbing.	334 km from *Porto Esperidião*, to *Porto Velho*, BR-364/MT.
143	*Philodendron (brasiliensis?)*	Araceae	Full sun.	408 km from *Porto Esperidião*, to *Porto Velho*, BR-364/MT.
144	*Passiflora*	Passifloraceae	Red flowers, green oval fruits. PCH 8597.	201 km from *Porto Esperidião*, to *Porto Velho*, BR-364/MT.
145	*Philodendron*	Araceae	Climber, sagitted leaves, crawling, half shade. PCH 8614.	23 km from *Vilhena*, to *Porto Velho*, BR-364/RO.
146	*Philodendron*	Araceae	Seems PCH 8610. Erect, leaves sagitted, narrower than 8614. PCH 8615.	23 km from *Vilhena*, to *Porto Velho*, BR-364/RO.
147	*Epiphyllum phyllanthus*	Cactaceae	Seems Rhipsalis, 640 m.a.s.l. approx. PCH 8616.	38 km from *Vilhena*, to Porto Velho, BR-364/RO.
148	*Heliconia*	Musaceae	Semi-umbrophile, marshy place, 2 m tall, distic leaves, thorny dorsal face, slightly rough flowers, green color, distal inflorescence, occasionally polistic.	Collected in the city of *Pimenta Bueno*, RO.
149	*Philodendron*	Araceae	Seeds, same as 143.	*Collected in the city of Pimenta Bueno*, RO.
150	*Heliconia*	Musaceae	Young, red border, 0.40 m tall.	*Pimenta Bueno*, RO.
151	*Philodendron maximum*	Araceae	Trunk, leaf 1 x 0.50 m.	Between *Pimenta Bueno* and *Ji-Paraná*, RO.
152	-	Orchidaceae	Small fluted bulbs, thin leaves.	Between *Pimenta Bueno* and *Ji-Paraná*, RO.
153	*Aechmea fernandae*	Bromeliaceae	Large leaf with thorns.	Between *Pimenta Bueno* and *Ji-Paraná*, RO.
154	*Monstera*	Araceae	Stakes and seeds.	Between *Pimenta Bueno* and *Ji-Paraná*, RO.
155	*Syngonium*	Araceae	-	Between *Pimenta Bueno* and *Ji-Paraná*, RO.
156	*Philodendron*	Araceae	-	Between *Pimenta Bueno* and *Ji-Paraná*, RO.
157	*Philodendron*	Araceae	Thin leaf.	Between *Pimenta Bueno* and *Ji-Paraná*, RO.
158	*Philodendron*	Araceae	Climber.	Between *Pimenta Bueno* and *Ji-Paraná*, RO.
159	*Philodendron*	Araceae	-	Between *Pimenta Bueno* and *Ji-Paraná*, RO.
160	*Philodendron*	Araceae	-	Between *Pimenta Bueno* and *Ji-Paraná*, RO.
161	-	Cyclanthaceae	Shade.	Between *Pimenta Bueno* and *Ji-Paraná*, RO.
162	*Monstera*	Araceae	Same as 139.	Between *Pimenta Bueno* and *Ji-Paraná*, RO.
163	*Philodendron*	Araceae	-	Between *Pimenta Bueno* and *Ji-Paraná*, RO.
164	*Monstera*	Araceae	Large leaf.	Between *Pimenta Bueno* and *Ji-Paraná*, RO.

56 I. BURLE MARX'S EXPEDITION TO THE AMAZON

165	Monstera	Araceae	Small, thin stem.	Between Pimenta Bueno and Ji-Paraná, RO.
166	Philodendron	Araceae	-	Between Pimenta Bueno and Ji-Paraná, RO.
167	-	Marantaceae	Half shade, height 6 m.	Between Pimenta Bueno and Ji-Paraná, RO.
168	Urospatha?	Araceae	Deep forest shadow. 260 m.a.s.l. approx. PCH 8620.	24 km from Ji-Paraná, to Porto Velho, BR-364/RO.
169	Astrocaryum?	Palmaceae	Fruits. PCH 8622.	24 km from Ji-Paraná, to Porto Velho, BR-364/RO.
170	Monstera	Araceae	PCH 8621.	24 km from Ji-Paraná, to Porto Velho, BR-364/RO.
171	Xanthosoma	Araceae	Leaf 1 x 0.60 m height 3 m. PCH 8624.	38 km from Ji-Paraná, to Porto Velho, BR-364/RO.
172	Philodendron	Araceae	310 m.a.s.l. approx., trepador. PCH 8623.	38 km from Ji-Paraná, to Porto Velho, BR-364/RO.
173	Aechmea sprucei	Bromeliaceae	Green, gray.	38 km from Ji-Paraná, to Porto Velho, BR-364/RO.
174	Clusia	Guttiferae	PCH 8626.	38 km from Ji-Paraná, to Porto Velho, BR-364/RO.
175	-	Orchidaceae	PCH 8628.	38 km from Ji-Paraná, to Porto Velho, BR-364/RO.
176	Maxillaria?	Orchidaceae	PCH 8627.	38 km from Ji-Paraná, to Porto Velho, BR-364/RO.
177	Attalea (or Orbygnia?)	Palmaceae	12 m high, 360 m.a.s.l. approx. PCH 8629.	41 km from Ji-Paraná, to Porto Velho, BR-364/RO.
178	Anthurium	Araceae	Giant. PCH 8630.	41 km from Ji-Paraná, to Porto Velho, BR-364/RO.
179	Caladium?	Araceae	No leaves, hardly the inflorescence, Less than 0.30 m high. PCH 8631.	6 km from Jaru, to Porto Velho, BR-364/RO.
180	Mauritiella armata or echinata?	Palmaceae	Caranaí. Thorns on the trunk, green seeds, 160 m.a.s.l. approx. PCH 8634.	4 km from Porto Velho, to Humaitá, BR-316/RO.
181	Montrichardia	Araceae	2 m tall, marsh, sun.	10 km from Porto Velho, to Humaitá, BR-316/RO.
182	Heliconia	Musaceae	Marsh, partial shade. PCH 8636.	10 km from Porto Velho, to Humaitá, BR-316/RO.
183	Bambusa	Gramineae	4 m tall thicket. PCH 8638.	10 km from Porto Velho, to Humaitá, BR-316/RO.
184	Melastomateceae	-	Red leaves, pink flowers, grass, next to small stream, exposed to the sun. PCH 8637.	10 km from Porto Velho, to Humaitá, BR-316/RO.
185	Aechmea mertensii?	Bromeliaceae	PCH 8645.	44 km from Porto Velho, to Humaitá, BR-316.
186	Philodendron	Araceae	Climber, sun, 210 m.a.s.l. approx. PCH 8641.	44 km from Porto Velho, to Humaitá, BR-316.
187	Philodendron	Araceae	Climber, sun, 210 m.a.s.l. approx. PCH 8642.	44 km from Porto Velho, to Humaitá, BR-316.
188	Palicourea	Rubiaceae	Bush, red flowers, purple stem, near to the flowers, 230 m.a.s.l. approx. PCH 8646.	48 km from Porto Velho, to Humaitá, BR-316.
189	Philodendron	Araceae	Purple leaf behind, climber.	83 km from Porto Velho, to Humaitá, BR-316.
190	Philodendron	Araceae	Leaf 0.25 x 0.55 m, liana.	83 km from Porto Velho, to Humaitá, BR-316.
191	Heliconia	Musaceae	Sun, pink, orange and yellow.	10 km from the intersection of Humaitá.
192	Calathea	Marantaceae	-	10 km from the intersection of Humaitá, BR-316/AM.

193	Philodendron	Araceae	Shade.	10 km from the intersection of Humaitá, BR-316/AM.
194	Philodendron	Araceae	-	10 km from the intersection of Humaitá, BR-316/AM.
195	Philodendron	Araceae	Shade.	20 km from the intersection of Humaitá, BR-316/AM.
196	Calathea	Marantaceae	Green with light stretch marks.	20 km from the intersection of Humaitá, BR-316/AM.
197	Philodendron	Araceae	Shade, climber.	20 km from the intersection of Humaitá, BR-316/AM.
198	Clusia	Guttiferae	1 m tall, medium shade, 190 m.a.s.l. approx.	39 km from the intersection of Humaitá, BR-316/AM.
199	Philodendron	Araceae	Quite frequent, creeper, 190 m.a.s.l. approx., flowers in the sun, sagittate leaves. PCH 8657.	39 km from the intersection of Humaitá, BR-316/AM.
200	Philodendron	Araceae	Climber, deep shadow, inflorescence 0.20 m, rough petiole, magenta, soft leaves, pale green, uncommon, 190 m.a.s.l. approx. PCH 8658.	39 km from the intersection of Humaitá, BR-316/AM.
201	Philodendron	Araceae	LCG 1338.	39 km from the intersection of Humaitá, BR-316/AM.
202	Philodendron	Araceae	LCG 1339.	-
203	Philodendron	Araceae	LCG 1340.	-
204	Philodendron	Araceae	LCG 1343.	-
205	Philodendron	Araceae	LCG 1341.	-
206	Philodendron o Syngonium?	Araceae	LCG 1345.	-
207	Ischnosiphon	Marantaceae	Erect grass, 1.50 m tall, red bracts, light lilac petals, dry ground plant, frequent. PCH 8665. WR 10454.	165 km from Humaitá, to Manaus, BR-316/AM.
208	Dieffenbachia	Araceae	-	165 km from Humaitá, to Manaus, BR-316/AM.
209	Anthurium	Araceae	Palms, 19 Leaflets. PCH 8660.	165 km from Humaitá, to Manaus, BR-316/AM.
210	Philodendron	Araceae	-	165 km from Humaitá, to Manaus, BR-316/AM.
211	Aechmea?	Bromeliaceae	Low, light green. PCH 8664.	165 km from Humaitá, to Manaus, BR-316/AM.
212	Philodendron ou Monstera?	Araceae	Small leaf with marbled spots, scaly. PCH 8663.	165 km from Humaitá, to Manaus, BR-316/AM.
213	Duguetia	Annonaceae	With fruits. PCH 8661.	165 km from Humaitá, to Manaus, BR-316/AM.
214	Palicourea	Rubiaceae	Corimbosa? 5 m tall, Intense golden yellow flowers, large striated leaves. PCH 8670.	185 km from Humaitá, to Manaus, BR-316/AM
215	Isertia hypoleuca	Rubiaceae	3 m tall, large flower, red, large green leaf, in the light green verse.	185 km from Humaitá, to Manaus, BR-316/AM.
216	-	Bromeliaceae	Leaf 3 m, green, with thorns, deep shade, 140 m.a.s.l. approx. PCH 8671.	185 km from Humaitá, to Manaus, BR-316/AM.
217	Norantea	Marcgraviaceae	Red, stakes.	-

58   I. BURLE MARX'S EXPEDITION TO THE AMAZON

	218	*Morenia*	Palmaceae	Black seeds, 2 m tall, shade, quite frequent. PCH 8672.	272 km from *Humaitá*, to *Manaus*, BR-316/AM (*São João* farm).
220	219	*Leptocarya tenue?*	Palmaceae	Small fruit, oranged red, with scales, leafy population. PCH 8673.	272 km from *Humaitá*, to *Manaus*, BR-316/AM (*São João* farm).
	220	*Philodendron tripartitum*	Araceae	PCH 8677.	272 km from *Humaitá*, to *Manaus*, BR-316/AM (*São João* farm).
	221	*Asplenium*	Polypodiaceae	PCH 8679.	272 km from *Humaitá*, to *Manaus*, BR-316/AM (*São João* farm).
	222	*Philodendron*	Araceae	Big. PCH 8678.	272 km from *Humaitá*, to *Manaus*, BR-316/AM (*São João* farm).
	223	*Philodendron*	Araceae	Lacinate leaves, growing on PCH 8673, small. PCH 8674.	272 km from *Humaitá*, to *Manaus*, BR-316/AM (*São João* farm).
223	224	*Heliconia*	Musaceae	Red flower, big leaves.	432 km from *Humaitá*, to *Manaus*, BR-316/AM.
	225	*Philodendron*	Araceae	Epiphyte, nesting habit, 0.90 m high. PCH 8684.	432 km from *Humaitá*, to *Manaus*, BR-316/AM.
	226	*Philodendron*	Araceae	Climbing. PCH 8686.	432 km from *Humaitá*, to *Manaus*, BR-316/AM.
226	227	*Dieffenbachia*	Araceae	Green leaves, 0.90 m high PCH 8685.	432 km from *Humaitá*, to *Manaus*, BR-316/AM.
230	228	*Philodendron*	Araceae	Scandent, small.	432 km from *Humaitá*, to *Manaus*, BR-316/AM.
229	229	*Philodendron*	Araceae	Climbing.	432 km from *Humaitá*, to *Manaus*, BR-316/AM.
	230	*Philodendron*	Araceae	Climbing.	432 km from *Humaitá*, to *Manaus*, BR-316/AM.
231	231	*Philodendron*	Araceae	Eliptic leaves, rounded petiole. PCH 8689. Could be a juvenile form from PCH 8688, see 232.	432 km from *Humaitá*, to *Manaus*, BR-316/AM.
	232	*Philodendron*	Araceae	Climbing, cordate leaves. PCH 8688.	432 km from *Humaitá*, to *Manaus*, BR-316/AM.
	233	*Philodendron*	Araceae	Long leaves, 0.55 x 0.25 cm.	434 km from *Humaitá*, to *Manaus*, BR-316/AM.
233	234	*Clusia*	Guttiferae	Eliptic-ovate leaves, very long, 1.50 m hugh, half shadow. PCH 8692.	434 km from *Humaitá*, to *Manaus*, BR-316/AM.
	235	*Pitcairnia?*	Bromeliaceae	Red flower, leaves with thorns.	434 km from *Humaitá*, to *Manaus*, BR-316/AH.
	236	*Saxo-fridericia (sclerocarpa?)*	Rapateaceae	Leaves 2 x 0.08 m, thorns on the edges.	434 km from *Humaitá*, to *Manaus*, BR-316/AM.
237	237	*Philodendron*	Araceae	Type "*cocar*", 130 m.a.s.l. approx. PCH 8694.	474 km from *Humaitá*, to *Manaus*, BR-316/AM.
	238	*Philodendron*	Araceae	-	474 km from *Humaitá*, to *Manaus*, BR-316/AM.
	239	*Heliconia tarumanensis*	Musaceae	LCG 1353.	*Porto Velho/Manaus.*
	240	*Heliconia*	Musaceae	LCG 1344.	*Manaus/Porto Velho.*
	241	*Heliconia tarumanensis*	Musaceae	Red flower. LCG 1331.	*Manaus/Porto Velho.*
	242	*Heliconia*	Musaceae	LCG 1360	Next to Iguapó-Açu river.
	243	*Heliconia tarumanensis*	Musaceae	Yellow flower. LCG 1334.	Nexto to *Humaitá*, to *Manaus.*
	244	*Heliconia*	Musaceae	Yellow flower. LCG 1323.	Next to *Porto Velho.*

245	Heliconia	Musaceae	LCG 1361.	Next to Iguapó-Açu river.
246	Heliconia	Musaceae	LCG 1346.	Next to Iguapó-Açu river.
247	Heliconia tarumanensis	Musaceae	Red flower. LCG 1321.	Manaus/Porto Velho.
248	Heliconia	Musaceae	LCG 1354.	Porto Velho/Manaus.
249	Heliconia	Musaceae	LCG 1363.	Next to Tapana river.
250	-	Araceae	Climber, dark green leaf, lighter back. PCH 8709.	Km 45 from BR-174 (INPA Reserve).
251	Philodendron	Araceae	Epiphyte, purple back on the young form, young plants in the soil of the forest, clean, long leaves, sagitted, acuminate, with reddish margins. PCH 8701.	Km 45 from BR-174 (INPA Reserve).
252	Philodendron af. melinoni	Araceae	Epiphyte. PCH 8704A.	Km 45 from BR-174/AM.
253	Anthurium	Araceae	Elliptical-ovate leaf, hard, 0.45 x 0.15 m, dark green, long petiole. PCH 8708.	Km 45 from BR-174/AM (INPA Reserve).
254	Philodendron	Araceae	Leaf lacinia and small, epiphyte. PCH 8702.	Km 45 from BR-174/AM (INPA Reserve).
255	-	Araceae	Wide petiole, flexible leaf.	Km 45 from BR-174/AM (INPA Reserve).
256	Philodendron	Araceae	Wide petiole, flexible leaf, 0.40 x 0.18 m, leaf dark green, lighter back, crepe, and reddish joint, striking ribs. PCH 8706.	Km 45 from BR-174/AM (INPA Reserve).
257	Philodendron	Araceae	Wide and triangular petiole, leaf cordata, dark green, small, red joint, epiphyte. PCH 8703.	Km 45 from BR-174/AM (INPA Reserve).
258	Philodendron	Araceae	Large rosettes, long petiole, rounded on the back, large deltoid leaves, dark green, larger than PCH 8705.	Km 45 from BR-174/AM (INPA Reserve).
259	-	Orchidaceae	No flowers, epiphyte.	-
260	-	Orchidaceae	No flowers, epiphyte.	Km 45 from BR-174/AM (INPA Reserve).
261	Heliconia	Musaceae	Dark red squirrels, white flowers, 1 m tall, swamp, rare. PCH 8713.	Km 45 from BR-174/AM (INPA Reserve).
262	Philodendron	Araceae	Yellow petioles, climber. PCH 8711. Maybe adult of PCH 8701 (251).	Km 45 from BR-174/AM (INPA Reserve)
263	Philodendron	Araceae	Climbing, hairy, hard, green leaves, 0.25 x 0.08 m. PCH 8714.	46 km from BR-174/AM, to Boa Vista.
264	Clusia	Guttiferae	Sandy soil, sun. PCH 8715.	Km 58 from BR-174/AM, to Boa Vista.
265	Heliconia	Musaceae	Big leaves, 0.80 x 0.30 m, green with white back, 2.50 m tall. PCH 8721.	Km 60 from BR-174/AM, to Boa Vista.
266	Heliconia	Musaceae	White flowers, red bracts, red central nerve on the back, leaf 0.50 x 0.10 m. PCH 8722.	Km 60 from BR-174/AM, to Boa Vista.
267	Philodendron melinoni?	Araceae	Red back, width petiole. PCH 8725.	Km 60 from BR-174/AM, to Boa Vista.
268	Cecropia	Moraceae	Pelted leaf, white on the back, hirsute, red nerves, velvety green. PCH 8726.	60 km from BR-174/AM, to Boa Vista.
269	Cecropia	Moraceae	6 bald segments. PCH 8727.	Km 60 from BR-174/AM, to Boa Vista.
270	Clusia	Guttiferae	Ovate leaves. PCH 8720.	Km 60 from BR-174/AM, to Boa Vista.

271	-	Orchidaceae	Small leaves. 170 m.a.s.l. approx. PCH 8717.	*Anaconda* farm. 60 km from BR-174/AM, to *Boa Vista*.
272	*Pitcairnia*	Bromeliaceae	Leaf 0.60 m, light green. PCH 8718.	60 km from BR-174/AM, to *Boa Vista*.
273	*Clusia*	Guttiferae	Narrow, elliptical-lanceolate leaves. PCH 8730.	60 km from BR-174/AM, to *Boa Vista*.
274	*Ananas?*	Bromeliaceae	Grayish green, thorns on the edges. PCH 8719.	60 km from BR-174/AM, to *Boa Vista*.
275	*Clusia*	Guttiferae	Elliptical leaves, 0.18 x 0.07 m. PCH 8724.	60 km from BR-174/AM, to *Boa Vista*.
276	*Philodendron*	Araceae	Long petiole, elliptical leaves, deep green. PCH 8729.	60 km from BR-174/AM, to *Boa Vista*.
277	*Aechmea?*	Bromeliaceae	Light green, thorns on the edge. PCH 8728.	60 km from BR-174/AM, to *Boa Vista*.
278	*Clusia*	Guttiferae	Obovate leaves. 170 m.a.s.l. approx. PCH 8731.	Km 100 from BR-174/AM, to *Boa Vista* (*Igarapé das Lajes*).
279	*Sobralia liliastrum?*	Orchidaceae	Thicket, 1.20 m tall. PCH 8738.	Km 120 from BR-174/AM, to *Boa Vista* (*Igarapé das Lajes*).
280	*Clusia*	Guttiferae	Thin, branched leaf, 0.40 m tall (seedlings).	Km 120 from BR-174/AM, to *Boa Vista* (*Igarapé das Lajes*).
281	-	Gesneriaceae	Hairy leaf, radius 0.30 m. PCH 8732.	Km 120 from BR-174/AM, to *Boa Vista* (*Igarapé das Lajes*).
282	*Philodendron*	Araceae	Climber.	Km 120 from BR-174/AM, to *Boa Vista* (*Igarapé das Lajes*).
283	*Philodendron*	Araceae	Leaf 0.65 x 0.30. PCH 8743.	Km 120 from BR-174/AM, to *Boa Vista* (*Igarapé das Lajes*).
284	*Philodendron*	Araceae	PCH 8744.	Km 120 from BR-174/AM, to *Boa Vista* (*Igarapé das Lajes*).
285	*Anthurium*	Araceae	Elliptical-lanceolate leaf, petiole short. PCH 8741.	Km 120 from BR-174/AM, to *Boa Vista* (*Igarapé das Lajes*).
286	*Clusia*	Guttiferae	0.40 m tall (seedlings) without ramifications.	Km 120 from BR-174/AM, to *Boa Vista* (*Igarapé das Lajes*).
287	*Philodendron*	Araceae	Epiphyte, green leaf, purple back.	Km 120 from BR-174/AM, to *Boa Vista* (*Igarapé das Lajes*).
288	-	Orchidaceae	Epiphyte.	Km 120 from BR-174/AM, to *Boa Vista* (*Igarapé das Lajes*).
289	*Philodendron*	Araceae	Epiphyte, small leaves.	Km 120 from BR-174/AM, to *Boa Vista* (*Igarapé das Lajes*).
290	-	Orchidaceae	-	Km 120 from BR-174/AM, to *Boa Vista* (*Igarapé das Lajes*)
291	-	Orchidaceae	-	Km 120 from BR-174/AM, to *Boa Vista* (*Igarapé das Lajes*).
292	*Tillandsia*	Bromeliaceae	Grayish green leaves, red flowers.	Km 120 from BR-174/AM, to *Boa Vista* (*Igarapé das Lajes*).
293	*Tillandsia*	Bromeliaceae	Flexible leaf, grayish green.	Km 120 from BR-174/AM, to *Boa Vista* (*Igarapé das Lajes*).
294	*Philodendron*	Araceae	Hard leaves, dark green, narrow, with lighter nerves, rupicolous, white spates. PCH 8739.	Km 120 from BR-174/AM, to *Boa Vista* (*Igarapé das Lajes*).

295	*Heliconia*	Musaceae	Yellow, orange bracts internally, sun, leaf 0.50 x 0.12 m, golden yellow, glauscescent on the back. PCH 8745.	214 km from BR-174/AM.
296	*Heliconia (psittacorum?)*	Musaceae	0.80 m tall, fine leaves, 0.30 x 0.06 m. PCH 8747.	214 km from BR-174/AM, to *Boa Vista*.
297	*Cecropia*	Moraceae	0.50 m tall (seedlings), Velvety leaves, when young, dark green with light green spots, grey back with red nerves.	214 km from BR-174/AM, to *Boa Vista*.
298	*Heliconia*	Musaceae	Green bracts at the base, and reds on top, some cases with green apex, yellow ovary, narrow at the base and then orange, light green leaves, purple main nerve, large. 160 m.a.s.l. approx. PCH 8749.	Jundiaí Station, 339 km from BR-174/RR, to *Boa Vista*.
299	*Heliconia*	Musaceae	Yellow bracts, orange with dark blackheads, bright orange ovary. PCH 8750.	353 km from BR-174/RR, to *Boa Vista*.
300	-	Piperaceae	Leaves 0.04 x 0.08 m.	353 km from BR-174/RR, to *Boa Vista*.
301	*Cassia*	Leguminosae	Yellow, arboretum 5/8 m tall. PCH 8753.	353 km from BR-174/RR, to *Boa Vista*.
302	*Heliconia*	Musaceae	Red nerve on the back, flower yellow and orange, bracts greener than the PCH 8749 (See 298). PCH 8751.	355 km from BR-174/RR, to *Boa Vista*.
303	-	Melastomataceae	Greenish-white flowers, 2 m tall. PCH 8752.	364 km from BR-174/RR, to *Boa Vista*.
304	*Anthurium*	Araceae	Violet flower (purple) green leaf, compound, purple spates, sun. PCH 8754.	417 km from BR-174/RR, to *Boa Vista*.
305	*Philodendron*	Araceae	Epiphyte, trilobed. PCH 8755.	417 km from BR-174/RR, to *Boa Vista*.
306	*Philodendron*	Araceae	Corded leaves, long and soft. PCH 8757.	417 km from BR-174/RR, to *Boa Vista*.
307	*Philodendron*	Araceae	Climbing, lanceolate leaves. PCH 8756.	417 km from BR-174/RR, to *Boa Vista*.
308	-	Orchidaceae	Micro. PCH 8758.	417 km from BR-174/RR, to *Boa Vista*.
309	*Syngonium*	Araceae	Light greenish-yellow spathe. PCH 8760.	417 km from BR-174/RR, to *Boa Vista*.
310	*Philodendron*	Araceae	Epiphyte.	417 km from BR-174/RR, to *Boa Vista*.
311	*Philodendron*	Araceae	Climber, sagittate lanceolate leaf, rugged. PCH 8759.	417 km from BR-174/RR, to *Boa Vista*.
312	*Heliconia*	Musaceae	Wide leaf, flowerless. PCH 8766.	497 km from BR-174/RR, to *Boa Vista*.
313	*Heliconia*	Musaceae	Thin leaf, reddish orange bracts: 2 m tall. PCH 8765.	497 km from BR-174, to *Boa Vista*.
314	*Furcraea*	Amaryllidaceae	With thorns, no flowers, local rocky. PCH 8763.	497 km from BR-174/RR, to *Boa Vista*.
315	*Begonia*	Begoniaceae	Light green, shade. PCH 8764.	497 km from BR-174/RR, to *Boa Vista*.
316	*Costus*	Zingiberaceae	Big flowers, with blue sedes, sun. PCH 8767.	497 km from BR-174/RR, to *Boa Vista*.
317	*Cyrtopodium*	Orchidaceae	PCH 8769.	534 km from BR-174/RR, to *Boa Vista*.

295

304

305

307

306

309

310

311

318	*Ananas*	Bromeliaceae	PCH 8768.	534 km from BR-174/RR, to *Boa Vista*.
319	*Cattleya*	Orchidaceae	Epiphyte, in Ipê, with fruits. PCH 8771.	12 km from *Caracaraí*, to *Boa Vista*, BR-174/RR.
320	*Cereus*	Cactaceae	120 m.a.s.l. approx. PCH 8772.	12 km from *Caracaraí*, to *Boa Vista*, BR174/RR.
321	*Ipomoea*	Convolvulaceae	White flower, small, leaves small, creeping, pelted leaf, 2 x 2 cm.	17 km from *Caracaraí*, to *Manaus*, BR-174/RR.
322	*Philodendron*	Araceae	Climber, leaf 12 x 20 cm.	17 km from *Caracaraí*, to *Manaus*, BR-174/RR.
323	*Clusia*	Guttiferae	White flower with pink center, leaf 0.06 x 0.12 m, 3 m tall.	17 km from *Caracaraí*, to *Manaus*, BR-174/RR.
324	?	-	White flowers with a petal, altered leaves, orange fruit, black seed, white aril.	17 km from *Caracaraí*, to *Manaus*, BR-174/RR.
325	*Heliconia*	Musaceae	Bright red bracts, orange flower with the tip black, ovary red, light green leaf.	42 km from *Caracaraí*, to *Manaus*, BR-174/RR.
326	*Abacaxi*	Bromeliaceae	Reddish, with spaced thorns.	108 km from *Caracaraí*, to *Manaus*, BR-174/RR.
327	*Abacaxi*	Bromeliaceae	Green, reduced thorns.	109 km from *Caracaraí*, to *Manaus*, BR-174/RR.
328	*Philodendron*	Araceae	Seeds, leaves 0.90 x 0.50 m.	112 km from *Caracaraí*, to *Manaus*, BR-174/RR.
329		Bromeliaceae	Red tip.	156 km from *Caracaraí*, to *Manaus*, BR-174/RR.
330	-	Iridaceae	Type Trimezia (Neomarica), fan leaf.	156 km from *Caracaraí*, to *Manaus*, BR-174/RR.
331	-	Cactaceae	Triangular, 1.80 m tall.	156 km from *Caracaraí*, to *Manaus*, BR-174/RR.
332	-	Solanaceae	Shrubby climber, alternating leaves, highly branched nerves, clustered flowers.	504 km from *Caracaraí*, to *Manaus*, BR-174/RR.
333	-	Rubiaceae	Red bracts, 22 cm long, purple flowers, leaf 0.25 x 0.60 m, petiole 0.20 m, 8 m tall.	505 km from *Caracaraí*, to *Manaus*, BR-174/RR.
334	*Clusia*	Guttiferae	Dark green leaf, hard.	505 km from *Caracaraí*, to *Manaus*, BR-174/RR.
335	*Bellucia?*	Melastomataceae	Flower on the trunk. Common name: Goiaba de Anta.	505 km from *Caracaraí*, to *Manaus*, BR-174/RR.
336	*Ouratea*	Ochnaceae	Yellow flowers, clustered, coming out of the apex of the bouquets, hard leaf, cordata, Leathery, 0.50 m tall.	Km 120 from BR-174/AM (*Igarapé das Lajes*).
337	-	Apocynaceae	Light to dark pink flower, terminal, green and ripe fruits, opposite leaves (perhaps two distinct species).	Km 120 from BR-174/AM (*Igarapé das Lajes*).
338	-	Malpighiaceae	White flower with pink major petal, small, in terminal clusters, hard leaves.	Km 120 from BR-174/AM (*Igarapé das Lajes*).
339	*Securidaca*	Polygalaceae	Purple flowers in clusters, leaves dwellings when young, semi-scaly.	Km 120 from BR-174/AM (*Igarapé das Lajes*).
340	-	Cyperaceae	Leaves 0.01 x 0.50 m, golden inflorescence with 1 m tall.	Km 120 from BR-174/AM (*Igarapé das Lajes*).
341	*Philodendron*	Araceae	-	522 km from *Caracaraí*, to *Manaus*, BR-174/AM (*Igarapé das Lajes*).

342	*Ficus*	Moraceae	-	522 km from *Caracaraí*, to *Manaus*, BR-174/AM (*Igarapé das Lajes*).
343	-	Bromeliaceae	Light green, thin leaves, thornless.	522 km from *Caracaraí*, to *Manaus*, BR-174/AM (*Igarapé das Lajes*).
344	-	Orchidaceae	With bulbs.	522 km from *Caracaraí*, to *Manaus*, BR-174/AM (*Igarapé das Lajes*).
345	?	-	2 m tall, long leaf.	522 km from *Caracaraí*, to *Manaus*, BR-174/AM (*Igarapé das Lajes*).
346	*Catasetum*?	Orchidaceae	-	522 km from *Caracaraí*, to *Manaus*, BR-174/AM (*Igarapé das Lajes*).
347	-	Orchidaceae	Fine leaf.	522 km from *Caracaraí*, to *Manaus*, BR-174/AM (*Igarapé das Lajes*).
348	*Anthurium*	Araceae	Shadow, long leaf, nerves striking.	522 km from *Caracaraí*, to *Manaus*, BR-174/AM (*Igarapé das Lajes*).
349	-	Palmaceae	-	522 km from *Caracaraí*, to *Manaus*, BR-174/AM (*Igarapé das Lajes*).
350	?	-	-	522 km from *Caracaraí*, to *Manaus*, BR-174/AM (*Igarapé das Lajes*).
351	*Clusia*	Guttiferae	Diverse.	522 km from *Caracaraí*, to *Manaus*, BR-174/AM (*Igarapé das Lajes*).
352	-	Leguminosae	Purple flower.	522 km from *Caracaraí*, to *Manaus*, BR-174/AM (*Igarapé das Lajes*).
353	*Epidendron*	Orchidaceae	-	522 km from *Caracaraí*, to *Manaus*, BR-174/AM (*Igarapé das Lajes*).
354	?	-	3/4 m tall, smooth, reddish trunk.	522 km from *Caracaraí*, to *Manaus*, BR-174/AM (*Igarapé das Lajes*).
355	-	Palmaceae	Thorns on the trunk, 1 m tall.	522 km from *Caracaraí*, to *Manaus*, BR-174/AM (*Igarapé das Lajes*).
356	*Philodendron*	Araceae	-	522 km from *Caracaraí*, to *Manaus*, BR-174/AM (*Igarapé das Lajes*).
357	*Billbergia*	Bromeliaceae	Dark green with light spots.	522 km from *Caracaraí*, to *Manaus*, BR-174/AM (*Igarapé das Lajes*).
358	-	Bromeliaceae	Dark green, greyish-green back.	522 km from *Caracaraí*, to *Manaus*, BR-174/AM (*Igarapé das Lajes*).
359	*Philodendron*	Araceae	Type *Speciosum*, seeds.	522 km from *Caracaraí*, to *Manaus*, BR-174/AM (*Igarapé das Lajes*).
360	-	Leguminosae	4 m tall, 4 m of diameter, sand and stones, green or black sheath, when ripe.	522 km from *Caracaraí*, to *Manaus*, BR-174/AM (*Igarapé das Lajes*).
361	*Warzewiczia coccinea* (Vahl.) Klotzch.	Rubiaceae	Common name: *Rabo from Arara*. Dark green leaf, 0.50 x 0.20 m, apical inflorescence, red bracts, tiny flowers.	522 km from *Caracaraí*, to *Manaus*, BR-174/AM (*Igarapé das Lajes*).
362	*Syagrus*	Palmaceae	6 m tall.	3 km from *Açailândia*, to *Imperatriz*, BR-010/MA.
363	*Turnera*	Turneraceae	Light yellow flower, 5 petals, brown core, 0.30 m tall, sun.	4 km from *Imperatriz*, to *Colinas de Goiás*, BR-010/MA.
364	*Turnera*	Turneraceae	Light yellow flower, darker yellow core, 0.30 m tall, sun.	4 km from *Imperatriz*, to *Colinas de Goiás*, BR-010/MA.

346

348

356

365	*Acrocomia*	Palmaceae	Fruit diameter 0.05 m, 6 m tall.	13 km from *Imperatriz*, to *Colinas de Goiás*, BR-010/MA.
366	*Dieffenbachia*	Araceae	2 m tall, thick trunk up to 0.10 m.	15 km from *Imperatriz*, to *Colinas de Goiás*, BR-010/MA.
367	-	Marantaceae	0.70 m tall, green leaf with wine color center.	15 km from *Imperatriz*, to *Colinas de Goiás*, BR-010/MA.
368	-	Marantaceae	Wine back with green nerve, leaf 0.30 x 0.15 m 0.70 m tall.	15 km from *Paragominas*, to *Açailândia*, BR-010/PA.
369	*Clusia*	Guttiferae	0.60 m tall (buds).	15 km from *Paragominas*, to *Açailândia*, BR-010/PA .
370	*Anthurium*	Araceae	Leaf 0.20 x 0.025 m, in trunk, shade.	15 km from *Paragominas*, to *Açailândia*, BR-010/PA .
371	*Anthurium*	Araceae	-	15 km from *Paragominas*, to *Açailândia*, BR-010/PA .
372	*Heliconia*	Musacea	Orange flower, leaf 0.40 x 0.12 m, red border, very smooth back, half shade.	40 km from *Imperatriz*, to *Colinas de Goiás*, BR-010/MA.
373	*Philodendron*	Araceae	Epiphyte, partial shade.	40 km from *Imperatriz*, to *Colinas de Goiás*, BR-010/MA.
374	*Vellozia*	Velloziaceae	Stone formation with *Cerrado*, sandstone, clay, sun.	159 km from *Imperatriz*, to *Colinas de Goiás*, BR-226/GO.
375	*Hippeastrum*	Amaryllidaceae	Stone formation with *Cerrado*, sandstone, clay, sun.	159 km from *Imperatriz*, to *Colinas de Goiás*, BR-226/GO.
376	-	Bromeliaceae	Stone formation with *Cerrado*, sandstone, clay, sun.	159 km from *Imperatriz*, to *Colinas de Goiás*, BR-226/GO.
377	*Evolvulus*	Convulvulaceae	-	118 km from *Imperatriz*, to *Colinas de Goiás*, BR-226/GO.
378	*Acrocomia*	Palmaceae	7 m tall, maintains remains of pods on the trunk, round seeds.	241 km from *Imperatriz*, to *Colinas de Goiás*, puerto from *Vanfromrlândia*, BR-226/GO.
379	*Syagrus*	Palmaceae	Fine trunk, oval seeds, leaves, long and thin, recurved, well transparent.	243 km from *Imperatriz*, to *Colinas de Goiás*, BR-226/GO.
380	*Cyperus*	Cyperaceae	Light green inflorescence, fine and long leaf, humid location.	243 km from *Imperatriz*, to *Colinas de Goiás*, BR-226/GO.
381	*Cyperus*	Cyperaceae	White inflorescence, humid location.	243 km from *Imperatriz*, to *Colinas de Goiás*, BR-226/GO.
382	-	Velloziaceae	Hard leaf, plane moving on the nerve, sawn at the edges, 0.60 m tall.	134 km from *Colinas de Goiás*, to *Goiânia*, BR-153/GO.
383	*Manihot*	Euphorbiaceae	-	135 km from *Colinas de Goiás*, to *Goiânia*, BR-153/GO.
384	-	Orchidaceae	Hard leaf, shade, epiphyte, bright green.	152 km from *Colinas de Goiás*, to *Goiânia*, BR-153/GO.
385	*Griffinia*	Amaryllidaceae	Bulb.	152 km from *Colinas de Goiás*, to *Goiânia*, BR-153/GO.
386	-	Marantaceae	Cream flower.	152 km from *Colinas de Goiás*, to *Goiânia*, BR-153/GO.
387	*Costus*	Zingiberaceae	Red flower, long leaf.	152 km from *Colinas de Goiás*, to *Goiânia*, BR-153/GO.
388	*Costus*	Zingiberaceae	Red stem, yellow flower.	152 km from *Colinas de Goiás*, to *Goiânia*, BR-153/GO.
389	*Dorstenia*	Urticaceae	Green leaf, elongated.	152 km from *Colinas de Goiás*, to *Goiânia*, BR-153/GO.
390	*Heliconia*	Musaceae	Light green leaf, 1.80 m tall.	152 km from *Colinas de Goiás*, to *Goiânia*, BR-153/GO.
391	*Dorstenia*	Urticaceae	Dark green leaf.	152 km from *Colinas de Goiás*, to *Goiânia*, BR-153/GO.

392	Philodendron	Araceae	-	148 km from Colinas de Goiás, to Goiânia, BR-153/GO.	392
393	Pitcairnia?	Bromeliaceae	Thin and malleable leaf.	148 km from Colinas de Goiás, to Goiânia, BR-153/GO.	
394	-	Aristolochiaceae?	Dark green leaf, light green back.	152 km from Colinas de Goiás, to Goiânia, BR-153/GO.	
395	Syagrus	Palmaceae	Tall, fine trunk, seeds, stone with Cerrado.	221 km from Colinas de Goiás, to Goiânia, BR-153/GO.	
396	-	Bromeliaceae	Long, hard leaves, sawn at the edges, longitudinally ribbed leaf.	221 km from Colinas de Goiás, to Goiânia, BR-153/GO.	394
397	Griffinia	Amaryllidaceae	-	221 km from Colinas de Goiás, to Goiânia, BR-153/GO.	
398	Heliconia	Musaceae	Strong orange flower, wet place.	379 km from Colinas de Goiás, to Goiânia, BR-153/GO.	
399	-	Marantaceae	Large leaf, yellow flower.	666 km from Colinas de Goiás, to Goiânia, BR-153/GO.	400
400	-	Marantaceae	Leaf 0.20 x 0.06 m, dark green with light green spots, back all green (Ctenanthe?).	666 km from Colinas de Goiás, to Goiânia, BR-153/GO.	
401	-	Marantaceae	Small leaf, lilac flower, small.	666 km from Colinas de Goiás, to Goiânia, BR-153/GO.	
402	-	Velloziaceae	Thin leaf when new, hairy.	666 km from Colinas de Goiás, to Goiânia, BR-153/GO.	
403	Encholirium	Bromeliaceae	All green, thorns on the edges.	666 km from Colinas de Goiás, to Goiânia, BR-153/GO.	
404	Manihot?	Euphorbiaceae	-	666 km from Colinas de Goiás, to Goiânia, BR-153/GO.	
405	-	Araceae	Small, dark green leaf with light green spots.	666 km from Colinas de Goiás, to Goiânia, BR-153/GO.	
406	Hippeastrum	Amarillidaceae	-	666 km from Colinas de Goiás, to Goiânia, BR-153/GO.	401
407	Kielmeyera	Guttiferae	White flower, seeds.	666 km from Colinas de Goiás, to Goiânia, BR-153/GO.	
408	Tillandsia	Bromeliaceae	Silver green, epiphytic.	666 km from Colinas de Goiás, to Goiânia, BR-153/GO.	
409	Pseudobombax	Bombaceae	Seedlings.	666 km from Colinas de Goiás, to Goiânia, BR-153/GO.	
410	Aspidosperma	Apocynaceae	Seeds (winged).	666 km from Colinas de Goiás, to Goiânia, BR-153/GO.	
411	Hymenaea	Leguminosae	20 m tall.	840 km from Colinas de Goiás, to Goiânia, BR-153/GO.	
412	-	Myrtaceae	Orange fruit, twelve, 2.5 cm diameter fruit, 15 m tall.	840 km from Colinas de Goiás, to Goiânia, BR-153/GO.	
413	Inga	Leguminosae	Pods 0.30 m, light green when ripe, glabrous, 15 m tall.	840 km from Colinas de Goiás, to Goiânia, BR-153/GO.	415
414	Aspidosperma	Apocynaceae	15 m tall, seeds winged.	840 km from Colinas de Goiás, to Goiânia, BR-153/GO.	
415	-	Sapotaceae	Fruit orange, hairy, calyx very evident. 2 cm diameter, 20 m tall.	840 km from Colinas de Goiás, to Goiânia, BR-153/GO.	416
416	-	Sapotaceae	Green or yellow fruit, velvety, 1.50 cm in diameter.	840 km from Colinas de Goiás, to Goiânia, BR-153/GO.	417
417	-	Sapotaceae	Fruit yellow, glabrous, 1 cm in diameter, round.	840 km from Colinas de Goiás, to Goiânia, BR-153/GO.	
418	Acrocomia	Palmaceae	Fruiting from 3 m tall, round fruits.	Between Ceres and Anápolis, BR-1S3/GO.	418

Figure 16. Expedition to the Amazon. Roberto Burle Marx and botanist Paul Hutchinson preparing material herbalized for identification. Sapé Gas Station, *Cuiabá-Porto Velho*, Brazil. Photograph: Oscar Bressane, Koiti Mori and José Tabacow, 1983.

List of Herbalized Plants.*
Dr. Paul Hutchison

Collection No.	Family	Name
8458	Bromeliaceae	*Encholyrium*
8475	Bromeliaceae	*Dyckia*
8477	Bromeliaceae	*Dyckia*
8479	Verbenaceae	-
8480	-	*Erythroxylon?*
8480 A	-	-
8481	Samydaceae	*Casearia*
8482	Liliaceae	*Smilax*
8483	Turneraceae	-
8484	Sapindaceae	*Paulinia*
8489	-	-
8490	Melastomataceae?	-
8491	-	-
8492	Melastomataceae	-
8493	Melastomataceae	-
8494	Melastomataceae	-
8495	-	-
8495 A	-	-
8496	-	-
8498	Musaceae	*Heliconia hirsuta*
8499	Amaryllidaceae	*Hippeastrum*
8500	Palmaceae	-
8501	Bromeliaceae	*Bromelia*
8502	Bromeliaceae	*Bromelia*
8503	Amarylliaceae	*Hippeastrum*
8504	Bromeliaceae	*Bromelia*
8505	Araceae	*Anthurium*
8506	-	-
8507	Araceae	*Philodendron*
8508	-	-
8509	Malpighiaceae	-
8510	Capparidaceae	-
8511	Bromeliaceae	-
8512	Bromeliaceae	*Dyckia*
8513	Velloziaceae	-
8514	Orchidaceae	-
8515	Bromeliaceae	*Dyckia pumila*
8516	Verbenaceae	-
8517	-	-
8518	Liliaceae	*Smilax*
8519	Malpighiaceae	*Byrsonima verbascifolia*
8520	Labiateae	*Salvia*
8521	Myrtaceae	*Myrcia?*
8522	Melastomataceae	-
8523	Compositae	-
8524	Bombacaceae	*Eriotheca*
8525	Apocynaceae	*Mandevilla*
8526	Amaryllidaceae	*Hippeastrum*
8526 A	Orchidaceae	-
8527	Iridaceae	-
8528	Melastomataceae	-
8529	Melastomataceae	-
8530	-	-
8531	Malvaceae	-
8532	Rubiaceae	*Cephaelis*
8533	Zingiberaceae	*Costus*
8534	Graminea	*Andropogon*
8535	Liliaceae	*Smilax*
8536	Bromeliaceae	*Dyckia*
8537	Amaryllidaceae	*Hippeastrum*
8538	Bignoniaceae o Apocynaceae	-
8539	Apocynaceae	*Mandevilla*
8540	Graminea	-
8541	Velloziaceae	-
8542	Melastomataceae	-
8543	Velloziaceae	-
8544	Palmaceae	-
8545	Palmaceae	*Bactris?*
8546	Euphorbiaceae	*Manihot*
8546 A	Euphorbiaceae	*Manihot*
8547	Euphorbiaceae	*Manihot*
8548	Araceae	*Anthurium*
8549	Velloziaceae	-
8550	Orchidaceae	*Cyrtopodium or Catasetum*
8551	Amaryllidaceae	*Hippeastrum*
8552	Bromeliaceae	*Dyckia*
8553	Araceae	*Anthurium*
8553 A	Araceae	*Anthurium*
8554	Orchidaceae	-
8554 A	-	-
8555	Musaceae	*Heliconia*
8555 A	Palmaceae	*Acrocomia*
8556	Bromeliaceae	*Bromelia*
8556 A	Palmaceae	*Acrocomia*
8557	Araceae	*Philodendron*
8557 A	Amaryllidaceae	*Hippeastrum*
8558	Bromeliaceae	-
8559	Palmaceae	*Bactris*
8560	Araceae	*Philodendron*
8561	Orchidaceae	*Cattleya nobilior*
8562	Sterculiaceae	*Guazuma ulmifolia*
8563	Malvaceae	-
8564	Amaryllidaceae	-
8565	Cycadaceae	*Zamia*
8566	Bromeliaceae	-
8567	Bromeliaceae	*Dyckia*
8568	Bromeliaceae	-
8569	Amaryllidaceae	*Hippeastrum*
8570	Orchidaceae	-
8571	Musaceae	*Heliconia episcopalis*
8572	Bromeliaceae	*Dyckia*
8573	Cactaceae	-
8574	Araceae	*Anthurium*
8575	Bromeliaceae	-

* Table prepared cataloguing information according to collection number, family, and name. Spaces without information are marked with a hyphen (-). Question marks (?) are from the original text.

I. BURLE MARX'S EXPEDITION TO THE AMAZON

8576	Bignoniaceae	-		8624	Araceae	*Xanthosoma*
8577	Marantaceae	*Calathea*		8625	Cactaceae	*Rhipsalis*
8578	Bromeliaceae	-		8626	Guttiferae	*Clusia*
8579	Orchidaceae	-		8627	Orchidaceae	*Maxillaria?*
8580	Palmaceae	*Acrocomia*		8628	Orchidaceae	-
8581	Palmaceae	*Acrocomia*		8629	Palmaceae	*Attalea*
8582	Bignoniaceae	-		8630	Araceae	*Anthurium*
8582 A	-	-		8631	Araceae	*Caladium*
8583	Araceae	*Philodendron*		8632	Leg. *Caesalpinioideae*	*Cassia spruceana*
8584	Bignoniaceae	*Tabebuia*		8633	Palmaceae	-
8585	Araceae	*Syngonium?*		8634	Palmaceae	*Mauritiella*
8586	Orchidaceae	-		8635	Melastomataceae	-
8587	Leg. *Caesalpinioideae*	*Bauhinia*		8636	Araceae	*Montrichardia*
8588	Guttiferae	*Clusia*		8637	Melastomataceae	-
8589	Palmaceae	*Attalea*		8638	Graminea	*Bambusa*
8590	Palmaceae	*Mauritiella*		8639	Musaceae	*Ravenala guianensis*
8591	Amaryllidaceae	*Hippeastrum*		8640	Anacardiaceae	*Cupania*
8592	Palmaceae	*Syagrus*		8641	Araceae	*Philodendron*
8593	Araceae	*Philodendron*		8642	Araceae	*Philodendron*
8594	Palmaceae	*Astrocaryum*		8643	Araceae	*Anthurium?*
8595	Palmaceae	*Bactris*		8644	Musaceae	*Heliconia*
8596	Bromeliaceae	*Bromelia*		8645	Bromeliaceae	-
8597	Passifloraceae	*Passiflora*		8646	Rubiaceae	*Palicourea*
8598	Palmaceae	*Syagrus*		8647	Melastomataceae	-
8599	Palmaceae	*Iriartea exorrhiza*		8648	Melastomataceae	-
8600	Palmaceae	*Sheelea*		8649	Palmaceae	*Mauritiella*
8601	Musaceae	*Heliconia*		8650	Musaceae	-
8602	Araceae	*Anthurium*		8651	Euphorbiaceae?	-
8603	Araceae	*Philodendron*		8652	-	-
8604	Araceae	*Philodendron*		8653	Melastomataceae	-
8605	Melastomataceae	*Miconia*		8654	Araceae	*Philodendron*
8606	Malpighiaceae	-		8655	Melastomataceae	-
8607	-	-		8656	Melastomataceae	-
8608	Euphorbiaceae	*Jatropha?*		8657	Araceae	*Philodendron*
8608 A	Euphorbiaceae	*Jatropha?*		8658	Araceae	*Philodendron*
8609	Lecythidaceae	*Eschweilera*		8659	Marcgraviaceaea	*Norantea*
8610	Araceae	*Philodendron*		8660	Araceae	*Anthurium*
8611	Araceae	*Philodendron*		8660 A	Araceae	*Anthurium*
8612	Leguminoseae	*Dioclea*		8661	Annonaceaea	*Duguetia*
8613	Araliaceae	*Schefflera*		8662	Araceae	*Philodendron*
8614	Araceae	*Philodendron*		8663	Araceae	*Philodendron*
8614 A	Musaceae	*Heliconia*		8664	Bromeliaceae	*Aechmea*
8615	Araceae	*Philodendron*		8665	Marantaceae	*Ischnosiphon*
8616	Cactaceae	*Epiphyllum phyllantus*		8666	Araceae	*Philodendron speciosum?*
8617	Bignoniaceae	*Jacaranda*		8667	Flacourtiaceae	*Lindackeria?*
8618	Leguminoseae	*Dioclea*		8668	Bignonciaceae	-
8619	Musaceae	*Heliconia*		8669	Malastomataceae	-
8620	Araceae	*Urospatha?*		8670	Rubiaceae	*Palicourea corymbosa*
8621	Araceae	*Monstera*		8671	Bromeliaceae	*Bromelia*
8622	Palmaceae	*Astrocaryum?*		8672	Palmaceae	*Morenia*
8623	Araceae	*Philodendron*		8673	Palmaceae	*Leptocarya tenue?*

8674	Araceae	Philodendron		8724	Guttiferae	Clusia
8675	Bromeliaceae	Aechmea		8725	Araceae	Philodendron melinoni?
8676	Euphorbiaceae	Mabea occidentalis		8726	Moraceae	Cecropia
8677	Araceae	Philodendron tripartitum		8727	Moraceae	Cecropia
8678	Araceae	Philodendron		8728	Bromeliaceae	-
8679	Polypodiaceae	Asplenium		8729	Araceae	Philodendron
8680	Marcgraviaceaea	Norantea		8730	Guttiferae	Clusia
8681	Araceae	Philodendron		8731	Guttiferae	Clusia
8682	Passifloraceae	Passiflora		8732	Gesneriaceae	-
8683	Melastomataceae			8733	Apocynaceae	Mandevilla
8684	Araceae	Philodendron		8734	Apocynaceae	Mandevilla?
8685	Araceae	Dieffenbachia		8735	Bromeliaceae	Tillandsia
8686	Araceae	Philodendron		8736	Orchidaceae	Maxillaria
8687	Araceae	Philodendron		8737	Moraceae	Ficus
8688	Araceae	Philodendron		8738	Orchidaceae	Sobralia liliastrum
8689	Araceae	Philodendron		8739	Araceae	Philodendron
8690	Rubiaceae	Palicourea		8740	Araceae	Philodendron
8691	Araceae	Philodendron		8741	Araceae	Anthurium
8692	Guttiferae	Clusia		8742	Araceae	Philodendron
8693	Bromeliaceae	Pitcairnea?		8743	Araceae	Philodendron
8694	Araceae	Philodendron		8744	Araceae	Philodendron
8695	Araceae	Philodendron		8745	Musaceae	Heliconia
8696	Araceae	Philodendron		8746	Rubiaceae	-
8697	Bromeliaceae	-		8747	Musaceae	Heliconia psittacorum?
8698	Araceae	Philodendron		8748	Legum. Mimosoideae .	Acacia
8699	Araceae	Philodendron		8749	Musaceae	Heliconia
8700	Bromeliaceae	-		8750	Musaceae	Heliconia
8701	Araceae	Philodendron		8751	Musaceae	Heliconia
8702	Araceae	Philodendron		8752	Melastomataceae	-
8703	Araceae	Philodendron		8753	Leg. Caesalpinioideae	Cassia
8704	Gramineae	-		8754	Araceae	Anthurium
8704 A	Araceae	Philodendron aff. melinoni		8755	Araceae	Philodendron
8705	Araceae	Philodendron		8756	Araceae	Philodendron
8706	Araceae	Philodendron		8757	Araceae	Philodendron
8707	Araceae	Philodendron aff melinoni		8758	Orchidaceae	-
8708	Araceae	Anthurium		8759	Araceae	Philodendron
8709	Araceae			8760	Araceae	Syngonium
8710	Sapindaceae	Paullinia cupana		8761	-	
8711	Araceae	Philodendron		8762	Araceae	Philodendron
8712	Araceae	Urospatha		8763	Amaryllidaceae	Furcraea
8713	Musaceae	Heliconia		8764	Begoniaceae	Begonia
8714	Araceae	-		8765	Musaceae	Heliconia hirsuta
8715	Guttiferae	Clusia		8766	Musaceae	Heliconia
8716	Malastomataceae	-		8767	Zingiberaceae	Costus
8717	Orchidaceae	-		8768	Bromeliaceae	Ananas
8718	Bromeliaceae	-		8769	Orchidaceae	Cyrtopodium
8719	Bromeliaceae	-		8770	Melastomataceae	-
8720	Guttiferae	Clusia		8771	Orchidaceae	Cattleya
8721	Musaceae	Heliconia		8772	Cactaceae	Cereus
8722	Musaceae	Heliconia		8773	Palmaceae	Astrocaryum
8723	Guttiferae	Clusia		8774	Leguminoseae	-
				8775	Onagraceae	-

Figure 17. Workers of *Sítio Roberto Burle Marx* collecting live plants, in a gnaisse-granite formation during another expedition, this time it is during the expedition to *Espírito Santo*, Brazil. Photography: Koiti Mori, 1976.

Field Annotations.*
Dr. Paul C. Hutchison and Fátima de Souza Menezes

#	Family	Name	Notes	Localization
8501	Bromeliaceae	-	Very fragile, "snowy" shoots with white hairs before the flowers, red bracts; small formations on the edge of the road, full sun. Altitude: near 830 m.a.s.l. approx.	Municipality of *Jataí* - GO, 10 km from *Jataí* to *Caiapônia* (BR-158). *Serra do Caiapó*.
8502	Bromeliaceae	-	Terrestrial, heliophilic, bracts totally red when in bloom, pink flowers, erect petals. Stream at the bottom of a canyon. Altitude: 920 m.a.s.l. approx.	*Estância* - GO, BR-158. *Serra do Caiapó*.
8503	-	*Hippeastrum*	No flowers, two bulbs, terrestrial, heliophilic. Altitude: 820 m.a.s.l. approx.	40 km to the north of *Estância*, 42 km to the south of *Caiapônia*, BR-158 *Serra do Caiapó*.
8504	Bromeliaceae	-	Species of great size, low central inflorescence, green leaf dark, when in red flower, hairiness next to the flowers and at the base of the leaves, leaves 2 m approx., pendulous apical part or recurved strongly, although sub-erect, hasteless inflorescence, 20 cm of diameter approx., apparently flowers for long period, shade, and half sun, relatively frequent. See 8511, same as (no pressed), in *Cerrado*.	*Caiapônia*, BR-158, *Serra do Caiapó* - GO.
8505	-	*Anthurium*	No flowers. Altitude: 720 m.a.s.l. approx.	12 km to the south of *Caiapônia*, BR-158, *Serra do Caiapó* - GO.
8506	-	-	Tree (?) Lilac flowers, purple filaments, soft and oblong fruits, purple, black when ripe.	12 km to the south of *Caiapônia*, BR-158, Serra do *Caiapó* - GO.
8507	-	*Philodendron*	Scandent, red fruit, in *Schinus* sp.	12 km to the south of *Caiapônia*, *Serra do Caiapó*, BR-158 - GO.
8508	-	-	Climber (?). Winged seed, with three wings, soft, pubescent leaves, green onsets.	17 km to the south of *Caiapônia*, BR-158, *Serra do Caiapó* - GO.
8509	Malpighiaceae	-	Yellow flowers, 3 m approx.	22 km to the south of *Caiapônia*, BR-158 *Serra do Caiapó* - GO.
8510	Capparidaceae	-	-	26 km to the south of *Caiapônia*, BR-158, *Serra do Caiapó* - GO.
8511	Bromeliaceae	-	Pubescent leaves, brown, bright red center, magenta flowers, petals with whitish edge.	26 km to the south of *Caiapônia*, BR-158, *Serra do Caiapó* - GO.
8512	-	*Dyckia*	Altitude: 880 m.a.s.l. approx.	50 km from *Caiapônia*
8513	-	*Vellozia*	Terrestrial, with fruits.	50 km to the south of *Caiapônia*, BR-158 *Serra do Caiapó* - GO.
8514	Orchidaceae	-	Terrestrial.	50 km to the south of *Caiapônia*, BR-158 *Serra do Caiapó* - GO.
8515	-	*Dyckia Pumila*	Heliophile, *rupicolous*, orange flowers. Altitude: 920 m.a.s.l. approx.	50 km to the south of *Caiapônia*, BR-158 *Serra do Caiapó* - GO.
8516	Verbenaceae	-	-	50 km to the south of *Caiapônia*, BR-158 *Serra do Caiapó* - GO.
8517	-	-	Shrub (?) White flowers, 0.50 m.	50 km to the south of *Caiapônia*, BR-158 *Serra do Caiapó* - GO.
8518	-	*Smilax*	Leathery leaf, infrequent.	50 km to the south of *Caiapônia*, BR-158 *Serra do Caiapó* - GO.
8519	-	*Byrsonima verbascifolia*	Erect leaves.	50 km to the south of *Caiapônia*, BR-158 *Serra do Caiapó* - GO.
8520	-	*Salvia*	Red flower, partial shade.	50 km to the south of *Caiapônia*, BR-158 *Serra do Caiapó* - GO.
8521	-	*Myrcia (?)*	Medium shade.	50 km to the south of *Caiapônia*, BR-158 *Serra do Caiapó* - GO.
8522	Melastomataceae	-	Tree, 2.50 m.	50 km to the south of *Caiapônia*, BR-158 *Serra do Caiapó* - GO.
8523	Compositae	-	Exposed strands.	50 km to the south of *Caiapônia*, BR-158 *Serra do Caiapó* - GO.
8524	-	*Eryotheca*	-	50 km to the south of *Caiapônia*, BR-158 *Serra do Caiapó* - GO.
8525	-	*Mandevilla*	Pink flower.	50 km to the south of *Caiapônia*, BR-158 *Serra do Caiapó* - GO.
8526	-	*Hippeastrum*	Bulb 4.5 cm, diameter 3.5 cm.	50 km to the south of *Caiapônia*, BR-158 *Serra do Caiapó* - GO.
8526 A	Orchidaceae	-	*Encyclia* (?)	50 km to the south of *Caiapônia*, BR-158 *Serra do Caiapó* - GO.
8527	Iridaceae	-	White flowers, thin green leaf, width 1.5 cm, infrequent.	47 km from *Jataí*, to *Rondonópolis*, BR-364.
8528	Melastomataceae	-	-	47 km from *Jataí*, to *Rondonópolis*, BR-364.

* Table prepared cataloguing information according to collection number, family, and name. Spaces without information are marked with a hyphen (-). Question marks (?) are from the original text.

72 I. BURLE MARX'S EXPEDITION TO THE AMAZON

8529	Melastomataceae	-	-	47 km from *Jataí*, to *Rondonópolis*, BR-364.
8530	?	-	-	-
8531	Malvaceae	-	60 cm, pale pink, deep brown at the base, red pistil and filament.	47 km from *Jataí*, to *Rondonópolis*, BR-364.
8532	Rubiaceae	*Cephaelis*	1,50 m, leathery flowers, red-orange bracts, blue fruits, yellow flowers, hirsutes, with stipules between the leaves, fruits feed birds, hygrophile, flooded place.	47 km from *Jataí*, to *Rondonópolis*, BR-364.
8533	-	*Costus*	Leaves 25 x 10 cm, 2 m tall, internodio 6 cm, in the base, up to 1 cm, above, red flower, yellow edges.	47 km from *Jataí*, to *Rondonópolis*, BR-364.
8534	Gramineae	*Andropogon?*	White flower.	67 km from *Jataí*, to *Rondonópolis*, BR-364.
8535	-	*Smilax*	-	116 km from *Jataí*, to *Rondonópolis*, BR-364.
8536	-	*Dyckia*	Orange petal, light red sepal splashed.	171 km from *Jataí*, to *Rondonópolis*, BR-364.
8537	-	*Hippeastrum*	Red flower, with clear core, greenish central list, occasionally whitish, above, clay soil with stones, *Cerrado*.	171 km from *Jataí*, to *Rondonópolis*, BR-364.
8538	Bignoniaceae (or Apocynaceae?)	-	-	171 km from *Jataí*, to *Rondonópolis*, BR-364.
8539	-	*Mandevilla*	Tube green pale yellow, limbus white to pale yellow, yellow throat.	171 km from *Jataí*, to *Rondonópolis*, BR-364.
8540	Gramineae	-	-	171 km from *Jataí*, to *Rondonópolis*, BR-364.
8541	Velloziaceae	-	Purple blue, few flowers, leaves with10 x 1 cm, 0.40 m tall.	171 km from *Jataí*, to *Rondonópolis*, BR-364.
8542	Melastomataceae	-	Woody, 1.50 m tall, white petals, bright green leaves above, burnt and pubescent below.	171 km from *Jataí*, to *Rondonópolis*, BR-364.
8543	Velloziaceae	-	Flowerless, small leaves.	171 km from *Jataí*, to *Rondonópolis*, BR-364.
8544	Palmaceae	-	-	171 km from *Jataí*, to *Rondonópolis*, BR-364.
8545	Palmaceae	*Bactris?*	Flowers creamy yellow, lint seeds, brown burnt ripe.	62 km from *Alto Araguaia*, to *Rondonópolis*, BR-364.
8546	-	*Manihot*	1.50 m tall, large leaves, plant diameter 2.50 m.	62 km from *Alto Araguaia*, to *Rondonópolis*, BR-364.
8547	-	*Manihot*	Fine leaves, 0.50 m tall, sun, newly burned area newly burned area.	62 km from *Alto Araguaia*, to *Rondonópolis*, BR-364.
8546 A	-	*Manihot*	-	
8548	-	*Anthurium*	Rupicolous, semi-ubiquitous, oval leaves, crawling rhizome, short petiole. 1 km away from the road.	84 km from *Alto Araguaia*, to *Rondonópolis*, BR-364.
8549	Velloziaceae	-	Sandy soil, flat area, sun.	84 km from *Alto Araguaia*, to *Rondonópolis*, BR-364/MT.
8550	-	*Cyridpodium* (or *Catasetum*)	Terrestrial, soil.	84 km from *Alto Araguaia*, to *Rondonópolis*, BR-364/MT.
8551	-	*Hippeastrum*	Long, greenish or white or yellow tube, flowers and buttons, green filaments, with aroma. Altitude 580 m.a.s.l. approx.	133 km from *Alto Araguaia*, to *Rondonópolis*, BR-364/MT.
8552	-	*Dyckia*	Dry inflorescence c/1 m tall, plant c/0.30 m, sun, orange flowers. *Serra da Petrovina*, altitude 580 m.a.s.l. approx.	133 km from *Alto Araguaia*, to *Rondonópolis*, BR-364/MT.
8553	-	*Anthurium*	Donated by José Guilherme Lima.	Original from *Chapada dos Guimarães*/MT.
8553 A	-	*Anthurium*	Gigantic, similar to 8.542, although larger, local more shaded, long petiole, in rich soil, red, sandy. Altitude: 550 m.a.s.l. approx. in grotto with vegetation.	135 km from *Alto Araguaia*, to *Rondonópolis*, BR-364/MT.
8554	-	-	Orchid?	-
8554 A	?, like Passifloraceae. Posibble Cucurbitaceae or Crescentia (Bignoniaceae)	-	Fruits with 0.50 m in length, hard, yellow and fine.	161 km from *Alto Araguaia*, to *Cuiabá*, BR-070 (BR-364)/MT.
8555	-	*Heliconia*	3 m tall, next to the estrada, growing in flooded terrain, full sun.	*Municipality from Pedra negra, 4 km to the south of Córrego Torrencinho.*
8555 A	-	*Acrocomia*	Seed purchased in the market.	
8556	Bromeliaceae	-	Pink inflorescence with 0.60 m size, full sun, terrain clay-sandy, in *Cerrado* alterado. Altitude: 840 m.a.s.l. approx.	42 km from *Alto Araguaia*, to *Rondonópolis*, BR-364/MT.
8556 A	-	*Acrocomia*	Only seeds.	
8557	-	*Philodendron*	*Serra da Petrovina*, grotto with vegetation on white soil with grava.	135 km from *Alto Araguaia*, to *Cuiabá*, BR-364/MT.
8558	Bromeliacae	-	-	
8559	-	*Bactris*	0.90 m tall, thorns on the central nerve, serrated leaves, brown fruit, black gola.	120 km from *Cuiabá*, to *Cáceres*, BR-070/MT.
8560	-	*Philodendron*	Epiphyte, in *Scheelea* sp., large leaf.	120 km from *Cuiabá*, to *Cáceres*, BR-070/MT.
8561	-	*Cattleya nobilior*	Lilac flower, large labellum and yellow.	122 km from *Cuiabá*, to *Cáceres*, BR-070/MT.
8562	-	*Guazuma ulmifolia*	12 m tall, diameter 6 m. Oasis Station. Altitude 250 m.a.s.l. approx.	160 km from *Cuiabá*, to *Cáceres*, BR-070/MT.
8563	Malvaceae	-	3 m tall, tubular red flowers, half shade.	-

8564	Amaryrellidaceae	-	-	-
8565	-	*Zamia*	Bolivian? 0.60 m tall, shrub acaule. Thin leaf, with rhizome, light yellow fruit when young and brown when ripe.	182 km from *Cuiabá*, to *Cáceres*, BR-070.
8566	Bromeliaceae	-	Red bracts, red and white inflorescence, 0.50 m tall, diameter 0.70 m.	182 km from *Cuiabá*, to *Cáceres*, BR-070.
8567	-	*Dyckia*	Often prostrate.	182 km from *Cuiabá*, to *Cáceres*, BR-070.
8568	Bromeliaceae	-	0.30 m diameter, nidular, central inflorescence, with fruits.	182 km from *Cuiabá*, to *Cáceres*, BR-070.
8569	-	*Hippeastrum*	Lemon cream flower, leaf 2 cm long, mate green.	182 km from *Cuiabá*, to *Cáceres*, BR-070.
8570	Orchidaceae	-	Terrestrial, leaf 0.07 x 0.02, pseudo-small bulbs.	182 km from *Cuiabá*, to *Cáceres*, BR-070.
8571	-	*Heliconia episcopalis*	Giant shape (new?), 3 m tall, long leaf, orange flower and red. Altitude: 280 m.a.s.l. approx.	182 km from *Cuiabá*, to *Cáceres*, BR-070.
8572	-	*Dyckia*	No flowers, giant, with shoots, fruits and seeds.	203 km from *Cuiabá*, to *Porto Velho*.
8573	-	*Mediocactus*	Triangular section, epiphyte, sun.	203 km from *Cuiabá*, to *Porto Velho*.
8574	-	*Anthurium*	Large leaves, in stone.	203 km from *Cuiabá*, to *Porto Velho*.
8575	Bromeliaceae	-	Nest type, long leaves, light green.	203 km from *Cuiabá*, to *Porto Velho*.
8576	-	*Tabebuia*	New seedlings, with fruit.	203 km from *Cuiabá*, to *Porto Velho*.
8577	-	*Calathea*	-	-
8578	-	*Aechmea bromelioides*	-	221 km from *Cuiabá*, to *Porto Velho*.
8579	Orchidaceae	-	-	221 km from *Cuiabá*, to *Porto Velho*.
8580	-	*Acrocomia*	Green seeds, 10 m tall.	221 km from *Cuiabá*, to *Porto Velho*.
8581	-	*Acrocomia*	-	*Porto Esperidião.*
8582	Bignoniaceae	-	-	6 km from *Porto Esperidião*, to *Porto Velho*, BR-364/MT.
8583	-	*Philodendron*	Leaf 0.40 x 0.25 m, clay-sandy soil.	53 km from Porto Esperidião, to *Porto Velho*, BR- 364/MT.
8584	-	*Tabebuia*	White, yellow throat.	53 km from *Porto Esperidião*, to *Porto Velho*, BR- 364 /MT.
8585	-	*Syngonium* (or *Philodendron?*)	Climber.	53 km from *Porto Esperidião*, to *Porto Velho*, BR-364/MT.
8586	Orchidaceae	-	Dam on dry branch, on the edge of the road.	53 km from Porto Esperidião, to *Porto Velho*, BR-364/MT.
8587	-	*Bauhinia*	White flowers.	53 km from *Porto Esperidião*, to *Porto Velho*, BR-364/MT.
8588	-	*Clusia*	Roadside, 1 m tall.	53 km from *Porto Esperidião*, to *Porto Velho*, BR-364/MT.
8589	-	*Attalea*	-	57 km from Porto Esperidião, to *Porto Velho*, BR-364/MT.
8590	-	*Mauritiella aculeata*	4 m tall, 4 m diameter, oval fruits with 2 x 3 cm, with scales.	57 km from Porto Esperidião, to *Porto Velho*, BR-364/MT.
8591	-	*Hippeastrum*	Orange flowers, light core.	67 km from *Porto Esperidião*, to *Porto Velho*, BR-364/MT.
8592	-	*Syagrus*	Canopy 1 m diameter approx., trunk with 2 a 4 m tall, trunk only 0.10 m in diameter, cream flowers.	71 km from Porto Esperidião, to *Porto Velho*, BR-364/MT.
8593	-	*Philodendron*	Giant leaves, growing on *Orbygnia.*	97 km from Porto Esperidião, to *Porto Velho*, BR-364/MT.
8594	-	*Astrocaryum*	Orange fruits, black seed, long trunk, 4 m tall, with thorns. *Sapê* farm.	192 km from Porto Esperidião, to *Porto Velho*, BR-364/MT.
8595	-	*Bactris*	Small fruits purple, small inflorescence, trunk and leaves with thorns, 2 a 3 m tall. *Sapê* farm.	192 km from Porto Esperidião, to *Porto Velho*, BR-364/MT.
8596	Bromeliaceae	-	Red bracts, dark purple flowers, lighter in the edges, on stones.	194 km from Porto Esperidião, to *Porto Velho*, BR-364/MT.
8597	Passifloraceae	-	Red flowers, oval fruits, greens.	201 km from Porto Esperidião, to *Porto Velho*, BR-364/MT.
8598	-	*Syagrus*	Green fruits, black seeds, 7 m tall.	203 km from Porto Esperidião, to *Porto Velho*, BR-364/MT.
8599	-	*Iriartea exorrhiza*	Yellow-orange fruits, brown seed, 15 m tall.	204 km from Porto Esperidião, to *Porto Velho*, BR-364/MT.
8600	-	*Scheelea*	3 a 4 m tall.	208 km from Porto Esperidião, to *Porto Velho*, BR-364/MT.
8601	-	*Heliconia*	Red bracts, yellow-green flowers.	241 km from Porto Esperidião, to *Porto Velho*, BR-364/MT.
8602	-	*Anthurium*	-	286 km from Porto Esperidião, to *Porto Velho*, BR-364/MT.
8603	-	*Philodendron*	Elliptical leaves, shoots.	290 km from *Porto Esperidião*, to *Porto Velho*, BR- 364/MT.
8604	-	*Philodendron*	No flowers.	290 km from *Porto Esperidião*, to *Porto Velho*, BR- 364/MT.
8605	-	*Miconia*	White flowers, 1 a 2 m.	*Comodoro* Station 337 km from *Porto Esperidião*, to *Porto Velho*, BR-364/MT.

74 I. BURLE MARX'S EXPEDITION TO THE AMAZON

8606	Malpighiaceae	-	Yellow flowers, 2.5 a 4 m.	*Comodoro* Station 337 km from *Porto Esperidião*, to *Porto Velho*, BR-364/MT.
8607	Lysisternaceae	-	-	*Comodoro* Station 337 km from *Porto Esperidião*, to *Porto Velho*, BR-364/MT.
8608	-	*Jatropha*	0.40 m tall.	*Comodoro* Station 337 km from *Porto Esperidião*, to *Porto Velho*, BR-364/MT.
8608 A	-	*Jatropha*	-	*Comodoro* Station 337 km from *Porto Esperidião*, to *Porto Velho*, BR-364/MT.
8609	-	*Eschweilera*	Pale yellow petals, leathery leaf, 1 m tall.	*Comodoro* Station 337 km from *Porto Esperidião*, to *Porto Velho*, BR-364/MT.
8610	-	*Philodendron*	Small petiole shape, maybe juvenil from 8.611.	406 km from *Porto Esperidião*, to *Porto Velho*, BR-364/MT.
8611	-	*Philodendron speciosum* (or *brasiliensis*?)	3 m tall, multiple and erect petioles.	438 km from *Porto Esperidião*, to *Porto Velho*, BR-364/MT.
8612	-	*Dioclea*	Shrubby. Altitude: 690 m.a.s.l. approx. *Vilhena.*	473 km from *Porto Esperidião*, to *Porto Velho*, BR-364/MT.
8613	Araliaceae	-	Schefflera. 1 a 1.5 m tall, quite frequent, although few in flowering, brown flowers, green fruit. Altitude: 730 m.a.s.l. approx.	361 km from *Porto Esperidião*, to *Porto Velho*, BR-364/MT.
8614	-	*Philodendron*	Sagitated leaves, crawling, half shade.	23 km from *Vilhena*, to *Porto Velho*, BR-364/RO.
8614 A	-	*Heliconia*	-	-
8615	-	*Philodendron*	Looks like 8.610, erect, sagittate leaves, - but narrower than 8.614.	-
8616	-	*Epiphyllum phyllanthus*	640 m.a.s.l. approx.	38 km from *Vilhena*, to *Porto Velho*, BR-364/RQ.
8617	-	*Jacaranda?*	Mauve leaves.	38 km from *Vilhena*, to *Porto Velho*, BR-364/RQ.
8618	-	*Dioclea*	Bush or climber, purple, 1 a 2 m tall, in devastated area.	33 km from *Vilhena*, to *Porto Velho*, BR-364/RQ.
8619	-	*Heliconia*	Erect, red, pubescent green leaves, 2 m tall, partial shade, floodable place, distic leaves, pruinous dorsal face, slightly hirsute flowers, with green color, distal inflorescence, occasionally polystichous.	-
8620	-	*Urospatha?*	Deep forest shadow, 260 m.a.s.l. approx.	24 km from *Ji-Paraná*, to *Porto Velho*, BR-364.
8621	-	*Monstera*	-	24 km from *Ji-Paraná*, to *Porto Velho*, BR-364.
8622	-	*Astrocaryum*	-	24 km from *Ji-Paraná*, to *Porto Velho*, BR-364.
8623	-	*Philodendron*	310 m.a.s.l. approx.	38 km from *Ji-Paraná*, to *Porto Velho*, BR-364.
8624	-	*Xanthosoma*	Leaf 1 x 0.60 m, 3 m tall.	38 km from *Ji-Paraná*, to *Porto Velho*, BR-364.
8625	-	*Rhipsalis*	-	38 km from *Ji-Paraná*, to *Porto Velho*, BR-364.
8626	-	*Clusia*	-	38 km from *Ji-Paraná*, to *Porto Velho*, BR-364.
8627	-	*Maxillaria*	-	38 km from *Ji-Paraná*, to *Porto Velho*, BR-364.
8628	Orchidaceae	-	-	38 km from *Ji-Paraná*, to *Porto Velho*, BR-364.
8629	-	*Attalea*	12 m tall. Altitude: 360 m.a.s.l. approx.	41 km from *Ji-Paraná*, to *Porto Velho*, BR-364.
8630	-	*Anthurium*	Gigant.	41 km from *Ji-Paraná*, to *Porto Velho*, BR-364.
8631	Araceae	*Caladium?*	Less than 0.30 m tall, no leaves.	6 km from *Jaru*, to *Porto Velho*, BR-364.
8632	-	*Cassia spruceana*	Deep yellow flowers, remanescent in burned area, 6 m aprox.	114 km from *Jaru, São João Station*, to *Porto Velho*, BR-364.
8633	-	*Palmaceae*	Leaves 3.5 m length, long petiole at the base, black pubescent, yellow flowers on orange spikes.	*Porto Velho.*
8634	-	*Mauritiella* (*armata or echinata?*)	Thorns on the trunk, green seeds. Altitude: 160 m.a.s.l. approx.	4 km from *Porto Velho*, to *Humaitá*, BR-316.
8635	Melastomataceae	-	Pink flowers, stouts also pink, 4 m tall. Altitude: 120 m.a.s.l. approx.	10 km from *Porto Velho*, to *Humaitá*, BR-316.
8636	-	*Montrichardia*	2 m tall approx., marsh, sun.	10 km from *Porto Velho*, to *Humaitá*, BR-316.
8637	Melastomataceae	-	Red leaves, pink flowers, grass, next to small stream, exposed to sun.	10 km from *Porto Velho*, to *Humaitá*, BR-316.
8638	-	*Bambusa*	Matorral, 4 m tall approx.	10 km from *Porto Velho*, to *Humaitá*, BR-316.
8639	-	*Ravenala guianensis. Phenakospermum?*		24 km from *Porto Velho*, to *Humaitá*, BR-316.
8640	-	*Cupania* (*guaraná*)	2 m tall approx., showy fruits, red, black seeds, covered by whitish pulp, going for blue, general gray appearance.	-
8641	-	*Philodendron*	Altitude: 210 m.a.s.l. approx.	44 km from *Porto Velho*, to *Humaitá*, BR-316.
8642	-	*Philodendron*	Altitude: 210 m.a.s.l. approx.	44 km from *Porto Velho*, to *Humaitá*, BR-316.
8643	-	*Anthurium* (?)	Altitude: 210 m.a.s.l. approx.	44 km from *Porto Velho*, to *Humaitá*, BR-316.

8644	-	*Heliconia*	Glaucous leaves on the bottom page, red bracts, green flowers.	44 km from *Porto Velho*, to *Humaitá*, BR-316.
8645	Aechmea mertensis (?)	*Bromeliaceae*	-	-
8646	-	*Palicourea*	Red flowering bush, purple stem, near flowers. Altitude: 230 m.a.s.l. approx.	48 km from *Porto Velho*, to *Humaitá*, BR-316.
8647	Melastomataceae	-	Shrub, in shaded area.	83 km from *Porto Velho*, to *Humaitá*, BR-316.
8648	Melastomataceae	-	On the roadside, shadow, radius 0.50 m.	83 km from *Porto Velho*, to *Humaitá*, BR-316.
8649	Palmaceae	Probably *Mauritiella*	-	83 km from *Porto Velho*, to *Humaitá*, BR-316.
8650	-	*Heliconia*	Red bracts, yellow flowers, glaucous leaves.	83 km from *Porto Velho*, to *Humaitá*, BR-316.
8651	Euphorbiaceae	-	Grass erect, soft, pubescent. Altitude: 160 m.a.s.l. approx.	10 km from *the intersection of Humaitá*, to *Manaus*, BR-316 (BR-230?).
8652	-	*Odonteronia* (or *Fosteronia*?)	Altitude: 160 m.a.s.l. approx.	10 km from *the intersection of Humaitá*, to *Manaus*, BR-316 (BR-230?).
8653	Melastomataceae	-	0.50 to 1 m tall, mauve flowers, hirsute leaves, rugged.	10 km from *the intersection of Humaitá*, to *Manaus*, BR-316 (BR-230?).
8654	-	*Philodendron*	-	10 km from *the intersection of Humaitá*, to *Manaus*, BR-316 (BR-230?).
8655	Melastomataceae	-	1 m tall, pink flowers.	10 km from *the intersection of Humaitá*, to *Manaus*, BR-316 (BR-230?).
8656	Melastomataceae	-	Approx. 2 a 3 m tall, pink flowers.	-
8657	-	*Philodendron*	Quite frequent, climber, approx. 2 m tall, flowers not sun, sagitted leaves. Altitude: 190 m.a.s.l. approx.	39 km from *Humaitá*, to *Manaus*, BR-316.
8658	-	*Philodendron*	Climber, in deep shade, inflorescencia ca. 0.20 m, rough petiole, magenta. Soft leaves, pale green, infrequent. Altitude: 190 m.a.s.l. approx.	39 km from *Humaitá*, to *Manaus*, BR-316.
8659	-	*Norantea*	Orange flower "dyed" red, 1.5 to 2 m tall.	-
8660	-	*Anthurium*	Palms, 19 leaflets.	165 km from *Humaitá*, to *Manaus*, BR-316.
8660 A	-	*Anthurium*	-	165 km from *Humaitá*, to *Manaus*, BR-316.
8661	-	*Duguetia*	With fruits.	165 km from *Humaitá*, to *Manaus*, BR-316.
8662	-	*Philodendron*	Climber.	165 km from *Humaitá*, to *Manaus*, BR-316.
8663	-	*Philodendron*	Small leaf, scaly, leaves with marbled spots.	165 km from *Humaitá*, to *Manaus*, BR-316.
8664	-	*Aechmea?*	Low, light green.	165 km from *Humaitá*, to *Manaus*, BR-316.
8665	-	*Ischinoziphon*	1 m tall, pink/red flowers, green leaves with marked nerves.	165 km from *Humaitá*, to *Manaus*, BR-316.
8666	-	*Philodendron speciosum*	2 a 3 m tall. Altitude: 140 m.a.s.l. approx.	169 km from *Humaitá*, to *Manaus*, BR-316.
8667	-	*Lindackeria*	Altitude: 140 m.a.s.l. approx.	174 km from *Humaitá*, to *Manaus*, BR-316.
8668	Bignoniaceae	-	White flowers.	174 km from *Humaitá*, to *Manaus*, BR-316.
8669	Melastomataceae	-	Corrugaded leaves, hirsute, red on the back. Altitude: 140 m.a.s.l. approx.	174 km from *Humaitá*, to *Manaus*, BR-316.
8670	-	*Palicourea corimbosa?*	5 m tall, deep golden yellow flowers, large striated leaves.	185 km from *Humaitá*, to *Manaus*, BR-316.
8671	-	*Bromelia*	Leaf 3 m, green, with thorns, in deep shade. Altitude: 140 m.a.s.l. approx.	185 km from *Humaitá*, to *Manaus*, BR-316.
8672	-	*Morenia*	Black seeds, 2 m tall, in shade, very frequent.	272 km from *Humaitá*, to *Manaus*, BR-316.
8673	-	*Leptocarya tenue?*	Small fruit, orange-red, with scales, leafy popullation.	272 km from *Humaitá*, to *Manaus*, BR-316.
8674	-	*Philodendron*	Laciniated leaves, growing on 8.673.	272 km from *Humaitá*, to *Manaus*, BR-316.
8675	-	*Aechmea*	Epiphyte.	272 km from *Humaitá*, to *Manaus*, BR-316.
8676	-	*Mabea occidentalis*	-	272 km from *Humaitá*, to *Manaus*, BR-316.
8677	-	*Philodendron tripartitum*	-	272 km from *Humaitá*, to *Manaus*, BR-316.
8678	-	*Philodendron*	-	-
8679	-	*Asplenium*	-	-
8680	-	*Norantea*	Red, 3 to 4 m tall, it seems 8.659. Altitude: 150 m.a.s.l. approx.	*São João* farm, 284 km from *Humaitá*, to *Manaus*, BR-316.
8681	-	*Philodendron*	-	284 km from *Humaitá*, to *Manaus*, BR-316.
8682	-	*Passiflora*	-	284 km from *Humaitá*, to *Manaus*, BR-316.
8683	-	*Melastomataceae*	Altitude: 115 m.a.s.l. approx.	432 km from *Humaitá*, to *Manaus*, BR-316.
8684	-	*Philodendron*	Epiphyte, nest habit, 0.90 m tall.	432 km from *Humaitá*, to *Manaus*, BR-316.

8685	-	*Dieffenbachia*	Leaf all green, 0.90 m tall.	432 km from *Humaitá*, to *Manaus*, BR-316.
8686	-	*Philodendron*	Climber.	432 km from *Humaitá*, to *Manaus*, BR-316.
8687	-	*Philodendron*	Climber, laciniated leaf.	432 km from *Humaitá*, to *Manaus*, BR-316.
8688	-	*Philodendron*	Climber, roped leaf.	432 km from *Humaitá*, to *Manaus*, BR-316.
8689	-	*Philodendron*	Elliptical leaves, perched petiole, may be juvenile of 8.688.	432 km from *Humaitá*, to *Manaus*, BR-316.
8690	-	*Palicourea*	Yellow flower, 2 a 4 m tall.	434 km from *Humaitá*, to *Manaus*, BR-316.
8691	-	*Philodendron*	Base of the inner face of the reddish spathe.	434 km from *Humaitá*, to *Manaus*, BR-316.
8692	-	*Clusia*	Oval elliptical leaves, very long, 1.5 m tall, half shade.	434 km from *Humaitá*, to *Manaus*, BR-316.
8693	-	*Pitcairnia*	Red flower, leaf with thorns.	434 km from *Humaitá*, to *Manaus*, BR-316.
8694	-	*Philodendron*	Type "*penacho*". Altitude: 130 m.a.s.l. approx.	474 km from *Humaitá*, to *Manaus*, BR-316.
8695	-	*Philodendron*	Sagitted corded leaves.	474 km from *Humaitá*, to *Manaus*, BR-316.
8696	-	*Philodendron*	Leaves sagitated, short, climber.	474 km from *Humaitá*, to *Manaus*, BR-316.
8697	Bromeliaceae		-	474 km from *Humaitá*, to *Manaus*, BR-316.
8698	-	*Philodendron*	Climber, rosette arrangement.	474 km from *Humaitá*, to *Manaus*, BR-316.
8699	-	*Philodendron*	-	474 km from *Humaitá*, to *Manaus*, BR-316.
8700	Bromeliaceae	-	No flowers, with 8.694 and 8.699.	474 km from *Humaitá*, to *Manaus*, BR-316.
8701	-	*Philodendron*	Epiphyte, purple back in the young forms, young plants on the floor of the clean forest, long leaves, sagitted, acuminate, with reddish edges.	Km 45 from BR-174 (*INPA Reserve*).
8702	-	*Philodendron*	Laciniated leaves, small, red joint, epiphyte.	Km 45 from BR-174 (*INPA Reserve*).
8703	-	*Philodendron*	Long and triangular petiole, roped leaf, dark green, small, red articulation, epiphyte.	Km 45 from BR-174 (*INPA Reserve*).
8704	Gramineae	-	In the sub-forest.	Km 45 from BR-174 (*INPA Reserve*).
8704 A	-	*Philodendron*	*Aff. melinoni*, epiphyte.	Km 45 from BR-174 (*INPA Reserve*).
8705	-	*Philodendron*	Large rosettes, petiole long rounded on the back. Large deltoid leaves, dark green, longer than 8.703.	Km 45 from BR-174 (*INPA Reserve*).
8706	-	*Philodendron*	Petiole with hard hairs, leaves 0.40 x 0.18 m, dark green, lighter back, fresh and reddish joint, marking ribbing.	Km 45 from BR-174 (*INPA Reserve*).
8707	-	*Philodendron*	*Aff. melinoni*, concave petiole, purple leaves.	Km 45 from BR-174 (*INPA Reserve*).
8708	-	*Anthurium*	Elliptical leaf ovate, hard, 0.45 x 0.15 m, dark green, long petiole.	Km 45 from BR-174 (*INPA Reserve*).
8709	Araceae?	-	Climber, dark green leaves, lighter back.	Km 45 from BR-174 (*INPA Reserve*).
8710	-	*Paullinia cupana*		Km 45 from BR-174 (*INPA Reserve*).
8711	-	*Philodendron*	Yellow petioles, climber, perhaps adult of 8.701.	Km 45 from BR-174 (*INPA Reserve*).
8712	-	*Urospatha?*	Espate pale yellow, green inside, brown purple bright, on the outside, very leathery, very rough petioles.	Km 45 from BR-174 (*INPA Reserve*).
8713	-	*Heliconia*	Dark red bracts, white flower, 1 m tall, marsh, infrequent.	Km 45 from BR-174 (*INPA Reserve*).
8714	Araceae	-	Climber, haste hairy, hard, green leaves 0.25 x 0.08.	46 km from BR-174, to *Boa Vista*.
8715	-	*Clusia*	Sandy soil, sun.	58 km from BR-174, to *Boa Vista*.
8716	Melastomataceae	-	-	58 km from BR-174, to *Boa Vista*.
8717	Orchidaceae	-	No flowers, epiphyte. Altitude: 170 m.a.s.l. approx. *Anaconda* farm.	60 km from BR-174, to *Boa Vista*.
8718	Bromeliaceae	*Pitcairnia*	Leaves 0.60 m, light green.	60 km from BR-174, to *Boa Vista*.
8719	-	*Bromelia (or Ananas)*	Grayish green, thorns on the edges.	60 km from BR-174, to *Boa Vista*.
8720	-	*Clusia*	Ovate leaves.	Km 60 from BR-174, to *Boa Vista*.
8721	-	*Heliconia*	Large leaf, 0.80 x 0.30 m, green, white back, 2.50 m tall.	Km 60 from BR-174, to *Boa Vista*.
8722	-	*Heliconia*	White flowers, red bracts, red central blackness on the back. Leaf 0.50 x 0.10 m.	Km 60 from BR-174, to *Boa Vista*.
8723	-	*Clusia*	Ovate leaves.	Km 60 from BR-174, to *Boa Vista*.
8724	-	*Clusia*	Elliptical leaves, 0.18 x 0.07 m.	Km 60 from BR-174, to *Boa Vista*.
8725	-	*Philodendron melinoni*	Red back, long petiole.	Km 60 from BR-174, to *Boa Vista*.
8726	-	*Cecropia*	Pelted, white on the back, hirsute, red nerves.	Km 60 from BR-174, to *Boa Vista*.
8727	-	*Cecropia*	6 glabrous segments.	Km 60 from BR-174, to *Boa Vista*.
8728	Bromeliaceae	*Aechmea*	Light green, thorns on the edge.	Km 60 from BR-174, to *Boa Vista*.
8729	-	*Philodendron*	Long petiole, elliptical leaves, deep green.	Km 60 from BR-174, to *Boa Vista*.
8730	-	*Clusia*	Narrow, elliptical-lanceolate leaves.	Km 60 from BR-174, to *Boa Vista*.
8731	-	*Clusia*	Obovate leaves. Altitude: 170 m.a.s.l. approx.	Km 60 from BR-174, to *Boa Vista*.

8732	Gesneriaceae	-	Hairy leaves, white, moles, 0.30 m tall.	*Igarapé das Lajes*, 120 km from BR-174, to *Boa Vista*.
8733	-	*Mandevilla*	Yellow climber.	120 km from BR-174, to *Boa Vista*.
8734	-	*Mandevilla?*	Pale pink.	Km 120 from BR-174, to *Boa Vista*.
8735	-	*Tillandsia*	Closed flowers, pinkish red, grayish green leaves.	Km 120 from BR-174, to *Boa Vista* (*Igarapé das Lajes*).
8736	-	*Maxillaria*	-	Km 120 from BR-174, to *Boa Vista* (*Igarapé das Lajes*).
8737	-	*Ficus*	-	Km 120 from BR-174, to *Boa Vista* (*Igarapé das Lajes*).
8738	-	*Sobralia liliastrum?*	Thicket, 1.20 m tall.	Km 120 from BR-174, to *Boa Vista* (*Igarapé das Lajes*).
8739	-	*Philodendron*	Leaves hard, dark green, narrow, with lighter nerves, rupicolous, white spathes.	Km 120 from BR-174, to *Boa Vista* (*Igarapé das Lajes*).
8740	-	*Philodendron*	Climber, leaf 0.50 x 0.60 m, tripartite.	Km 120 from BR-174, to *Boa Vista* (*Igarapé das Lajes*).
8741	-	*Anthurium*	Lanceolate elliptical leaves, short petioles.	Km 120 from BR-174, to *Boa Vista* (*Igarapé das Lajes*).
8742	-	*Philodendron*	Climber, brown leaves in the lower part.	Km 120 from BR-174, to *Boa Vista* (*Igarapé das Lajes*).
8743	-	*Philodendron*	Leaf 0.65 x 0.30 m, oval, elliptical, long petiole.	Km 120 from BR-174, to *Boa Vista* (*Igarapé das Lajes*).
8744	-	*Philodendron*	-	Km 120 from BR-174, to *Boa Vista* (*Igarapé das Lajes*).
8745	-	*Heliconia*	Yellow, orange bracts internally, sun. Leaf 0.50 x 0.12, golden yellow, glaucescent on the back.	214 km from BR-174, to *Boa Vista*.
8746	Rubiaceae	-	-	214 km from BR-174, to *Boa Vista*.
8747	-	*Heliconia psittacorum?*	0.80 m tall, thin leaves 0.06 x 0.30.	214 km from BR-174, to *Boa Vista*.
8748	-	*Acacia*	Yellowish-white inflorescence. Altitude: 130 m.a.s.l. approx.	229 km from BR-174, to *Boa Vista*.
8749	-	*Heliconia*	Green bracts at the base and red above, some cases with green apex, yellow ovary, narrow at the base and, later, orange color, light-large green leaves, main purple nervura. Altitude: 160 m.a.s.l. approx.	*Jundiá* Station, 339 km from BR-174, to Boa Vista.
8750	-	*Heliconia*	Orange yellow bracts with black dots, bright orange ovary.	353 km from BR-174, to *Boa Vista*.
8751	-	*Heliconia*	Red nerve on the back, yellow and orange flower, greener in the bracts than 8749. 1.50 m tall.	355 km from BR-174, to *Boa Vista*.
8752	Melastomataceae	-	White greenish flowers, 2 m tall.	364 km from BR-174, to *Boa Vista*.
8753	-	*Cassia*	Tree, 5-8 m, yellow flowers.	364 km from BR-174, to *Boa Vista*.
8754	-	*Anthurium*	Violet flower, green leaf, compound, purple spathe, place of sun.	417 km from BR-174, to *Boa Vista*.
8755	-	*Philodendron*	Epiphyte, trilobed.	417 km from BR-174, to *Boa Vista*.
8756	-	*Philodendron*	Climber, lanceolate leaves.	417 km from BR-174, to *Boa Vista*.
8757	-	*Philodendron*	Epiphyte, broad, soft chordate leaves.	417 km from BR-174, to *Boa Vista*.
8758	Orchidaceae	-	Micro.	417 km from BR-174, to *Boa Vista*.
8759	-	*Philodendron*	Climber, lanceolate sagittate leaf, rugged.	417 km from BR-174, to *Boa Vista*.
8760	-	*Syngonium*	Light greenish-yellow spathe.	417 km from BR-174, to *Boa Vista*.
8761	-	*Aroideae?*	-	417 km from BR-174, to *Boa Vista*.
8762	-	*Philodendron*	Climber, small leaf, lanceolate sagitated.	417 km from BR-174, to *Boa Vista*.
8763	-	*Furcraea*	With thorns, no flowers, rocky place.	497 km from BR-174, to *Boa Vista*.
8764	-	*Begonia*	Light green, shade.	497 km from BR-174, to *Boa Vista*.
8765	-	*Heliconia hirsuta*	Fine leaf, reddish orange bracts, 2 m tall.	497 km from BR-174, to *Boa Vista*.
8766	-	*Heliconia*	Long leaf, no flowers.	497 km from BR-174, to *Boa Vista*.
8767	-	*Costus*	Large flowers, with blue seeds, sun.	497 km from BR-174, to *Boa Vista*.
8768	-	*Ananas*	-	534 km from BR-174, to *Boa Vista*.
8769	-	*Cyrtopodium*	Purple flowers.	534 km from BR-174, to *Boa Vista*.
8770	Melastomataceae	-	-	597 km from BR-174, to *Boa Vista*.
8771	-	*Catleya*	Epiphyte (in Ipê), with fruits.	12 km from *Caracaraí*, to *Boa Vista*, BR-174.
8772	-	*Cereus*	Altitude: 120 m.a.s.l. approx.	12 km from *Caracaraí*, to *Boa Vista*, BR-174.
8773	-	*Astrocaryum*	Multiple trunks, yellowish orange fruit.	12 km from *Caracaraí*, to *Boa Vista*, BR-174.
8774	-	*Leguminosa*	White flowers, in spikes.	17 km from *Caracaraí*, to *Boa Vista*, BR-174.
8775	Onagraceae	-	1 m tall, yellow flowers, very frequent.	12 km from *Caracaraí*, to *Boa Vista*, BR-174.

Figure 18. *Passiflora* L. collected in the Amazon, Brazil. Photography: Oscar Bressane, Koiti Mori and José Tabacow, 1983.

Field Notes.*
Dr. William A. Rodrigues and Rosangela Cunha Rocha

Collection No.	Family	Name
10320	Dillentaceae	*Doliocarpus*
10321	Vochysiaceae	*Vochysia*
10322	Simarubeceae	*Simaruba*
10323	Compositae	-
10324	Leguminoseae	*Andira humilis* Mart. ex Benth.
10325	Malpighiaceae	*Banisteria*
10326	Myrtaceae	*Eugenia*
10327	Rubiaceae	*Basanacantha*
10328	Myrtaceae	-
10329	Annonaceae	*Xylopia*
10330	Melastomataceae	*Miconia*
10331	Polygonaceae	*Coccoloba*
10332	Tiliaceae	*Lueheopsis*
10333	Caricaceae	*Jaracatia*
10334	Bignoniaceae	-
10335	Leguminoseae	*Andira humilis* Mart. ex Benth.
10336	Lauraceae	*Mezilaurus cf. crassiramea* (Meissn.) Taubert.
10337	Vochysiaceae	*Erisma*
10338	Cucurbitaceae	*Gurania*
10339	Leg. *Caesalpinioideae*	*Bauhinia*
10340	Loganiaceae	*Antonia ovata*
10341	Styracaceae	*Styrax*
10342	Myrcinaceae	*Rapania*
10343	Rubiaceae	-
10344	Rubiaceae	*Tocoyena formosa* (Cham. & Schl.) K. Schum
10345	Rubiaceae	*Tocoyena formosa* (Cham. & Schl.) K. Schum
10346	Apocynaceae	*Forsteronia*
10347	Leg. Mimosoideae	*Inga*
10348	Boraginaceae	*Geracanthos*
10349	Gramineae	*Andropogon*
10350	Vochysiaceae	*Qualea*
10351	Oxalidaceae	*Oxalis*
10352	Sterculiaceae	*Guazuma*
10353	Compositae	-
10354	Leg. *Caesalpinioideae*	*Hymenaea stigonocarpa*
10355	Malpighiaceae	-
10356	Simarubaceae	*Simaruba*
10357	Leg. Mimosoideae	*Calliandra*
10358	Compositae	-
10359	Bignoniaceae	*Anemopaegma arvense* (Vell.) Stelff
10360	Compositae	-
10361	Verbenaceae	*Lippia lupulina* Cham.

* Table prepared cataloguing information according to: Collection number, name, family, notes and location. Spaces without information are marked with a hyphen (-). Question marks (?) are typical of the original.

80 I. BURLE MARX'S EXPEDITION TO THE AMAZON

10362	Apocynaceae	*Mandevilla*
10363	Loranthaceae	-
10364	Malpighiaceae	*Byrsonima*
10365	Velloziaceae	-
10366	Compositae	*Baccharis*
10367	Euphorbiaceae	*Euphorbia*
10368	Myrtaceae	-
10369	Euphorbiaceae	*Dalechampia*
10370	Malpighiaceae	*Banisteriopsis*
10371	Rubiaceae	-
10372	Bombacaceae	*Eryotheca*
10373	Sterculiaceae	*Helycteres*
10374	Musaceae	*Heliconia*
10375	Malpighiaceae	-
10376	Malpighiaceae	*Byrsonima*
10377	Leguminoseae	*Hymenaea stigonocarpa* Mart. Ex Hayne var.
10378	Cochlospermaceae	*Cochlospermum*
10379	Marcgraviaceae	*Norantea*
10380	Legum. Papilionaceae	-
10381	Acanthaceae	*Ruellia*
10382	Euphorbiaceae	*Croton*
10383	Compositae	-
10384	Turneraceae	*Turnera*
10385	Euphorbiaceae	*Croton*
10386	Myrtaceae	-
10387	Euphorbiaceae	*Jatropha*
10388	Leg. Papilionaceae	-
10389	Meliaceae	*Guarea*
10390	Euphorbiaceae	*Dalechampia*
10391	Malvaceae	*Pavonia*
10392	Euphorbiaceae	*Manihot*
10393	Zingiberaceae	*Renealmia*
10394	Malpighiaceae	-
10395	Rubiaceae	*Psychotria*
10396	Vochysiaceae	*Vochysia*
10397	Urticaceae	-
10398	Malvaceae	*Pavonia*
10399	Bignoniaceae	-
10400	Malpighiaceae	*Byrsonima*
10401	Apocynaceae	-
10402	Leg. Papilionaceae	*Dioclea*
10403	Malpighiaceae	-
10404	Bignoniaceae	*Jacaranda cuspidifolia* Mart.
10405	Apocynaceae	*Forsteronia*
10406	Polygonaceae	*Triplaris pavonii* Meissn.
10407	Leg. Mimosoideae	*Pithecellobium*
10408	Bignoniaceae	*Tabebuia*
10409	Acanthaceae	*Ruellia*
10410	Verbenaceae	*Lantana*
10411	Annonaceae	*Annona*
10412	Sapotaceae	*Pouteria*

10413	Rubiaceae	*Faramea*
10414	Guttiferae	*Kielmeyera coriacea* Mart.
10415	Cycadaceae	*Zamia*
10416	Myrtaceae	-
10417	Rubiaceae	*Alibertia*
10418	Leg. Papilionaceae	*Erythrina*
10419	Amaryllidaceae	*Zephyranthes*
10420	Turneraceae	*Turnera*
10421	Bignoniaceae	*Tabebuia*
10422	Leg. Papilionaceae	*Platypodium elegans* Vog.
10423	Ochnaceae	*Ouratea castanaefolia* C. DC.
10424	Bignoniaceae	*Tebebuia*
10425	Cochlospermaceae	*Cochlospermum Regium* (Mart.) Pilger
10426	Bignoniaceae	*Tabebuia*
10427	Bignoniaceae	*Tabebuia*
10428	Compositae	*Vermonia scabra* Pers.
10429	Myrtaceae	*Psidium*
10430	Compositae	*Emilia sonchifolia* DC.
10431	Musaceae	*Heliconia*
10432	Cucurbitaceae	*Gurania spinulosa* (Poepp. & Endl) Cogn.
10433	Apocynaceae	*Himatanthus*
10434	Ochnaceae	*Ouratea*
10435	Compositae	*Asteracea*
10436	Rutaceae	*Spiranthera odoratissima* St. Hil.
10437	Leg. Papilionaceae	*Dioclea*
10438	Annonaceae	*Xylopia*
10439	Annonaceae	*Annona coriacea* Mart.
10440	Bignoniaceae	-
10441	Leg. *Caesalpinioideae*	*Cassia spruceana*
10442	Apocynaceae	*Odontafromnia nitida* (Vahl.) M. Arg.
10443	Melastomataceae	*Aciotis fragilis* (Rich.) Cogn.
10444	Araceae	*Montrichardia arborescens* (L) Schott.
10445	Melastomataceae	*Bellucia acutata* Pilger.
10446	Vochysiaceae	*Vochysia ferruginea* Mart.
10447	Sapindaceae	*Cupania*
10448	Annonaceae	*Guatteria*
10449	Vochysiaceae	*Vochysia obscura* Warm.
10450	Melastomataceae	*Miconia pileata* DC.
10451	Melastomataceae	*Tococa guianensis* Aubl.
10452	Melastomataceae	*Miconia tiliaefolia* Naud.
10453	Leg. Mimosoideae	*Entada polyphylla* Benth.
10454	Maranthaceae	*Ischnosiphon*
10455	Solanaceae	*Solanum rugosum* Dunal
10456	Rubiaceae	*Palicourea guianensis* Aubl.
10457	Lecythidaceae	*Eschweilera*
10458	Passifloraceae	*Passiflora foetida* L.
10459	Musaceae	*Heliconia*
10460	Bromeliacea	*Pitcairnia*
10461	Rapateaceae	*Saxofridericia aculeata* Koern.
10462	Leg. Papilionaceae	*Chaetocalyx*
10463	Musaceae	*Heliconia rostrata*

Figure 19. [Lower] *Clusia* sp. collected live plant No. 323. *Piedra Azul, Espírito Santo*, Brazil. Photography: Oscar Bressane, Koiti Mori and José Tabacow, 1983.

List of herbalized plants.*
Dr. William Rodrigues

#	Name	Family	Notes	Localization
10320	*Doliocarpus*	Dilleniaceae	Climber, red fruit, seed with white aril, dark green leaf, 0.15 m, low lighting, *Cerrado*, clay soil, dry.	9 km from *Caiapônia*, to *Piranhas*, BR-158/GO (*Serra do Caiapó*).
10321	*Vochysia*	Vochysiaceae	Tree, 2 m tall, little dense canopy, 1.50 diameter, green fruit, erect leaves, very frequent, *Cerrado*, lots of sun, clay soil, dry.	9 km from *Caiapônia*, to *Piranhas*, BR-158/GO (*Serra do Caiapó*).
10322	*Simaruba*	Simarubaceae	Tree, 4-5 m tall, canopy not very dense, 3-4 m in diameter, purple fruit, 0.01 m in diameter, very frequent, *Cerrado*, clay soil.	9 km from *Caiapônia*, to *Piranhas*, BR-158/GO (*Serra do Caiapó*).
10323	-	Compositae	Shrub, 1 m tall, cream fruit, whitish leaf in verse, greenish white flower, without characteristic aroma, occasional frequency, in stony place.	9 km from *Caiapônia*, to *Piranhas*, BR-158/GO (*Serra do Caiapó*).
10324	*Andira hurnilis* Mart. ex. Benth.	Leguminosae	Tree, 4 m tall, 3 m diameter, dense crown, greenish fruit, green leaf, rusty in the verse, thick bark and longitudinal fissures, rare, *Cerrado*, clay soil.	9 km from *Caiapônia*, to *Piranhas*, BR-158/GO (*Serra do Caiapó*).
10325	*Banisteria*	Malpighiaceae	Climber, very frequent, velvety textured leaf.	9 km from *Caiapônia*, to *Piranhas*, BR-158/GO (*Serra do Caiapó*).
10326	*Eugenia*	Myrtaceae	Shrub, 2 m tall, abundant flowering, white flower.	9 km from *Caiapônia*, to *Piranhas*, BR-158/GO (*Serra do Caiapó*).
10327	*Basanacantha*	Rubiaceae	Climber, white flower, occasional frequency.	9 km from *Caiapônia*, to *Piranhas*, BR-158/GO (*Serra do Caiapó*).
10328	-	Myrtaceae	Shrub, 1 m tall, white flower, occasional frequency.	9 km from *Caiapônia*, to *Piranhas*, BR-158/GO (*Serra do Caiapó*).
10329	*Xylopia*	Annonaceae	Tree, 5 m tall, 4 m diameter, verticillate canopy, white flower, very frequent, *Cerrado*, clay soil.	9 km from *Caiapônia*, to *Piranhas*, BR-158/GO (*Serra do Caiapó*).
10330	*Miconia*	Melastomataceae	Shrub, 1.50 m tall, little dense, rusty leaf in the verse, white flower, medium frequency.	9 km from *Caiapônia*, to *Piranhas*, BR-158/GO (*Serra do Caiapó*).
10331	*Coccoloba*	Polygonaceae	Climber, leaf 0.20 x 0.20 m, greenish flower, moderately frequent, *Cerrado*.	9 km from *Caiapônia*, to *Piranhas*, BR-158/GO (*Serra do Caiapó*).
10332	*Lueheopsis*	Tiliaceae	Tree, 3 m tall, little dense canopy, rusty fruit, rusty leaf in verse, 0.20 x 0.15 m, white flower, *Cerrado*, clay soil.	9 km from *Caiapônia*, to *Piranhas*, BR-158/GO (*Serra do Caiapó*).
10333	*Jaracatia*	Caricaceae	Grass, 0.50 m tall, white flower, *Cerrado*, clay soil.	9 km from *Caiapônia*, to *Piranhas*, BR-158/GO (*Serra do Caiapó*).
10334	-	Bignoniaceae	Climber, green pod fruit, orange flower, sun, very frequent, *Cerrado*.	São Simão Road/*Jataí*, BR- 365/GO.
10335	*Andira humilis* Mart. ex. Benth.	Leguminosae	Tree, 5 m tall, 6 m diameter, dense canopy, red leaf when young, blowing flowers, *Cerrado*, sandy-clay soil.	São Simão Road/*Jataí*, BR- 365/GO.
10336	*Mezilaurus cf. crassiramea* (Meissn.) Taubert.	Lauraceae	Medium size tree, 4 m tall, 0.15 m trunk diameter, dense crown, 3 m diameter, rusty leaf in the verse, with hairs, leathery, trunk w/thick bark and longitudinal fissures, *Cerrado*.	9 km from *Caiapônia*, to *Piranhas*, BR-158/GO (*Serra do Caiapó*).
10337	*Erisma*	Vochysiaceae	Tree, 4 m tall, 0.15 m trunk diameter, little dense canopy, flower purple, very frequent, *Cerrado*.	111 km *Jataí*, to *Caiapônia*, BR-158/GO.
10338	*Gurania?*	Cucurbitaceae	Climber, pink flower, occasional frequency, *Cerrado*.	111 km *Jataí*, to *Caiapônia*, BR-158/GO.
10339	*Bauhinia* (*Leg. Caesalpinoidea*)	-	Shrub, 1.80 m tall, little leafy, green leaf, white flower.	111 km *Jataí*, to *Caiapônia*, BR-158/GO.
10340	*Antonia ovata*	Loganiaceae	Tree, 3 m tall, slightly dense, 1 m diameter, straw-colored nut.	111 km *Jataí*, to *Caiapônia*, BR-158/GO.
10341	*Styrax*	Styracaceae	Tree, 2 m tall, little dense, green fruit, rusty leaf, flower white, yellow anthers.	111 km *Jataí*, to *Caiapônia*, BR-158/GO.
10342	*Rapania*	Myrcinaceae	Tree, 2 m tall, 0.04 m trunk diameter, little dense canopy, fruit green and young, occasional frequency.	111 km *Jataí*, to *Caiapônia*, BR-158/GO.
10343	-	Rubiaceae	Tree, 2 m tall, white flower, occasional frequency, *Cerrado*, sandy-clay soil.	111 km *Jataí*, to *Caiapônia*, BR-158/GO.
10344	*Tocoyena formosa* (*Cham. et Schl.*) K.Schum.	Rubiaceae	Tree, 2.5 m tall, 0.08 m trunk diameter, dense canopy, 2 m diameter, white flower, occasional frequency, sandy-clay soil.	111 km *Jataí*, to *Caiapônia*, BR-158/GO.

* Table prepared cataloguing information according to: Collection number, name, family, notes and location. Spaces without information are marked with a hyphen (-). Question marks (?) are typical of the original.

10345	*Tocoyena formosa* (*Cham. et Schl.*) *K.Schum.*	Rubiaceae	Tree, 2.5 m tall, 0.08 trunk diameter, dense canopy, diameter 2 m, green fruit, white flower, occasional frequency, sandy-clay soil.	111 km *Jataí*, to *Caiapônia*, BR-158/GO.
10346	*Forsteronia*	Apocynaceae	Climber, white latex, discolored leaf, opposites, white flower, occasional frequency *Cerrado*.	111 km *Jataí*, to *Caiapônia*, BR-158/GO.
10347	*Inga* sp.	Leguminosa mimosoidea	Shurb, 3 m tall, white flower, greenish fruit, occasional frequency, *Cerrado*.	111 km *Jataí*, to *Caiapônia*, BR-158/GO.
10348	*Gerascanthus* sp.	Boraginaceae	Shurb, 5 m tall, young fruit, white flower, frequent, *Cerrado*.	111 km *Jataí*, to *Caiapônia*, BR-158/GO.
10349	*Andropogon*	Gramineae	Herb, 0.40 m tall, white flower, abundant, *Cerrado*.	116 km *Jataí*, to *Rondonópolis*, BR- 364/GO.
10350	*Qualea*	Vochysiaceae	Tree, 8 m tall, 0.30 m trunk diameter, dense, 4 m diameter, light green leaf, yellow flower, altered *Cerrado*.	116 km *Jataí*, to *Rondonópolis*, BR- 364/GO.
10351	*Oxalis*	Oxalidaceae	Herb, 0.15 m tall, yellow flower, occasional frequency, altered *Cerrado*, sandy-clay soil.	116 km *Jataí*, to *Rondonópolis*, BR- 364/GO.
10352	*Guazuma*	Sterculiaceae	Tree, 4 m tall, cream flower, aromatic, occasional frequency, roadside, *Cerrado*.	116 km *Jataí*, to *Rondonópolis*, BR- 364/GO.
10353	-	Compositae	Greenish flower, rock field in *Cerrado*, stony ground.	171 km *Jataí*, to *Rondonópolis*, BR- 364/GO.
10354	*Hymenea stigonocarpa?*	Leg. Caesalpinoideae	Tree, 6 m tall, 0.15 m trunk diameter, 6 m canopy diameter, large fruit, dark brown, occasional frequency.	171 km *Jataí*, to *Rondonópolis*, BR- 364/GO.
10355	-	Malpighiaceae	Herb, 0.10 m tall, opposite leaves, yellow flower, infrequent, rock field, *sandstone*.	171 km *Jataí*, to *Rondonópolis*, BR- 364/GO.
10356	*Simaruba*	Simarubaceae	Occasional tree, 3 m tall, 0.10 m of trunk diameter, little dense canopy with 2 m diameter, discolored leaf, greenish flower, sandstone, rupestrian field.	171 km *Jataí*, to *Rondonópolis*, BR- 364/GO.
10357	*Calliandra*	Leguminoseae mimosoideae	Shrub, full sun, medium frequency, 3 m tall, fruits greenish, few leaves, leaflets 2 x 5 mm, white flower, center reddish, gray trunk, erect and thin.	171 km *Jataí*, to *Rondonópolis*, BR- 364/GO.
10358	-	Compositae	Occasional herb, 0.50 m tall, purple flower, sandstone, rupestrian field.	171 km *Jataí*, to *Rondonópolis*, BR- 364/GO.
10359	*Anemopaegma arvense* (Vell.) Stelff.	Bignoniaceae	Occasional herb, 0.30 m tall, cream flower.	171 km *Jataí*, to *Rondonópolis*, BR- 364/GO.
10360	-	Compositae	White flowers, occasional herb, 0.30 m tall, rupestrian.	171 km *Jataí*, to *Rondonópolis*, BR- 364/GO.
10361	*Lippialupulina* Cham.	Verbenaceae	Herb 0.50 m tall, occasional, rupestrian, purple bracts, lilac flower.	171 km *Jataí*, to *Rondonópolis*, BR- 364/GO.
10362	*Mandevilla*	Apocynaceae	Climber, white latex, yellow flower with red center, frequent, rock, rupestrian.	171 km *Jataí*, to *Rondonópolis*, BR- 364/GO.
10363	-	Loranthaceae	Herb, semi-parasitic, in *Hymenaea*, greenish flowers, rupestrian field.	171 km *Jataí*, to *Rondonópolis*, BR- 364/GO.
10364	*Byrsonima*	Malpighiaceae	Shurb, 1.50 m tall, frequent, yellow flowers, rupestrian.	171 km *Jataí*, to *Rondonópolis*, BR- 364/GO.
10365	-	Velloziaceae	Lilac flower, 0.40 m tall, rupestrian.	171 km *Jataí*, to *Rondonópolis*, BR- 364/GO.
10366	*Baccharis*	Compositae	Herb, 0.50 m tall, light cream flowers, occasional, roadside.	171 km *Jataí*, to *Rondonópolis*, BR- 364/GO.
10367	*Euphorbia*	Euphorbiaceae	White flowers, green fruits, 0.40 m tall, ocassional, roadside.	171 km *Jataí*, to *Rondonópolis*, BR- 364/GO.
10368	-	Myrtaceae	0.40 m tall, white flowers, pink blooms, ocassional, *Cerrado*, roadside.	171 km *Jataí*, to *Rondonópolis*, BR- 364/GO.
10369	*Dalechampia*	Euphorbiaceae	Herb, 0.30 m tall, frequent, frequent, *Cerrado*, flowers with bracts yellow and orange glands, green fruits.	171 km *Jataí*, to *Rondonópolis*, BR- 364/GO.
10370	*Banisteriopsis*	Malpighiaceae	Shurb, 2 m tall, occasional, pale pink flowers, glands dark red, *Cerrado*.	171 km *Jataí*, to *Rondonópolis*, BR- 364/GO.
10371	-	Rubiaceae	Shurb, 2 m tall, little dense cup, white flower, occasional, *Cerrado*.	*Caiapônia* Road/*Jataí*, BR-158/GO.
10372	*Eryotheca*	Bombacaceae	Tree, 6 m tall, trunk diameter 0.20 m, fruit w/seeds colour of straw, occasional in the *Cerrado*.	21 km from *Caiapônia*, to *Jataí*, BR-158/GO.
10373	*Helycteres*	Sterculiaceae	Shurb, 2 m tall, red flower, showy, roadside, *Cerrado*, ocassional.	*Caiapônia* Road/*Jataí*, BR-158.
10374	*Heliconia*	Musaceae	Herb, 1.80 m tall, bract orange, flor yellow, local, wet, occasional, *Cerrado*.	*Caiapônia* Road/*Pírenhas*, BR-158.
10375	-	Malpighiaceae	Liana, red fruit, by the roadside, frequent.	*Serra da Caiapó*.

10376	*Byrsonima*	Malpighiaceae	Small tree, flor yellow, frequent in the *Cerrado*.	*Serra da Caiapó.*
10377	*Hymenaea stigonocarpa* Mart. ex Hayne var.	Leguminoseae	Tree, 8 m tall, 0.25 m trunk diameter, occasional in the *Cerrado*, dark brown fruit.	*Caiapônia* Road/*Jataí*, BR-158.
10378	*Cochlospermum*	Cochlospermaceae	Shurb, 1.50 m tall, yellow flower, frequent in the *Cerrado*.	*Serra da Caiapó.*
10379	*Norantea*	Marcgraviaceae	Shrub, woody, scaly, dark wine inflorescence, young and green fruit, bracts of the same color as the flower (nectaries).	*Serra da Caiapó.*
10380	*Leguminosae papilionoidea*	-	Herb, 0.40 m tall, purple flower, roadside, occasional in the *Cerrado*.	41 km from *Jataí*, to *Mineiras*, BR-364/GO.
10381	*Ruellia* sp.	Acanthaceae	Herb, 0.10 m tall, flor blue, sandy soil, edge of the road, local recently burned, sun, frequent, *Cerrado*.	62 km *Alta Araguaia*, to *Cuiabá*, BR-364/MT.
10382	*Croton* sp.	Euphorbiaceae	Sub-Shrub, 0.30 m tall, white flower, roadside, local recently burned, sun, frequent, *Cerrado*.	62 km *Alta Araguaia*, to *Cuiabá*, BR-364/MT.
10383	-	Compositae	Shrub, 0.20 m tall, white flower, roadside, local recently burned, sun, occasional, *Cerrado*.	62 km *Alta Araguaia*, to *Cuiabá*, BR-364/MT.
10384	*Turnera*	Turneraceae	Herb, 0.30 m tall, yellow flower, roadside, local recently burned, sun, occasional, *Cerrado*.	62 km *Alta Araguaia*, to *Cuiabá*, BR-364/MT.
10385	*Croton?*	Euphorbiaceae	Sub-shrub, 0.20 m tall, white flower, roadside, local freshly burned, sun, frequent, *Cerrado*.	62 km *Alta Araguaia*, to *Cuiabá*, BR-364/MT.
10386	-	Myrtaceae	Sub-shrub, 0.15 m tall, white flower, roadside, local recently burned, occasional, *Cerrado*.	62 km *Alta Araguaia*, to *Cuiabá*, BR-364/MT.
10387	*Jatropha*	Euphorbiaceae	Sub-shrub, 0.10 m tall, white flower, white latex, roadside, local burned, sun, frequent, *Cerrado*.	62 km *Alta Araguaia*, to *Cuiabá*, BR-364/MT.
10388	-	Leguminoseae	Herb, 0.30 m tall, pink flower, immature fruit, green, roadside, local recently burned, sun, occasional, *Cerrado*.	62 km *Alta Araguaia*, to *Cuiabá*, BR-364/MT.
10389	*Guarea*	Meliaceae	Shurb, 0.30 m tall, pale cream flower, roadside, local recently burned, occasional, *Cerrado*.	62 km *Alta Araguaia*, to *Cuiabá*, BR-364/MT.
10390	*Dalechampia*	Euphorbiaceae	Shrub, 0.30 m tall, yellow bracts, greenish flower, orange glands, roadside, newly burned local, frequent, *Cerrado*.	62 km *Alta Araguaia*, to *Cuiabá*, BR-364/MT.
10391	*Pavonia*	Malvaceae	Shrub, 0.50 m tall, red flower, roadside, sun, ocasional, *Cerrado*.	79 km *Alta Araguaia*, to *Cuiabá*, BR-364/MT.
10392	*Manihot*	Euphorbiaceae	Herb, 0.40 m tall, greenish flower, roadside, local freshly burned, occasional, *Cerrado*.	62 km *Alta Araguaia*, to *Cuiabá*, BR-364/MT.
10393	*Renealmia*	Zingiberaceae	Herb, 0.20 m tall, yellow flower, moist ground, occasional, *Cerrado*.	*Caiapônia* Road/*Piranhas*, BR-158/GO.
10394	-	Malpighiaceae	Shrub, 0.40 m tall, yellow flower, red winged fruit, roadside, local recently burned, sun, frequent, *Cerrado*.	62 km *Alta Araguaia*, to *Cuiabá*, BR-364/MT.
10395	*Psychotria*	Rubiaceae	Shrub, 0.40 m tall, sulfur yellow inflorescence, roadside, local recently burned, sun, occasional, *Cerrado*.	62 km *Alta Araguaia*, to *Cuiabá*, BR-364/MT.
10396	*Vochysia* sp.	Vochysiaceae	Tree, 20 m tall, 0.40 m trunk diameter, dense canopy, 8,00 m diameter, yellow flower, sun, frequent, riparian forest, *Cerrado*.	79 km *Alta Araguaia*, to *Cuiabá*, BR-364/MT.
10397	-	Urticaceae	Shrub, 0.50 m tall, white-green flower, roadside, local recently burned, ocassional, *Cerrado*.	79 km *Alta Araguaia*, to *Cuiabá*, BR-364/MT.
10398	*Pavonia*	Malvaceae	Shrub, 1.50 m tall, lemon yellow flower, roadside, sun, occasional, *Cerrado*.	79 km *Alta Araguaia*, to *Cuiabá*, BR-364/MT.
10399	-	Bignoniaceae	Scandent bush, 0.50 m tall, calyx greenish (flowerless), white-green leaf, waxy, occasional, altered *Cerrado*.	79 km *Alta Araguaia*, to *Cuiabá*, BR-364/MT.
10400	*Byrsonima*	Malpighiaceae	Shrub, 0.20 m tall, yellow flower, sun, occasional, between stones, on the slope of the mountains, sandstone formation.	*Serra da Petrovina*, Km 130 *from* BR-364/MT.
10401	-	Apocynaceae	Shrub, 0.40 m lactescent, pale rose flower, occassional in mountain slope, between rocks, sun.	*Serra da Petrovina*, km 130 *from* BR-364/MT.
10402	*Dioclea*	Leg. papilionoideae	Shurb semi-scan, showy flower, purple blue, roadside, occasional, altered *Cerrado*.	Km 120 *from* BR-364/MT.
10403	-	Malpighiaceae	Shrub, 1.50 m tall, yellow flower, sun.	*Cuiabá.*
10404	*Jacaranda cuspidifolia* Mart.	Bignoniaceae	Tree, 6 m tall, purple blue flower, slightly dense canopy, 3 m diameter.	*Cuiabá.*
10405	*Forsteronia*	Apocynaceae	Climber, white latex, yellow flower with red center.	*Cuiabá.*
10406	*Triplaris pavonii* Meissn.	Polygonaceae	Tree, 3 m tall, pink-purple fruit, without ants, rusty male inflorescence (collected from another specie), frequent, riparian forest in the *Cerrado*.	130 km from *Cuiabá*, to *Cáceres*, BR-070/MT.

86 I. BURLE MARX'S EXPEDITION TO THE AMAZON

10407	*Pithecellobium* sp.	Leguminosa mimosoidea	Tree, 8 m tall, 0.20 trunk diameter, greenish flower, red stomas, white corolla, chestnut fruit (collected from another individual by Roberto Burle Marx), used in local arborization, sandy-clay soil, abundant, altered *Cerrado*.	Km 160 da BR-070 - *Oasis* Station (count from *Cuiabá*).
10408	*Tabebuia* sp.	Bignoniaceae	Purple *ipê*. Tree, 1.80 m tall, lilac flower, sandy-clay soil, occasional, *Cerrado*.	Km 163 from BR-070.
10409	*Ruellia* sp.	Acanthaceae	Herb, 0.30 m tall, blue flower, local shaded, frequent, foot of a nose, sandy-clay soil, stony, *Cerrado*.	km 182 from BR-070 (count from *Cuiabá*).
10410	*Lantana* sp.	Verbenaceae	Shurb, 0.60 m tall, blue flower, sun, sandy-clay soil occasional stony local.	182 km from *Cuiabá*, to *Cáceres*, BR-070/MT.
10411	*Annona* sp.	Annonaceae	Shurb, 1 m tall, yellow flowers, sun, occasionally in place.	182 km from *Cuiabá*, to *Cáceres*, BR-070/MT.
10412	*Pouteria* sp.	Sapotaceae	Tree, 3 m tall, many tortuous branches, rusty flower, occasional.	182 km from *Cuiabá*, to *Cáceres*, BR-070/MT.
10413	*Faramea* sp.	Rubiaceae	Tree, 2 m tall, white flower, green fruit, occasional, *Cerrado*. *Guettaria*?	182 km from *Cuiabá*, to *Cáceres*, BR-070/MT.
10414	*Kielmeyera coriacea* Mart.	Clusiaceae	*Caraipa*? Tree, 1.50 m tall, white flowers, stamens yellow, frequent, open area (sun).	182 km from *Cuiabá*, to *Cáceres*, BR-070/MT.
10415	*Zamia*	Cycadaceae	Shrub acaulescent, 0.80 m tall, mature infrutescence and rusty, with red seeds, local partially shaded, frequent.	182 km from *Cuiabá*, to *Cáceres*, BR-070/MT.
10416	-	Myrtaceae	Shrub, 1 m tall, white flower, local partially shaded, frequent.	182 km from *Cuiabá*, to *Cáceres*, BR-070/MT.
10417	*Alibertia* sp.	Rubiaceae	Tree, 2 m tall, with few branches, white flower, occasional.	182 km from *Cuiabá*, to *Cáceres*, BR-070/MT.
10418	*Erythrina* sp.	Leg. papilionoideae	Tree, 1.50 m tall, red flower (*Erythrina cf. daminguesii* Hassler), ocasional, occasional, sandy-clay soil, stony, in the *morro* base, *Cerrado*.	203 km from *Cuiabá*, to *Cáceres*, BR-070/MT.
10419	*Zephyranthes* sp.	Amaryllidaceae	Herb, bulbous, 0.20 m tall, white flower, recently burned area, sun, abundant.	203 km from *Cuiabá*, to *Cáceres*, BR-070/MT.
10420	*Turnera* sp. (*Piriqueta* sp.?)	Turneraceae	Shurb, 1.50 m tall, yellow flower, shaded place, *morro* base, stony ground, abundant.	205 km from *Cuiabá*, to *Cáceres*, BR-070/MT.
10421	*Tabebuia ochracea* (Cham.) Standley	Bignoniaceae	Tree, 6 m tall, 0.25 trunk diameter, green fruits covered by dense rusty coating (collected by Roberto Burle Marx), sandy-clay soil, altered *Cerrado*.	206 km from *Cuiabá*, to *Cáceres*, BR-070/MT.
10422	*Platypodium elegans* Vog.	Leg. papilionoideae	Tree, 7 m tall, yellow flower, old brown fruits, roadside, sandy-clay soil, occasional, *Cerrado*.	210 km from *Cuiabá*, to *Cáceres*, BR-070/MT.
10423	*Ouratea castanaefolia* C. DC.	Ochnaceae	Tree, 4 m tall, yellow flower, roadside, sandy-clay soil, occasional, *Cerrado*.	6 km from *Porto Esperidião*, to *Porto Velho*, BR-364/MT.
10424	*Tabebuia* sp.	Bignoniaceae	Tree, 2 m tall, 2 cm trunk diameter, white flower, roadside, sandy-clay soil, frequent.	6 km from *Porto Esperidião*, to *Porto Velho*, BR-364/MT.
10425	*Cochlospermum regium* (Mart.) Pilger.	Cochlospermaceae	Tree, 4 m tall, yellow flower, green fruit, roadside, sun, frequent, *Cerrado*.	55 km from *Porto Esperidião*, to *Porto Velho*, BR-364/MT.
10426	*Tabebuia*	Bignoniaceae	Tree, 10 m tall, white flower with inner tube gives corolla yellow stripe, green fruit (collected by Roberto Burle Marx) roadside, frequent, *Cerrado*.	68 km from *Porto Esperidião*, to *Porto Velho*, BR-364/MT.
10427	*Tabebuia* sp.	Bignoniaceae	Tree, 8 m tall, 20 cm trunk diameter, yellow flower, frequent along the way, *Cerrado*.	69 km from *Porto Esperidião*, to *Porto Velho*, BR-364/MT.
10428	*Vernonia scabra* Pers.	Compositae	Shurb, 2 m tall, fruit with cream bristles, damp local, roadside, frequent, *Cerrado*.	57 km from *Porto Esperidião*, to *Porto Velho*, BR-364/MT.
10429	*Psidiurn* sp.	Myrtaceae	Tree, 2 m tall, white flower, roadside, occasional, *Cerrado*.	60 km from *Porto Esperidião*, to *Porto Velho*, BR-364/MT.
10430	*Emilia sonchifolia* DC.	Compositae	Herb, 0.60 m tall, white flower, roadside, ocassional, *Cerrado*.	60 km from *Porto Esperidião*, to *Porto Velho*, BR-364/MT.
10431	*Heliconia*	Musaceae	Herb, 2 m tall, red bract, green flower, leaf bottom face in wax white, waterlogged terrain, semi-shade, secondary vegetation, roadside.	BR.-364/MT, to *Vilhena*.
10432	*Gurania spinulosa* (Poepp. & Endl.) Cogn.	Cucurbitaceae	Climber, herbaceous, orange flower, roadside, ocassional in the bush.	BR.-364/MT, to *Vilhena*.
10433	*Himatanthus* sp.	Apocynaceae	Tree, 3 m tall, abundant white latex, white flower, trunk 0.15 m diameter, sandy-clay soil, occasional, *Cerrado*.	337 km from *Porto Esperidião*, to *Porto Velho*, BR-364/MT (Comodoro Station).
10434	*Ouratea* sp.	Ochnaceae	Shurb, 1.50 m tall, yellow flower, sandy-clay soil, occasional, *Cerrado*.	337 km from *Porto Esperidião*, to *Porto Velho*, BR-364/ MT (Comodoro Station).

10435	*Asteracea* sp.	Compositae	Shurb, 1 m tall, old fruit, straw color, clay-sandy soil, ocassional, *Cerrado*.	337 km from *Porto Esperidião*, to *Porto Velho*, BR-364/MT (*Comodoro* Station).
10436	*Spiranthera odoratissima* St. Hil.	Rutaceae	Shurb, 1 m tall, white flower, aromatic, clay-sandy soil, *Cerrado*.	In *Vilhena*, near the airport, RO.
10437	*Dioclea* sp.	Leguminosae	Woody climber, purple flower, green fruit, roadside, frequent, *Cerrado*.	*Vilhena*, RO.
10438	*Xylopia*	Annonaceae	-	BR-364/ RO near *Vilhena*.
10439	*Annona coriacea* Mart.	Annonaceae	Tree, 2.50 m tall, 0.10 m trunk diameter, flower with greenish external petals, internally orange, edible fruit, cultivated in the city.	*Vilhena*, RO.
10440	-	Bignoniaceae	Liana, yellow flower, roadside, occasional in the forest of the mainland.	25 km from *Ji-Paraná*, to *Porto Velho*, BR-364/RO.
10441	*Cassia cf. spruceana*	Leg. caesalpinoidea	Tree, 5 m tall, yellow flower, in hanging clusters, occasional in the mainland forest.	254 km from *Porto Velho*, to *Humaitá*, BR-316/RO.
10442	*Odontafromnia nitida* (Vahl.) M.Arg.	Apocynaceae	Liana, white latex, yellow flower, flooded terrain, frequent, roadside.	4 km from *Porto Velho*, to *Humaitá*, BR-316/RO.
10443	*Aciotis fragilis* (Rich.) Cogn.	Melastomataceae	Herb, 0.20 m tall, the whole purple plant, lilac flower, wet ground, bare soil, sandy-clay soil, frequent.	10 km from *Porto Velho*, to *Humaitá*, BR-316/RO.
10444	*Montrichardia arborescens* (L.) Schott.	Araceae	Shurb, 1.80 m tall, cream inflorescence, green bract, waterlogged ground, roadside, frequent.	10 km from *Porto Velho*, to *Humaitá*, BR-316/RO.
10445	*Bellucia acutata* Pilger	Melastomataceae	Shurb 3 m tall, pink white flower, pink button, secondary vegetation, roadside, frequent.	33 km from *Porto Velho*, to *Humaitá*, BR-316/RO.
10446	*Vochysia ferruginea* Mart.	Vochysiaceae	Tree, 2.50 m tall, yellow flower, secondary vegetation, roadside, frequent.	34 km from *Madeira river*, to *Humaitá*, BR-316/AM.
10447	*Cupania*	Sapindaceae	Shurb, 1.70 m tall, red fruit, black seed, wrapped partially with white aril, low secondary vegetation, roadside, occasional.	34 km from *Madeira river*, to *Humaitá*, BR-316/AM.
10448	*Guatteria*	Annonaceae	Tree, 3 m tall, 5 cm shaft diameter, flower button greenish, scrub on moist soil, roadside, occasional.	44 km from *Madeira river*, to *Humaitá*, BR-316/AM.
10449	*Vochysia obscura* Warm.	Vochysiaceae	Tree, 3 m tall, 8 m trunk diameter, smooth bark and yellow, old fruit, dirty field, frequent.	10 km from *Humaitá*, to *Manaus*, BR-316/AM.
10450	*Miconia pilcata* DC.	Melastomataceae	Shurb, 1.50 m tall, lilac flower, purple stames, secondary forest, roadside, occasional.	10 km from *Humaitá*, to *Manaus*, BR-316/AM.
10451	*Tococa guianensis* Aubl.	Melastomataceae	Shurb 1 m tall, lilac flower, yellow stames, myrmecophile, roadside, occasional.	10 km from *Humaitá*, to *Manaus*, BR-316/AM.
10452	*Miconia tiliaefolia* Naud.	Melastomataceae	Shurb, 1.50 m tall, greenish fruit, roadside, occasional.	10 km from *Humaitá*, to *Manaus*, BR-316/AM.
10453	*Entada polyphylla* Benth.	Leguminosae mimosoidea	Liana scandent, greenish flower, roadside, occasional.	Km 500 from BR-316, *Manaus - Porto Velho*.
10454	*Ischnosiphon*	Maranthaceae	Erect herb, 1.50 m tall, red bract, light lilac petal, mainland forest, frequent.	Km 498 from BR-316, *Manaus - Porto Velho*.
10455	*Solanurn rugosum Dunal.*	Solanaceae	Shurb, 3 m tall, blue flowers, yellow stilettos, secondary vegetation, roadside, occasional.	Km 484 from BR-316, *Manaus - Porto Velho*.
10456	*Palicourea guianensis* Albl.	Rubiaceae	Tree, 3 m tall, yellow flower, secondary vegetation, frequent at roadside.	Km 484 from BR-316, *Manaus - Porto Velho*.
10457	*Eschweilera*	Lecythidaceae	Medium tree, collapsed, greenish flower bud, forest of mainland, occasional.	Km 490 from BR-316, *Manaus - Porto Velho*.
10458	*Passiflora foetida* L.	Passifloraceae	Scandent herb, white petal, white staminates, with purple base, deforested terrain, roadside.	Km 250 from BR-316, *Manaus - Porto Velho* (Petroselva Station).
10459	*Heliconia*	Musaceae	Erect herb, 2 m tall, pink bracts, white petals with green and dark green stripes almost black, forest of mainland, frequent.	Km 245 from BR-316, *Manaus - Porto Velho*.
10460	*Pitcaimia* sp.	Bromeliaceae	Epiphyte, red bracts, yellow flower, mainland forest.	14 km from Iguapó-Açu river, to *Manaus*, BR-316/AM.
10461	*Saxofridericia aculeata* Koern.	Rapateaceae	Erect herb, 1.80 m tall, yellow flower, mainland forest, occasional.	14 km from Iguapó-Açu river, to *Manaus*, BR-316/AM.
10462	*Chaetocalyx* sp.	Leguminosae papilionoidea	Creeping liana, wine flower, forest edge, roadside.	Km 205, road between *Cáceres* and *Porto Esperidião* / MT.
10463	*Heliconia rostrata*	Musaceae	Erect herb, 2 m tall, red and yellow bract, dry land forest, frequent (in front of the forest).	25 km from *Ji-Paraná*, to *Porto Velho*, BR-364/RO.

Figure 20. *Heliconia burle-marxii.* Photo: Haruyoshi Ono, date not available. *Instituo Burle Marx Collection.*

List of herbal plants* by Luiz Antonio Ferraz Mathes.
Field Annotations: Fátima de Souza Menezes

Observation: The numbers refer to the ratio of living plants collected.

Collection No.	Name	Family	Notes	Localization
294	*Philodendron*	Araceae	Hard leaves, dark green with lighter nerves, nerves in grid, equal to PCH 8739.	115 km from *Manaus*, to *Caracaraí* (count from the intersection with BR-174/AM). *Igarapé das Lajes.*
321	*Ipomoea*	Convolvulaceae	Small white flower, leaves small (0.02 x 0.02 m), peltadas, creeping.	13 km from *Caracaraí*, to *Manaus*, BR-174/RR.
322	*Philodendron*	Araceae	Climber, leaf 0.12 x 0.20 m.	13 km from *Caracaraí*, to *Manaus*, BR-174/RR.
323	*Clusia*	Guttiferae	White flower with pink center, leaf 0.06 x 0.12 m, 3 m tall.	13 km from *Caracaraí*, to *Manaus*, BR-174/RR.
324	?	-	White flowers with a petal, alternate leaves, orange fruit, black seed, white aril.	13 km from *Caracaraí*, to *Manaus*, BR-174/RR.
325	*Heliconia*	Musaceae	Live red bract, orange flower with the tip black, red ovary, light green leaf.	42 km from *Caracaraí*, to *Manaus*, BR-174/RR.
332	-	Solanaceae	Shrubby climber, altered leaf, well-branched nerves, cluster flower.	504 km from *Caracaraí*, to *Manaus*, BR-174/RR.
333	-	Rubiaceae	Red bract, 0.22 m long, purpure flower, leaf 0.25 x 0.60 m, petiole 0.20 m, 8 m tall.	505 km from *Caracaraí*, to *Manaus*, BR-174/RR.
336	*Ouratea*	Ochnaceae	Yellow flower in cluster, leaving from the apex of the bouquets, hard leaf, cordiform, leathery, 0.50 m tall.	Km 120 from BR-174/AM. *Igarapé das Lajes.*
337	-	Apocynaceae	Light to dark pink flower, terminals, green and ripe fruit, opposite leaves (maybe two different species).	Km 120 from BR-174/AM. *Igarapé das Lajes.*
338	-	Malpighiaceae	White flower with rose petal, small, terminal clusters, hard leaves.	Km 120 from BR-174/AM. *Igarapé das Lajes.*
339	*Securidaca*	Polygalaceae	Purple flower in clusters, purple leaf when young, semi-scandent.	Km 120 from BR-174/AM. *Igarapé das Lajes.*
340	-	Cyperaceae	Leaf 0.01 x 0.50 m, golden inflorescence, 1 m tall.	Km 120 from BR-174/AM. *Igarapé das Lajes.*

* Table prepared cataloguing information according to: Collection number, name, family, notes and location. Spaces without information are marked with a hyphen (-). Question marks (?) are typical of the original.

Visão, 12 de dezembro de 1983

AMBIENTE

DESMATAMENTO

Uma região devastada

Expedição de paisagistas à Amazônia observa devastação.

Burle Marx e a Amazônia devastada: catorze paisagistas contra a falta de critérios

Foram, ao todo, 11 mil km de estradas, 1.800 km de rios, em 53 dias de viagem — de 26 de setembro a 17 de novembro passado. Ao final do percurso, com início e término no Rio de Janeiro e que incluiu passagens por Uberlândia, Cuiabá, Porto Velho, Manaus, Boa Vista, Belém, Goiânia e Ribeirão Preto, os catorze paisagistas e botânicos, liderados por Roberto Burle Marx, haviam feito "um corte transversal na formação botânica brasileira", em busca de vegetais passíveis de ser utilizados em projetos de paisagismo.

Divididos em três grupos, responsáveis pela cata de mudas e sementes, pelas fotografias e pela coleta de plantas vivas e a embalagem do material que ia sendo reunido, os pesquisadores trouxeram um arsenal de mais de trezentas espécies de várias famílias botânicas, sob forma de plantas, mudas, sementes, ou de simples registro fotográfico. As plantas vivas foram levadas para o sítio de Burle Marx, no Rio de Janeiro, aí rapidamente replantadas. Após a classificação, serão transferidas para herbários no Rio de Janeiro e em São Paulo.

Devastação — Organizada com o principal objetivo de colher material botânico e conhecer as plantas em seu próprio habitat, a expedição patrocinada pelo Conselho Nacional de Desenvolvimento Científico e Tecnológico (CNPq) pôde observar, ao longo do itinerário, os resultados de algumas intervenções do homem na região amazônica. E o que eles viram só fortalece as denúncias de que a região vem sendo devastada num ritmo inquietante.

Já a partir de Cuiabá, conta o paisagista Koiti Mori, de São Paulo, a expedição deparou com vários caminhões carregados de carvão vegetal. Na mata amazônica, presenciaram o transporte de enormes toras. "Num só dia", confessa o arquiteto paulista José Tabacow, "foram contadas 98 carretas carregadas de madeira", a maior parte cortada com permissão do Instituto Brasileiro de Desenvolvimento Florestal, que, em contrapartida, oferece incentivo para o replantio de eucalipto e pinheiro, como forma de estimular a produção de matéria-prima para a siderurgia e as fábricas de celulose.

A arquiteta Cíntia Chamas, outra integrante da expedição, viu a reserva dos waimiri-atroari cortada ao meio por uma estrada e teve informação de que os 3 mil índios que formavam a tribo estão reduzidos a pouco mais de quinhentos, vivendo à custa de um artesanato à base de miçangas e fios de náilon. O paisagista Oscar Bressane conta que ficou alarmado com a situação de Roraima. "Por ser o local mais distante de todos os que visitamos", diz ele, "esperávamos encontrar farta vegetação, mas só vimos um buritizal no meio de um alagado que se salvou porque o fogo não conseguiu atingi-lo."

Ao relatar a viagem na Faculdade de Arquitetura e Urbanismo da Universidade de São Paulo, no dia 28 de novembro, em conferência que intitulou "Paisagismo e devastação", Burle Marx não poupou críticas a vários órgãos governamentais que, em vez de coibir, patrocinam a devastação. Segundo ele, o INCRA, por exemplo, considera o desmatamento uma benfeitoria, para efeito de redução na cobrança de impostos. "Não sou contrário à colonização nem à derrubada de árvores", confessou o renomado paisagista, "desde que acompanhadas de estudos para avaliar os impactos dessas atividades e as suas conseqüências a curto e longo prazos." Repetindo advertências dos cientistas que se reuniram este ano no encontro da Associação Brasileira para o Progresso da Ciência, em Belém, Burle Marx reclamou maior participação da comunidade científica nos planos para a Amazônia, como forma de conter a devastação da floresta. □

Results:

In consensus, the team considers the results of the expedition to be less than satisfactory when compared with the results of similar shorter trips taken previously. In terms of development, the project was ambitious in its itinerary, taking into account the available resources and time. Thus, the design of the trip should have accounted for the possibility of an alternative itinerary, substantially shorter in length, that would have allowed for a more detailed exploration of certain areas.

The participants, committed to following a predetermined route, did not have enough time for deeper penetrations and explorations that might have resulted in a truly representative collection. As a result, the collection points were limited almost exclusively to the roadsides, often in secondary formations or in places demonstrating a significantly altered state.

Again, in relation to the organization of the trip, it became clear that certain field tasks required more time or a greater number of supervisors than was initially stipulated. This fact was especially evident when it came to packaging live plants and recording field data. This situation was corrected by reassigning each participant's responsibilities.

The observation of the various phytophysiognomies was important, especially in the transition areas, where we focused on the emergence of the first botanical elements characteristic of the subsequent formation, as well as the disappearance of dominant species from the previous formation. The enclaves are also worth commenting, especially in the rocky countryside of the *Igarapé das Lajes*,[14] at km 115.

---

[14] José Tabacow describes this Amazonian terrain like the bottom of the sea, with plants similar to those of the *restingas*, growing in sandy soil. Small trees grow in these places, since the water table's location so close to the surface seems to restrict the growth of larger clusters of trees.

Figure 21. Article: *"A Devastated Region. Landscape Architects on an Expedition to the Amazon Observe the Devastation"*, in *Revista Visão* (12/12/1983). Various members of the expedition team (14 landscape architects) offered their impressions on the destruction, deforestation, excessive extraction, reforestation with non-native plants, and restricted indigenous territories.

Personal statement by Luiz Carlos Gurken

The Amazonian flora is still practically unknown, with a fantastic potential in terms of usable plants for landscape architecture. It mainly comprises herbaceous plants, possessing a rare beauty, belonging to the families of the Araceae, Heliconiaceae, Marantaceae, and Rubiaceae, among others. This herbaceous flora, beyond its ornamental appearance (whether due to the shape or the color of its inflorescences) plays a vital role in the balance of the ecosystem.

Heliconias, belonging to the Heliconiaceae family, are one example, existing in a wide variety of species with colorful flowers. They have a notable presence in our humid forests and play an important role in maintaining the ecological balance.

On the American continent, heliconias are pollinated exclusively by hummingbirds, which are also the main biological controllers of the *Phlebotomus* sandfly, transmitter of *Leishmaniasis,* so widespread in the deforested Amazon.

During the species' flowering season, up to 80% of the nectar hummingbirds eat comes from heliconia. With few herbaceous species and the majority of them large in size, palm trees have an exuberant presence in the riparian forest, the flooded forests and the mountains, with a particular importance in the Amazonian landscape.

Despite their ornamental beauty, many of the Amazonian palm trees have never been used in landscape design, such as the *tucumã, inajá, buritirana, pupunha, caioué*[15] and other species that have never been classified and whose material was collected for scientific identification. Collecting fruits from many of the Amazonian palm species was of vital importance for studying germination, acclimation and future uses in urban landscaping.

As for the trees, the vast green sea of the Amazon contains an incalculable number of species. Certain regions of the forest are home to endemic species, many of which are unfortunately being indiscriminately destroyed, without their properties being known.

The best known trees for use in landscape design include *visgueiro,*[16] *ingás, sumauma,* many species of *figueiras, taxizeiros, moela de mutum, seringueira* and the Santos mahogany.

It was with great sadness that I described the destruction of hundreds of trees that produce the *Castanha do Pará* [Brazil nut]. A very rich source of food, of great value on the international market, produced by gigantic trees that began growing at a time when the climate still allowed, is being criminally cut or destroyed by fires. There can be no doubt that this is causing an ecological imbalance, mainly in the fauna, which will become irreversible and irrecoverable in the near future since the climate no longer favors the germination and the growth of young and medium-sized seedlings of the *Castanheiras do Pará*. Epiphytic plants such as those of the Bromeliaceae, Orchidaceae, Araceae and Cactaceae families also grow on Amazonian trees. They are important for the survival of the fauna that live exclusively in the branches and crowns of those trees. The animals that make up the epiphytic community include *macacos, saguis, jaguatiricas,* mountain cats, lizards, and birds such as *araras*, parrots, toucans,[17] and many others that, over time, have adapted to this habitat above the ground.

With the cutting of the trees, the epiphytic plants disappear, and so does the fauna associated with them.

Many of these epiphytic plants were portrayed beautifully by the painter Margaret Mee[18] during her travels through the Amazon forests.

Today, the populations of these plants, which were once abundant in certain regions, have been drastically reduced. As for the fauna observed during the expedition, the most valuable occurrence was the presence of small flocks of the rare *arara azul* (*Anodorhynchus glaucus* Viellot),[19] found in the *Vale do Guaporé* region and in the vicinity of the *Jamari* River, a tributary of the *Madeira*, both in the state of *Rondônia*.

In the *Vilhena* region, also in the state of *Rondônia*, at an altitude of ±680 m above sea level, where there is an interesting abrupt transition from the *Cerrado* to the Amazon forest, the fauna is very rich and you can still find the arpía and the crested hawk-eagle, the king vulture and the *anta*,[20] all animals that are disappearing from our forests and that are currently in danger of extinction.

Conclusion:

No doubt, the Amazon region has a gigantic potential for wood, for plants that can be used in landscape architecture, and plant species with properties for medicinal use. But we have to maintain natural resources in a renewable way. The Amazon forest shows us that extractive practices lead to desertification because it is maintained by a layer of *humus* in poor soil that is often sandy.

In consequence, we need to use the forest in a rational way. Using it, but also renewing it with the same native species and, especially, preserving the regions that are sanctuaries for flora and fauna, which are of great value to us both for maintaining the ecological balance and for rainfall, as well as in their use for tourism.

[15] These palms were used by the locals for their ritual, nutritional, medicinal and artisanal production values. The *tucumã* (*Astrocaryum vulgare* Mart.) is a food source and has medicinal value as a source of vitamins, as well as for oil production and for personal care (Portal Amazonia, 2021). The *inajá* (*Maximiliana Maripa* Aublet Drude) is used for food, medicinal purposes, and oil production as well as cosmetic use and, according to recent studies, it can be a source of energy generation (Portal Amazonia, 2020). The *buriti* (*Mauritia sp.*) has food value and is used for oil production, medicinal use, as a source of vitamin C, and as a healing agent (Portal Amazonia, 2020). The *pupunha* (*Bactris gasipaes* Kunth var. gasipaes Henderson) is known for the food value of the heart of palm and is used for oil extraction and for flour production (Portal Amazonia, 2020). The collection and classification of these plants for subsequent propagation has been the foundation for adding to their value as ornamental species and their possible incorporation and use in landscape design.

[16] *Visgueiro: Parkia pendula* (Willd.) Benth. ex Walp. Ingá: *Inga edulis* Mart. Sumaúma: *Ceiba pentandra* (L.) Gaertn. *Figueiras* from the genus Ficus. *Taxizeiros* from the Leguminosae family. Moela de mutum from the Loganiaceae family. *Seringueira: Hevea brasiliensis* L. from the Euphorbiaceae family, and *Bálsamo: Myroxylon balsamum* (L.) Harms. For more information, see Reflora, 2020.

[17] Several animal species are associated with life in the treetops, such as *macacos* (macaques of the genus Macaca) and *saguis* (marmosets) (*Callithrix* sp.); among the felines we find the *jaguatirica* (*Leopardus pardalis*) and the *gato-do-mato* (*Leopardus tigrinus*); among reptiles, there are various lizards; and there are birds such as araras (macaws) (from the genera Ara, Anodorhynchus and Cyanopsitta), parrots (the Psittacidae family), and toucans (the Ramphastidae family). For more information, see the *Catálogo Taxonômico da Fauna do Brasil* (PNUD, 2020).

[18] Margaret Mee was an artist, explorer, conservationist and political activist born in Chesham, Buckinghamshire, United Kingdom. Mee was a lover of the Amazon region, where she did most of her work. Before Margaret Mee, no woman had traveled the Amazon so extensively. Mee made a total of 15 botanical expeditions. The last expedition was just a few months before her death at the age of 79. Venezuela was part of Margaret's travels when, in 1967, the *National Geographic Society* financed her partial ascent of the Pico de Neblina (on the border of Brazil and Venezuela). *"Even in remote and dangerous regions, she usually traveled alone with the help of local guides. Most of her paintings were done along the Rio Negro and its tributaries, and most of the time in situ (some were painted from live specimens brought back to her studio). As her travels coincided with the beginning of the commercial exploitation of the Amazon, she focused not only on discovering new plants but also on making a record of a world that was rapidly disappearing. She became famous in Brazil and abroad for her efforts to save the Brazilian rain forests and brought international attention to the cause of the Amerindians. She found some of the rarest plant species, many of which were unknown to science, and some of which are now extinct as a result of deforestation. Several have been named in her honor, including Aechmea meeana E. Pereira & Reitz, Nidularium meeanum Leme, Wand. & Mollo, and Neoregelia margaretae L.B. Sm. Since she sometimes neglected to collect specimens of the plants she painted, her folios include some plants that have never been seen alive by other botanists. On her final expedition, she painted the rare Selenicereus wittii (Schum.) G. D. Rowley, the Amazonian moonflower that blooms for a single night. Having searched in vain since 1965, she finally came across a plant with a bud near Manaus in May 1988. She watched it until it bloomed, then drew it by the glow of a fluorescent flashlight. The painting appears as the final plate in her memoir."* Margaret Mee: In Search of Flowers of the Amazon Forests (1988). (JSTOR, Mee, Margaret Ursula (1909-1988), 2021). For more information, see: L. Gamlin, 1989, "Mourning the World's Loveliest Garden: Review of 'Margaret Mee in Search of the Flower of the Amazon Forests", New Scientist, 1693; A. McConnell, 2004, "Mee, Margaret Ursula (1909-1988)", Oxford Dictionary of National Biography; T. Morrison, 1988, "Before the Amazon", *Margaret Mee in Search of the Amazon Forests*: 18-27; R. Schultes, 1990, "Margaret Mee and Richard Spruce", *Naturalist*, 115: 143-148.

[19] The *Glaucous macaw* (*Anodorhynchus glaucus* Viellot), is currently listed in the *Red Book of Threatened Brazilian Fauna* as a regionally extinct species, adding to the growing number of threatened species in the various biomes of Brazil (*Instituto Chico Mendes* de *Conservação da biodiversidade*, 2016).

[20] The *anta (Brazilian tapir)* (*Tapirus terrestres*) and the *arpia (harpy eagle)* (*Harpia harpyia*) are both endangered according to the report by the *Instituto Chico Mendes de Conservação da biodiversidade* (ICMBio), 2016.

Figure 22. *Sobralia margaritae*, collected and illustrated by Margaret Mee in the Amazon, 1977. The plant is named in honor of the artist and scientist. Published in: Mee, Margaret, *Flowers of the Brazilian Forest*; Burle Marx, Roberto (prologue), Tryon Gallery, London, 1968.

LANDSCAPE ARCHITECTURE AND DEVASTATION   1983

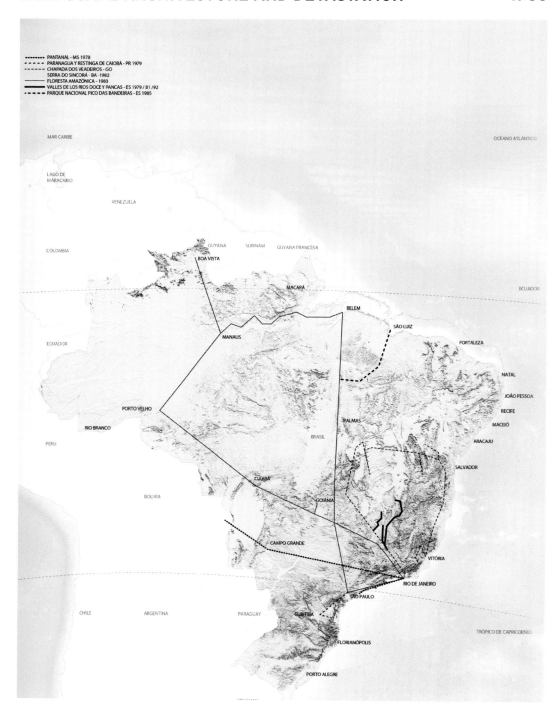

Figure 23. Map of botanical expeditions by Roberto Burle Marx and collaborators: 1978, 1979, 1981, 1982, 1983, 1985, 1992. Map based on information from Oscar Bressane and José Tabacow and developed by María A. Villalobos H. and Gu Yuxuan, 2019-2021.

The invitation I received from the Brazilian Botanical Society to give this lecture, through the remarkable figure of Nanuza Menezes, is a great opportunity.

I have just returned from an extensive expedition in the Amazon, where my team and I covered a distance of approximately 11,000 kilometers.

With financing from CNPq and the support of Varig and Petrobras, our main objective was to survey vegetation that could potentially be used in landscape design projects. And that goal was pursued through the collection of live plants, herborized plant material for later identification, annotations that could support their identification, and the essential photographic documentation. Just for information, on our itinerary, starting from *Rio de Janeiro*, we passed through *Uberlândia*, *Jataí* and *Caiapônia*, where we quickly and superficially explored the *Serra do Caiapó*, *Cuiabá*, *Porto Velho*, *Manaus* and *Boa Vista*. From there, we descended the Amazon River to *Belém*, *Goiânia*, *Riberão Preto*, *São Paulo*, and finally returned to *Rio de Janeiro*.

We will be able to assess the definitive results of our efforts once all the collected plants have been identified. However, an initial approximation reveals the collection of nearly 300 species never used in landscaping projects. The seedlings will become part of my collection of tropical plants and, after the long period required for their development, they will be the mother plants that will provide new seedlings for use in landscape design projects.

The spirit of the trip, which we began developing few decades ago, and which was the same for other similar but shorter expeditions, was to get to know the plants in their habitat, understand them as elements in the landscape, understand their associations, their phytosociological importance – in short, how they form part of their natural setting.

As landscape architects, it was fundamental for us to observe the different phytophysiognomies that appeared along the way, as well as – and especially – the transitions between those formations.

The idea of valuing the flora of Brazil, through the use of our native plants in parks and gardens, mainly seeks to expose city-dwellers to the knowledge of our natural riches while helping, in some way, to bolster species threatened with extinction.

On the other hand, in this respect, with each trip our astonishment grows at the lack of respect for nature, and the utter lack of concern for the environment. Over 11,000 kilometers there was no evidence to indicate any efforts at conservation. On the contrary, what you see all around is pure empiricism and the immediate occupation of natural areas. The road construction techniques are extremely aggressive and brutal.

Plant life is viewed as an undesirable obstacle, which must be eliminated entirely. In areas where material is taken for infill, the layer of organic soil is removed and lost, preventing any chance of spontaneous regrowth. The craters left behind favor erosion, resulting in huge bare cliffsides, like wounds that testify to the depths of the aggression. The cost of recovering these spaces will be much greater than the investment it would take to prevent these damages in the first place. The material that is removed is used as infill; in turn, this prevents water from circulating freely. So the water pools, which completely obliterates the vegetation, thus creating new wounds in the landscape that are difficult to heal. Likewise, the cuts that are made for the roads are carried out without any consideration. Inclines of up to 100% are an invitation to erosion and, left unprotected, these slopes threaten to collapse onto the roadbed at any moment.

The full picture of this destructive method is rounded out by the abandonment of service roads, traced without any criteria for observing the flows of water or maximum slopes. Used as detours during construction, the soil becomes compacted, eliminating the possibility of spontaneous regrowth, or even secondary planting.

Whereas the roads themselves and their construction are already highly destructive, following their introduction wide swaths of devastation run along both sides, which can spread unlimited unless they come up against some eventual natural barrier, like a wide river or a break in the terrain. Rarely does the natural forest still reach up to the edges of the road. Normally the vegetation is at a distance of several kilometers. The vision of these highways through the Amazon is depressing. It no longer looks like a thin red line cutting through the forest, as in the photographs from the early days of the Transamazonian Highway. Instead, what you see are vast swaths of embers and smoking tree trunks – an image of desolation, a portrait of chaos.

I refuse to believe that it is impossible to develop a road engineering technique with less of an impact on the environment or where the impact is almost entirely limited to just the tracks and curbs. Allegations of traffic safety are meant to justify the total clear cutting of the roadsides. And yet, depending on the type of vegetation, it could serve as a kind of shock absorber for a possible uncontrolled vehicle.

Figure 24. [Top] Provisional river crossing on the *Porto Velho-Manaus* highway, Brazil. Photograph: Oscar Bressane, Koiti Mori and José Tabacow, 1983. **Figure 25.** [Center] *Porto Velho-Manaus* highway, Brazil. Photograph: Oscar Bressane, Koiti Mori and José Tabacow, 1983. **Figure 26.** [Bottom] Brazilian mahogany (Swietenia macrophylla) logs in a sawmill yard, in *Rondônia*. Photograph: Oscar Bressane, Koiti Mori and José Tabacow, 1983.

The clearcutting of these strips merges, both visually and physically, with the limits of the nearby *haciendas* [farms]. The pasturelands generate vast areas that are completely devastated and thus remain at the mercy of the sun, raising temperatures and augmenting the repercussions of the rain, worsening erosion and favoring winds that, forming huge clouds of dust, make certain stretches of the roads extremely dangerous.

In contrast, when the forests reach all the way up to the sides of the road, travelers feel safer and protected from these effects. My intent is not to offer road engineering solutions. That said, although I am ignorant in the matter, I am convinced that it is possible to build a road without paying such a high price. Installing plaques with conservationist messages on roadsides is just cheap demagoguery. Over hundreds of kilometers of roadsides, we saw a single tree, which had been named the *Pau do Juscelino*.[21]

At the very least, a joke in poor taste. If there was a real interest in preservation, there would be no need for plaques or *Paus* [poles] dedicated to our presidents. Further accentuating the panorama of devastation, we continually crossed paths with trucks carrying gigantic trunks that once were majestic trees. The main participants in this activity are former residents of Paraná who have been displaced from their home state, which has given them the *know-how* of devastation. In a single day, we counted 98 trucks transporting logs. It is a sinister procession, harnessing power and speed in the disposal of natural resources that are labelled renewable but are never renewed. Planting pines or eucalyptus is not renewal. It is simply replacing original primary forests with forests of raw materials to make charcoal to feed steel mill furnaces and to produce cellulose. The Forest Code allows an owner of land in the Amazon to remove 50% of the original forests. Then, the remaining 50% of land is sold and a new owner, protected by law, can demolish half of that area, and so on, until the property reaches a size that is no longer of interest economically. What is more, the laws drawn up in the offices in Brasília are entirely disconnected from the reality of the Amazon. To give just one example: there is a law that prohibits the cutting of the *Castanheira-do-Pará*[22] because of the economic interest associated with the Brazil nuts and the trees themselves.

[21] *The Pau do Juscelino* makes reference to the former president of Brazil (1956-1961): Juscelino Kubistchek.

[22] Almost 30 years after this lecture, the *Castanheira-do-Pará* (*Bertholletia excelsa* Bonpl.) was listed as vulnerable (VU) on the IUCN Red List, 2011.

Figure 27. [Top] Representation of the Brazilian landscape, with a wide variety of palm trees that caught the attention of the explorers Martius and Spix (Martius & Spix, 1829). **Figure 28.** [Center] River landscape, Amazon, Brazil. Photograph: Oscar Bressane, Koiti Mori and José Tabacow, 1983. **Figure 29.** [Bottom] Landscape in a riverside community. Stilt houses among *açaís. The açaí* (*Euterpe oleracea*) is a species of palm tree that provides fruits that are an important food source for the inhabitants of the *Estreito de Breves, Pará*, Brazil. Photograph: Oscar Bressane, Koiti Mori and José Tabacow, 1983.

To create pastureland, the landowners clear the forests, keeping only the Brazil nut trees, which are left standing alone in the middle of the pastures. Brazil nut trees are fertilized by a kind of wild bee. In isolation, when they are set apart from the forest, these trees can't be visited by those insects and thus never bear fruit. This fact was already denounced by botanists from the National Research Institute of the Amazon (INPA), but no measures were taken. While, on the one hand, the laws are misguided or inadequate, on the other, the government actually encourages destruction through unilateral measures like the ones adopted by the INCR,[23] espousing the perspective of colonization and regarding the felling of trees as beneficial for the purpose of calculating taxes. Mind you, clearcutting is only justified when the land can be worked immediately. The simple removal of the vegetation merely favors the loss of fertile soil, increased erosion and excess sediment in rivers. Considering such problems as an improvement is worse than ignorance. It's a crime! As a result, the fauna is decimated, and the epiphytic and subforest flora disappears. With the differences in sun exposure, the new edges of the forest are also altered, resulting in a much larger area being affected negatively by the clearcutting.

I am not against colonization, or harnessing natural resources, or even felling forests. But actions in nature should be preceded by studies that provide knowledge, which can help us assess the impacts, the immediate and long-term consequences. Above all, it is fundamental to consult the scientific community in developing laws and other control mechanisms for the use of natural resources, so that the interventions are founded on concepts rooted in scientific knowledge and not, as is the case presently, on interference from politicians bent on favoring minority interests.

During our trip, we focused intently on those kinds of problems – that is, the various forms of human interference. But we also aimed to observe the lessons nature has to offer, seeking to understand the structure of the landscape, the dominant elements in the natural composition that define a given space. In this regard, our interest was piqued by the distribution of palm trees, with the presence of different species depending on the ecological conditions. The *buritizales*, with their majestic presence, were visible on almost the entire route beginning from *Minas Gerais*; damper slopes or areas with standing water were more often associated with *buritiranas*,[24] delicate miniatures with roughly the same shape and frond distribution.

In the areas with the highest elevations, in *Minas*, *Goiás*, *Mato Grosso*, *Pará* and *Maranhão*, there are spectacular formations of *Attalea* and *Scheelea*. In the transition between the *Cerrado* and the Amazon Forest in the vicinity of Cáceres, the *pupunhas*[25] begin to appear, the fruits of which are edible when cooked; the *bacaba*[26] with its characteristic fan-shaped collections of leaves, rising above the forest canopy; the *tucuns*,[27] with their stems covered in enormous black thorns; the *açaís*,[28] forming large patches in the forest; and many other species of palm, which makes it easy to understand why this family garnered so much attention from botanists, especially Martius and Barbosa Rodrigues.

At other points, there is a clear presence of *visgueiros*, the *Parkia pendula*, with its unusual proportions and characteristic crown. Or the *sumaúma* (*Ceiba pentandra)*, with its spectacular *sapopembas*,[29] buttress roots that distribute the trees' weight over the unstable ground. At each bend in the road, something new caught our attention. Whether it was an impressive flowering climber, or the hairy fruit of a Bombacaceae, or even a massive growth of *imbaúbas*,[30] invaders of deforested lands. To the landscape architect intent on observing, on understanding, nature offers countless lessons. The *imbaúbas*, for example, are easy to spot in the landscape because they appear in large groups. In contrast, the *visgueiros* are almost always isolated by themselves, yet they have a marked presence and stand out due to the structure of their crowns and, at a certain time of year, the light coloring of their new leaves. The *buritis* are associated with water, while the *attaleas* seek out the driest slopes or ones that have been devastated by fire. The *sumaumeiras*, due to their colossal size, can create a spectacular impact in the landscape with just three or four individuals.

The rocky formations are a chapter in themselves. Because these areas are normally better preserved – since they are unsuitable for economic exploitation – they are characterized by a richness of flora that would warrant a separate expedition all by itself.

Observing these and countless other examples, it is striking that they have never been adopted for use in man-made landscapes. The squares in the small cities of the Amazon are identical to the ones found in *Espírito Santo* or in the interior of *Paraná*.

[23] *Instituto Nacional de Colonização e Reforma Agrária.*

[24] *Buritiranas: Mauritiella armata* (Mart.) Burrett. For more information about this and other species mentioned below, see: Reflora, 2020.

[25] *Pupunhas: Bactris gasipaes* Kunth. *Ibid.*

[26] *Bacaba: Oenocarpus bacaba* Mart. *Ibid.*

[27] *Tucuns: Bactris setosa* Mart. *Ibid.*

[28] *Açaís: Euterpe oleracea* Mart. *Ibid.*

[29] *Sapopembas* is the indigenous name given to the buttress roots that support the structure of trees like *Sterculia apetala* (Jacq.) H. Karst or *Ceiba pentandra* (L.) Gaertn.

[30] *Imbaúbas: Cecropia pachystachya* Trécul. For more information, see: Reflora, 2020.

The vegetation used is conventional, almost always exotic, such as *amendoeiras*,[31] *casuarinas* and a few others. And that's only if there are any trees at all – because, in most cases, the squares are completely devoid of shade and, as a result, they are underutilized. These places take their inspiration from larger cities, deferentially copying their mistakes: painting the bases of the trees white, installing aggressive lighting, importing non-native plants into the landscape.

In the new state of *Rondônia*, specifically in *Vilhena*, a colossal tree stump was installed in the city square, a testimony to the pride and arrogance with which this country is being destroyed. And yet, introducing plants and minerals from the surrounding landscape into the urban environment would be more coherent in terms of landscape design and cheaper in terms of execution and maintenance, as well as more balanced in terms of the interaction between people and the environment. Rather than in ardent speeches, the love for the land should be demonstrated through an appreciation of regional elements. If elements of the regional landscape were brought into the urban environment of every city, those cities would be better integrated with their surroundings and the native flora – and at least part of that flora would be preserved.

In this testimony, I have tried to relate just a fraction of what we saw. There is much more to tell. In truth, this expedition was not that different from others that we have made, except for the great length of the journey. We witnessed once again, with perplexity, the indifference, shortsightedness, and brutality of humanity in using nature as though it were inexhaustible. Except, on this trip, the devastation we observed was immense. As we descended the Amazon River, our raft was forced to stop for four hours waiting for the smoke from the fires to clear. Between *Manaus* and *Santarém*, a stretch of some 800 km, we hardly saw the forest, due to the extent of the destruction along the roadside.

What I'm left with is the ability to devote all my strength to raising awareness of this disaster. And I'm left with the possibility that someone with decision-making power will listen to me. And, mainly, I'm left with the hope that humanity will realize that we are not the masters of an inexhaustible nature. On the contrary, we depend on it for balance and for our own survival.

São Paulo, November 26, 1983.

---

[31] The common name *Amendoeiras* refers to two species: *Terminalia catappa* L. (known as the *Tropical almond*, *Amendoeira-de-praia*, in Brazil or *Almendrón* in Venezuela) a tree native to Asia; and *Prunus dulcis* (Mill.) D.A. Webb, syn. *Prunus amygdalus* var. *sativa* (Mill.) (Almond) Focke, a tree native to Iran (Hassler M, 2021). The species *Terminalia catappa* L. is a large tree, widely planted and used in Brazil, particularly on ships in the era of Portuguese colonization, which used the trunks as a counterweight. The conditions on the Brazilian coast favored its growth. For more information, see: Lemos, 2014; *Global Invasive Species Database*, 2021; Ribeiro, Marquet, & Loiola, 2020.

Brasa, troncos
queimados, a vegetação aniquilada.
Caos e desolação

'Dados os meios terríveis de que dispomos, nunca se destruiu tanto'

MARIA JULIETA DRUMMOND DE ANDRADE

Burle Marx:
'Temos de lutar, mesmo sabendo que não seremos ouvidos'

— Gostaria que os que viessem depois de mim pudessem, pelo menos, ver alguma coisa que ainda lembrasse o País fabuloso que é o Brasil, do ponto de vista botânico, dono da flora mais rica do globo.

Com essa frase de sombrio esperança, o paisagista, pintor, tapeceiro, decorador e artesão de jóias Roberto Burle Marx, nascido em São Paulo em 1909, resume o pessimismo que o acomete, ao comprovar, por onde passa, uma "destruição geral da natureza". E acrescenta, com a sua maneira peculiar de escandir e acentuar certas sílabas, prolongando-as como se estivesse cantando:

— Dados os meios terríveis de que dispomos, nunca se destruiu tanto. É muito perturbador ver isso tão forma acelerada. Dói saber que, depois da construção da usina nuclear entre o Rio e São Paulo, qualquer descuido pode provocar o desaparecimento das duas cidades. Levantaram até um belvedere — palavra tão linda, que significa bela visão — para essa usina ser contemplada, como se pudéssemos nos encantar diante de uma guilhotina... Parece coisa de sádicos.

Confessa não entender de política; seu mundo são as cores, as formas, a flor. Afirma, entretanto, que existem hoje mais políticos ambiciosos e mal orientados do que políticos professando um verdadeiro conceito patriótico, e que não basta algum leigo proclamar seu patriotismo para conseguir resolver problemas que exigem soluções específicas. Acha também indispensável que nossas crianças as desde cedo um claro conhecimento da agressão que se pratica contra os recursos naturais de que dispomos. Sente, portanto, a obrigação moral de, com os meios a seu alcance, denunciar e combater o que julga errado — lição que aprendeu com o arquiteto alemão Walter Gropius quando, certa vez, a caminho de Petrópolis, iam visitar o jardim que Burle Marx fizera para Odete Monteiro, o paisagista brasileiro protestou contra os cortazes que enfeavam a paisagem:

— Ele me perguntou se eu já tinha dito aquilo publicamente e, diante de minha resposta dubitativa ("Será que adianta alguma coisa?"), me fez ver que temos de lutar, mesmo sabendo que não seremos ouvidos.

Esse espírito pelejador leva permanentemente Burle Marx a protestar, cada vez que depara com um crime, por menor que seja, cometido contra a natureza. Assim, em novembro último escreveu uma carta de irônica indignação a um dirigente do Banco do Brasil, por ter tido conhecimento da eliminação de uma clúsia — por ele plantada há 20 anos nos jardins brasilienses que rodeiam a sede daquele organismo — sob a alegação de que a árvore estaria impedindo a visão da nossa Bandeira em dias de luto, "ou seja, apenas quando estivesse hasteada a meio pau".

Em expedição à Amazônia, um encontro com a 'tragédia ambiental'

Em dezembro, proferiu palavras mais duras na carta que enviou a Carlos Castelo Branco e que foi por este transcrita em sua coluna, contra "a tragédia ambiental" que encontrou na Amazônia, ao percorrê-la, retornando destes se restringir aos gabinetes do poder decisório, teremos verdadeiros abortos, sob a forma de leis inadequadas ou que o pior — da necessidade tâneo. E, como o aterro impede a livre circulação das águas, formam-se represamentos que aniquilam completamente a vegetação.

Nos 11 mil quilômetros que percorreu com a sua equipe, o viajante buscou inutilmente a imagem que recordava, fixada em fotografias da época em que se iniciou a construção da Transamazônica: uma linha vermelha cortando a floresta. Novas imagens, de caos e desolação, as haviam substituído; extensas superfícies cobertas de brasa e troncos fumegantes. Num só dia, chegou a contar 98 carretas, que passavam conduzindo toras, em "sinistra procissão", reveladora do poder e velocidade que temos para esgotar recursos naturais, erroneamente chamados de renováveis, já que nunca foram renovados. Lembrou-se também com desânimo dos quatro rios em que a balsa, na qual desciam o Amazonas, teve de ficar parada, devido à cortina de fumaça, proveniente das queimadas, que enegrecia o ambiente.

Para confirmar a inoperância dos dirigentes brasileiros, que ditam leis, sem o menor conhecimento da realidade amazônica e ra como benfeitoria o desmatamento das terras", esquecido de que este só se justifica quando aquela pode ser imediatamente trabalhada:

— A simples remoção da capa vegetal favorece apenas o carreamento das camadas férteis, a erosão e o assoreamento, protegendo esse ativo defensor da natureza —, provocando ainda outras conseqüências deploráveis, com a extinção parcial da flora e da fauna e a alteração, pela entrada de luz, dos limites da floresta. Tudo isso é criminoso!

Revoltou também o paisagista verificar que as praças das cidadezinhas amazônicas eram idênticas às do Espírito Santo, por exemplo, ou do Paraná, com uma vegetação convencional, composta quase exclusivamente de amendoeiras e casuarinas, todas com a base pintada de branco. Cúmulo do ufanismo disparatado e destruidor: o colossal tronco morto, exibido, à guisa de escultura, numa praça de Vilhena, em Rondônia.

Além das plantas, o amor pelos peixes, que sabem sofrer com discrição

Esse saldo negativo não transformou, no entanto, Burle Marx num homem ácido. De calça e blusão brancos, combinando com a cabeleira alva, abundante e rebelde, ele lamenta, em seu escritório de Laranjeiras, que a entrevista não tenha podido realizar-se no Sítio Santo Antônio da Bica, situado em Campo Grande, onde mora. Mostra o val do Prado Valladares, Carlos Leão, Henrique de Melo Barreto. No sítio, onde mora em companhia de alguns empregados e de um cachorro, cultiva uma rara coleção de plantas, trazidas de suas viagens. Com o que também sabe exteriorizar uma ternura e uma capacidade de afeto enormes e, julgando-se dono do próprio Burle Marx, não lhe permitem.

contra. Esta tanto pode estar na toalha de mesa, que acaba de pintar, quanto no broto da vitória-amazônica, emergindo de repente da terra, ou na visão inesperada de uma viuvinha (árvore venezuelana, que nada tem de "alheira de defunto"), em contraste com o verde do fundo. A pureza dessa floração o faz comentar, emocionado:

— Aquele branco estava cantando para mim.

Sempre foi sensível às plantas. Recorda o deslumbramento que o invadia aos quatro anos quando, depois de acompanhar a mãe, podando as roseiras, via uma flor surgir daqueles esqueletos; mais tarde, o impacto que, adolescente, sentiu ao encontrar, no Jardim Botânico de Dahlem, na Alemanha, uma série de plantas brasileiras, desconhecidas entre nós. De volta à terra, reagiu contra a topiaria, que é a arte — então em moda na Europa — de dar às plantas configurações bizarras: pães, cadeiras, camelos, etc., como se observara, há alguns anos, na Praça Paris. Sofrendo a influência inicial do famoso Glaziou, engenheiro hidráulico que se tornara paisagista e autor dos jardins, de cunho inglês, do Passeio Público, fez seu primeiro trabalho em 1933, por encomenda de Lúcio Costa.

Um bom jardim, para Burle Marx, é aquele que revela compreensão especial e justaposição de formas e volumes, como na pintura e na arquitetura, sendo capaz de criar surpresas; passa a ser de fato jardim quando as plantas que o compõem atingem as proporções desejadas. Assim, uma palmeira imperial jovem é bonita, só quando chega aos 30 metros de altura atinge seu esplendor. Aprecia especialmente os jardins de floração permanente, feitas de canteiros que dão, sucessivamente, flores durante o ano inteiro. Não demonstra preferência por nenhum dos quase 80 que já fez (entre os quais se destacam, no Brasil, o do edifício do Ministério da Educação e do Museu de Arte Moderna, do Aterro do Flamengo, no Rio, da Pampulha, em Belo Horizonte, do parque Ibirapuera, em São Paulo, do Itamaraty, em Brasília), embora admita que, apesar das decepções que sempre o aguardam, é mais reconfortante criar jardins públicos, que servem a inúmeras pessoas, do que particulares.

Falar sobre as plantas e seu órgãos sexual, que é a flor, é para Burle Marx um trabalho e uma alegria: não assim falar com as plantas. Ao contrário do que hoje em dia virou moda, afirma que o importante é sabermos criar um ambiente adequado para elas, com a água, a luz e o adubo necessários.

"Não é com conversinha fiada que uma planta cresce, nem descobrindo se ela gosta de Bach ou se detesta Beethoven, diz, com convicção, entendo não se aninha e negar a existência de certas vibrações ou forças positivas ou negativas, unindo a desunindo homens e vegetais, porque já ouviu pessoas elogiarem uma planta e esta, depois, amanhecer morta.

Figure 30. In his testimony, Burle Marx asserts the importance of fighting, even when you know your demands will fall on deaf ears. Roberto Burle Marx, in *O Globo*, 05/01/1984, p. 29. *O Globo* digital archive.

II. LANDSCAPE, BOTANY AND ECOLOGY: INTERVIEWS WITH ROBERTO BURLE MARX FROM THE BOOK *DANS LES JARDINS DE ROBERTO BURLE MARX*
1994

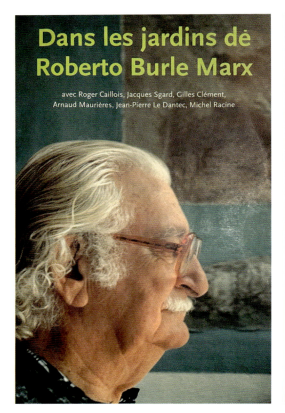 

Figure 31. [Left] Cover of the book Leenhardt, J. (2016). *Dans les jardins de Roberto Burle Marx* Actes Sud, Paris; [Right] Cover of the book Leenhardt, J. (2010). *Nos jardins de Burle Marx*, Perspectiva, *São Paulo*.

This section contains Jacques Leenhardt's interview of Roberto Burle Marx, *"Landscape, Botany and Ecology"*. The interview was originally published as the result of an interdisciplinary seminar on nature and art in the design of urban spaces, organized by Jacques Leenhardt in France at the Crestet Centre d'Art from October 16-18, 1992. The seminar was organized with the collaboration of Roberto Burle Marx, Beatriz Berinson, Janete Ferreira da Costa and Véronica de Jullian, Brigitte Navelet-Noualhier and Renata Proença.

The Spanish translation on which this English version is based was produced in collaboration with Jacques Leenhardt, using the French and Portuguese versions published respectively in: Leenhardt, J. (2016). *Dans les jardins de Roberto Burle Marx*, Actes Sud, Paris, pp. 65–87 and Leenhardt, J. (2010). *Nos jardins de Burle Marx*, Perspectiva, *São Paulo*, pp. 47–67.

The production team for the Portuguese version was as follows: Pérola de Carvalho (translation), Eliane Levinsky and Sérgio Coelho (proofreading), Adriana García (cover design), Ricardo W. Neves, Sergio Kon and Lia N. Marques (production).

Photo credits for the original publications belong to Jacques Leenhardt and Marcel Gautherot, all rights reserved.

This interview offers the reader a conversation between friends. Interviewer and interviewee focus on the longstanding role of nature and culture in the process of landscape design throughout history. They examine a landscape that is *"made by man and for man"* while also seeking to protect and expand natural and cultural diversity at a time when Brazil was looking to emphasize its character as a country of tropical peoples.

The dialogue leads the reader through historical landscapes; theological, compositional, and botanical notions; and feverish descriptions of diverse experiences in landscape design. These gestures demonstrate the generosity of someone hoping to plant curiosity in the reader's mind, along a path that offers any number of tools and invites reflection and the reinvention, both individual and collective, of new questions.

Figure 32. Roberto Burle Marx in the *Atelier* during the construction process. *Sítio Burle Marx, Santo Antônio da Bica*, Brazil. Photograph: *O Globo* Archives. Published in the book *Roberto Burle Marx: Uma Fotobiografia* by Soraia Cals (Cals, 1995. p. 79) and in the *dossier* submitted to support the nomination of the *Sítio Roberto Burle Marx* for inscription on the World Heritage List, by the Ministry of Citizenship and Culture, Secretariat of Culture, National Institute of History and Heritage (IPHAN), 2019, p. 301.

LANDSCAPE, BOTANY AND ECOLOGY:
JACQUES LEENHARDT'S INTERVIEW OF ROBERTO BURLE MARX

1994

Figure 33. *Baobab (Adansonia digitata* L.), Monumental plant in the Maracaibo Botanical Garden, Maracaibo, Venezuela. Photograph: Carla Urbina, 2013. **Figure 34.** [Opposite page] *Baobab (Adansonia digitata* L.*),* Monumental plant in the *Praça da República, Recife,* Brazil. Photograph: María A. Villalobos H., 2021. Both trees were part of Roberto Burle Marx's professional life, some 50 years apart. These projects highlight the value of monumental plants in the design of public spaces.

JACQUES LEENHARDT -

How would you define the concept of a garden?

ROBERTO BURLE MARX -

Today, my extensive and longstanding experience as a landscape gardener, creator, producer, and curator of gardens allows me to formulate the concept of the garden, as I have laid out for myself, as an adaptation of the ecological environment to the natural requirements of civilization.

This concept, which shapes my vision, is supported by a long practice that does not make any claim to originality, in essence since all my work is based on historical evolution and observation of the natural environment.

What is the source of this concept?

It is the same one that underlies the behavior of Neolithic man: transforming nature and its topography to make room for human existence – individual and collective – for both utilitarian and recreational ends. There are two landscapes: one is natural and given; the other is humanized and, therefore, constructed. The latter results from all the factors imposed by necessity. Yet, beyond the implications derived from economic demands (transportation, agriculture, culture, housing, manufacturing, etc.), let us not forget that the landscape is also defined by an aesthetic demand, which is not a luxury or a prodigality, but an absolute necessity for human life and without which civilization itself would be emptied of its purpose.

Figure 35. *Parque do Flamengo, Rio de Janeiro*, Brazil. Photograph: Marcel Gautherot, c. 1966. Archive of the *Instituto Moreira Salles*.

Figure 36. *Copacabana, Rio de Janeiro*, Brazil. Photograph: Marcel Gautherot, c. 1976. Archive of the *Instituto Moreira Salles*.

[32] "The difference I see between his painting and his drawing translates into a thematic progression. In his current phase, the composition derives from the plant's structure, which is isolated and outlined against the space. This results from his vast experience as a gardener, as a botanist, as an ecologist capable of seeing and understanding the interior world of plants. But for a different reason, it might be considered a purely aesthetic aspect of the artistic expression. By exhaustively observing and noting the overlapping plant structures, while adding to nature Roberto Burle Marx was also able to construct a fully individual language in drawing. In terms of its stylistic affiliation, at the most it could be said to be contemporary to Picasso, Braque, and Matisse, but we must recognize that Roberto Burle Marx was able to capture the intricacies of the plant world, discovering spaces, planes, and lights/darknesses never revealed by anyone before". Valladares, Clarival do Prado. *Roberto Burle Marx em 1974* in Marx, Burle. *Roberto Burle Marx*. São Paulo: MAM, 1974. [English version based on the Spanish translation].

Figure 37. *Pão de Açúcar* from the *Parque do Flamengo*, Rio de Janeiro, Brazil. This section of the park was designed by Roberto Burle Marx and collaborators. Photograph: María A. Villalobos H., 2021. **Figure 38.** [Opposite page] Natural and humanized landscape. View of the Cerro El Ávila from the Parque del Este in Caracas, Venezuela. "The Parque del Este (PDE) is the most important urban park in Venezuela. The PDE combines landscape design and qualities with exceptional environmental educational values and has been recognized by international experts as one of the most valuable modern parks in the Western Hemisphere, with conditions that merit its nomination as a UNESCO World Heritage Site" (Henriquez, et al., 2009, pp. 18–19). For more detail on the importance of the Parque del Este in the world and in the work of Burle Marx, see Berrizbeitia, Anita *"Defesa do Parque del Este"*. October 2, 2008 (Berrizbeitia, 2008). Photograph: Venezuela Tuya, n.d. Available in: Venezuela Tuya, 2017–2021.

Did the idea of a garden come to you as a result of your painting practice?

As a visual artist, I received stringent training in the disciplines of drawing and painting, and the idea of the garden came from a combination of circumstances. I have applied the principles of plastic composition to nature, in accordance with the aesthetic sensibility of my era. In short, the garden has provided a way for me to organize and compose my pictorial works using unconventional materials.

To a large extent, I can explain this evolution by the shock that my generation experienced, with the impact of Cubism and abstract art. The confrontation of the visual characteristics of these aesthetic movements with the natural elements gave rise to my desire to develop new experiences. I decided, therefore, to use the natural topography as a surface on which to compose, and the plant and mineral elements of nature became the materials in a plastic composition, in the same way that every artist seeks to compose their canvases using colors and brushes.

The critics who are most interested in my work have repeatedly highlighted the aesthetic relationship between my painting and my methods of landscape design. Geraldo Ferraz and Clarival Valladares[32] noted the correspondences between the different aspects of my work, and I am the first to recognize that I do not distinguish between the object *"painting"* and the object *"landscape"* when I construct them. It is just a question of different means of expression.

Figure 39. Children's playground in the *Parque da Cidade* in *Brasília*, Brazil, designed by Roberto Burle Marx and collaborators, awaiting restoration. Photograph: María A. Villalobos H., 2021. **Figure 40.** [Opposite page] Restored playground (2013) at the Maracaibo Botanical Garden, Maracaibo, Venezuela, designed by Roberto Burle Marx and collaborators and inaugurated in 1983. Photograph: Carla Urbina, 2014.

Do you consider yourself a pioneer, an innovator?

Over time, my experience of nature and the work we can do with it deepened, and I became more aware of the work I developed in relation to and because of nature. It isn't my place to judge this experience, but I do reflect on it to better understand its reasons, its purpose and to situate it in its medium and in its time. I flatly refuse to accept the most frequent and common assessment of my work, which is to call it *"original"*. Originality never concerned me as much as quality or respect for the function of landscape design. Whether it is a garden, a park or the configuration of urban spaces, my idea of the construction of the landscape always ties in with the historical orientation, according to which each era has its own aesthetic thought that emerges and manifests itself in all forms of artistic expression. In that sense, my work reflects modernity, the period in which I'm producing it, without losing sight of the considerations that are passed down by tradition, which are also valid.

Figure 41. Adolpho Ducke Botanical Garden, *Manaus* Brazil. Ducke described more than 900 species and 50 genera of plants. His travels and research on Amazonian flora were published in more than 180 articles and monographs. Since its creation in 2000, this botanical garden, considered the largest in Brazil (including the forest reserve), pays tribute to Adolpho Ducke, a renowned Austrian botanist, born in Trieste, Italy, whose career was dedicated to promoting the creation of biological reserves in Brazil and in the tropics to protect living things. For more information see Archer, 1962. Photograph: Neil Palmer, International Center for Tropical Agriculture (CIAT), 2011.
Figure 42. [Opposite page] Tropical dry forest in the Maracaibo Botanical Garden, Maracaibo, Venezuela, designed by Roberto Burle Marx and collaborators. Photograph: Andry Jons, 2018.

From your point of view, can this form of artistic expression – garden design – play an educational or social role?

No doubt, the social mission of the landscape architect includes an educational component. It is up to the landscape designer to help people understand and love what nature represents, through their gardens and parks. In Brazil, where historically there has been a dislike of vegetation that has been planted, experience has taught me to always keep working to changing people's mindset. We can contribute to this through our actions. Moreover, our approach must assert, loud and clear, a forward-looking dimension: it must express that someone took the care to leave an aesthetic and useful legacy, worthy of the name, for future generations.

The prevailing conditions in Brazil, and, possibly in other tropical countries – demand that we draw broad lines for a policy of investigating what exists. The idea would be to create a series of botanical reserves drawing on private, public, and international contributions with the aim of maintaining, and preserving for the future, samples of nature in an original, or at least a minimally altered, state. Given the diversity of the flora, these areas should be distributed throughout the various botanical provinces. These veritable natural gardens could preserve the rarest as well as the most typical botanical communities.

Thus, landscape designers would have access to broader means of expression, made of these plants that would serve as a vocabulary they can use in their compositions. With this abundant and expressive material at their disposal, they would have the possibilities of creating, in landscape design too, the magnificent works that the human spirit has been capable of, following the laws of aesthetic composition, harmony, contrast and proportion. The idea gives the matter its form, hence the need for a raw material – plants in all their diversity – that can embody the idea.

Aren't there many difficulties in a country like Brazil, which is particularly affected by deforestation and the destruction of natural sites?

From an anthropocentric point of view, we could say that plants were created for man. That is the attitude the Bible takes. Based on this point of view, the European world, with its highly domesticated flora, maintained a fairly balanced relationship between humans, trees and forests. But with the conquest of the New World, the Europeans were struck by fear, especially in the face of the tropical forests. For them those forests were an impenetrable refuge for indigenous peoples and aggressive beings such as panthers, snakes, spiders, crocodiles, and mosquitoes.

Hence the overwhelming need in people's minds to open strategic clearings, the anxious urge to cut down trees and destroy the forest. The clearing of spaces for livestock and agriculture required extensive deforestation. Soon enough, *"civilized"* man took up the traditional technique of the indigenous peoples of planting on burned areas. But this practice was associated with the nomadic migrations of indigenous peoples. The sedentary *"civilized"* people implemented it over extensive spaces, and today it is practiced with an intensity never seen in the past, in proportion to the power of the machines being used (tractors), which are more and more efficient every day. In a single day, one of these machines can destroy millennia of biological evolution.

This is the sad panorama that reveals how powerless we are in the face of the terrible violence of the moral, technical, social, economic, and psychological logic of the contemporary world. And yet there is still a whole universe of plant life to be preserved which, for lack of appropriate techniques and a sufficiently large number of specialists in the field, remains relatively unknown to us to this day.

Figure 43. Parque Nacional Canaima, Venezuela. The landscape plan for the Parque Nacional Canaima was created by Roberto Burle Marx and collaborators in 1986, according to the list published in: Leenhardt, Jacques. 2016. *Nos jardins de*

In commercial terms, the noble task of cultivating, preserving and disseminating the treasure of tropical plants is not profitable. In addition, unbridled population growth leads to extremely serious problems – particularly in terms of a shortage of food resources – which in turn gives rise to a collective attitude among the population lacking in respect for nature, trees, and gardens.

Despite all the misunderstandings that affect the relationship between humans and plants, the interdependence is so great that the desire for the presence of nature remains. This often shows up in nearly unconscious customs, like in the case of plastic flowers. Today, these simulacra have taken over our markets. In a large hotel in Miami, I even saw an entire winter garden without a single real plant: they were all made of plastic! This has taken hold to such an extent that the owner of a nursery in that city was closed, due to the strong competition from the plastic flower producers. People have lost the notion that plants are permanently undergoing transformations and are subject to cycles that result in changes, which is what gives them their charm – and is sorely absent from the plastic simulacra, inert and inexpressive.

But to return to the issue of deforestation, which is undoubtedly more serious in tropical countries than in temperate climates, one of its main effects is the transformation of climates and microclimates, as well as the destruction of the collective capital represented by the fertility of the soil. Deforestation leads to the disappearance of the fauna and thus begins a process of desertification that is difficult to reverse. It is a type of attack perpetrated by humankind against the sources of life and a form of destruction that affects future generations.

Burle Marx. São Paulo: Editora Perspectiva, 2016, p. 136. Photograph: Carla Urbina, 2010. **Figure 44.** Deforestation, mining, and extraction processes in the Parque Nacional Canaima, Bolívar State, Venezuela. Photograph: Carla Urbina, 2010.

And the fundamental material you work with plants!

Whatever their philosophical differences, creationists and anti-creationists agree on the fact that creation or the appearance of life did not occur in a single moment but in successive stages. Genesis details the acts of creation; first the earth, then the parting of the waters and only after that came the plants, animals, and humans. Science, for its part, has shown that plants, through photosynthesis, create the conditions for the continuation of the evolutionary process; they modify the composition of the Earth's atmosphere and fulfill Prometheus's dream, capturing solar energy and making way for the appearance of insects, birds, mammals and, finally, humans and the higher plant forms, with their varied shapes, colors, and structures. It is through them that life, the phenomenon of reproduction, is transmitted, directing a spectacle of a thousand riches that culminates in their blooming. It cannot be overemphasized that the Earth's atmosphere, with its 21% oxygen, is a requisite for life, and that this atmosphere is maintained and balanced by the activity of plants – particularly algae.

Plants are our reason for being. But how do we understand them? On the one hand, they are living beings that obey a determinism linked to the laws of growth, physiology, biophysics, and biochemistry. On the other hand, every plant is the result of a long historical process that incorporates, in its present state, all the experiences of a long lineage of ascendants in which those indistinct first beings are lost to time.

Figure 45. Parque del Este, Caracas, Venezuela. Photographs: José Tabacow, 1970s.

This perfection of forms, colors, rhythms, and structures puts them in another type of category, that of aesthetic beings, which makes them a mystery to us.

Plants can be considered unstable beings to the highest degree. They remain alive even when they are transformed. They undergo constant mutation, creating a permanent imbalance, yet their purpose is always the search for a new balance. As we deepen our knowledge of plants, the field of the unknown grows almost exponentially larger. Knowledge uncovers more problems than it solves. The more answers we find, the more questions accumulate. To give one example, I remember a spectacle. I witnessed in the depths of the *Caatinga* in the northeast of Brazil. At a certain time of night, over a large area, all the *Cereus jamacaru* DC (*Mandacaru*) opened their large glowing white flowers as if to the rhythm of a metronome.

In the moonlight the corollas of various petals came unbuttoned, exposing their throats, attracting a swarm of insects. As I contemplated this spectacle, I was reminded of the movement of anemones in the sea, and I could not stop thinking about the mysterious reasons for that strange coincidence.

I thought to myself that a plant, like a color, takes on its full meaning when juxtaposed with another color or another plant.

Figure 46. *Mandacaru* (*Piptanthocereus jamacaru* DC.). Photograph: Alexander Arzberger, 2018. Available in: Arzberger, 2018.

So, your models are the natural associations between plants?

In nature, groupings don't occur by chance: they are the result of a complex interplay of compatibility involving the climate, the soil, the integration of plants with animals, and plants with one another. Environmentalists refer to these groupings as associations.

The phenomenon of associations is intimately linked to one of the most fascinating biological processes: adaptation. It is impossible to address such a vast and complex subject as adaptation in just a few sentences. In passing, we can at least touch briefly on mutual adaptation, in line with modern biologists, which shows the simultaneous and associated development of flowers and pollinating insects.

At the beginning, in the Mesozoic era, the first plants, like flowers, were pollinated by slow-moving, *"clumsy"* insects of the coleoptera type. The evolution of flowers to the bilateral state (orchids) or asymmetrical state (reeds) was accompanied by the emergence of improved, more agile insects (butterflies and Hymenoptera). Not to mention the advent of pollination by hummingbirds. There is no region on the earth richer in plant associations than the tropics. And among those who have seen it, this

Figure 47. Collection of butterflies at the Brasília Botanical Garden, *Brasília,* Brazil. Photograph: María A. Villalobos H., 2021.

spectacle is even more stunning and impressive for the inhabitants of temperate countries.

The shock of this hectic world of activity, heat and life left a profound impression on many naturalists from the era of great discoveries, such as von Martius, Geoffroy Saint-Hilaire, Gardner or Prince Wied-Neuwied.[33] Even today, the richness of the flora of the tropical zones is such that, from my own experience, I can say that I have never made an excursion without having found or collected plants previously unknown to me, some of which were unknown to science itself.

It is evident that the gardens have an ecological foundation, especially in a country like Brazil where the climatic and geological conditions are extremely varied. Anyone wishing to study the problem of the introduction, cultivation and domestication of wild plants will find a field that is little developed and, in some respects, unexplored.

[33] Additional information on the botanical explorers mentioned here is available in the third part of this book.

Figure 48. [Left] Dragonfly (insect of the order *Odonata*) and butterfly (insect of the order *Lepidoptera*) [right] in the Maracaibo Botanical Garden, Maracaibo, Venezuela, designed by Roberto Burle Marx and collaborators. Photographs: Ligia Ararat, 2014.

Figure 49. Association of tubular plants in the *Praça dos Cristais, Brasília* Brazil, designed by Roberto Burle Marx and collaborators. In the background are the crystal-shaped sculptures designed by Haruyoshi Ono. Photograph: Maria A. Villalobos H., 2021.

[34] *Platanus* is a genus consisting of a small number of species native to the northern hemisphere. It has a height between 30 and 50 m, and small flowers with between 3 and 7 petals. The leaves are simple and alternate. There are two subgenera: *Castaneophyllum* which contains the anomalous P. kerrii, and the subgenus *Platanus*. These trees are common in European cities such as Madrid, Paris and Rome. For more information see Floyd, Sandra K. *et al.*, "A developmental and evolutionary analysis of embryology in Platanus (Platanaceae), a basal eudicot" in American Journal of Botany, 1999;86:1523–1537. Available in: Floyd, Lerner, & Friedman, 1999.

Figure 50. [Left] *Laelia flava* Lind. on rocks, Brazil. Photograph: J. Cascavel, 2010. **Figure 51.** [Right] Lichens on rocks in *Goiás*, Brazil. Photograph: Carla Urbina, 2019.

In a country with a flora as rich as Brazil's, what does it mean for a landscape designer to invent new forms?

In Brazil, the landscape designer is free to work and build gardens based on an immensely rich floral foundation. While respecting the requirements of ecological and aesthetic compatibility, the landscape designer can create very expressive artificial associations. Creating artificial associations does not mean rejecting or merely imitating nature. It means transposing and associating the results of an attentive and prolonged observation, based on selective and personal criteria. From my own experience, I can tell you what I have learned from my contact with botanists. Their collaboration is essential for anyone aspiring to acquire a mastery of the conscious and profound art of landscape design, for anyone who wants to learn to take advantage of the immense heritage that is the exuberant Brazilian flora, so unfortunately misunderstood by landscape designers and nature lovers alike.

Despite the fact there are nearly 5,000 tree species and an estimated 50,000 different flora species native to Brazil, our gardens offer, above all, a domesticated and cosmopolitan flora. In addition, the streets are often planted with exotic species: *Platanus*[34] for example. I strongly oppose this,

Figure 52. [Left] *Purple glory tree* (*Tibouchina granulosa* (Desr.) Cogn.), *Rio de Janeiro*, Brazil. Photograph: María A. Villalobos H., 2021. **Figure 53.** [Right] Red mimosa (*Calliandra dysantha* Benth.), in the *Parque do Flamengo*, *Rio de Janeiro*, Brazil, by Roberto Burle Marx and collaborators. Photograph: María A. Villalobos H., 2021.

and for a long time I have been fighting against certain forms of urban development in which the existing landscape is destroyed to make way for plant compositions that are completely disconnected from the true local landscape. This destroys the original work, represented by a biotype, as a stage of equilibrium acquired over thousands of years of activity through the interplay of the forces of nature.

Our landscape designs must be based on an interpretation and understanding of natural associations. I could, for example, cite my research on the flora of the *canga*, the ecosystem of iron-rich materials that make up the subsoil of extensive regions of central Brazil. In the middle of the mountains, I discovered a new world: an extraordinary association of the yellows of the lichens[35] and *Laelia flava* Lind.[36] with the violets of the quaresmeiras[37] and the Venetian red of the *Mimosa calodendron* Mart,[38] a plant known for the defensive movements of its leaves. All that mix of colors stands out against a background in which shapes, rhythms, and colors act together to highlight, in each season, a particular kind of bloom.

Figure 54. [Left] *Ficus drupacea* Thunb. in the *Sítio Roberto Burle Marx, Santo Antônio da Bica*, Brazil. Photograph: María A. Villalobos H., 2021. **Figure 55.** *Ficus drupacea* Thunb. in the *Sítio Roberto Burle Marx, Santo Antônio da Bica*, Brazil. Photograph: Carla Urbina, 2009.

[35] Lichens are living organisms that arise from the symbiosis between a fungus and an alga, or a cyanobacterium. Several species of lichens may contain a third element such as yeast. The ability to adapt *"to nutrient-poor environments allows them to develop early and begin forming soil ready for the subsequent arrival of other plant organisms."* (Mehrotra & Aneja, 1990, p. 708).

[36] *Laelia flava* Lind. (synonym of *Cattleya crispata* (Thunb.) Van den Berg) is a species of lithophyte orchid that belongs to the *Cattleya* genus. Common in the state of *Minas Gerais*, it has a basal sheath and a single, apical, erect leaf that is coriaceous, narrowly oblong, and obtuse. It flowers in late winter and early spring. For more information see Jones, H., *Orchidaceae Americanae Caldasia*, 10(50), 1970, pp., 491–495. Available in: Jones, 1970.

[37] *Quaresmeira*, or purple glory tree, is the common name of the *Tibouchina granulosa* (synonym of *Pleroma granulosum* (Desr.) D. Don). It belongs to the family of *Melastomataceae*. The plant lives 60 to 70 years, and usually reaches 8 to 12 m in height. The trunk can be simple or multiple, with a diameter of 30 to 40 cm. *"The leaves are simple, elliptic, pubescent, coriaceous, with well-marked longitudinal nerves and entire margins. Flowering occurs twice a year, from February to April and from August to October, when abundant simple pentamerous flowers emerge which have a maximum of 5 cm diameter, long stamens, and purple corolla"* (Forzza, 2010).

[38] *Mimosa calodendron* Mart belongs to the Leguminosae family, commonly found in south-eastern and central-western Brazil. *"These contribute to the growth of other species under their crown (positive interactions). These plants can provide shade, build-up of organic matter, milder temperatures, and humidity, and reduce grazing, factors that favor a microhabitat for the germination and development of seedlings of other species"* (Padilla & Pugnaire, 2006).

Figure 56. Polychromatic landscape of the *Sítio Roberto Burle Marx, Santo Antônio da Bica*, Brazil. Photograph: María A. Villalobos H., 2014.

[39] *Acrocomia aculeata* (Jacq.) Lodd. ex Mart, belonging to the family Arecaceae. This is a palm tree native to Brazil, known by many names, including *corozo*, *coyol*, *macaúba*, *macaíba*, *coco-de-catarro* and *coco-de-espinho*. In terms of height, this palm can reach 13 to 20 m with a crown diameter of 3 to 4.5 m. The bark is smooth and dark with strong, straight spines up to 15 cm long (Caldas, 2006).

[40] *Ficus calcicola* Corner belongs to the family *Moraceae*. In the book *As figueiras no Brasil*, Ernani Diaz explains that in Brazil there are 80 native species and about 40 exotic species of fig. *"In Rio, fig trees can be seen in places like Campo de Santana, one of the most concentrated areas of Ficus in the city. On the beaches of Botafogo and Flamengo, there are streets lined with Ficus microcarpa interspersed with Ficus benjamina, both exotic species. In Leblon, there are many Ficus religiosa, which are also exotic. One of the main figures responsible for spreading the use of native plants in landscaping in the country was Roberto Burle Marx."* (Fundação Carlos Chagas Filho de Amparo, 2004). For more information see Carauta J. P. P. & Diaz, B. E., *Figueiras no Brasil* ed. UFRJ, 2002.

[41] An alternative description of the flora of the *Pancas valley* and its vegetation is given in the lecture *"Gardens and Ecology"* which is included in the third part of this book.

Figure 57. *Vale de Pancas, Espírito Santo*, Brazil. Photograph: Oscar Bressane, 2013. **Figure 58.** [Opposite] Expedition to *Diamantina - Serra do Cipó, Minas Gerais*, Brazil. Photograph: Oscar Bressane, 2013.

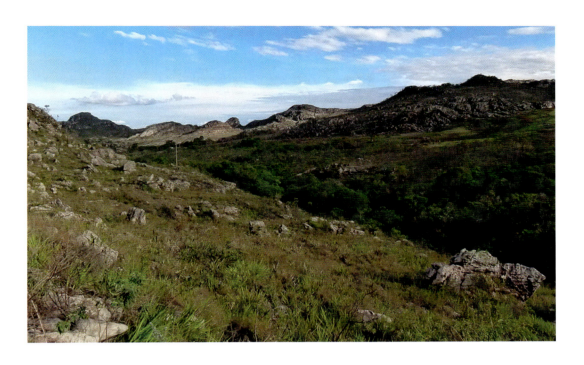

This instability is one of nature's great secrets: nature engages in constant renewal thanks to the effects of light, rain, wind, and shade, which give it new shapes in the form of limestone massifs, whose rock has fissures that provide access routes for a rich biogenic sediment, into which roots delve in search of the build-up of nutrients within. This produces a spectacle marked by clusters of palms (Acrocomia aculeata[39] [Jacq.] Lodd. Ex-Mart) and Ficus calcicola,[40] whose intertwined roots have the curious feature of wrapping around their support, whether rocks, trees, or other palms.

I have visited regions of rare beauty such as the Vale de Pancas, which, 30 years ago, was home to indigenous tribes. The region is a valley enclosed by conical-shaped mountains arranged like the stage of a theater, and on whose precipices perches a flora that is completely *sui generis*, from *villosas* to bombacaceae, orchids, *meriânias*, *Mandevilla flowers*, *amendoeiras*, and so on.[41] From these heights, we see the long ribbon of the winding course of the river unravel through the *Vale de Pancas*, fed by the waters that flow down from the basin. It is a pity that these elemental formations are not given the protection afforded to a sanctuary. Little by little they are being destroyed by the local population, who fail to understand that it is a treasure, and by European immigrants, who are transplanted without adapting, who have maintained the criteria for beauty from their countries of origin.

How does the landscape designer play with that other natural element: the climate?

Beyond the general action of the climate in a region as a whole, it is subdivided and diversified into a series of microclimates based on various factors (topography, altitude, etc.) that can have a very significant influence on the evolution of a garden.

Indeed, garden design often involves *"creating"* microclimates and harmonizing them following the idea that, in plant associations, each plant finds its place, side-by-side with others, in a relationship of mutual dependence.

The value of plants in composition, like the value of color in painting, is always relative. Plants are valued for their contrasts or for the harmony that they establish with the other plants they interact with.

Speaking of microclimates, I remember one region, the *Serra do Cipó*, about 100 km from *Belo Horizonte* (in the state of *Minas Gerais*), where the flora is mainly determined by the existence of a sandy, quartz-rich soil. The journey there involves traveling from microclimate to the next, and from one surprise to another.

Thus, in these climatic conditions, we can find plants that are modified in such a way by the action of the environmental forces that representatives of genetically distant families and strong resemblances to one another in their external appearance.

Figure 59. *Lagoa de Araruama, Cabo Frio, Rio de Janeiro*, Brazil. Photograph: María A. Villalobos H., 2021.

Such is the case of the *Sipolisia* (Compositae family), which has the appearance of a *Vellozia* (*Eryngium* family, in the form of a Bromeliaceae), or the *Lychnophora*, which takes on the appearance of a *Vellozia*. There (as in other regions of Brazil, such as *Cabo Frio*, characterized by an intense and constant prevailing wind), we can gain an understanding of the modulating effect of the wind on the plants.

In protected depressions, trees can grow to their fullest and, in that microclimate, a build-up of fertile debris together with good moisture retention creates an unspoiled world of orchids, lichens and epiphytes which, although dependent on moisture, are loathe to overly depend on their roots. In the highest altitudes there is a very particular botanical group, a *"nebulous"* flora characterized by small trees, almost without branches, bearing small leaves and covered with epiphytes and brightly colored woody vines, which coordinate with red flowers like the *Sophronis* (orchids).

The *Usneas* form a belt of varying thickness all around. It is a truly phantasmagorical, changing landscape.

The plants fade and disappear in the mist, or they stand out in their abundance until the light reveals the various planes on which the vegetation is anchored.

Figure 60. Modulating effect of wind and mist in *Cabo Frio, Rio de Janeiro*, Brazil. Photograph: Carla Urbina, 2020.

Like the natural arrangements you've talked about, is the art of gardening an age-old, primeval tradition?

During certain historical periods and in certain countries, the balance of the social order is projected in the art of shaping the landscape. We can say without exaggeration that the history of the garden (that is, the built landscape) ties in with the history of the ethical and aesthetic ideas of each era.

It is true that Westerners have had a different experience of landscape than Eastern cultures – and certainly, a poorer and more recent one. For a start, we know that the landscape in the West followed the influence of the East from the 14th century onwards, through Italy and – much later – the Iberian Peninsula.

Beginning in the Neolithic period, in every region, there is a clear presence of elements that prove the existence of the idea of the garden. Hence, we can affirm that the garden dates to the most distant of times.

Indeed, from the earliest stages of civilization up to the time of human sedentism, the development of agricultural activity and utilitarian forms of craft (linked to construction, protection, and the development of ceramic techniques), the presence of what could be called the "notion" of the garden is evident.

Figure 61. Pottery from the collection of Roberto Burle Marx, *Sítio Roberto Burle Marx, Santo Antônio da Bica*, Brazil. Photograph: María A. Villalobos H., 2021.

The shape of Neolithic vessels and utensils, as well as their decorative elements, display biomorphic motifs with a predilection for plant and animal elements from the natural world.

So even then there was participation in an aesthetic sphere. That is why objects took the form of their natural models, which are controlled by human perception in the context of an emotional relationship. Thus, objects were understood not only as useful, but also as beautiful.

Almost all Neolithic examples of stylized representations of plant and animal figures reveal the existence of a contemplative attitude, and even an artistic consciousness on the part of their maker, whose goals for the representation of an object went beyond its physical reality. Through an organization of visual form, this stylization gave the object the form and power of a symbol.

As civilization became organized in more strongly defined social and political structures (Egypt and Mesopotamia), the influence of artistic creation on the natural topographic surface became more precise.

Figure 62. "Useful and beautiful" pottery collected by Roberto Burle Marx during his lifetime, as exhibited at the *Sítio Roberto Burle Marx, Santo Antônio da Bica*, Brazil. Photograph: Carla Urbina, 2009.

Architecture emerged at the moment when human thought and will imposed themselves on physical nature, seeking to transform and undermine it. The emergence of civilization is characterized, therefore, not only by the first testimony of the first code recorded on tablets, but also by the conscious transformation of a physical landscape into a constructed landscape, with an eye to generating a visual impact based on ethical concepts (religious, political) and aesthetic concepts (predilection of forms, definition of noble materials, formation of styles belonging to the culture of each community).

Both architecture and landscape management are defined in accordance with the natural environment. The materials chosen and the solutions adopted by the artistic work are turned into an effect that corresponds to the physical reality of the environment. It is noteworthy, and symptomatic of this, that the founding mythological texts of every civilization are very specifically connected to an idea of the landscape or even directly to a description of a garden. The three Hesperides were the garden nymphs who protected the orchard where the golden apples grew, near Agadir – a garden protected by a dragon that never sleeps. Also, in a tomb in the Valley of the Kings in Upper Egypt, an inscription was found that mentions the pharaoh's gardener.

Dreamlike gardens and botanical knowledge served as a frame for a large part of Greek mythology. According to legend, the ornamental motif of the Corinthian column, the acanthus leaf, participates in this aesthetic interaction between man and his natural landscape, serving as a truly architectural motif. The Dionysian lifestyle (and the figure of Bacchus), the legend of Artemis (and Diana) as well as Aphrodite (Venus), all imply the idea of a world conceived as a landscape.

From the origins of the most ancient empires of the Assyrian-Chaldean civilization and from the famous Babylon onwards, we find texts about fabulous gardens, illustrating pomposity and power. It is worth recalling the legendary example of the Hanging Gardens of Semiramis, characterized by the inclusion of landscape designs in the architectural ensemble. And the various civilizations that developed in Asia Minor (Iran, Iraq, the Mediterranean coast of Syria) have influenced the history of landscape thinking. The Sumerians, Babylonians and Chaldeans, Hittites, Hebrews, Assyrians, Persians and all the peoples who inhabited the region have written their own passages in the history books about the relationship between humankind and landscape.

Figure 63. [Top] The Goddess of Discord Choosing the Apple of Contention in the Garden of the Hesperides, Joseph Mallord William Turner, 1806. Technique: Oil on canvas. Dimensions: 155 x 218.5 cm. Tate Britain, Turner Gallery, Room T7 (as of 1910). **Figure 64.** [Center] *Diana and Calisto* c. 1556–1559, Tiziano Vecelli. Oil on canvas. National Gallery, London. Digital version available at: Vecelli, 1556–1559. **Figure 65.** [Bottom] *The Birth of Venus* Sandro Botticelli, 1480. Oil on canvas. Dimensions: 172.5 x 278.9 cm. Gallerie degli Uffizi, Florence, Italy. Digital version available at: Botticelli, 1480.

Figure 66. [Top] Amphitheatre of Babylon, UNESCO World Heritage Site. Photograph: Khalid Mohammed, AP Photo, 2019. Available in: Schnessel, 2019. **Figure 67.** [Center and bottom] Amphitheatre in the Parque do Flamengo, *Rio de Janeiro*, Brazil. Photograph: Carla Urbina, 2014.

Figure 68. [Top left] Gardens of Babylon. Engraving. Available in: Kircheri, Lairesse, Munnichuysen, Decker, & Cruyl, 1679. **Figure 69.** [Center and bottom] Terraced gardens of the *Praça das Fontes*, awaiting restoration, *Parque da Cidade, Brasília*, Brazil. Photograph: María A. Villalobos H., 2021.

As a naturally fertile region situated between the Tigris and Euphrates, Mesopotamia became the legendary cradle of civilization, the place where Adam and Eve lived: Eden. Turning back to the history of Western civilization, we will find, in the Hebraic tradition, the Bible's description of the genesis of the world, set in a framework entirely inspired by categories of gardens. God, creator of the world and life, is presented in the Hebrew text as a builder, an artist creating a landscaped universe, which he gives to man in the form of a paradise, a garden full of greenery. The expulsion of Adam and Eve from this garden brings about the conflicts and eternal sufferings that contrast with the ideal memory and the dreams nourished by the visions of that lost landscape. The loss of paradise becomes a permanent frustration, and the visual arts take on the role of remembering those origins.

In the Middle Ages and early Renaissance, Christian religious paintings depicted landscapes that seemed to be just that: images of the lost paradise. Only after the Renaissance took hold among the elites who developed new behaviors and aesthetic demands did the great examples of artificial landscapes emerge, creating an ideal medium between architecture and the natural environment.

The Renaissance Garden was governed by a concept of visual composition, architectural treatment and a perfect mastery of forms and proportions. Thereafter, the French-style garden was based on the use of space as a building element, in a design that was aimed at provoking ecstasy, accompanied by a monumental impact. It is clear: every period in the history of styles is reflected, in one way or another, in the garden – and so much so that there is an exact historical correspondence all the way through to the present.[42]

---

[42] An alternative description of the historical evolution of the garden can be found in the lecture *"Concepts in Landscape Composition"*.

Figure 70. [Top] Gardens of Versailles, France. Photograph: María A. Villalobos H., 2010. **Figure 71.** [Center] *The Garden of Eden with the Fall of Man*, Jan Brueghel the Elder and Peter Paul Rubens, 1615. Oil on canvas. Dimensions: 74.3 x 114.7 cm. Geheugen can Nederland. Digital version available at: Rubens & Brueghel the Elder, 1615. **Figure 72.** [Bottom] *The Annunciation* Leonardo Da Vinci, 1472. Oil on canvas. Dimensions: 98.00 x 217.00 cm. Available at the Gallerie degli Uffizi, Florence, Italy. Digital version available at: Da Vinci, 1472.

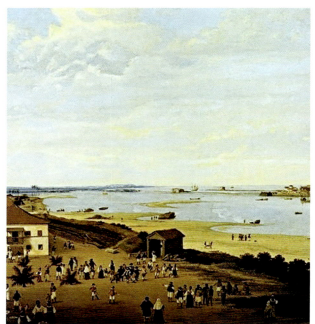 

Figure 73. [Left] *Recife* seen from the island of *Santo Antônio*, Brazil. Painting by Frans Post, 17th century. Digital version available at: Post, 17th century. **Figure 74.** [Right] Neighborhood of *Santo Antônio*. In the background you can see the Church of the *Divino Espírito Santo*, which was built over the Calvinist church erected by the French in 1642 and which stood until 1654. After the Pernambucan revolt in 1654, the priests of the Companhia de Jesus in *Olinda* asked the King of Portugal to establish a school in Recife. The school, the Jesuit College of *Recife* opened in 1690 and operated until 1759, when the Marquis of *Pombal* expelled the Jesuits from Portugal and its colonies. The Jesuit College was handed over to the Confraternity of the *Divino Espírito Santo* in 1855, with the condition that they restored the church. The second floor of the building served as a jail and housed the Court of Appeals. The church is in front of the *Parque Dezessete*, which was renovated by Roberto Burle Marx and collaborators. For more information see *Igreja do Divino Espírito Santo – Recife, Pernambuco. Histórias, Fotografías e significados das igrejas mais bonitas do Brasil*. (Sanctuaria.art, n.d.). Photograph: María A. Villalobos H., 2021. **Figure 75.** [Opposite] Parque *Dezessete*, *Recife*, Brazil, reformed by Roberto Burle Marx and collaborators. The square is characterized by the presence of multiple specimens of *Ficus benjamina* L., arranged geometrically along the lines of the historical layout. For more information on the work of Roberto Burle Marx in *Recife*, see the Official Gazette of the state of Recife, Decree No. 29.537 of March 23, 2016, *Provisions on the classification as Historic Gardens by Burle Marx of the planted public spaces in Recife*, which specifies their integration into the municipal system of protected areas – SMUP Recife, instituted by Municipal Law 18.014. Available in: Diário Oficial, 2016. Photograph: María A. Villalobos H., 2021.

What about the Brazilian tradition, if there is one?

In the case of Brazil, the history of the garden and the landscape could be presented in the following way: from the first accounts of the *"discovery"* of the garden to the rise of the Empire at the start of the last century, the natural landscape is what prevails.

There are hardly any organized landscapes. Nevertheless, special mention should be made of the urbanization work carried out by the Dutch in Recife and Olinda during the first half of the 17th century, as well as the initiative of Prince Johann-Maurits of Nassau and the gardens or landscaped spaces of *Rio de Janeiro* in the late 18th century, when the city became (beginning in 1753) the capital of Brazil. From another perspective, Brazilian sociologists – and in particular Gilberto Freyre – are part of a tradition of native gardens that replicate the lifestyles of rural civilization, associated the exploitation of sugar cane in the north-eastern Brazilian states, such as *Pernambuco*, *Alagoas*, *Paraíba*, *Sergipe* and *Bahia*. These lifestyles are based around an architectural unit consisting of a house, a chapel and production buildings (mills), embellished by a landscape treatment designed to enhance the property using decorative plants.

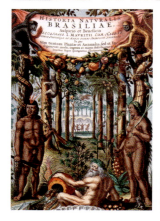

Meanwhile, plenty is known about the cloisters, monasteries, and convents of Brazilian religious architecture from the first three centuries of the period (16th–18th centuries). This mode featured ornamental plants in movable trays destined to decorate the church on holidays. Records from the period document urban and rural spaces alike, since both were dealt with regularly in the organization of gardens, which at the very least clearly demonstrates the equivalent of a composition and gives the impression of a conscious selection of plants. These are insufficient and poorly documented examples, nonetheless.

So, we cannot speak of an established type of traditional Brazilian garden, either in urban planning or from the point of view of private models. On the contrary, in this first phase we can identify an artificial landscape contributing to the embellishment of private, urban, and rural life, dominated by orchards, imported fruit trees (mango, avocado, sapotes, lemons), corrals for poultry and pastureland for grazing domestic animals. These practices gave rise what we call in Brazil the *quintal* (orchard), the *sítio* (small rural property) and the *roça* (farm), which correspond to small or medium-sized private properties eventually situated in urban areas.

The practice of burning to obtain arable land is a particularly noteworthy rural phenomenon in Brazil from the point of view of the natural landscape. Indeed, very early on, the idea of an untouched, exuberant, and excessive nature took hold throughout the country from the perspective of the occupation and cultivation of the land. However, in rural exploitations, areas of virgin forest have always been preserved, either to maintain water supplies using agricultural mechanical devices or as spaces to enjoy and, eventually, as hunting reserves.

Figure 76. [Top] Church of *São Francisco de Assis* one of the major works by Antônio Francisco Lisboa (Aleijadinho), *Ouro Preto, Minas Gerais, Brazil.* Photograph: María A. Villalobos H., 2021. **Figure 77.** [Center left] Garden of the Museum of the Ordem Terceira do Carmo, *Salvador da Bahia,* Brazil, built in the mid-18th century. Photograph: María A. Villalobos H., 2021. **Figure 78.** [Center right] Ruins of the old sugar mill of Santo Amaro, *Salvador da Bahia,* Brazil, testimony of a past of slavery and exploitation, where flowers grow from among the stones. Photograph: María A. Villalobos H., 2021. **Figure 79.** [Bottom left] Cover page of *Historia Naturalis Brasiliae* from 1648, by Georg Marcgrave. Marcgrave carried out three expeditions in the states of *Alagoas, Pernambuco, Paraíba, Rio Grande do Norte* and *Ceará.* For more information see Phaf-Rheinberge, Ineke, Luanda, *"Precisão do olhar e canibalismo: Georg Marcgrave e a história do Atlântico Sul",* in *Viagens, Viajantes e Deslocamentos,* projeto História No. 42, June 2011. Available in: Phaf-Rheinberge, 2011. **Figure 80.** [Bottom center] Bananas, guavas, and other fruits. Brazil. 1641–1643. Albert Eckhout. Oil on canvas. Dimensions: 91.0 x 91.0 cm. National Museum of Denmark. Digital version available at: Eckhout, 1641–1643. **Figure 81.** [Bottom right] Plan of *Recife* in 1644. For more information see Barleus, Caspar: *História dos feitos recentemente praticados durante oito anos no Brasil,* Cláudio Brandão (trac.), Mário Guimarães Ferri (pref.). *Belo Horizonte:* Livraria Itatiaia editora Ltda., 1974.

Figure 82. Coffee exploitation landscape with enslaved workers. Ferrez, Marc. 1882. *Indivíduos escravizados em terreiro de uma fazenda de café na região do Vale do Paraíba. Instituto Moreira Salles* Collection, *Paraíba* Valley. Gelatin and silver print photograph. *Instituto Moreira Salles*. Digital version available at: Ferrez, c. 1882.

The geographic immensity of Brazil (8 million km^2) and the concentration of the population in the cities are the main factors that explain why the built landscape is so diverse and dispersed. At the beginning of the 19th century, King John VI of Portugal, intent on imposing the models of European civilization on the Brazilian Empire through fundamental reforms, decided to completely transform Brazilian cultural practices. He decreed the opening of the ports, thereby connecting the country to the world. Although he lived in Lisbon before the Napoleonic campaigns, he moved to Brazil, where he built enormous agricultural operations. He created schools for engineering and for the teaching of the arts and showed an immense interest in the study of local nature, as evidenced by the creation of the fantastic Rio de Janeiro Botanical Garden.

Figure 83. Building of the Imperial School of Fine Arts, by Auguste François Marie Glaziou. Ferrez, Marc. 1891. Black and white photograph, gelatin, and silver print. Dimensions: 24 x 18 cm. *Instituto Moreira Salles, Rio de Janeiro*: 1891. Digital version in: Ferrez, Escola Nacional de Belas Artes, c. 1891. The original work by Grandjean de Montigny was inaugurated in 1926 on the former *Travessa do Sacramento* now known as Avenida *Passos*. For more information see Pereira, Sônia Gomes. 2008. "A Escola Real de Ciências, Artes e Ofícios e a Academia Imperial de Belas Artes do Rio de Janeiro". In: *Ipanema*, Rogéria Moreira. D. *João e a cidade do Rio de Janeiro. Rio de Janeiro*: Instituto Histórico e Geográfico do Rio de Janeiro 2008. pp. 383–370.

A certain knowledge of the natural science first dates from his reign: it had never been developed before then, except for the Dutch period (1600–1625) which saw contributions from scholars of the quality of Barlaeus, Willem Piso and Georg Marcgrave, illustrated in the paintings and designs of Frans Post, Albert Eeckhout and Zacharie Wagner.[43]

The imperial court, the French mission and the naturalists who came to Brazil in the 19th century (Martius, Spix, Humboldt, Geoffroy Saint-Hilaire, Gardner, and others) completely changed the conditions for the construction of the landscape. Numerous wild plants were selected for cultural and private decorative uses. Others came from the West Indies,

[43] An alternative description of the artists named here is presented in the third part of this publication.

Figure 84. Portico of the Academia Imperial de Belas Artes, recovered from the demolition of the building in 1938 and transferred to the Rio de Janeiro Botanical Garden, *Rio de Janeiro*, Brazil. Photograph: Carla Urbina, 2020.

Africa, the Orient and various provinces. These were imported and acclimatized with immediate success. Great botanists also emerged in Brazil: Rodrigues, Vellozo, etc.[44]

In fact, agriculture, which had attracted many immigrants during the development of coffee growing in the regions of *São Paulo* and *Rio de Janeiro*, was once again an important factor influencing the built landscape.

At the time of the royal court and during the Empire (1822–1889), private and public architecture developed on a remarkable scale. Particularly noteworthy are the works of Grandjean de Montigny in *Rio*, Vauthier in *Recife*, and the works of the landscape architect Glaziou, who designed the park of the imperial palace (*Quinta da Boa Vista*) and the *Campo Santa Ana*, both in *Rio de Janeiro*.

But the second half of the century is characterized by works in the European academic style, in which the essential concern was to keep pace with the creative work of the *"civilized"* centers of the world, and to showcase recently acquired wealth and the appearance of nobility.

Because of the abolition of slavery and the economic crisis that followed, the fall of the Empire ushered in a period that profoundly changed the distribution of private wealth, which was henceforth established in the southern states thanks to the contribution of a new agricultural workforce. The period from 1890 to 1920 saw the rise and fall of natural rubber production in the Amazon and the development of agriculture and livestock, which resulted in an uptick in movement to import materials and European workers. There also emerged an elite and a bourgeoisie eager to emulate behaviors copied from *"civilized"* European models rather than originating from a local artistic production. At that moment a considerable number of constructions were erected in the main cities of Brazil thanks to the European craftsmen (Portuguese, Italians, Germans, and others) who had recently settled in the country. They brought with them the techniques and materials characteristic of the European modernity and the *Art Nouveau style*, which in Brazil was given the moniker *estilo floral* (floral style) to signify its dominant aesthetic motif.

[44] For more information on the botanists mentioned here see the lecture *"The Involvement of Botanists in My Professional Training"*, included in the third part of this book.

Figure 85. [Top] *Quinta de Boa Vista* and lake designed by Auguste François Marie Glaziou, in 1874, *Rio de Janeiro*, Brazil. Photograph: María A. Villalobos H., 2018. **Figure 86.** [Centre] Historical Garden of the Museu da República, *Rio de Janeiro*, Brazil, designed by Glaziou. Photograph: María A. Villalobos H., 2018. **Figure 87.** [Bottom] *Campo Santa Ana* designed by Glaziou, in 1874, *Rio de Janeiro*, Brazil. Photograph: María A. Villalobos H., 2018.

Undoubtedly, it is possible to establish a correspondence between the *"floral style"* and the *Belle Époque* of decadent European Romanticism. We can thus observe that the exaggeration that reigned in Brazil almost annihilated our historical and artistic heritage, demolishing ancient palaces and religious buildings, all in the name of the whims of the nouveau riche and a morbid anxiety on the part of people who needed to be perceived as *"civilized"*.

The fashion for gardening and the passion for the culture of flowers and exotic plants in Brazil dates to this period. The rose invaded all the arts, from poetry to ceiling decorations. Chinese bamboo, ferns, dwarf palms, carnations, chrysanthemums, dahlias, and many other species were the object of intense botanical consumption for decorative purposes. This residue of Romanticism of the *Belle Époque* persisted until the 1940s.

Such were the legacies and the artistic experience with which I was confronted when I returned from Germany, bringing with me in my head the fixed idea of simply becoming a visual artist of my generation and my home country. So, when someone asks where I first perceived the aesthetic qualities of the native Brazilian flora, what drove my desire to construct a new order of visual composition using the native plants of this land, frankly I can only answer: it came from studying painting in the exhibits of Brazilian tropical plants at the Botanical Garden in Berlin!

Figure 88. [Top] *Sítio Roberto Burle Marx, Santo Antônio da Bica*, Brazil. Photograph: María A. Villalobos H., 2021. **Figure 89.** [Centre] Granite arches from the demolition of a 14th-century building in downtown Rio de Janeiro, Brazil. Arches installed at a height of 45 m at the *Sítio Roberto Burle Marx, Santo Antônio da Bica*, Brazil. Photograph: María A. Villalobos H., 2014 and 2021. **Figure 90.** [Bottom left] Features recovered from demolition work in the center *of Rio de Janeiro*, Brazil, used in the *Sítio Roberto Burle Marx, Santo Antônio da Bica*, Brazil. Photograph: Carla Urbina, 2018. **Figure 91.** [Bottom right] Concert by Mariana Tabacow and Larissa Galvão in the *Atelier* of the *Sítio Roberto Burle Marx, Santo Antônio da Bica*, Brazil. Commemoration of the 110th anniversary of Robert Burle Marx's birth (August 4, 1909). Photograph: Carla Urbina, 2019.

Figure 92. Xerophytic plants in the Dahlem Botanical Garden, Berlin, Germany. The garden was built between 1897 and 1910 under the direction of Adolf Engler, author of *Die natürlichen Pflanzenfamilien*. Adolf Engler collaborated with several other great botanists, including C.F.P. von Martius, on the work *Flora Brasiliensis*, 1840–1906. Photograph: María A. Villalobos H., 2013.

It was there that I truly grasped the force of the nature of the tropics; where I understood that, within my reach, there was a material ready to serve an artistic project all my own, which was still poorly defined at that time. From then on, I used native natural elements, with all their strength and qualities, as a material in my artistic compositions.

At least that is my understanding landscape art: as an artistic affirmation.

Figure 93. Jacques Leenhardt at the Botanical Garden in *São Paulo*, Brazil, for the documentary series *Expedições Burle Marx*. In the film, Leenhardt states that Roberto Burle Marx *"discovered Brazilian nature in the greenhouses of the Dahlem gardens. That was the first trip he made. Afterwards, he undertook several trips in the Amazon and Brazil. I believe that this distancing from the Brazilian reality was the starting point for his developing a new point of view on gardens and nature. I find that a garden is always about the journey. This began with botanical gardens, which are the gardens of travelers."* Jacques Leenhardt, in *Coleccionador* (min 05:23 – 6:10), as part of the documentary series *Expedições Burle Marx* directed by João Vargas, in Brazil, in 2013.

Jacques Leenhardt is a philosopher and sociologist. He is Director of Studies at the *École des hautes études en sciences sociales (EHESS)*, Paris, France. Leenhardt is honorary president of the International Association of Art Critics (AICA), founding member of the Art Critics Archives (GIS, *Rennes*), and president of the Association of Friends of Wifredo Lam. His expertise in sociology, literature, landscaping, history, art, urban, narrative and Latin America is evident in publications and exhibitions such as *Les Amériques latines en France* (1992), *Dans les Jardins de Roberto Burle Marx* (1994– 2011), *Villette-Amazone. Manifeste pour l'environnement au XXIe siècle* (1996), *Michel Corajoud, paysagiste* (2000), *Érico Veríssimo, Conscience du paysage* (2002), *Reinventar o Brasil: Gilberto Freyre entre história e ficção* (J.L. org. 2006), *Jardins verticaux dans le monde entier*, with Anna Lambertini (2007). Notable exhibitions he has curated include: *Des Forêts et des Hommes* (Muséum National d'Histoire Naturelle, 1996), *Villette-Amazone, Manifeste pour l'environnement au XXIe siècle* (Grande Halle de la Villette, 1996), *Pavillon Environnement de l'Exposition universelle* (Hanovre, 2000), *Arte Frágil, Resistências* (MAC, São Paulo, 2009), *Debretea Missão Artística Francesa no Brasil, 200 anos* (Museus Castro Maya, Rio de Janeiro, Brazil, 2016).

III. SELECTED LECTURES FROM THE BOOK
ARTE & PAISAGEM: CONFERÊNCIAS ESCOLHIDAS
1954-1983

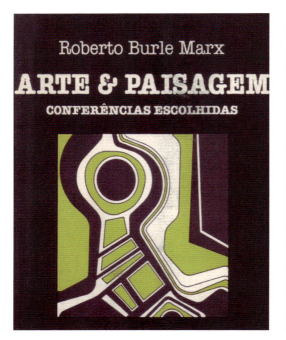 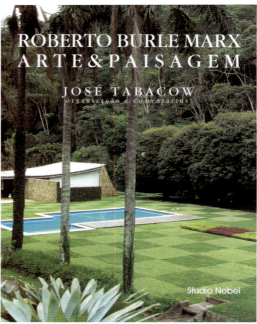

Figure 94. [Left] The book *Arte e Paisagem: Conferências escolhidas* by Roberto Burle Marx, edited by José Tabacow. Cover design: Roberto Burle Marx. Logo: Lacy M. Tsukumo Andrade. Photographic productions: Haruyoshi Ono. Publisher: Livros Studio Nobel Ltda., 1987. **Figure 95.** [Right] The book *Arte e Paisagem* by Roberto Burle Marx, organized and with commentary by José Tabacow. Cover design: Moema Calvacanti. Cover photo: Luiz Claudio Marigo. Publisher: Livros Studio Nobel Ltda., 2004.

This section offers the English translation of a selection of lectures compiled, organized, edited, and commented on by José Tabacow. These lectures were originally published in Portuguese in the book by Roberto Burle Marx, *Arte e Paisagem: Conferências escolhidas* (São Paulo: Livros Studio Nobel Ltda, 1987). The preface, as well as the selection, organization, and revision of the lectures were undertaken by José Tabacow. The book was included in the Ciudad Abierta collection, and the production team included María Viera de Freitas, Renan Morais Figueredo, and María Aparecida Amaral. The original cover design was by Roberto Burle Marx. The logo was designed by Lacy M. Tsukumo Andrade. The photographs were assembled by Haruyoshi Ono.

In the preface to the edition published in 1987, Tabacow highlights the value of repetition in the process of understanding a living work, which evolved over time and depending on the collaborators, and the urban and environmental circumstances of the tropics. Likewise, Tabacow draws attention to the importance of plants as a decisive element in the publication process as part of the path to understanding the work of a man who transformed his home into one of the most relevant collections of living plants in the world.

Finally, Tabacow recalls that: *"The aim is for this book to help the reader understand, perceive why the content of Roberto Burle Marx's work offers so much more than physical beauty, since his landscape designs and his conservation work meld together without clearly defined limits. Plants are, at the same time, the materials used in his compositions and the symbol of his love for living things"* (Tabacow, 1987. p. 5).

166 III. SELECTED LECTURES FROM THE BOOK *ARTE & PAISAGEM: CONFERÊNCIAS ESCOLHIDAS*

Figure 96. *Parque del Este*, Caracas, Venezuela. Photograph: Carla Urbina, 2012.

LANDSCAPE DESIGN IN LARGE AREAS 1962

At the moment, I am excited about the new gardens I have been put in charge of developing. That's because they are large parks, which, because of their size, offer landscape architects a higher degree of freedom when it comes to choosing solutions and developing new ideas. They are: in Venezuela, the grand *Parque del Este*; in *Brasília*, the Zoological and Botanical Garden, which combines the qualities of a zoo and a botanical garden over a huge area; in *Rio de Janeiro*, the *Parque do Flamengo*, which encompasses an exceptional area of immense value, and I consider it miraculous that the administration has been able to protect it from commercial interests; and, finally, the São Paulo Botanical Garden, which has the characteristics of a scientific garden, a reserve for the conservation of flora and fauna, and a recreation area for the people of that immense and hard-working metropolis.

In carrying out these new projects, I draw on the experience I have accumulated over the years I have spent planning and building gardens.

I look back as far as my first commissions, like the gardens I did in *Pernambuco* at the beginning of my career. There are two in particular, however, that I'd like to comment on: the first is an ecological garden where, drawing on my experiences and observations from the *Caatinga*, I was able to introduce and combine species from those environments. The other is a water garden, divided into three sections: exotic plants, American plants, and Amazonian plants. The idea that inspired me was taken from a photograph of the aquatic plant tanks at Kew Gardens. In the project, I was meant to modify a pre-existing garden, my first contribution being the removal of a *"monument"* made from stone dust, in questionable taste, dedicated to the heroes of *Pernambuco* or the like. As expected, there was an outcry from local *"patriots"*, and the only argument I could offer was that, because it was cheap and ugly, the monument was not worthy of the distinguished heroes it honored. Funnily enough, many years later, on a visit to Kew Gardens, I was surprised to find that the water garden was entirely different from what I had imagined.

Figure 97. [Top] Parque del Este, Caracas, Venezuela. Photograph: Andrés Manner, s.f.P. The Parque del Este is an urban park project developed by Roberto Burle Marx and Associates (a company that operated from 1955 to 1965), with a team made up of Roberto Burle Marx, Mauricio Monte, Julio César Pessolani, John Godfrey Stoddart and Fernando Tábora. For the project, the botanist Leandro Aristeguieta oversaw the botanical aspects together with the horticulturists Louis Longchamp, Karl Wendlinger and Dante Bianchi. In association with the Faculty of Sciences and the Botanical Institute of the Central University of Venezuela, expeditions were carried out to national parks such as Henri Pittier (Rancho Grande), Guatopo, El Ávila, as well as to the south of Lake Maracaibo, the Orinoco Delta, Imataca Mountains, the plains of the Alto Apure and the Gran Sabana. See Tábora, Fernando. *Dos parques, un equipo: Parque del Este, Caracas, Venezuela y Aterro do Flamengo, Rio de Janeiro, Brazil. Caracas*, 2007. **Figure 98.** [Center] The *Parque do Flamengo* under construction, in volume I of the *Processo de Tombamento* no. 0748-T-64. IPHAN Central Archive, Rio de Janeiro. Available in Romeiro Chuva, 2017. **Figure 99.** [Bottom] Cobra habitat at the Zoological and Botanical Garden in *Brasília*, Brazil, 1958. Photograph: Brasília Zoological Garden Foundation, Public Archive of the Federal District. Available in *Imagem e Memoria Candangclandia*. The design for the Zoological and Botanical Garden in *Brasília* fulfills the function of preserving the *flora of the Cerrado*.

Figure 100. [Top, both pages] Xerophytic Garden in the *Parque del Este*. Caracas, Venezuela. Photographs: Carla Urbina, 2012. **Figure 101.** [Center, both pages] *Parque do Flamengo*, Rio de Janeiro, Brazil. Photographs: María A.

Villalobos H. 2021. **Figure 102.** [Bottom, both pages] Lakes in the Zoological and Botanical Garden, *Brasília*, Brazil. Photographs: María A. Villalobos H. 2021.

Figure 103. [Top] Ecological Garden in *Pernambuco, Praça Euclides da Cunha, Recife*, Brazil. Project designed by Roberto Burle Marx and collaborators. Collection of the *Instituto Burle Marx*. **Figure 104.** [Center and bottom] Ecological Garden in *Pernambuco, Praça Euclides da Cunha, Recife*, Brazil. Project designed by Roberto Burle Marx and collaborators in 1938. Photographs: María A. Villalobos H., 2021.

Figure 105. [Top] Drawing by Roberto Burle Marx, 1935. Water Garden in *Pernambuco, Praça Casa Forte, Recife*, Brazil. Archive of the *Instituto Burle Marx*. **Figure 106.** [Center and center left] Water Garden, *Kew Gardens*, London. Photographs: María A. Villalobos H., 2012. **Figure 107.** [Center right and bottom] Water Garden in *Pernambuco, Praça Casa Forte, Recife*, Brazil. Photographs: María A. Villalobos H., 2021.

When it comes to large parks, much of the experience I rely on comes from the work I did for the park in Araxá, in *Minas Gerais*, together with Mello Barreto. Working with a botanist was a real learning experience for me. He was the one who took me to visit and analyze, one by one, the different plant associations in the mountains of *Minas Gerais*. Together, we observed the flora associated with the *arenito* (sandstone), *canga* (ironstone), *calcário* (limestone), *gnaisse* (gneiss), *granito* (granite), and *basalto* (basalt). For my training, that contact with one of the greatest field botanists I have ever known was of immense value.

[45] Santana, Rivânia María Trotta. *"O movimento Modernista Verde, de Cataguases – MG".* Em Tese, Belo Horizonte, v. 10, p. 172-177, Dec. 2006. [Quote from the author of the original text].

[46] Silva, Gustavo Santos. *O botânico Henrique Lahmeyer de Mello Barreto e sua contribuição para o conhecimento da flora de Minas Gerais* [manuscript]. 2018. 79 f. Dissertação (Mestrado em Biologia Vegetal). Mestrado em Biologia Vegetal. Universidade Federal de Minas Gerais, Belo Horizonte, 2018. [Quote from the author of the original text] (Silva, 2018).

Figure 108. [Top] Garden of local rocks in the Zoo and Botanical Garden in the *Parque das Mangabeiras*, located in the *Serra do Curral, Minas Gerais*, Brazil, designed by Roberto Burle Marx and collaborators in 1982. Photograph: María A. Villalobos H., 2012. **Figure 109.** [Center] *Orthophytum mello-barretoi* L.B.Sm., native to the *Serra do Cipó, Minas Gerais.* Discovered by Henrique Lahmeyer de Mello Barreto, first published in Bol. Mus. Nac. Rio de Janeiro, Bot., n.s., 15: 2 (1952). Photograph: Giulietti *et al.*, 2009, available in *Plantas raras do Brasil: 1-496. Conservação International, Belo Horizonte, Minas Gerais* (Kew Science, n.d.). *"Henrique Lahmeyer de Mello Barreto (1892-1962) was one of the most important Brazilian botanists and miners of the 20th century. Mello Barreto was a carioca [native of Rio de Janeiro] who was interested in the botanical aspects of nature from a young age. [...] In 1926 he was invited to be director of the Horto Florestal in the city of Cataguases, where he remained until 1931. In 1927, Cataguases was the setting for the Green Movement, a literary branch of the modernist movement, and Mello Barreto was no doubt involved in this moment in the history of Brazilian art.*[45] *In 1931, he moved to Belo Horizonte after he was invited to be director of the newly created Botanical Garden of Minas Gerais. [...] Self-taught, he did not hold a degree in botany, but his knowledge was recognized with a distinction from the then director of the National Museum of Rio de Janeiro, Adolpho Ducke. In addition to Portuguese, he spoke four other languages – English, Latin, German, and French – with great fluency. He became a professor of Natural History at the Faculty of Medicine in Minas Gerais and taught Systematics for the degree in Agricultural Engineering. He was a member of the Biological Society of Minas Gerais and of the Supervisory Council of Artistic and Scientific Expeditions in Brazil. In 1940, Mello Barreto met Burle Marx. The exchange of knowledge between the two made it possible for the new landscape designs to adopt a concept more focused on integrating native flora with the surroundings. Thus, the two partners planned more than 17 projects and ended up becoming lifelong friends [...] There were also other collaborations, for example in Cataguases, Ouro Preto, Pará de Minas, and one of the most famous: Barreiro, in Araxá. In the latter, a series of gardens were designed so that each one could represent a kind of biome present in Minas Gerais [...] The botanist ended up creating an extensive network, across various institutions around the world, which allowed for the exchange of information about botanical materials for different purposes. He studied the area of the Serra do Cipó, learning not only about the botanical formations, but also the phytogeographical interactions there. In 1946, Henrique Lahmeyer de Mello Barreto was invited to direct the Rio de Janeiro Zoological Garden [...] He died in 1962 of a massive heart attack, while hard at work, and, as reported by some newspapers at the time, he died as he would have wanted, 'in his garden'.*[46] (Museu Casa Kubitschek, 2018, p. 8). **Figure 110.** [Bottom] Amphitheater in the Zoo and Botanical Garden in the *Parque das Mangabeiras*, located in the *Serra do Curral, Minas Gerais*, Brazil. Photograph: María A. Villalobos H., 2012.

A trip to Berlin also contributed to my education; there, I was able to admire and examine the first ecological gardens built by Engler. I think I've laid out the antecedents that inspired me in the execution of the large projects that I intend to speak about.

The first decision that has to be made is the overall positioning – in other words, the meaning that the park should have. In the case of a botanical garden, we can choose between organizing it according to a systematic criterion, an ecological criterion, or a more or less eclectic criterion that lets us combine the advantages of one or the other. While, on the one hand, an ecological garden will be more harmonious, when it comes to certain plant groups creating collections offers such an important educational resource and aesthetic effect that they become fundamental elements. That is the case with collections of araceae, bromeliads, orchids, palm trees, etc.

The functions of a botanical garden, which is, in essence, a scientific institution, include research and dissemination, systematic and unsystematic teaching, the undertaking of botanical explorations, the curation of collections of living plants and herborized materials, the exchange of plants, seedlings and seeds, the organization of regular exhibitions, courses, etc. A garden of that kind is perfect for displaying plants, either isolated or in associations. It is a place where you can compare plants from the same family and understand their ability to adapt to extremely diverse environments and living conditions.

On the other hand, with respect to the needs of a zoo, the presence of animals introduces a certain discipline into the movement of the park's structure, which demands a series of precautions on the part of the landscape designer, such that the functional and aesthetic solutions can be developed simultaneously, without entering into conflict. For the Zoological and Botanical Garden in *Brasília*, for example, we opted for a distribution of the animals in an environment formed by the vegetation from the ecological groups of their respective habitats. That said, the idea is not just to create a copy of nature. It is necessary to design a composition that highlights and emphasizes the presence of the animals and plants so that they gain expressivity as elements of a particular landscape.

Figure 111. [Top] Berlin-Dahlem Botanical Garden, Germany. Photograph: María A. Villalobos H., 2012. **Figure 112.** [Center and bottom] Water gardens in the Zoological and Botanical Garden in *Brasília*, designed by Roberto Burle Marx and collaborators in 1957, *Brasília*, Brazil. Photographs: María A. Villalobos H., 2021.

The landscape designer must also account for adaptation, which demonstrates an accord between beings and their environment, animals and the planet, humans, and nature, and the city. We can understand that certain animal forms are the result of an environment. Our wolf, the *guará*,[47] with its long dark legs, is perfectly adapted to the *Cerrados*[48] and adopts fruitarian habits, foraging for fruits of the *Solanum lycocarpum* St. Hill., or *"wolf apples"*. And what about the mimicry that leads certain butterflies towards trees with grayish trunks, against which they blend in entirely?

There are plant associations that often take on a symphonic meaning. It's the idea that comes to mind when I think about how the *Mimosa calodendron* Mart. connects with the *Lychnophora* and the *Anthurium affine* Schott. The bizarre shape of a *baobab* responds to some reason in nature. And so, we enter an endless world of forms and reasons. How strange it is to observe certain primitive forms of art and see that they are based on an observation of nature. There are some enlightening analogies. A spoon is like the spathe of an aroid, a hook could be similar to a thorn, perhaps from a *Desmoncus*, a climbing palm that *"fishes"* for trunks, branches of vines to latch onto. In the same way, very elaborate forms, like the structures designed by Pier Luigi Nervi, exist in the intricate nervation of the leaves of the *Victoria regia*. And it is through observation that we come to understand the reasons behind the existence of many things.

[47] The *lobo-guará* (Chrysocyon brachyurus), or maned wolf, is a typical animal of the *Cerrado*, which has been listed as endangered. It can be found in Brazil, Argentina, Bolivia, Paraguay, Peru and Uruguay. For more information see: WWF, n.d.

[48] The *Cerrado* is a tropical savannah biome, located in the central west of Brazil, receiving water from three of the largest hydrographic basins in South America (*Tocantins, São Francisco* and *Prata*). This biome represents the second largest plant formation in Brazil (almost 23% of the territory). It is characterized by a broad heterogeneity of plant forms and densities, including herbaceous plants, shrubs, and trees, which coexist in a thick, mature soil with high levels of iron and aluminum. It is estimated that there are more than 10,000 species of plants in the region's flora and hundreds of animal species. Currently, it is threatened by erosion and mercury pollution, because of gold mining, as well as the unchecked expansion of monoculture farming and extensive livestock activity. For more information see: WWF, n.d.

Figure 113. [Top left] Butterfly mimicking the aerial roots (called pneumatophores) of a *Taxodium dicticum* (L.) Rich., or swamp cypress, in the Rio de Janeiro Botanical Garden, Brazil. Photograph: María A. Villalobos H., 2021. **Figure 114.** [Top right] *Mimosa calodendron* Mart. *Cidade das pedras, Goiás*, Brazil. Photograph: Carla Urbina, 2019. **Figure 115.** [Center left] *Lobo-guará* (Maned wolf) Chrysocyon brachyurus (Illiger, 1815). Photograph: Leonardo Leiva, 2021. **Figure 116.** [Center] *Solanum lycocarpum* A. St.-Hil., or the wolf apple. *Minas Gerais*, Brazil, on BR116 between Teófilo Otoni and Gov. Valadares, November 2013 (Knapp IM-10682). Photograph: Sandy Knapp, 2013. Available in: Knapp, 2013. **Figure 117.** [Center right] Flower of the *Solanum lycocarpum* A. St.-Hil. in La Gran Sabana on route toward Roraima, Venezuela. Photograph: Carla Urbina, 2013. **Figure 118.** [Bottom left] Structure of a *Victoria regia* Lindl. (also called *Victoria amazonica*, Poepp., Sowerby) in bloom on the lake in the Rio de Janeiro Botanical Garden, Brazil. Photograph: María A. Villalobos H., 2021. **Figure 119.** [Bottom right] Architectural structure that recalls the form of the *Victoria regia* Lindl. Pier Luigi Nervi, 1942. *Sala Mescita, Parque Acqua Santa Terme*, in *Chianciano*, Italy. Available in: Nervi, 1942.

The meaning behind the existence of some beings is in their beauty. I'd like to repeat that nature is a kind of symphony in which the elements are all closely related – size, shape, color, aroma, movement, etc. Given this conception, a plant or an animal is no longer just a systematic entity, a being in a collection. It is much more: a system endowed with an immense amount of spontaneous activity, possessing its own *modus vivendi* in the world around it. In zoological gardens as we know them, it is possible to demonstrate that natural reality: the existence of an intimate relationship between plants, animals, and minerals. Thus, the beak of a hummingbird is shaped in such a way that is seems like a tool that was specifically designed to collect nectar from the flowers of a bromeliad or a heliconia. But there are also visual analogies: the bracts of a different heliconia that recall, in both form and color, certain features of the *papagayo*[49] and the *arara*.[50] There is a mystery in the coordinating colors and shapes that combine to create a connection between the bird and the plant. There is also quantitative meaning that can be perceived in nature: how many times have we seen a splotch of yellow, or another color, against a large green surface that satisfies an aesthetic need. That splotch needed to be there because its presence makes the green sing, shine brighter, stand out against the whole.

The forces of nature operate entirely independently from the concepts created by man, which may seem naive at times, when examined in the light of the mechanisms that drive those forces. Nature wastes no time in eliminating what is useless and has no reason for existing. It exists beyond our philosophical notions of good and evil. And although I know this, I still sometimes feel pantheistic tendencies, and I am tempted to ask myself, like certain Hindu botanists, why, if plants don't suffer, if they can't feel, do they cloak themselves in so much joy with their blooms?

Again, regarding zoological gardens, the basic idea – contrary to what we find in so many museums – is not to create portraits of dead animals and wax plants, but rather of living animals among living plants. I have always been repulsed by what other people seem to find pleasing: keeping artificial plants, dead plants, barely even the image of a plant.

---

[49] The *papagayo* is a bird of the Psittacidae family, known in the Caribbean and America as the loro, and in English as the parrot. For more information about these birds, see: *The Cornell Lab of Ornithology*, 2021.

[50] The *arara* is a multicolored bird of the Psittacidae family. The various species of the genus *Ara* are characterized by their colorful plumage and large size. They can reach up to 90 cm in length. They are known in some regions of America as *guacamayos* (*The Cornell Lab of Ornithology*, 2021).

Figure 120. [Top] *Colibríes* (*Phaethornis guy* (Lesson, 1833)) and *Phaethornis syrmatophorus* (Gould, 1851) drinking nectar from a heliconia flower. Photograph: Enrique Ascanio, n.d. **Figure 121.** [Bottom] *Guacamayo bandera* (*Ara macao* (Linnaeus, 1758)) in the Parque del Este, Caracas-Venezuela. Photograph: Pedro Romero, 2016.

And they are content to deceive themselves and others. I reject the plastic models of plants that are the gaudy expressions of mass production. I believe that this spirit a far cry from that of Von Martius, a man of the humanistic tradition who, upon arriving in Brazil, fell in love with its exuberant nature and, in a mixture of science and poetry, divided the territory into phytogeographic regions identified by the names of Greek divinities like the naiads, oreads, and hamadryads.

He was a man with a finely tuned sensitivity, who combined the most advanced ecological ideas of his time with a strong artistic sentiment, which can be seen in his descriptions of the sunrise over a lake in Pará or a tropical storm in the heart of the Amazon jungle.

In the case of a zoo, another important issue is to ensure visitors are able to move around freely without getting too tired, while being able to take in the landscape from different angles and approach the animals and plants without interfering with their behavior and safety.

As we have seen so far, the work of a landscape architect is becoming increasingly complex. It is impossible to perform it in isolation. Only with the dedicated and clear participation of botanists and other experts can a landscape designer correctly interpret the natural landscape to be able to think harmonically about how to design and execute the built landscape. A comprehensive understanding of the problem comes from that collaboration. Only a well-rounded team can consider all the biological, social, artistic, and technical aspects of a large park. I would never have been able to develop these projects without the advice of my botanist friends. I have relied on them in pursuing one of the most constant aspects of my professional activity: the search for and introduction of new plants into gardens.

Figure 122. [Top] Tropical storm in the *Mata Atlântica, Rio de Janeiro*, Brazil. Photograph: María A. Villalcbos H., 2012. **Figure 123.** [Center left] Araceae (with the spadix and spathe) in one of the nurseries at the *Sítio* Roberto Burle Marx, *Santo Antônio da Bica*, Brazil. Photograph: Carla Urbina, 2014. **Figure 124.** [Center] Scientific illustration of *Desmonchus orthacanthos*. Martius, von C.F.P., *Historia Naturalis Palmarum* (1823-1853). Hist. Nat. Palm. vol. 2 (1839). Missouri Botanical Garden, Saint Louis, United States. Digital version available at: Martius C. v., *Desmoncus orthacanthos Mart.*, 1823-1853. **Figure 125.** [Center right] *Anthurium affine Schott* in the *Sítio Roberto Burle Marx, Santo Antônio da Bica*, Brazil, for the celebration of the centennial of Roberto Burle Marx's birth. Photograph: Carla Urbina, 2019. **Figure 126.** [Bottom] Map of the phytogeographic regions of Brazil. Martius, C. F. P. Von Martius (1858). *"Tabula geografica brasiliae et terrarum adjacentium exhibens itinera botanicorum [et florae brasiliensis quinque provincias]. Provinciae florae brasiliensis"*. In: Martius, C. F. P. Von, Eichler, A. W. & Urban, I. (ed.). *Flora brasiliensis*. Monacchi et Lipsiae: R. Oldenbourg, 1840-1906, v. 1, 1.

Figure 127. Demolition of Lago 9, Parque del Este in Caracas, Venezuela, as part of the construction process for the *El Leander* project (architectural design for the construction of a museum under the lake by Micucci and associates, Metro de Caracas and Odebrecht, 2008). Since its opening, the park has been a symbol of democracy and public urban life. Photograph: Dahlia Gutierrez. *"The Parque del Este is complete. Just as removing its trees and gardens would diminish and eventually destroy it, adding a program unrelated to its environmental and ecological mission would equally diminish and eventually destroy it. Moreover, the Park is currently among the cultural sites with certain possibilities of being added to the UNESCO World Heritage list, and this intervention damages it in such a way that will make this great achievement impossible. With the construction of the Leander project and the negative effects it will have on the park, its eventual inclusion on the World Heritage list would be impossible. The Parque del Este is too important on every level – national, international, ecological, and environmental – to be treated with such informality and such contempt."* (Berrizbeitia, 2008).

Figure 128. Current state of the *Parque del Este* in Caracas, Venezuela. Note the damage to the association of palm trees in Lago 9. Photograph: Eduardo Izaguirre, 2015. The destruction of the *Parque del Este* was prevented thanks to the action of the National Architects' Association of Venezuela, through the figure of its president, Dr. Marianella Genatios, with support from the International Federation of Landscape Architects (IFLA). At the world congress in 2009, held in *Rio de Janeiro*, Brazil, the IFLA released an international letter signed by all its members in support of the preservation of the *Parque del Este*. The video of the emotional reading of the IFLA's letter in defense of the recovery of the heritage of the *Parque del Este* in Caracas, which took place in *Rio de Janeiro*, Brazil in October 2009, can be consulted at: IFLA, 2009. In Caracas, on April 8, 2010, the Architects' Association of Venezuela expressed in an official statement *"its total rebuke of the institutions that are meant to defend heritage and environmental values as well as citizens' recreation (Ministry of the Environment, National Institute of Parks, Institute of Cultural Heritage), as well as the promoters of the Museum Project, who, by promoting this project, are officializing riding roughshod over a public asset, without giving citizens any say in the matter."* (Blackmore, 2010).

In Brazil we are witnessing a dangerous process of the destruction of nature. But there are still many things that cannot be destroyed. So, I consider it an obligation to preserve certain endangered species, aiming to guarantee the survival of their beauty for the future, which, in turn, represents their scientific importance. This hunt for species requires a knowledge of phytogeographic nature and a certain familiarity with the forests and other natural formations where we seek them out. In forests, the plants are adapted to different heights: there are plants that inhabit the understory, medium-height plants, trees with crowns, and epiphytes. The biology of these forests is still largely unknown. There are thousands of aspects about them yet to be studied. But, to guarantee that possibility, we need to prevent their destruction and attempt to restore them whenever possible.

Thus, I hope I have conveyed, briefly, my concerns when dealing with large projects, like the ones cited at the beginning of this lecture. I would like to draw attention to the fact that, beyond everything that has been said here, gardens are subject to certain laws that are not specific to them, but rather are inherent in any form of art. They are the same questions of form and color, of size and time, of rhythm. In landscape design, certain characteristics are sometimes of greater importance than in other forms of art. Three-dimensionality, temporality, and the dynamics of living beings have to be taken into account in the composition. And the other features have their own ways of participating in gardens. In nature, color can't have the same meaning as it does in painting. It depends on sunlight, clouds, rain, the time of day, location, and every other environmental factor. That is why I can consider the garden to be a manifestation of art with its own characteristics, with its own personality.

1962

Figure 129. *Baobab (Adansonia digitata* L.) in the Maracaibo Botanical Garden, Venezuela. Photograph: Carla Urbina, 2010.

Figure 130. Collection of Brazilian Art, *Sítio Roberto Burle Marx, Santo Antônio da Bica*, Brazil. Photograph: María A. Villalobos H., 2021.

CONSIDERATIONS ON BRAZILIAN ART

1966

Looking at the artistic production in monuments from Latin American countries gives a clear impression of the influence of indigenous peoples, of their personal way of interpreting and lending their own characteristics to the Baroque that arrived by way of Spain. However, the indigenous cultures already had a social organization and a status that allowed him to develop an artistic tradition in many different spheres: the ceramics of the Aymara and the sculpture from Tiwanaku, dating from centuries before the appearance of the Incas. That creativity can be found, for example, in the *continuum* that runs from abstraction to figuration and vice versa, readily apparent in so many ceremonial vessels.

It is important to note the integration that often takes place in architecture, where sculpture, relief and color come together, like in the constructions and funerary temples built by the Mayan civilization in the Yucatán.

Meanwhile, in Brazil, colonial art can be found in every facet: art from the metropolis, art brought over from Portugal and carried out mainly using local materials and labor that aims to adapt, as best it can, to the necessary techniques. The indigenous peoples in Brazil possessed a more diverse material culture than that of the Andeans. The materials used in their architecture were more fragile and their houses more temporary, due to an economy that was based, above all, on hunting and fishing, with the mechanisms that involved. As a result, although the Brazilian indigenous people possessed and still possess artisanal techniques of rare mastery and beauty through their connection with nature, their inventive participation in colonial constructions was limited.

When Brazil was discovered and is colonization began, the Manueline style was dominant in Portugal: a late Gothic style combined with Romanesque heritage, the deep roots left by Mozarabic culture, and the Eastern influences newly acquired through travel and trade.

The process of *mestizaje* took place practically since the beginning of colonization, forging deep ties between whites, indigenous peoples and *pretos*.

Figure 131. [Top] A convergence of art and architecture in the ceremonial playing field, or *Teotachtli*, representing the *juego de pelota* in the Mayan city of *Chichen Itzá*. In the background is the El Castillo pyramid, known as the Temple of *Kukulcan*, Yucatán, Mexico. Photograph: Carla Urbina, 2019. **Figure 132.** [Center] The Mayan water god *Chaac* is seen here represented in the temples of the Mayan city of *Uxmal*, Yucatán, Mexico. Photograph: Carla Urbina, 2019. **Figure 133.** [Bottom] Kalasasaya Temple, in the archaeological city of Tiahuanaco, located in the state of Tiahuanacota, 15 kilometers southeast of Lake Titicaca, in western Bolivia. Photograph: Pavel Špindler, 2012. Digital version available at: Špindler, 2012.

We will see that the latter left an imprint of great strength and expressivity.

In the fields of music, cuisine, spoken language and religion – which, despite being repressed, has managed to survive until today, as in the case of *candomblé*[51] and *umbanda*[52] – the *pretos* gave Brazilian civilization a contribution of the highest quality. However, the dominant groups prevented the manifestations of their material culture from prospering with the same creative impetus as the other arts that I cited just now. Only later was it possible to corroborate the importance of this fusion, through the work of Alejadinho,[53] Mario de Andrade, Machado de Assis, Cruz e Souza, Agnaldo Manoel dos Santos, Maurino, and Miguel dos Santos, among others.

In Italy, there were marked differences in the characteristics of the artistic production of the time, not only from north to south, but also from one region to another, or from one city to another, despite the limited size of the territory. These differences were the result of the regime of city-states and the need for self-expression, combined with an intense political instability.

Looking at the architecture of colonial Brazil, we immediately see that, despite the immense size of the territory, there is an apparent cultural homogeneity: the artwork from *Pernambuco* does not differ fundamentally from that of other areas, like *Bahia*, *Rio de Janeiro* or *Minas Gerais*.

[51] *Candomblé* is an Afro-Brazilian religion derived from traditional African forms of worship. It is a monotheistic religion that believes in the existence of a *'Supreme Being'* (*Olorum, Mawu* or *Zambi*, depending on the culture), in which the forces of nature are worshipped, personified in the form of deified ancestors: *Orixás, Voduns* or *Consultas*, depending on the country. The Africans who were trafficked as slaves to Brazil came from different places along the African Atlantic coast, from Senegal to Angola, Mozambique, and Madagascar. *"As a result, there was a broad variety of captives with different languages, habits, and beliefs. They had nothing in common but the misfortune of being reduced to slavery, far from their native lands"* (Fatumbi Verger, 2002).

[52] *Umbanda* is a Brazilian religion that combines African, indigenous, and Christian beliefs. This religion was formed at the beginning of the 20th century in the southeast of Brazil and is considered the *"quintessential Brazilian religion"* with a syncretism that combines Catholicism, the tradition of the African *orixás*, and spirits of indigenous origin. On November 8, 2016, *Umbanda* was added to the list of intangible heritage by virtue of a decree based on studies carried out by the Rio Heritage of Humanity Institute (IRPH). (*Prefeitura de Rio de Janeiro*, November 7, 2016).

[53] Antônio Francisco Lisboa (c. 1730 or 1738–1814), known as Aleijadinho, was a sculptor and architect from Brazil's colonial period. His most notable works include the sculptures for the *Santuário de Congonhas*, as well as the church of São Francisco de Assis in *Ouro Preto* and *São João del Rei*, in *Minas Gerais*, Brazil. For more information see: Martins, 1939, p. 179.

Figure 134. [Top] Exterior of the *Casa de Iemanjá, Salvador de Bahia*, Brazil. Photograph: María A. Villalobos H., 2021. **Figure 135.** [Center] interior of the *Casa de Iemanjá*, Salvador de Bahia, Brazil. Photograph: María A. Villalobos H., 2020. **Figure 136.** [Bottom] *Praça dos Orixás, Salvador de Bahia*, Brazil. The landscape project for the *Dique do Tororó* was carried out by José Tabacow and Oscar Bressane. Photograph: María A. Villalobos H., 2020.

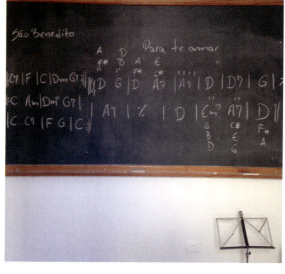

It differs somewhat from the Portuguese models, due to the difficulties with finding skilled workers and the need to adapt local materials both to the tropical environment and to the distance and isolation with respect to the metropolis. In Portugal, the echoes of renewal emerged more slowly. The novelties took even longer to arrive on our shores from countries like France and Italy, and they spread even more slowly across the immense stretches of the territory. This was not only because the colonizers, with all the difficulties they faced, were focused mainly on the essentials, but also because there was little incentive for the exchange of customs and ways of living in the social strata with no prospect of advancing in the short term. The extraordinary thing is that the Baroque and Rococo adapted admirably to the Brazilian landscape.

Figure 137. [Top left] Agnaldo Manoel dos Santos (1926-1962) was an Afro-Brazilian sculptor from the northeast. His work was characterized by its powerful expressivity and by its defense of the traditional African arts. The artist built his own vocabulary by exploring his context and his time. For more information see: Ribeiro da Silva Bevilacqua, 2015, pp. 107-122. Photograph: Oxóossi Caçador. n.d. Wood, Collection of the *Museu de Arte Moderna da Bahia*. **Figure 138.** [Top right] Cruz e Souza (1861-1891) was a Brazilian poet, a precursor of symbolism and known as *Dante Preto*. Among his best-known works are *Broquéis* (1893) and *Missal* (1893). His work is characterized by musicality, individualism, sensualism and an obsession with white, transparency, translucency, haziness, and sheen (Escola, Equipe Brasil, n.d.). Photograph: Santa Catarina Public Library, Florianopolis, Brazil. Digital version available at: *Acervo da Biblioteca Pública de Santa Catarina*, 1958. **Figure 139.** [Bottom left] Mario de Andrade (1893-1945) was a poet, musician, and one of the main ideologues of the modern movement in Brazil. His best-known works include *Paulicéia Desvairada* (1922), *Macunaíma* (1928) and *O Movimento Modernista* (1942). *"At 16, he began studying piano and dedicating his life to music. He began to read about the biographies of musicians, but his interest was already broader: 'I went to every art exhibition, I devoured art history books, I was troubled by a poorly understood aesthetic, I studied writers and the language, and despite my limited wages, I soon bought my first print.' In 1911, he began studying piano at the Conservatory for Theatre and Music and, the following year, he was asked to serve as a teacher's aide for the class on Music Theory."* Hall of musical and poetic education, Casa Mario de Andrade, São Paulo, Brazil. Casa Mário de Andrade, as part of the exhibition *Morada do Coração Perdido*, from the section Music Teacher. (*Poiesis*, n.d.). Photograph: Yasmine Luna, 2016. **Figure 140.** [Bottom right] Maurino Araújo was a 20th-century Brazilian baroque expressionist artist and sculptor from *Minas Gerais*. *"Maurino was born in the mining town of Rio Casca on May 28, 1943, into a family that, as he described it, did everything themselves: 'We planted our food, we built our houses, we made our own tools and everything we needed,' he says. Self-taught, he was a construction worker, a bricklayer's assistant, a shop attendant, and an accountant for construction sites. Under the influence of his grandparents, who were potters, Maurino began working with clay. As a child he moved to Paraná. Away from the clay work, he began drawing; at the school he attended in Paraná, the teacher asked him to draw on the blackboard, fascinated by the student's exceptional talent. In the 1960s, the artist discovered wood and was soon influenced by the Baroque style; he hadn't found the firmness he was looking for in clay. Maurino studied for six years at a Franciscan seminary in São João del-Rei-MG and it was there that he became acquainted with the works of Aleijadinho. Enchanted by the artist's pieces, he began to study them in detail. Nothing escaped his eye: from the expressions to how the wood was cut. The impression was so strong that it remained engraved in his mind for years, with traces of the powerful influence showing up in his work [...]. At the end of the 70s, his work took a turn after he visited Africa: 'It was like something inside me waking up, breaking through, and I began to understand myself better,' the artist said. Today it is easy to see what that 'awakening' did to Maurino's work. We need only look at his work: there, Africa shows through in each cut in the wood"* (Guia das Artes, 2015). Photograph: *Museu Afro Brasil* in *São Paulo*, Brazil, 2008. Available in: Araujo, n.d.

You couldn't imagine the cathedrals of Chartres or Cologne in Brazil: the country is so Baroque that it seems the style originated here.

We see this in the exuberant nature that, nonetheless, does not display the brilliant greens of the gorges of Galicia or the orgy of reds, coppers and oranges of a European autumn, or the gentleness of the landscapes of Umbria. Our green is dark, almost black and, by strange contrast, it joins together with two dominant colors: the yellow of the *cassias* and the *ipês* (which add variety to the chromatic composition) and the purple of the *quaresmeiras*, seemingly intended to create the ritual atmosphere of Easter, repeating the liturgical colors of the services and processions. Along with these unique colors, nature exhibits the pink tones of the *paineiras*, to even out the composition. Colors that can only be explained by this light and this sky, contrasting with the dark, dense green of the surrounding vegetation. In the forms and rhythm of the mountains, of the sierras, we find an *allegro vivace* that contrasts with the more contemplative moments, the *adagios* of the valleys and plains.

The miner artists had a similar understanding of the art of composition: how to create a white wall covered with lime to contrast with the *alizares*[54] made from *pedra-sabão*; how, inside the churches, they were able to create moments of eloquence in the gilded carved wooden altars that reflect light and silence, a pause in the white walls, unlike many Latin American churches, where the vehemence of the ornament leaves no room for rest and completely takes over walls, columns and ceilings.

[54] *Alizares* are used as a type of molding to hide the joints between a wall and a door or window, typical of Brazilian baroque architecture, in this case covered with *esteatito*, commonly known as *pedra-sabão* or soapstone (a type of stone widely used in Brazil). For more information see: Ávila *et al.*, 1996.

Figure 141. [Top left] *Church of Nossa Senhora do Rosario.* Antônio Pereira de Souza Calheros (1785), *Ouro Preto, Minas Gerais*, Brazil. Photograph: Carla Urbina, 2018. **Figure 142.** [Top right] Chartres Cathedral, in France, is considered the pinnacle of Gothic architecture in France. Photograph: Robin Poitou, 2013. **Figure 143.** [Center right] The Cathedral of Cologne, in Germany, is the largest Gothic church in Northern Europe. Photograph: Thomas Wolf, 2017. **Figure 144.** [Bottom left] Church of Matriz do Santíssimo Sacramento de Santo Antônio, *Recife*, Brazil. It sits atop the former trenches built by the Dutch invaders. The church was built between 1752 and 1790. The carvings in the presbytery are noteworthy, in addition to the panels painted by Sebastião da Silva Tavares. The painting and gilding were done by Manuel de Jesús Pinto between 1790 and 1805. For more information, see: Franca, Reubem. *Monumentos do Recife. Recife: Secretaria de Educação e Cultura*, 1977. Photograph: María A. Villalobos H., 2020. **Figure 145.** [Bottom right] Church and Convent of São Francisco, 18th century, *Salvador de Bahia*, Brazil. Located in front of the *Largo do Cruzeiro*, the church appears austere from the outside but is exuberant on the inside. The exteriors are made of limestone and the interiors are made of *arenisca* (sandstone). For more information, see: Bethell, Leslie. *Historia de América Latina: América Latina Colonial.* EdUSP, 1999, vol. II, p. 686. Photograph: María A. Villalobos H., 2020.

Figure 146. [Top] Lugnano in Teverina, Umbria, Italy. Photograph: Marcella Del Signore, 2020. For more information on the work of architect and urban planner Del Signore, see: Data, Matter, Design: *Strategies in Computational Design*. New York: Routledge, 2020. **Figure 147.** [Center] Autumn landscape in the *Dahlem* Botanical Garden, Berlin, Germany. Photograph: María A. Villalobos H., 2014. **Figure 148.** [Bottom] Bright green gorges in Galicia,

Spain. Photograph: Adrián Capelo Cruz, 2019. **Figure 149.** [Top] *Allegro vivace* in the forms of the *Serra dos Órgãos, Teresópolis-Petrópolis*, in the state of *Rio de Janeiro*, Brazil. Photograph: Carla Urbina, 2018. **Figure 150.** [Bottom] *Adagio*, the landscape as a gentle, contemplative movement in the plains of the *Chapada do Araripe*, Ceará, Brazil. Photograph: Carla Urbina, 2018.

Figure 151. [Top] Vivid combinations of dark greens and golden yellows in the *Serra do Petrópolis*, *Rio de Janeiro*, Brazil. Photograph: María A. Villalobos H., 2021. **Figure 152.** [Bottom] Association of golden flowering trees in the *Praça dos Cristais* in *Brasília*, designed by Roberto Burle Marx and collaborators, and inaugurated in 1970. Photograph: María A. Villalobos H., 2021. **Figure 153.** [Opposite page, top] Vivid combinations of dark greens, pinks, and purples in the *Serra do*

Petrópolis, Rio de Janeiro, Brazil. Photograph: María A. Villalobos H., 2021. **Figure 154.** [Center] *Ceiba speciosa* (A. St-Hil, A. Juss. & Cambess). Ravenna, Samambaia Institute of Environmental Sciences and Ecotourism, *Petrópolis, Rio de Janeiro*, Brazil. Gardens built by Roberto Burle Marx and collaborators in 1948. Photograph: María A. Villalobos H., 2021. **Figure 155.** [Bottom] *Tabebuias* and *Cuaresmeiras*, Maracaibo Botanical Garden, Venezuela. Photograph: Carla Urbina, 2012.

They even left us the exteriors of some churches, carefully designed and well proportioned; some with well-structured features, as seen in the production of Antonio Francisco Lisboa *"Aleijadinho"*, a rich, complex, and compelling work that results in entirely new elements in the chapel of the *Ordem Terceira de São Francisco* and that reaches its maximum expression in the church of *São Francisco de Assis*, one of the most flawless monuments from the colonial period.

The urban development in *Ouro Preto* is visually exquisite because of how the adaptation of its streets, the local topography, and its evenly distributed churches, certain forms of trees, such as the *Pinheiro de Paraná*,[55] for example, become an important element in the baroque composition.

In the extraordinary ensemble of *Bom Jesús de Matosinhos*, in Congonhas do Campo, Aleijadinho built the architecture and integrated the structural group of the prophets in the composition, through clearly defined planes. Thus, as we approach, it creates a play between volumes that contrast and relate to one another and with the body of the church. Here, it might be said that he takes on the quality of a primitive artist because, in the creation of these sculptures, he returns to the roots of the Gothic style, to the influence of prints from 1470 that he had probably seen and which, for their part, reflected the influence of German art.

It is curious how the imperial palm tree,[56] a new element, imported in 1808 by Dom João VI, seems specifically designed to complement Baroque architecture. The *Carmo*, from *São João del Rei*, illustrates this for us: in front of the church, a group of palm trees connects the construction with humanity, through the landscape; the ancient hues of the trunks

[55] The *Pinheiro de Paraná* is the common name in Brazil for the species *Araucaria angustifolia* (Bertol.) Kuntze, Araucariaceae family, which is known in other Latin American countries as the *pino misionero, pino candelabro* or *curí*. This species is native to Brazil and is in danger of extinction (EN) (IUCN, 2021).

[56] The imperial palm is the common name for the species *Roystonea oleracea* (Jacq.) O.F.Cook (Areacaceae family). In Brazil, the first specimen, brought from Mauritius, was planted in the *Rio de Janeiro* Botanical Garden by Don João VI in 1809, the origin for its common name in Brazil (*Jardim Botânico do Rio de Janeiro*, n.d.). It is known in other Latin American countries as "*chaguaramo*" or "*palma real*". It is listed as "near threatened" (NT) (IUCN, 2021).

Figure 156. [Top] Sculptures of prophets in the *Bom Jesús de Matosinhos* complex, created by Aleijadinho. Photograph: Carla Urbina, 2021. **Figure 157.** [Center left] Imperial palm trees used by Burle Marx on the path to the Capilla de *Santo Antônio, Sítio Roberto Burle Marx, Santo Antônio da Bica*, Brazil. Photograph: María A. Villalobos H., 2021. **Figure 158.** [Center] The imperial palm tree as part of the Brazilian Baroque landscape, in the *Sántuario do Bom Jesús de Matosinhos*, in *Congonhas*, Brazil. Photograph: Carla Urbina, 2021. **Figure 159.** [Center right] *Sántuario Diocesano do Bom Jesús de Matosinhos* and sculptures of prophets. Photograph: Marcel, Gautherot, c. 1947-1957. Archive of the *Instituto Moreira Salles*. Digital version available at: *Instituto Moreira Salles*, n.d. **Figure 160.** [Bottom] Roberto Burle Marx and Luciano Amédée Peret working on the restoration of the *Santuário de Bom Jesus de Matosinhos*, in *Congonhas do Campo, Minas Gerais*, 1973-74. Photograph: Assis Alves, 1973-1974.

of the palm trees combine admirably with the pilasters and the portal made from *pedra-sabão*, which has gray and dark bluish tones, in contrast to the ocher tones of the sandstone.

Unfortunately, the state of their conservation is poor: the incomprehension on the part of a large number of administrators, who think they can solve the problems in a garden by painting the bases of the trees, is an evil that Brazil inevitably suffers from.

In *Congonhas do Campo*, for example, a spurious construction was built off to one side of the magnificent baroque architectural ensemble, distorting the value of the monument in the landscape and Aleijadinho's intention: for his statues to be seen against the blue sky, full of fat, plump, fluffy clouds. That *"ballet of statues"*, as Germain Bazin calls it, when lit by the last rays of the setting sun, transmits its message of intense poetic and rhythmic emotion. They say that an administrator hoped to build a bandstand there, an absurdity only possible in Brazil.

And yet, this is a country where 20th-century man coexists with the Stone Age: we went from the ox cart to the automobile and the airplane, without the mediations of the European tradition. We were isolated from the rest of the world for many years, but it was in that isolation, in that apparent calm, that the clash between cultures and the fusion of races took place. The result was a unique way of living, feeling, and thinking. In view of this, visual artists must take their vocabulary from the observation of human fauna, their habits, customs, and contradictions, situating them and relating them to nature and to the landscape, onto which they imprint their own character and shape them so that, through their own personal vision, their own way of expression, they can convey their message of poetic emotion.

That does not mean simply borrowing certain elements from folklore, believing that it will result in art with a national expression. That would offer just an *'appearance'* because the content would be divorced from the worldview. Instead, we need to look at the foundations of popular culture, to use that vocabulary to recreate a new syntax, a new language.

Figure 161. [Top] Path towards the entrance of the Capilla de *Santo Antônio, Sítio Roberto Burle Marx, Santo Antônio da Bica,* Brazil. Photograph: Carla Urbina, 2014. **Figure 162.** [Center] *Parque do Flamengo, Rio de Janeiro,* Brazil. Photograph: Carla Urbina, 2018. **Figure 163.** [Bottom] *Sántuario do Bom Jesus de Matosinhos. "Ballet of statues"* at sunset. Photograph: María A. Villalobos H., 2021.

Figure 164. [Top] João Guimarães Rosa (1908-1967) was a Brazilian novelist who was a member of the Brazilian Academy of Letters. Guimarães Rosa's work highlights popular phonetic and semantic systems. Guimarães Rosa paid special attention to the landscape of the Brazilian *sertão* region. This is how Guimarães Rosa described it in his *Biografía Irracional*: "*I miss the people who respond to the wind; I miss the generals. You'll see: the wind that blows through the fronds of the buritis palms when there is the threat of a storm. How could anyone forget that? The wind is green. Then, in a lull, you take the silence and put it in your lap*" (Guimarães, 2001, p. 306). The image of the *Grande Sertão Veredas* National Park, *Minas Gerais*, Brazil, evokes Guimarães Rosa's literary landscape. Photograph: Rodrigo Guimarães, 2021. Digital version available at: Guimarães, n.d. **Figure 165.** [Bottom] Heitor Villa-Lobos (1887-1959) was the most important Brazilian composer of the 20th century. March 5, the date of Villa-Lobos's birth, is celebrated in Brazil as National Classical Music Day. Villa-Lobos's music embraces the origins of Brazilian regional cultures, using sounds from nature and elements of popular and indigenous songs. For more information, see: Wright, 1992. The photograph shows a moment from the homage to Heitor Villa-Lobos held at City Hall in Caracas, Venezuela, 1953. Photograph: Archive of the *Museu Villa-Lobos*. Digital version available at: *Portal do Museu Villa-Lobos*, n.d.

It's no different from the experience of some Brazilian artists, like Guimarães Rosa who, observing and studying the speech of the inhabitants of the interior, its correspondence with certain moods and with the surrounding landscape, created a work of universal value. The experience of a Villa-lobos, who finds his inspiration in popular music, is the same. And so, many others, each in their own field, aimed to find the path that would lead to a new, unique, national language.

In my work as an artist, in the field of landscape architecture, I try to create a vocabulary based on the extremely rich Brazilian flora, its infinite variety, introducing native species into gardens; studying ecological associations with passion and constancy; observing the natural landscape and fighting for the preservation of that heritage that is being ruthlessly destroyed by burning and other even more terrifying methods. The few reserves of plant life are decimated, along with the cities, by hasty subdivisions and urban developments, where the land is completely razed to later plant exotic trees, giving the whole, in the vast majority of cases, the appearance of a cemetery for the living.

At a time when city-dwellers are squeezed in and suffocated in their homes, where the order is determined by a standard of minimums, there is a need to create large open spaces where people can breathe, get in touch with nature, have the opportunity to meditate, to contemplate a flower or the form of a plant in a peaceful place, where young people can have the pleasure of enjoying sports and life in the open air without worry. That means creating gardens with their own expressions, like a work of art, but which also satisfy the need for contact with nature, which is increasingly unfulfilled by the lives we lead in a technological civilization.

Still, the work does not end there. We have to fight against greed and the desire for immediate profit, to preserve the flora, the vegetation – in short, what remains of the magnificent heritage that we should be leaving as a legacy to the coming generations."

Thus, we need to understand the past and learn the fundamental values of the present, to situate ourselves within it and become aware of the meaning of tradition. Fight for the preservation of creative expression in all fields of knowledge and human activity, seeking out a language of our own that reflects all our desires for a better, more balanced life where we can grow together, while encapsulating the feeling of contemporaneity, which lends value to art as a contribution to universal culture: that is the work of the Brazilian artist.

Alongside the sophistication of technology like electricity, the automobile, the airplane, and going to the moon, there is the threat of nuclear power, the threat of the disintegration of nature and, with it, that of man.

We are witnesses to the minimal, tragic lives of the poor lost in the hardship of daily life, which rapidly leads toward an anonymous death. And it is compelling to see how, even in such adverse conditions, many men and women still seek out communication expressed through a desire for beauty, and they create order in matter, they organize their own aesthetic parameters, they stand up for creation and against agglomeration, with their revelations of form and a new worldview. Faced with this dramatic, limited horizon, it is imperative to find a space, an opening for man, for the children of man, for the generations to come. Artists must find the courage to accept and live with the anxiety of their time and understand it in all its manifestations, without forgetting joy and fulfilment, however rare they may be.

Through gardens, through Brazilian flora, I experiment with building a space for breath and for reflection; I find a way to resemble those who look for greater possibilities for balance in life or, at least, a willingness to pursue that end.

An ordered garden in today's urban spaces is an invitation to coexistence, to return to the real time of the nature of things, in contrast to the deceptive speed of the rules of consumer society.

Gardens can and should be a means of raising awareness of an existence in the true measure of man, of what it means to be alive. They are an example of the peaceful coexistence of various species, a place for respecting nature and respecting others, respecting difference: in short, the garden is an instrument of pleasure and a means of education.

In a predatory society like ours, devoid of resources, gardens, collective spaces, invite individuals to preserve what belongs to us all.

Out of solidarity for the daily suffering of so many, it is essential for me to open a space for greenery, areas where anyone can get out from under the weight of our times, by searching for or finding a bit of our lost paradise.

April 1966

Figure 166. *Praça da República* renovated by Roberto Burle Marx, *Recife*, Brazil. In 1937, Roberto Burle Marx maintained the imperial palms and incorporated new types of palms. Photograph: María A. Villalobos H., 2021.

Figure 167. Composition of usnea, bromeliads and orchids at the *Sítio Roberto Burle Marx, Santo Antônio da Bica* Brazil. Photograph: María A. Villalobos H., 2021.

GARDEN AND ECOLOGY 1967

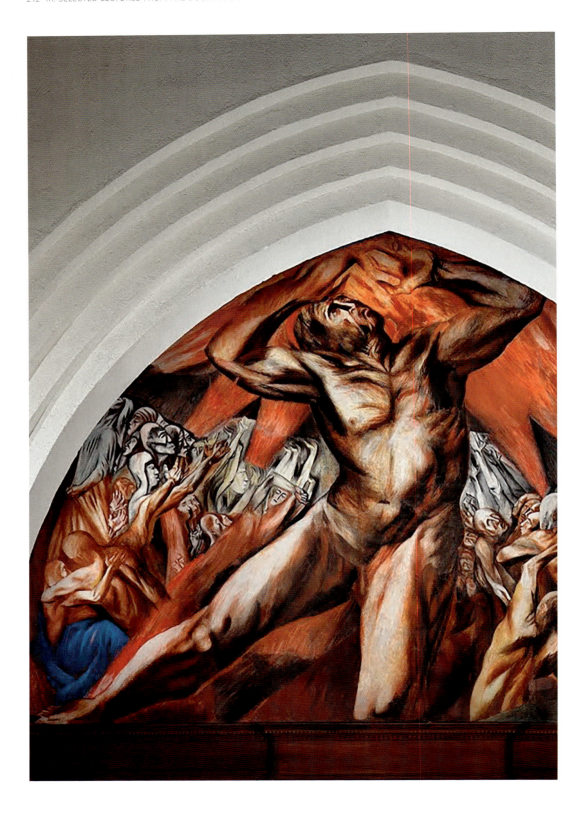

Creationists and non-creationists, whatever their philosophical differences, can fully agree that creation or the beginning of life did not occur in a single act, but in successive stages. The book of Genesis explains the acts of creation in detail: first the earth, then the separation of the waters and, later, the creation of plants, animals and human being. On the other hand, science has shown that plants, through photosynthesis, create the conditions for the continuity of the evolutionary process and they alter the composition of the Earth's atmosphere, just as they enact Prometheus' dream, capturing the energy of sunlight and permitting the appearance of insects, birds, mammals, human being and the higher plants, with their wealth of shapes, colors, and structure. It is through them that life, the phenomenon of reproduction, is transmitted, directing a spectacle of riches that culminates in their blooming. It cannot be overemphasized that the Earth's atmosphere, with 21% oxygen, is a requisite for life, maintained and kept in balance by the activity of plants, particularly algae.

Figure 168. *Prometeo* is a mural by the Mexican painter José Clemente Orozco, located in the cafeteria of *Pomona College* in Southern California. It was painted in 1930 as a metaphor for the challenges faced by those seeking to expand their knowledge. Orozco's *Prometeo* steals fire from the gods to give it to humans. Photograph: Fredrik Nilsen (Nilsen, n.d.).

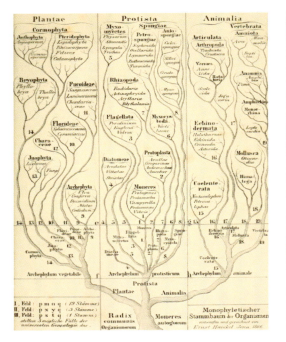 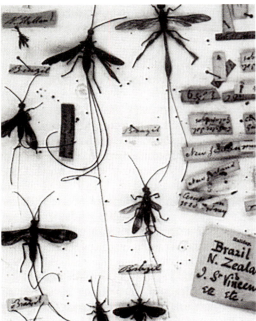

Plants are our object. And how do we understand plants? On the one hand, a plant is a living being that obeys a determinism conditioned by the laws of growth, physiology, biophysics, and biochemistry. On the other hand, any plant is the result of a long historical process that incorporates, in its present state, all the experiences of a long line of ascendants in which those indistinct first beings are lost to time. This perfection of shapes, colors, rhythm, structures, puts them in another type of category: the level of aesthetic beings, which makes them a mystery to us. Plants have the property of being unstable. They are alive, and as such they change. They undergo constant mutation, a permanent imbalance, the purpose of which the search for a new balance. As we deepen our knowledge of plants, the field of the unknown grows almost exponentially larger. Learning reveals even greater mysteries. The more questions we answer, the more *"whys"* and *"what fors"* we accumulate. As an example, I remember a spectacle I witnessed in the middle of the *Caatinga*, in the northeast of Brazil. At a certain time of night, over a large area, all the *Cereus jamacaru* DC. (*mandacaru*), opened their large white flowers as if to the rhythm of a metronome. In the moonlight, the multi-petalled corollas opened, exposing their throats, into which a swarm of insects were drawn. Seeing them reminded me of the movements of sea anemones and I couldn't help thinking

Figure 169. [Left] Haeckel, Ernst, 1834-1919. *Monophyletisher Stammbaum der Organismen (Taf I)* in *Generelle morphologie der organismen. Allgemeine grundzüge der organischen formen-wissenschaft, mechanisch begründet durch die von Charles Darwin reformirte descendenztheorie*. Berlin, G. Reimer, 1866. MBLWHOI Library. Digital version available at: Haeckel, 1866, p. 463. **Figure 170.** [Right] Hymenopteran pollinators on display in *"Box 73"* as part of the Haliday Collection at the National Museum of Ireland, Dublin. Darwin's specimens include *Hymenoptera* from the

about the intangible reasons for that strange coincidence. Plants, like colors, are enriched with meaning when they are contrasted with another color or another plant. In nature, associations don't happen by chance. They respond to the compatibilities that depend on a complex series of factors including the climate, the soil, and the interactions between plants and animals and among the different plants themselves. Ecologists call these defined groupings *"associations"*.

The phenomenon of association is closely linked to one of the most fascinating biological phenomena: adaptation. It would be impossible to address a subject as vast and profound as that of adaptation in just a few pages. However, I admit that we should at least briefly discuss mutual adaptation, which is so popular with modern biologists and students of evolution, showing the simultaneous and associated development of flowers and pollinating insects.

At the beginning of the Mesozoic era, the first flowering plants were pollinated by slow, *"clumsy"* insects like beetles. The evolution of flowers to the bilateral state (as in orchids) or asymmetrical state (as in reeds) is accompanied by the appearance of improved, more agile insects (butterflies and Hymenoptera). Not to mention the advent of that utmost refinement: pollination by hummingbirds.

subfamily Braconinae (from Brazil and the Galápagos Islands) and *Diptera* (*Chloropidae* and *Agromyzidae*) (from New Zealand). Available in: Smith, 1987, p. 33. **Figure 171.** [Top left] *Cereus jamacaru DC.* Photograph: Danilo Alvarenga Zavatin, 2017. Inaturalist. Available in: Alvarenga Zavatin, 2017. **Figure 172.** [Bottom left] Anemones (*Actinothoe sphyrodeta* (*Gosse, 1858*)). Photograph: Bernard Picton, 2013. Inaturalist United Kingdom. Available in: Pickton, 2013. **Figure 173.** [Right] *Cereus hildmannianus* K. Schum. Barcelona Botanical Garden, Spain. Photograph: Carla Urbina, 2015.

No region on the Earth's surface is richer in plant associations than the tropical zone. This impression is even greater and more stunning for people from temperate countries in their first contact with the tropics. The astonishment caused by this raucous world of activity, heat, and life, changed the lives of many naturalists during the period of great revelations, such as Martius, Saint-Hilaire, Gardner, Prince Wied-Neuvied, and others.[57] Today the richness of the flora of the tropical zones is still such that, speaking from my own experience, I can say that I have never made an excursion in which I failed to find or collect plants unknown both to me and to science. In consequence, it is clear that gardens should have an ecological foundation, especially in a country like Brazil, with extraordinarily varied conditions. Anyone wishing to study a simple problem like planting crops or the domestication of wild plants will

Figure 174. [Left] Scientific illustration of the life of pollinating insects. The watercolor by María Sibylla Merian shows a *Heliconia acuminata* A.Rich. in association with the life cycle of the *Southern Armyworm Moth* and two unidentified insects. A version of print number 54 published in Merian's book: *Metamorphosis Insectorum Surinamensium*. Royal Collection. Available in: Merian, 1702-03. **Figure 175.** [Top right] Live insect in the Professor Mello Barreto Nature Education Park, *Rio de Janeiro*, Brazil. The park was designed by the landscape architect Fernando Chacel. Photograph: María A. Villalobos H., 2021. **Figure 176.** [Bottom right] Live insects in the *Dois Irmãos* Municipal Natural Park, *Rio de Janeiro*, Brazil. The park was created in 1992 by the architect Sérgio

find a field that is little developed and, in some respects, unexplored.

In Brazil, landscape architects have the freedom to build gardens based on a floristic reality of abundant richness. While respecting the requirements of ecological and aesthetic compatibility, they can create enormously expressive artificial associations. Creating artificial landscapes does not mean either rejecting or subserviently imitating nature. It means knowing how to transpose and associate the results of a slow, intense, and prolonged observation, by implementing a selective, personal criterion.

[87] To learn more about traveler botanists and the influence they had on the work of Roberto Burle Marx, see the lecture "The Involvement of Botanists in My Professional Training" from 1983, in Part Three of this book.

Bernardes and the landscape architect Fernando Chacel, who worked alongside Roberto Burle Marx and was considered by many to be his successor. For more information, see the article by Estêvão Bertoni, "*Fernando Chacel (1931-2011) - Paisagista sucessor de Burle Marx*", in *Folha de São Paulo*. Available in: Bertoni, 2011. Photograph: María A. Villalobos H., 2021. **Figure 177.** [Left] Live butterfly camouflaged in the flora of the *Dois Irmãos* Municipal Natural Park, *Rio de Janeiro*, Brazil. Photograph: María A. Villalobos H., 2021. **Figure 178.** [Right] Live insect from the Coenagrionidae family in the *Rio de Janeiro* Botanical Garden, Brazil. Photograph: María A. Villalobos H., 2021.

From my personal experience, I still remember everything I have learned from the time I have shared with botanists, and I consider those collaborations to be fundamental. Anyone wishing to practice conscious and profound landscape design should take advantage of the immense heritage of the exuberant Brazilian flora, which has been so poorly understood by landscape designers and garden lovers.

Although there are nearly 5,000 tree species within an array made up of some 50,000 different flora species, our gardens offer, above all, a domesticated and cosmopolitan flora and our streets are often planted with exotic species, such as *platanus*,[58] *ligustrum*,[59] etc. I reject this concept of landscaping and have fought against certain forms of urbanization in which the natural landscape is totally destroyed in order to immediately create a plant composition using species that are alien to the local landscape reality. What is destroyed is the magnum opus, the state of equilibrium in an activity that has gone on for millions of years carried out by the forces of nature.

Our conceptions and experiences are the result of a long process of interpreting and

---

[58] *Platanus*, genus of the Platanaceae family. Distribution: North and Central America, Mediterranean, Central Asia and Western Himalayas, Indochinese Peninsula. For more information, see: Hassler, Michel, 2004-2021. *Platanus*. World Plants. Synonymic Checklist and Distribution of the World Flora (Hassler, Platanus L., 2021).

[59] *Ligustrum*, genus of the Oleaceae family. Global distribution. For more information, see: Govaerts, R. (ed.), 2021. *Eup Ligustrum*. WCSP: World Checklist of Selected Plant Families (version Aug 2017). Catalogue of Life, *et al.* (2021). Species 2000 & ITIS Catalogue of Life, 2021-04-05 (Govaerts, Ligustrum, 2021).

understanding natural associations. From among my experiences, I could cite my observations on the flora of the canga a conglomerate of iron-rich material that makes up the soil of vast areas of central Brazil. Climbing the mountains, after passing through fields of grass, I came upon a grayish patch of rocks, and as I drew nearer, I discovered a world entirely new to me: an extraordinary association of plants that seem created to coexist with one another, the vivid cadmium yellow of the lichens and the *Laelia flava* Lindl. contrasting with the dark purple of the *quaresmeiras*, harmonizing with the Venetian red of the back side of the leaves of the *Mimosa calodendron* Mart., a plant that is remarkable for the defensive movements of its leaves. All that mix of colors stands out against a background in which shapes, rhythms, and colors act together to highlight, in each season, a particular kind of bloom.

This instability is precisely one of the great secrets of nature: it never bores us, and is constantly changing with the effects of light, rain, wind, and shadows, which generate new forms. I would also like to mention the epilithic flora on the limestone outcroppings where the rocks are characterized by prominent stratification: a rich biogenic

Figure 179. [Opposite page] Vivid combinations of dark greens and purples at the *Praia do Pontal*, Paraty, Brazil. Photograph: María A. Villalobos H., 2021. **Figure 180.** [Top left] Golden blooms in the *Praça do Derby*, Recife, Brazil. Photograph: María A. Villalobos H., 2021. **Figure 181.** [Bottom left] Purple blooms, *Goiás*, Brazil. Photograph: Carla Urbina, 2018. **Figure 182.** [Right] Contrast of yellows and purples in *Praça do Derby*, Recife, which was renovated by Roberto Burle Marx in 1936. For more information see Municipality of Recife, Decree No. 29,537, March 23, 2016, Recife, Brazil. Available in: *Diario Oficial Prefeitura do Recife*, 2016. Photograph: María A. Villalobos H., 2021.

220 III. SELECTED LECTURES FROM THE BOOK *ARTE & PAISAGEM: CONFERÊNCIAS ESCOLHIDAS*

sediment accumulates in the cracks, and roots dig down in search of the nutrients concentrated there. The panorama is characterized by groups or communities of palm trees (*Acrocomia aculeata* (Jacq.) Lodd. ex Mart.) and by the *Ficus calcícola* with its intertwined roots and its special ability to envelop and overlie different types of supports, whether they are rocks, trees, or palm trees.

I visited regions of rare beauty, such as the *Vale do Rio Pancas*, which was still home to indigenous tribes 30 years ago. The region is a valley, enclosed by conical-shaped mountains arranged like stage in a theatre on whose slopes lives a flora that is entirely *sui generis*, with *vellózias, bombax, orchids, meriânias, mandevilas, alamandas*, etc. From these heights, it is possible to look down at the winding courses of the rivers, fed by the runoff from the slopes.

It is a pity that these primary formations are not given the protection that is afforded to a sanctuary, and they are gradually being destroyed at the hands of local people, who fail to understand that they are treasures, and by European immigrants, who are transplanted but do not adapt, and whose standards of beauty, are imported from their native lands.

I also want to offer my testimony about one of the most impressive plant formations in Tropical America: the *buritizal*. The *buriti* (*Mauritia vinifera* Mart.) is the largest of the palm trees of the Brazilian flora, and its trunk can grow to a height of 50 meters. It grows in groups of hundreds or thousands of individuals, gathered in damp or flooded depressions. There are few examples of excessive efforts toward the perpetuation of the species as violent as the immense clusters, a few meters long, that produce thousands of copper-colored fruits with a scaly covering.

Figure 183. [Top left] *Merianthera burle marxii* in the *Vale de Pancas, Espírito Santo*, Brazil. Photograph: Oscar Bressane, 2013. **Figure 184.** [Top right] *Alamandas* at the *Sítio Roberto Burle Marx, Santo Antônio da Bica*, Brazil. Photograph: María A. Villalobos H., 2021. **Figure 185.** [Center left] *Brassavola nodosa* (L.) Lindl, in the Maracaibo Botanical Garden, Venezuela. Photograph: Carla Urbina, 2014. **Figure 186.** [Center right] Trunk of a tree from the *Bombax* genus, known as the ceiba in Venezuela and in the rest of Latin America, located in the Professor Mello Barreto Nature Education Park, *Rio de Janeiro*, Brazil. Photograph: María A. Villalobos H., 2021. **Figure 187.** [Bottom left] *Brassavola nodosa* (L.) Lindl., the orchid known in Venezuela as the *dama de la noche*. Photograph: Marcos Vinicio Antonio Villalobos H., 2017. **Figure 188.** [Bottom right] *Vellozia* gardenat the *Sítio Roberto Burle Marx, Santo Antônio da Bica*, Brazil. Photograph: María A. Villalobos H., 2021.

Figure 189. [Opposite page] Canaima Lagoon, Moriche palms *Mauritia flexuosa* L.f. (synonym of the *Mauritia vinifera* Mart.), Canaima National Park, Venezuela. Photograph: Carla Urbina, 2010. **Figure 190.** [Center left] Parque Burle Marx, *São Paulo*, Brazil. Photograph: Carla Urbina, 2014. **Figure 191.** [Center right] *Sítio Roberto Burle Marx*, Santo Antônio da Bica, Brazil. Photograph: María A. Villalobos H., 2021. **Figure 192.** [Bottom] *Plaza de las Fuentes* in the *Parque da Cidade* in *Brasilia*, Brazil. Photograph: María A. Villalobos H., 2021.

Figure 193. [Top] *Buritizal, "jalapão" Tocantins*, Regional Park, Brazil. Photograph: Ronaldo Vieira de Carvalho, 2017. Available in: Vieira de Carvalho, 2017. **Figure 194.** [Center left] Ministry of Justice and Public Security, *Brasília*, Brazil. Photograph: María A. Villalobos H., 2021. **Figure 195.** [Center right] 308 South, model superblock in *Brasília*, Brazil. Photograph: María A. Villalobos H., 2021. **Figure 196.** [Bottom] *Parque do Flamengo, Rio de Janeiro*, Brazil. Photograph: María A. Villalobos H., 2021.

Figure 197. [Bottom] Original sketch of the phylogenetic layout for the Maracaibo Botanical Garden, Maracaibo, Venezuela, from the archive of the *Instituto Roberto Burle Marx*. Photograph: María A. Villalobos H., 2012.

Figure 198. [Opposite page top, center, and current page] Restoration of the Arecidae section from the phylogenetic layout for the Botanical Garden of Maracaibo, Venezuela. Photographs: Trisgel Labrador, 2016.

Figure 199. Group of palm trees in the *Praça dos Cristais, Brasília*, Brazil. This public space was designed by Roberto Burle Marx and collaborators and inaugurated in 1970. Photograph: María A. Villalobos H., 2021.

Here and there, a pair of macaws, with their showy plumage, crosses the landscape looking to perch among the leaves. The form of propagation of this palm tree, whose fruits are carried by water, means that it grows in rows, sometimes in straight lines, and it follows the paths of rivers.

Rounding out the panorama of the *buritizal*, other delicate plants appear throughout, such as the *buritirana*, a palm tree that is a miniaturized replica of the *buriti* and the *Urospatha*, araceae with sagittate leaves and inflorescences with a spiral form that looks more like a baroque decoration.

Plants live in resonance with the environment, and there is a correspondence between the conditions of the niches they occupy and their requirements for birth, growth, and reproduction.

Plant life is a cyclical activity with pauses marked by death and germination, made crystal clear in the case of annuals and monocarpic plants, like the immensely beautiful *Corypha umbraculifera* L.[60] that waits 50 years to produce a spectacular bloom.

Aside from the more global action on a region, the climate is subdivided and diversified into a series of microclimates resulting from various factors – topography, soil, altitude, etc. – which may have serious importance from the standpoint of a garden.

In truth, many times building a garden entails *"creating"* microclimates, balancing them, always maintaining the conception that, in these associations, the plants are placed side by side almost in a relationship of necessity.

The value of each plant in the composition, like the value of color in painting, is always relative. The plant has value in the contrast or harmony it generates with the other plants it relates to.

Regarding the problem of microclimates, I remember a region where I was able to make observations

The *Corypha umbraculifera* L. is a monocarpic species (it only bears fruit once in its life), with pale yellow terminal inflorescence (which can reach more than 3 meters in height). Its leaves are fan-shaped. The inflorescence is racemose and produces minute flowers with thin anthers, which do not reveal traces of pollen grains. When the *Coryphas* near the Rio Botanical Garden bloomed in 1981, between 23 and 26 clusters were reported in the process of producing fruit (Toledo Rizzini & de Mattos Filho, 1984). The *Coryphas* collected, planned, and planted by the landscaper in the *Parque do Flamengo* in *Rio de Janeiro* in the 1960s bloomed 50 years later, in 2019. The Director of the *Instituto Burle Marx*, Isabela Ono, said in an interview conducted with Globo (2019) that, although the *Coryphas* are native to southern India, they do not know with certainty on which expedition or trip they were collected (Ono, 2019). The head of the Technical Division at the *Sítio Roberto Burle Marx*, Marlon da Costa Souza, reported in an interview with the newspaper *Estadão* in 2019 that, 20 years earlier, other specimens had bloomed at the *Sítio* and in the *Parque do Flamengo* itself, where Burle Marx had planted them (Jansen, 2019). The exceptional moment of flowering offers everyone in person and the international community (through different media) the opportunity to appreciate the *unstable permanence* of nature and to experience it with a special intensity. Today, hundreds of germinating seeds lie under the growing palms. Those plants could be collected, propagated, and replanted, in order to provide favorable conditions for the development of the plant's life cycle.

Figure 200. [All] *Corypha umbraculifera* L. flowering in 2019, located on pedestrian walkways in the *Parque do Flamengo*, *Rio de Janeiro*, Brazil. Photographs: María A. Villalobos H., 2021.

Figure 201. *Corypha umbraculifera* L. at the *Sítio Roberto Burle Marx, Santo Antônio da Bica*, Brazil. Photograph: Marlon de Souza and Caetano Troncoso, 2019.

Figure 202. [Top] Sequence from a study of botanical provinces which shows how the reflection on microclimatic relationships translates into the landscape design for the Maracaibo Botanical Garden, Venezuela. Illustration: *Botanical City*, 2015. **Figure 203.** [Bottom] Plant contrasts in the lagoon area of the *Sítio Roberto Burle Marx, Santo Antônio da Bica*, Brazil. Photograph: Carla Urbina, 2014.

that were central to my understanding. I am referring to the *Serra do Cipó*, about 100 kilometers from *Belo Horizonte*, in *Minas Gerais*, where the flora is mainly determined by the soil that is rich in quartzite and sandstone.

Making that trip implies walking from microclimate to microclimate, from one surprise to the next. Under these conditions, there are plants that are altered to such an extent by the action of common environmental forces, that plants from families that are extremely distant in phylogenetic terms show a marked resemblance in their external appearance. This is the case of the *Sipolisia*[61] which look like *Vellozia*,[62] *Eryngium*, in the form of a bromeliad and *Lychnophora*[63] which also look like Velloziaceae. Likewise, in other parts of Brazil (the *Cabo Frio* region, characterized by its intense wind that always blows in the same direction) the effect of the wind is visible on the plants. In sheltered depressions, the trees can thrive to the fullest, and, in this microclimate, the accumulation of biogenic debris and a greater retention of moisture supports an unexpected world of orchids, lichens and epiphytes that, although dependent on humidity, can't survive an excess of it on their roots. At the highest elevations we find a peculiar community of plants, the nebular flora, marked by low trees, with multiple branches and small leaves, with an unprecedented wealth of epiphytes and corticulous lichens, in intense colors, that combine with red flowers like the *Sophronitis*.[64] The *Usneas*[65] form undulating strings. It's an otherworldly landscape. There, either the plants are blurred and disappear into the mist, or they emerge in all their fullness, as the light enhances the various layers where the blooms follow one after the other.

[61] *Sipolisia lanuginosa* Glaz. ex Oliv. is a genus of the Asteraceae family, native to southeastern Brazil. For more information, see: Hassler, Michel, 2004-2021. *Sipolisia* Glaz. ex Oliv, Plants. Synonymic Checklist and Distribution of the World Flora (Hassler, Sipolisia Glaz. ex Oliv., 2021).

[62] *Vellozia*, a genus of herbaceous plants in the Velloziaceae family (Govaerts, Vellozia, 2021). Species endemic to South America. Its habitat is rocky fields (Embrapa, n.d.).

[63] *Lychnophora*, genus of the Asteraceae family. For more information, see: Monge, M.; Semir, J. (*in memoriam*); Loeuille, B.F.P. 2020. *Lychnophora* in Flora do Brasil 2020. *Jardim Botânico do Rio de Janeiro* (Reflora: Jardím Botânico do Rio de Janeiro, 2020).

[64] *Sophronitis* are a genus of orchids with very striking colors distributed in dry areas, mountains, and cloud forests of Brazil (American Orchid Society, 2019).

[65] *Usnea* is a genus of the Fungi kingdom, in the Parmeliaceae family. For more information, see: Kirk P. M. (ed.) (2021). Species Fungorum Plus: Species Fungorum for CoL+ (version Feb. 2020). In: Catalogue of Life, *et al.* (2021). Species 2000 & ITIS Catalogue of Life, 2021-04-05 (Kirk, 2021). Lichen species such as *Usnea barbata*, a synonym for *Usnea articulata* (L.) Hoffm., commonly known as *"old man's beard"* due to its characteristic form of thin hanging threads.

Figure 204. [Top left] *Heterocoma ekmaniana* (Philipson) Loeuille, J. N. Nakaj. & Semir in *Goiás*, Brazil. Photograph: Rodolph Delfino Sartin, 2016. **Figure 205.** [Top right] *Lychnophora* in *Palmeiras, Bahia*, Brazil. Photograph: Matt Lavin, 2014 (Lavin, 2014). **Figure 206.** [Bottom left] Orchid *Sophronitis. Cattleya* sp., Rio de Janeiro Botanical Garden, Brazil. Photograph: Carla Urbina, 2018. **Figure 207.** [Bottom right] *Trianthema portulacastrum* L., *Cabo Frio*, Brazil. Photograph: María A. Villalobos H., 2021.

Figure 208. [Top] *Usnea articulata* (L.) Hoffm. (synonym of Usnea barbata) at the Samambaia Institute of Environmental Science and Ecotourism, *Petrópolis, Rio de Janeiro*, Brazil. Gardens built by Roberto Burle Marx in 1948. Photograph: María A. Villalobos H., 2021. **Figure 209.** [Bottom left] *Solanum* sp., *Cabo Frio, Rio de Janeiro*, Brazil. Photograph: María A. Villalobos H., 2021. **Figure 210.** [Bottom right] *Crotalaria* sp., *Cabo Frio, Rio de Janeiro*, Brazil. Photograph: María A. Villalobos H., 2021.

These same landscapes, on the same journey I took with my dear friend, the botanist Mello Barreto, now deceased, were visited with the same admiration by illustrious figures like Saint-Hilaire, who left such erudite documentation, hardly mentioning the difficulties of the time.

From an anthropocentric point of view, we could say that plants were created for man. That is the attitude the Bible takes. In the European world, with its highly domesticated flora, man was able to maintain a relative balance in relation to trees and forests. With the conquest of the New World, the forests, especially the tropical forests, filled him with fear. It was the refuge of natives and aggressive animals: leopards, snakes, spiders, alligators, and mosquitos. Thus, the need to open strategic clearings came into the inhabitants' minds along with the combination of demolition and destruction. The need to create pastureland and farmland required extensive clearcutting.

And so "civilization" adopted the technique of *coivara*, which the indigenous peoples used in their nomadic agriculture. And the *coivara* was expanded, amplified, and today it is implemented with an unprecedented intensity, as the means of destruction, the machines (*bulldozers*) keep getting bigger and bigger. In under an hour one of those mechanical

Figure 211. A controlled *coivara* carried out by inhabitants of the *Quilombola Calungas* along the road to the Santa Bárbara Waterfall, Goiás, Brazil. *Coivara* is an indigenous practice that consists of the programmed burning of the land as a method of clearing and preparing the earth for cultivation. The ashes are used as fertilizer. Photograph: Carla Urbina, 2019.

monsters can destroy the work of millennia of evolution. It is the melancholy image that people see, powerless against the greater violence of the moral, economic, social, and psychological influences of the contemporary world. Despite all this, there is still a universe of plant life to be preserved – a universe that remains partially unknown to this day, due to the lack of techniques and specialists in sufficient numbers.

The commercialism of our perspective undercuts the value of the noble task of cultivating, preserving and disseminating the treasure of tropical plants. The chaotic increase in population fuels extremely serious problems, including a cultural shortcoming that undermines collective attitudes regarding issues of nature conservation, respect for trees and how to behave in a garden.

As for the pairing between humans and plants, the dependency is so profound that, despite all the failures in our understanding, there is still a feeling, a desire for their presence. Reality is often replaced by a simulacrum or even a custom that people may follow almost unconsciously. It is the case for plastic plants and flowers, which have invaded and tainted today's markets. In North America, I witnessed the winter garden of a large international hotel in Miami without a single living plant: it was made entirely of plastic models. A great horticulturist in that country was forced to close his nursery because it couldn't withstand competition from the manufacturers of pseudo-plants. Millions of human beings are unable to understand that plants are mutable, cyclical, and their lives entail a series of modifications, which is what gives them their charm, something non-existent in plastic models, which are static and express nothing. Returning to the issue of devastation, more serious in tropical countries than in temperate zones, we should highlight that one of the main effects has to do with climatic and microclimatic alterations, as well as in the destruction of the social capital represented by the fertility of the soil.

This is compounded by the extinction of the fauna and the desertification of extensive areas that are difficult to recover. It is an attack on the part of humanity against the sources of life, and it is a form of destruction that affects future generations.

The social mission of a landscape architect has the educational aspect of communicating the feeling of admiration and the understanding of the value of nature to the public through contact with gardens and parks. In Brazil, where there is a certain dislike of vegetation that has been planted, experience has taught me that we have to keep insisting over and over so that, through the clash between positions, people can come to understand the importance of our actions and our contributions, which can lead to a shift in their mindset. Our attitude also has a meaning in terms of projection, for the future, to show that someone took the care to leave a valuable legacy for posterity, in terms of both aesthetics and use.

The prevailing conditions in Brazil, and possibly in other tropical countries, permit laying out policies to preserve what still exists through the creation of a series of nature reserves – drawing on private, public, and international resources – for the main purpose of maintaining portions of nature, for the present and the future, in an original or minimally altered state.

Given the diversification of the flora, these reserves, authentic natural gardens, should be distributed throughout the different botanical provinces, preserving the most typical communities or the most valuable endemic species. Thus, landscape designers would have access to broader and more representative means of expression, like a vocabulary they can use in their compositions. With this abundant and expressive material at their disposal, they would have the possibilities of creating, in landscape design too, the magnificent works that the human spirit has been capable of, following the laws of aesthetic composition: for example, the laws of contrast, of harmony, and of proportion. The idea gives the matter its form, hence the need for a raw material that can embody the idea. In conclusion, we assert that landscape design is an art, albeit a highly elaborate art resulting from a web of conceptions and knowledge, woven together through the evolution of the artist's own life, with all their experiences, doubts, anxieties, desires, mistakes, and successes.

June 1967

Figure 212. Tropical Dry Forest Reserve and Botanical Garden, Maracaibo, Venezuela. Photograph: Andry Jons, 2018.

Figure 213. Sequence of microclimates at the *Sítio Roberto Burle Marx, Santo Antônio da Bica*, Brazil. Photograph: María A. Villalobos H., 2021.

LANDSCAPE ARCHITECTURE AND BRAZILIAN FLORA 1975

The exuberant nature, the rich flora and fauna of our territory, thriving for centuries, has meant that Brazilians often think of them as inexhaustible, eternal assets. However, shortly after the discovery, an exploration process began that, although it had shifting objectives and target areas, left deep scars on the face of our land over the years. Beginning from the 17th century there is direct evidence of essences that spread and how large areas disappeared, which were ruined due to misuse. Saint-Hilaire denounced the indiscriminate exploration. On his travels, Martius documented the violent fires he saw, also writing in his diary about other irrational behaviors, like criminal self-serving hunting. And yet, despite a whole series of complaints, the destruction never ceased. On the contrary, its rhythm has only accelerated with each new decade.

Some specific figures will better illustrate what we are saying: in the last 10 years, the forestland in the state of *Espírito Santo* has been reduced to 3% of the territory it originally occupied. Recent news from the newspapers shows that 10 years of colonization in the Amazon resulted in the disappearance of 3% of its forests, equivalent in figures to 7,800,000 hectares. *São Paulo* was nearly entirely covered with rich forests. A few decades were enough to almost wipe out its natural green cover completely. In 1854, almost 80% of the total area of the region was covered with forests. In 1907, that percentage was 58%. In the following 45 years, that percentage dropped to 18%. Two years ago, the coverage was 8%. More or less swiftly, the process of destruction throughout the country follows these same patterns.

Figure 214. [Top] The colonial practice of deforestation and burning as a quick way to prepare the land for planting crops, affecting the soil and the biodiversity. Bosset De Luze (between 1820 and 1840). *Fazenda Pombal, Colônia Leopoldina, Bahia. Fundação Estudar. Doação da Fundação Estudar*, 2007 / Collection of the *São Paulo* state picture gallery, Brazil. *Coleção Brasiliana*. Digital version available at: Luze, 1820-1840. **Figure 215.** [Center] Relationship between fires and deforestation in the Amazon for indiscriminate exploitation of the soil, a practice still present and exacerbated in the 21st century. Brazil. Photograph: Adriano Gambarini, 2020. Digital version available at: Gambarini, 2020. **Figure 216.** [Bottom] Representation of deforestation in *Rio de Janeiro*, Brazil, reported during the Martius expeditions (19th century). Carl Friedrich Philipp von Martius, c. 1842. *Silva Caesa, Cum Ficu Grandaeva, ad S. Joannen Marcum, Prov. Rio de Janeiro* / Clearcut forest, *com uma velha figueira*, in *São João Marcos*, province of Rio de Janeiro. Two-color lithograph (black and sepia) on paper. Martha and Eric Stickel Collection. Archive of the *Instituto Moreira Salles*. Digital version available at: Martius, c. 1842.

In 1928, I took a study trip to Germany, where I became a regular visitor to the Dahlem Botanical Garden. The collections of plants grouped according to geographical criteria were, for me, living lessons in botany and ecology. It was there that I was able to systematically observe many specimens typical of the Brazilian flora. They were beautiful species and almost never used here in gardens. The fact impacted me deeply and, when I returned, I prepared to defend our flora by all the means at my disposal. I understood that any effort would be justified given of the value and potential of what I was setting out to defend.

The face of the country was changing rapidly. Many of the forested areas that I was familiar with lost their vegetation over a short period. Obviously, the research work, of botanical collection, could not counteract the rhythm of those transformations. Much of it was no doubt lost forever. There was also a lack of official and private entities to help preserve the native flora, as well as a dearth of interest, capabilities, or incentives to carry out that function. The range of botanical materials available to landscape designers was extremely small, limited to the easiest and most conventional plants, most of which were imported. In part, society itself was responsible for this situation: the desire to imitate the Old World prevented people from seeing the beauty that was all around them.

Saving at least a part of our decimated flora, collecting specimens from nature, discovering their potential for landscape design, reproducing species to be able to use them properly in gardens, showing their immense value (when used correctly) in harmony with their surroundings, became my goal as a landscape designer.

That was the beginning of the idea of creating a nursery that would make it possible for me to achieve that goal. The land where the collection would be kept had to fulfill a series of prerequisites, associated with its function: a varied geography, the presence of abundant water, rocks, suitable soil, etc.

Figure 217. [Top] Adolpho Ducke Environmental Protection Area, *Manaus*, Brazil. Photograph: *Prefeitura de Manaus*, 2017. Available in: *Prefeitura de Manaus*, 2017. **Figure 218.** [Center left] *Sítio Roberto Burle Marx, Santo Antônio da Bica*, Brazil. Photograph: Carla Urbina, 2019. **Figure 219.** [Center and center right] tropical vegetation in the Dahlem Botanical Garden, Berlin, Germany, which was built between 1897-1910, under the direction of Adolf Engler. He is notable for his work on plant taxonomy and phytogeography in *The Natural Plant Families* (*Die natürlichen Pflanzenfamilien*). Engler collaborated with several other great botanists, including C.F.P. von Martius, on the book *Flora de Brasil* (*Flora Brasiliensis*), 1840-1906. More information in the digital version, available at: Engler, 1844-1930. Photographs: María A. Villalobos H., 2012. **Figure 220.** [Bottom] *Euterpes* sp. in the lagoon of the *Sítio Roberto Burle Marx, Santo Antônio da Bica*, Brazil. Photograph: María A. Villalobos H., 2021.

The work, which began with the acquisition of the land, was carried out in stages over the years, and it is my hope to protect the collections and to preserve the specimens and plants. After a long search, we found an area that fulfilled those basic requirements, and that could support the native species from the most varied regions, as well as providing different conditions in terms of lighting, humidity, etc.

The *Sítio Santo Antônio da Bica*, in Guaratiba, included an area on a slope that was still forested. It had a varied topography and included a section of lowlands influenced by brackish water.

The plant life on the slopes was intact. Little by little, the vegetation was built up. Today, in addition to the species characteristic of the *Serra do Mar*, it houses valuable specimens of the Amazonian flora, collected on various expeditions.

They include the *Couroupita guianensis* Aubl. or *Abricó-de-macaco*, and the *Euterpe oleracea* Mart., the açaí from soft drinks and ice cream, an elegant palm tree that I have frequently used for ornamental purposes in gardens. Various specimens from other regions were planted there, always in areas of the *Sítio*, with similar habitat characteristics.

Some were collected on excursions with the botanist, and my friend, Adolpho Ducke. He had studied the region in depth, and he was a keen observer who had an amazing memory when it came to plants. He oriented himself with incredible ease in areas he had traveled through previously, and he remembered the exact location of species that he had observed years before in the same way that we remember the arrangement of the furniture in our homes.

In order to assert the importance of these qualities and to give a more vivid idea of a group excursion, it is worth talking about some of the conditioning factors and some of the human requisites. First, you need to have botanical knowledge or information about the region to be covered, at least in general terms. You need to know which of the larger botanical provinces it belongs to and what the typical species are. You need to have an idea of what to look for going in, what the most interesting plants should be, but without passing over possible new discoveries with unexpected value. You also need to be a good observer.

Figure 221. [Top] Roberto Burle Marx next to the *Congea tomentosa* Roxb. in front of the main building at the *Sítio Roberto Burle Marx, Santo Antônio da Bica*, Brazil. Photograph: Clauss Meier, n.d./ Tyba. Published in the nomination dossier for the inclusion of the *Sítio Roberto Burle Marx* on the World Heritage List (IPHAN, 2019). **Figure 222.** [Center] *Abricó-de-macaco* is the common name in Brazil for the species *Couroupita guianensis* Aubl. Photograph: María A. Villalobos H., 2021. **Figure 223.** [Bottom] *Abricó-de-macacos* promenade, *Parque do Flamengo, Rio de Janeiro*, Brazil. Photograph: María A. Villalobos H., 2020.

A collection can be lost almost entirely if it isn't accompanied by on-site observations of the conditions in which the plants were found. The location and light conditions must be identified, and the type of soil and its moisture level must be observed. There can be a broad diversity in the physical conditions of plants, even within a very small area, due to a small variation in altitude, the presence of rocks, or other conditioning factors. You also need to know the appropriate technique for collecting each plant. Whether it can be propagated by cuttings or if seeds need to be collected. Whether the specimen should be removed from the ground with soil or if it will survive a bare root transplant. How the plants are conditioned is very important so that they can survive being transported and eventually replanted.

The physiognomy of a region varies intensely from one season to the next. Plants that may seem devoid of any charm at one time of year may be beautiful at another. Thus, two collections in the same region, at different times of year, can offer quite different results.

In that sense, I owe a lot to the botanists with whom I had the pleasure of sharing my travels. With them, I learned to explore our territory, open to the beauties that are offered, at every step, to those who want to see them.

The first plant collections took place in *Pernambuco*, in the *Caatinga*. I took trips with the botanist Brade, almost always on foot, in the *Serra do Mar* region. On another occasion, I had the pleasure of working with the remarkable botanist Henrique Lahmmeyer de Mello Barreto. He taught me to see that plants don't live in isolation, but in associations; they have their own logic and their own beauty. I learned that it's important to understand their natural habitat before trying to use them in gardens. With Mello Barreto, I travelled through several regions, learning about the flora of the *canga* with its iron crust, the areas of sandstone and quartz, the *Cerrado* and the limestone soils.

Figure 224. [Top] Alexander Curt Brade (1881-1971) was a German botanist who specialized in orchids and ferns from Brazil and Costa Rica. Brade studied architecture in Görlitz, Silesia. Much of his early tropical plant collections were destroyed in the bombing of the Berlin-Dahlem Museum during World War II. Brade worked at the Rio de Janeiro Botanical Garden until he was named head of the department of Systemic Botany. In *São Paulo* at the end of his life, he devoted his efforts to the classification of ferns and Melastomataceae. There are 628 names published by Brade, according to the International Plant Indexer (IPNI). For more information, see Pabst, G.F.J. (1967). Alexandre (sic) Curt Brade. Taxon, vol. 16, 161–167, June, 1967 (Pabst, 1967 pp. 161–167). The image shows, on the horizon, part of the *Serra do Mar* biodiversity corridor, where Brade and Roberto Burle Marx carried out joint expeditions, from Paraty, Brazil. Photograph: María A. Villalobos H., 2021. **Figure 225.** [Center] Plant life in the rocky areas of the *Cerrado* on quartzite formations in the *Cidade das Pedras*, *Pirenópolis*, *Goiás*, Brazil. Photograph: Carla Urbina, 2019. **Figure 226.** [Bottom] Collection of *Encholirium* sp. during the expedition to *Bahia*. Photograph: Oscar Bressane, 1982.

Figure 227. [Top] Plant life in the rocky areas of the *Cerrado* on quartzite formations in the *Cidade das Pedras*, *Pirenópolis*, *Goiás*, Brazil. Photograph: Carla Urbina, 2019. **Figure 228.** [Bottom] Limestone landscape in the *Caverna das Samambaias* (ferns) near *Vila Propício*, *Goiás*, Brazil. Photograph: Carla Urbina, 2019. **Figure 229.** [Opposite page, top left] *Milagres*, *Bahía*, Brazil. Photograph: María A. Villalobos H., 2020.

Figure 230. [Center left] Plant associations in rock formations, *Rio de Janeiro*, Brazil. Photograph: María A. Villalobos H., 2021. **Figure 231.** [Right] *Serra do Curral*, seen from the Mangabeiras Botanical Garden, *Minas Gerais*, Brazil. Photograph: María A. Villalobos H., 2012. **Figure 232.** [Bottom] Geological formation on the way to *Milagres*, *Bahia*, Brazil. Photograph: María A. Villalobos H., 2020.

In those years of working together, we completed several projects together that combined the ideals of landscape design and ecology to raise awareness about the formations specific to our country. But there were major difficulties, and the projects we developed and directed in his way were almost always met with misunderstanding or negative reactions. For the most part, the projects from that time were disfigured, cut short, only partially carried out, or they simply never got farther than the drawing board.

The creation of planting beds was one of the first tasks at the *Sítio*. It was essential to provide adequate shelter for a series of plants that, in general, survive under the protection of others. They are called understory plants and epiphytes, and they grow in the sunlight that is filtered through the tops of the largest trees. Still being expanded today, the beds are home to more than 400 species of *Philodendron*, a number of begonias, orchids and bromeliads from all over the country.

The lithophyte garden is another section that brings together a large number of specimens of the country's saxicolous flora. It shows the

Figure 233. [Left] *Sombral Graziela Barroso* at the *Sítio Roberto Burle Marx, Santo Antônio da Bica*, Brazil. Photograph: María A. Villalobos H., 2021. **Figure 234.** [Right] *Philodendron* at the entrance to the *Sombral Margaret Mee* at the *Sítio Roberto Burle Marx, Santo Antônio da Bica*, Brazil. Photograph: María A. Villalobos H., 2021.

many solutions found by plants, choosing which stones to grow on. They were built at the top of a hill devoid of large vegetation and partially covered by large blocks of granite. Both the geographical location and the sun exposure offer the plants the basic conditions necessary for their survival. Between large stones, certain specimens of *Ceiba* emerge aggressively, with their thorny branches. Nearby is the *Allamanda purpurea*, brought from *Ceará*, with its incredibly colorful flowers. They are joined by the *mandevillas*[66] from *Bahia* and *Espírito Santo*, along with various species of *clusias*,[67] with their thick leaves and well-defined shape.

[66] *Mandevilla* Lindl. is a genus of plants in the Apocynaceae family. It is widely distributed across Brazil in the following phytogeographic domains: Amazon, *Caatinga*, *Cerrado*, *Mata Atlântica*, Pampa, Pantanal. For more information, see: Mandevilla in Flora do Brasil 2020. Jardim Botânico do Rio de Janeiro (Reflora, 2020).

[67] *Clusia* L. is a genus of plants in the Clusiaceae family. It includes trees, shrubs and hemiepiphytes distributed across the neotropical realm, growing from the state of Florida in the United States to *Rio Grande do Sul* in Brazil. Widely distributed across Brazil in the following phytogeographic domains: Amazon, *Caatinga*, *Cerrado*, *Mata Atlântica*. For more information, see: Nascimento Jr, J.E.; Alencar, A.C. 2020. Clusia in Flora do Brasil 2020. Jardim Botânico do Rio de Janeiro (Nascimento Jr, et al., 2020).

Figure 235. Interior view of the shade house at the *Sítio Roberto Burle Marx*, *Santo Antônio da Bica*, Brazil. Photograph: María A. Villalobos H., 2021.

Figure 236. [Top] Nanuza Menezes. Photograph: Marcos Santos, USP. Available in: Santos, n.d. **Figure 237.** [Center] *Vellozia burle-marxii*. Photograph: Koiti Mori in Motta, Flávio Licfels, Gautherot, Marcel, (1984), p. 171. *Roberto Burle Marx e a nova visão da paisagem*. Brazil: Nobel, 1984, p. 171. **Figure 238.** [Bottom] *Vellozias* at the *Sítio Roberto Burle Marx*, *Santo Antônio da Bica*, Brazil. Photograph: María A. Villalobos H., 2021.

Figure 239. [Top left] Bromeliads. Photograph: María A. Villalobos H., 2021. **Figure 240.** [Top right] *Vellozias*. Photograph: Carla Urbina, 2019. **Figure 241.** [Center] Begonias. Photograph: María A. Villalobos H., 2021. **Figure 242.** [Bottom left and right] Orchids and bromeliads. Photographs: Carla Urbina, 2019. All photographs on this page are from the *Sítio Roberto Burle Marx*, *Santo Antônio da Bica*, Brazil.

Bromeliads of various origins were planted between and on the stones, along with orchids and cacti. There is also a series of Velloziaceae, collected in the regions of *Grão Mogol*, *Chapada dos Veadeiros*, *Serra do Espinhaço* and the northern part of the state of *Rio de Janeiro*, near the city of *Madalena*. In this collection, which includes 55 different species, two were identified that were hitherto unknown to science. Moreover, Nanuza Menezes, a specialist in the family, has asserted that this is the largest existing collection in the world.

Some of these plants were collected alongside large roads, like the beautiful *Euphorbia phosphorea* Mart.,[68] found along the BR-116, near *Jequié*, *Bahia*, or a new Velloziaceae, found in *Vitória da Conquista*.

Others were in more remote in areas, which, because of the difficult access, were preserved intact. This was the case of the *Wunderlichia*,[69] a little known Compositae that we found in the *Chapada dos Veadeiros*, in *Goiás*.

In low-lying areas, where the waters of a stream were partially dammed, a niche for aquatic plants was created. It is home to the *Eichhornias*,[70] collected in *Minas Gerais*, the *Hydrocleys*,[71] from along the banks in *Rio-Bahia*, the *Victoria Regia* from the Amazon, as well as the *Nymphaea*,[72] etc. The stones in the vicinity of the lake are once again home to lithophytes amid cacti, bromeliads, and others. The mass of vegetation there created a new environment for the fauna that had been pushed out of the region by clearcutting and fires, which are still frequent in the area today.

Figure 243. Lagoon habitat for flora and fauna at the *Sítio Roberto Burle Marx*, *Santo Antônio da Bica*, Brazil. Photograph: Carla Urbina, 2009.

Many insects, birds, mammals, reptiles and amphibians make their homes there, since they are protected, and the conditions are right for their survival.

[68] *Euphorbia phosphorea* Mart. Species belonging to the Euphorbiaceae family distributed throughout the northeast of Brazil. For more information, see: Govaerts R. (ed.), 2021. *Euphorbia phosphorea* Mart. WCSP: World Checklist of Selected Plant Families (version Aug. 2017). Catalogue of Life, et al. (2021). Species 2000 & ITIS Catalogue of Life, 2021-04-05 (Govaerts, 2021).

[69] The species *Wunderlichia* Riedel ex Benth. & Hook. fil. Cited in the text as belonging to the Compositae family, it is currently identified as belonging to the Asteraceae family, according to the information published in World Plants: Synonymic Checklists of the Vascular Plants of the World. For more information, see: Hassler, Michel. 2004-2021. *Wunderlichia* Riedel ex Benth. & Hook. fil. World Plants. Synonymic Checklist and Distribution of the World Flora (Hassler, 2021).

[70] *Eichhornia* Kunth is a genus of the Pontederiaceae family. A species of aquatic plants (rhizomatic or otherwise), annuals, perennials, whose geographical distribution in Brazil occurs in the phytogeographic domains of: Amazon, *Caatinga*, *Cerrado*, *Mata Atlântica*, Pampa, Pantanal. For more information, see: Sousa, D.J.L. 2020. Pontederiaceae in Flora do Brasil 2020. *Jardim Botânico do Rio de Janeiro* (Sousa, 2020).

[71] *Hydrocleys* Rich. is a genus in the Alismataceae family. Perennial aquatic herbaceous plants. It is not endemic to Brazil but has been naturalized. It is present in the geographical domains of: Amazon, *Caatinga*, *Cerrado*, *Mata Atlântica*, Pampa, Pantanal. For more information, see: Matias, L.Q. 2020. Alismataceae in Flora do Brasil 2020. *Jardim Botânico do Rio de Janeiro* (Matias, 2020).

[72] *Nymphaea* L. is a genus in the Nymphaeaceae family. Perennial aquatic plants with large rhizomes and leaves that usually float. Native of Brazil. Present in the phytogeographic domains of: Amazon, *Caatinga*, *Cerrado*, *Mata Atlântica*, Pampa, Pantanal. For more information, see: Pellegrini, M.O.O. 2020. Nymphaeaceae in Flora do Brasil 2020. *Jardim Botânico do Rio de Janeiro* (Pellegrini, 2020).

Figure 244. Lithophyte garden at the *Sítio Roberto Burle Marx*, *Santo Antônio da Bica*, Brazil. Photograph: María A. Villalobos H., 2021.

Figure 245. [Top] *Eichhornias* in the phylogenetic layout from the Maracaibo Botanical Garden, Maracaibo, Venezuela. Photograph: Carla Urbina, 2012. **Figure 246.** [Center] *Eichhornias* in the Mangabeiras Botanical Garden, *Minas Gerais*, Brazil. Photograph: María A. Villalobos H., 2012. **Figure 247.** [Bottom] *Nymphaeas* in the Mangabeiras Botanical Garden, *Minas Gerais*, Brazil. Photograph: María A. Villalobos H., 2012.

Figure 248. [Top] *Bauhinia* in the *Parque do Flamengo*, *Rio de Janeiro*, Brazil. Photographs: Carla Urbina, 2014.
Figure 249. [Center] *Pseudobombax ellipticum*, in the *Parque del Este*, Caracas, Venezuela. Photographs: Carla Urbina 2012. **Figure 250.** [Bottom] *Heliconia* in the shade house, which is used for plant care, propagation and experiments at the *Sítio Roberto Burle Marx*, *Santo Antônio da Bica*, Brazil. Photographs: Carla Urbina, 2014.

Figure 251. Célio, Roberto Burle Marx and Flamarion Soares de Gama, at the *Sítio Roberto Burle Marx, Santo Antônio da Bica*, Brazil. Photograph: Marcel Gautherot, ca. 1961. Archive of the *Instituto Moreira Salles*, Brazil. Digital version available at: Gautherot, c. 1961.

There are nests built by *João-de-barro*[73] in the trees, hummingbirds,[74] *paturis*,[75] *arapongas*,[76] magpies,[77] as well as a thousand butterflies and snakes. The fact is that the *Sítio* tends toward being a site of balance, where the fauna can also find its place free from the constant threats of fire and landslides.

The efforts going on at the *Sítio* always centered on reproducing and perpetuating our species. The collections grow from year to year, in a process that resembles the storage of live plants, saved from the generalized destruction. But that alone is not enough for their preservation. The *Sítio* is also an important work site, where those same plants are cared for, propagated, and where their behavior, growth, and various needs are observed, and experiments of a technical and aesthetic nature are carried out.

Here, we should open a parenthesis to talk about the non-native plants housed at the *Sítio*. Whether they have an affinity with our flora, or their inclusion is justified by their characteristics, I have introduced botanical elements from other countries, with the intention of enriching our gardens. Those species include *Bauhinia blakeana* D. Don,[78] a magnificent tree with large purple flowers, and the *Pseudobombax ellipticum* Dugand,[79] which lets us observe the opening movement of the flowers, with their bright colors.

---

[73] *João-de-barro* is the common name in Brazil for the bird species *Furnarius rufus* (Gmelin, 1788). For more information, see: Alan P. Peterson, M.D., 2006-11-29. *Furnarius rufus* (Gmelin, 1788). ITIS: The Integrated Taxonomic Information System (Peterson, 2006).

[74] Colibrí or *beija-flor* is the common name in Brazil for a wide variety of bird species of the Trochilidae family (hummingbirds). More information about the species in this family, their distribution, and images, see: eBird (eBird, n.d.).

[75] *Paturi* is the common name in Brazil for the bird species *Netta erythrophthalma* (Wied-Neuwied, 1833). For more information, see: ITIS: The Integrated Taxonomic Information System (Peterson, 2006).

[76] *Araponga* is the common name (of indigenous origin) in Brazil for the bird species *Procnias nudicollis* (Vieillot, 1817). For more information, see: Alan P. Peterson, M.D., 2006-11-29. *Procnias nudicollis* (Vieillot, 1817). ITIS: The Integrated Taxonomic Information System (Peterson, 2006).

[77] Garza is the common name of the bird genus *Ardea* Linnaeus (1758) of the Ardeidae family. For more information, see: Alan P. Peterson, M.D., Richard C. Banks, 2011-09-22. *Ardea* Linnaeus, 1758. ITIS: The Integrated Taxonomic Information System (Peterson, et al., 2011).

[78] *Bauhinia blakeana* Dunn., a species of the Fabaceae family. Its geographical distribution covers areas of: China, India, Indonesia, Malaysia, Mauritius, the Northern Marianas, Papua New Guinea, Reunion, and Rodrigues. For more information, see: Roskov Y., Bisby F., Zarucchi J., Novoselova M. (eds.) (2021). ILDIS: World Database of Legumes (version 12, May 2014). In: Catalogue of Life, et al. (2021). Species 2000 & ITIS Catalogue of Life, 2021-04-05 (Roskov Y., 2021).

[79] *Pseudobombax ellipticum* (Kunth) Dugand is a plant species of the Malvaceae family. Distribution in: Mexico (Campeche, Chiapas, Colima, Durango, Guanajuato, Guerrero, Hidalgo, Jalisco, State of Mexico, Michoacán, Morelos, Nayarit, Nuevo León, Oaxaca, Puebla, Querétaro, Quintana Roo, San Luis Potosí, Sinaloa, Tabasco, Tamaulipas, Veracruz, Yucatán, Zacatecas), Guatemala, Honduras, Nicaragua, Belize, Cuba, Hispaniola Island, Lesser Antilles. For more information, see: Hassler, Michael (2004 - 2021). *Pseudobombax ellipticum* (Kunth) *Dugand. World Plants. Synonymic Checklist and Distribution of the World Flora. Version* 12.1 (Hassler, 2021).

Figure 252. Sequence of microclimates at the *Sítio Roberto Burle Marx, Santo Antônio da Bica*, Brazil. Photographs: María A. Villalobos H., 2021.

Figure 253. [Top] Sun gardens at the *Sítio Roberto Burle Marx, Santo Antônio da Bica*, Brazil. Photograph: María A. Villalobos H., 2021. **Figure 254.** [Bottom] Gardens of the *Cozinha de pedra* at the *Sítio Roberto Burle Marx, Santo Antônio da Bica*, Brazil. Photograph: María A. Villalobos H., 2021.

Visiting the *Sítio* is always a rewarding experience, even for neophytes. The convergence of the different environments, the variety of blooms that alternate with the seasons, the pleasure of witnessing the different phases of the plants as they bud, and grow and produce fruit, are all factors that bring in countless visitors. The arrangement of the elements has an educational component, associated with an aesthetic pursuit.

The associations of diverse plants create harmonious atmospheres. Other times, beauty is created by repeating the same species to form homogeneous volumes. Sometimes, the flowers are valued more, when all the details of its structure are visible.

By providing aesthetic pleasure to those who contemplate them, through the path of art these environments accomplish what the *Sítio* sets out as a primary goal: to elevate our plants and contribute to people's respect and love for them.

The process of learning to recognize beauty is long; it is difficult to try to show it where it isn't usually expected. The areas that were treated as an obstacle to enrichment during the entire process of formation of a country, in the *Caatinga*, in the *Cerrados*, in the *"green hell"* – that even earned a pejorative name – as well as the elimination of the plant cover, even today, runs parallel to our supposed ideals of development and material progress.

By housing some plants from each of these regions, the *Sítio* is proof of the emotion felt in learning about them and the concern for preserving them, if not in all the aspects of the flora, at least in the qualities that are most significant from the point of view of landscape design.

November 1975

Figure 255. *Calathea Burle Marxii* H.Kenn. (synonym of *Goeppertia burle-marxii* (H.Kenn.) Borchs. & S.Suárez, at the *Sítio Roberto Burle Marx, Santo Antônio da Bica*, Brazil. Photograph: María A. Villalobos H., 2018.

Figure 256. *Ipanema, Rio de Janeiro,* Brazil. Photograph: Carla Urbina, 2009.

LANDSCAPE RESOURCES OF BRAZIL 1976

To help explain what I have come to talk about today, I would first like to delve, with the reader, into the meaning or meanings of the expression *"landscape resources"*.

Looking at the dictionary, we find the following: *"landscape"*, according to Aurélio Buarque,[80] refers to the expanse of land that can be perceived in a single glance. Antenor Nascentes[81] defines it as the extension of the country offered by an overview. According to Domingos Vieira,[82] it is a view or representation of land, fields, estates, etc. Caldas Aulete[83] expresses it as follows: the portion we can perceive of the place we are in: panorama, vista.

Now it is worth making some important observations based on these definitions:

a) What is constant is the reference to the sense of vision. It includes everything that we can take in with our gaze; it is not a selective or restrictive term. Nor does it contain any value judgment either. It that is true, we must accept that the urban environment is as much a landscape as the natural environment. And a degraded environment is also a landscape, in the same way as the one that has maintained its original features, or one that has been reconstructed to suit human needs.

b) As a direct consequence of this definition, the landscape, encompassing the entire visual environment from any point of observation, can be identified as a series of geographical formations within that portion of land. It is even more complex, however, in that it also includes the physical foundation, constituted by the corresponding portion of the lithosphere and local water resources: all the living beings that inhabit it – including humans.

c) The landscape is not static, since all its constituent elements are susceptible to their own transformations that also cause mutual alterations (the biotope and the biocenosis form a dynamic system).

---

[80] Aurélio Buarque de Holanda Ferreira (1910-1989). Trained as a lawyer, he was a prominent Brazilian philologist and writer, dedicated to the study of the Portuguese language. His notable works include *Dois mundos* (1942) and the *Diccionario Aurelio da Língua Portuguesa* (1975). One of his best-known works is the *Novo Dicionário da Língua Portuguesa* (1975). For more information, see: Buarque de Holanda, *et al.*, 2007.

[81] Antenor Nascentes (1886-1972) was one of the most important scholars of the Portuguese language in the 20th century and a founding member of the Brazilian Academy of Philology. His notable works include the *Dicionário de língua portuguesa da Academia Brasileira de Letras* (1967). For more information, see: Alves Pereira Penha, 2002, pp. 67-72.

[82] Dr. Frei Domingos Vieira dos Eremitas Calçados de Santo Agostinho published the *Grande Diccionario Portuguez ou Thesouro da Língua Portugueza* in 1871-1874. For more information, see: Braga, Vieira, & Coelho, 1871.

[83] Francisco Júlio Caldas Aulete (1826-1878), born in Lisbon, was a professor, lexicographer, politician, and author of the *Diccionario Contemporâneo de Língua Portuguesa*. For more information, see: Caldas Aulete, Nascentes, & Garcia, 1968.

d) A territory is made up of an infinite number of landscapes, partially overlapping. Certain areas, certain *"landscapes"* need to be distinguished from this whole, to which we give a certain aesthetic, cultural, scientific, or social meaning; and treating these areas as autonomous units could be a useful functional measure with an eye to certain purposes. The landscape, meanwhile, will always remain indivisible, continuous, where theoretical boundaries lose their substance.

But, although the term *"landscape"* does not offer any information about its characteristics, it is evident that any vista has a series of elements that define it for the observer and differentiate it from other myriad landscapes. The morphology of the terrain, the flora, the fauna, the local water resources, and the anthropic action are aspects that, in constituting the landscape, also characterize it in an unmistakable way.

The systematization of these elements, whether conscious or intuitive, is what makes it possible for someone to evoke their "homeland", for example, in contrast to any others that they may come to know.

That is also how the concept of a macro-landscape or landscape domain can be created, formulated by geographers and which corresponds not only to a visual domain but to a larger unit, characterized by its typical morphoclimatic features and its main patterns of vegetation.

When we hear about the *"cultural landscape"*, its meaning becomes clear by analogy as a vernacular term.

In contrast to these uses, rooted in the diversity, richness, and dynamism of the original meaning of *"landscape"*, there is also a colloquial meaning for the term, which is essentially contradictory. *"Landscape"*, in this sense, is a limited set of spaces, endowed with specific environmental characteristics – a definition that owes much of its origins to Romanticism. These landscapes are bucolic, or magnificent, or wild, and their common denominator is that they stand in opposition to the urban environment.

Static and passive, contrasted with the dynamism of "civilized" areas, these landscapes were understood as mere means for consumption. So much so that real estate advertising uses the term very successfully. When we talk about the *"landscape"* it should be clear that we are not referring only to this degraded concept, but to all environments in our territory, our visual domain.

"Resources", on the other hand, are goods, assets, possessions. In that sense, landscape resources can be understood as those landscapes that, due to specific characteristics – whether aesthetic, scientific or historical – constitute the cultural assets of a community. We see, then, that *"landscape"* doesn't denote any judgment about its object. To refer to a *"landscape resource"* is to assert that certain landscapes are endowed with qualities that put them in a category that is separate from their cultural value.

The IBGE – Brazilian Institute of Geography and Statistics – includes landscape resources among those resources that are practically inexhaustible, implying that they constitute durable and profitable assets for the community.

It is convenient, however, to explain a fact is often misunderstood: the landscape resources of a nation can be considered inexhaustible, since their proper use does not imply transformations that endanger their fundamental quality. However, undesirable interferences can cause them to cease to be resources; in other words, their basic qualities are degraded or completely lost. Some simple examples will help to clarify what I mean: the *Serra do Curral*, which surrounds *Belo Horizonte*, constituted one of its landscape resources because it characterized the landscape of the city. The invasion of the *Serra* by haphazard constructions and the mining operations that are currently devastating it will no doubt lead to the creation of a new landscape. But this new landscape that cannot be called, even with the utmost goodwill, a *"landscape resource"*. That landscape resource has been destroyed, ruined by human action, for the sake of material gain.

Because the merciless logging in the *Serra do Mar* eliminates plant life that is of great visual beauty, it threatens the existence of that landscape resource. The skyscrapers in *Gávea* damaged one of the most beautiful resources that we possessed in *Rio*, just as they violently defaced the area of the *Lagoa*, crossing the line of mountains.

Even though human action is already being felt in larger and larger areas, and that it is almost

Figure 257. Botanical Garden and *Parque das Mangabeiras*, *Minas Gerais*, Brazil. On October 14, 1966, by way of Decree No. 1,466, the *Parque das Mangabeiras* was created, for the purpose of preserving the *Serra do Curral* and creating a new recreation area for the city. In 1974, the construction of the park was authorized through Law No. 2,403. The landscape design was done by Roberto Burle Marx and collaborators. The park covers an area of 2.4

always in conflict with nature, Brazil still has a reasonable number of natural landscapes that possess great beauty.

The geological diversity from region to region; the vegetation that is characteristic of each of these areas; the vegetation with its varied volumes, textures and colors; its visual relationship with the surrounding rock formations; the rhythms of buds, of blooms; the size of the trees, tied in with the richness and exuberance of the epiphyte plants; the typical physiognomy of the mountains; the points where there is still a visual relationship between dry land and surface water (the mosaic land and water); the areas of exceptional diversity (*Pantanal*, *Hileia*); the various landscape enclaves that contrast with the regional standard; the different kinds of coastal regions – dunes, mangroves, mountain ranges; all of this, in a way, could constitute a landscape resource, an immense resource, which, if it coincides today with our physical boundaries, it is due to our negligence or carelessness. And strictlyspeaking, there is nothing new in this assertion. It is more of an attempt to return to the perspective of those naturalists who, beginning in the last century, visited our country and created true monuments in homage to the nature they found here.

I will only cite Martius who, when compiling his *Flora brasilensis*, worked toward that purpose: establishing the various Brazilian botanical provinces, describing with each region that he traveled through with precision and detail. His conception of our landscape, in general terms, persists today; his botanical provinces correspond to macrocommunities of the Brazilian landscape, which are defined as follows:

million m^2 and includes 59 springs in the *Córrego da Serra*, which is part of the *São Francisco River*. For more information, see: *Prefeitura Belo Horizonte*, 2021. Photograph: María A. Villalobos H., 2012. **Figure 258.** Skyscrapers in *Gávea* and *Leblón* seen from the northern edge of the *Lagoa Rodrigo de Freitas*, Rio de Janeiro, Brazil. Photograph: María A. Villalobos H., 2021.

Naiads – forested lowlands of the Amazon.

Hamadryads – low-lying areas between plateaus in the northeast.

Dryads – Atlantic forests of the *Serra do Mar*, the region of the *mares de morros*.

Oreads – cliffs covered by *Cerrados* and penetrated by gallery forests.

Napaeae – the *Planalto das Araucárias* and the mixed grasslands of southwestern *Rio Grande do Sul*.

Ferri[84] adds two areas not differentiated by Martius, which are the Pantanal wetlands and the various types of coastlines: rocky (sandstone) and silty.

As we have said earlier, each of these units has a series of unique characteristics, distinguishing them from the neighboring areas, which form their intrinsic character, their distinctiveness, and their value in landscape terms. Obviously, the understanding of these particular characteristics brings with it several problems when it comes to the approach.

It seems to me that this is the point that should concern our experts in tourism: How can we orient this still incipient activity in Brazil so that our landscapes are truly understood not only in their general appearance, but also in their most delicate details? At the same time, without preventing human interference, which is necessary for their survival. There need to be a series of criteria.

---

[84] Mário Guimarães Ferri (1918-1985). Born in *São Paulo*, he was a scientist, artist, and pioneering environmentalist in Brazil. For more information, see: Gil Martins, 1994. Using simple and precise language, Ferri communicated the importance of protecting the environment to the public. The list of Ferri's works is rich and varied. For more information, see: Guimaraes Ferri, Mario. 1985.; Guimarães Ferri, Mário. 1974.

Figure 259. [Top] Cover of *Vegetação Brasileira*, by Mário Guimarães Ferri. Editor: Itatiaia, 1980. **Figure 260.** [Center left] *Naiads*. Available in: Henrietta Rae. *Hylas and the Water Nymphs*. 1910. London Royal Academy (Rae, 1910). **Figure 261.** [Center right] *"Las aguas del Amazonas"*. Available in: Martius, Karl Friedrich Philipp von; Spix, Johann Baptist von. s.f. *Extração e Preparo dos Ovos de Tartaruga, no Rio Amazonas* (Martius & Spix, s.f.). In Greek mythology, naiads are nymphs (a female divinity) associated with fresh water, waterfalls, rivers, and lakes (Britannica, s.f.). Martius associates these divinities with the lowlands of the Amazon in northern Brazil. **Figure 262.** [Bottom left] *Hamadryads*. Available in: Bin, Émile, *Le Bûcheron et l'Hamadryade Aigeiros*. 1870. Musee d'Art Thomas Henry (Bin, 1870). **Figure 263.** [Bottom right] Brazilian *Caatinga*. Available in: Martius, Karl Friedrich Philipp von. *Sylva aestu aphylla, quam dicunt caatinga*, 1794-1868 (Martius K. F., 1794-1868). The hamadryads are the eight daughters of Oxylus and Hamadryas. Each one presided over a different species of tree, in addition to being able to take revenge on beings that threatened their protected species, which is why Martius associates them with the area of the *Caatinga* in northeastern Brazil.

Our territory is occupied or in the process of being occupied. Making human action compatible with nature, planning each intervention, should be a constant concern, especially since technological means have incremented enormously our capacity for sudden transformation of the landscape.

There are some basic criteria to be observed in relation to each of these associations: maintaining a landscape unity, in each of the corresponding units – which does not imply monotony or uniformity. We will see later that landscape design tends towards diversification. What we cannot accept for our interference to be synonymous with deterioration, dispossession, destruction, or disorder.

In one of his projects, Caldeira Cabral[85] systematizes the specific areas for the protection of nature and the landscape, presenting the following categories:

Integral Reserve – a zone of minimum intervention, set aside for scientific purposes.

Nature Reserve – comprehensive protection area, justified by scientific, historical, and aesthetic interests for purposes of culture and recreation.

Tourist Reserve – peripheral zone around the nature reserves, subject to the forest regime, and where the basic tourist facilities for the complex are located.

[85] Francisco Caldeira Cabral (1908-1992) was a Portuguese landscape architect dedicated to reflecting on and working for the preservation of the landscape. He was known for his contribution to the development of a landscape preservation policy and for the concept of a *"Continuum Naturale"* which he used to express the importance of the relationship of continuity between all living beings. For more information, see: Teresa Andresen (*Comissária*), *do Estádio Nacional ao Jardim Gulbenkian. Francisco Caldeira Cabral e a primeira geração de arquitectos paisagistas* (1940–1970). *Catalog of the exhibition the at *Fundação Calouste Gulbenkia*, from October 2, 2003, to January 21, 2004. Lisbon: FCG, 2003. (Andressen, 2003).

Figure 264. [Top left] *Dryads.* Available in: Evelyn DeMorgan. *The Dryad/Die Dryade.* 1884-1885. (De Morgan, 1884-1885). **Figure 265.** [Top right] *Mata Atlântica.* Available in: Martius, Karl Friedrich Philipp von; Spix, Johann Baptist von. *Silva Montium Serra dos Órgãos declivia obumbrans. Rio de Janeiro.* 1794-1868 (Martius & Spix, 1794-1868). The *dryads* were associated by Martius with the *Mata Atlântica* of southeastern Brazil, showing the relationship between the beings and the forests they live in. According to mythology, if a tree in that forest was cut down or killed, the divinity also died, and whoever destroyed it was punished by the gods. **Figure 266.** [Center left] *Oreads.* Available in: Bouguereau, Adolphe-William. *Les Oréades*, 1902 (Bouguereau, 1902). **Figure 267.** [Center right] Brazilian *Cerrado.* Available in: Martius, Karl Friedrich Philipp von; Spix, Johann Baptist von. *Cataracta rivi, qui dicitur Riberão do Palmital. Prope Sabará in Prov. Minarum.* 1794-1868 (Martius & Spix, 1794-1868). The oreads are the protectors of mountains, caves, and grottoes. Martius associates these figures with the phytogeography of the Brazilian *Cerrado.* **Figure 268.** [Bottom left] *Napaeae.* Available in: Henri-Edmond Cross. *Napéias.* 1908 (Cross, 1908). **Figure 269.** [Bottom right] *"O bosque araucária brasiliana na Provincia de Minas" [Gerais]* Available in: Martius, Karl Friedrich Philipp von; Spix, Johann Baptist von. *Lucus Araucariae Brasilianae.* 1794-1868 (Martius & Spix, 1794-1868). The napaeae are the nymphs of valleys, hills, and lowlands. The areas inhabited by Araucarias on the central plateau and the mixed grasslands of southern Brazil round out the phytogeographic zones characterized by Von Martius.

These first three special zones roughly correspond to our national parks and equivalent reserves. Although their value is changeable in both scientific and cultural terms because of their limited size, they are present in the country's overall visual context. Or, in other words: an immense sequence of deteriorated landscapes cannot be counterbalanced by a few protected areas, however beautiful they may be. Our landscape heritage (or resources) would be reduced to a minimum, consisting only of those reserves.

The fourth special zone encompasses more extensive territories because of its greater openness, which justifies a greater interest:

Landscape Reserve – an area of special landscape interest due to its aesthetic, historical or ecological value, in which human activity can continue but its development must be conditional upon approval from the administration, while its goal must also be the protection and social and economic promotion of the population, through opportune and economic aid. We find that the joint application of these four modes of protection would already provide for the maintenance of a good standard of quality for our landscapes. Despite this, I would like to add an additional aspect here, which would bring us even closer to our objective, as we have already said, the idea would be to guarantee a sequence of landscapes throughout the territory, which can maintain a basic quality or balance, despite being diversified and subject to a wide variety of uses and regimes, whether natural or humanized.

Figure 270. Flamboyán, *Delonix regia* (Hook.) Raf., Araruama, RJ, 1937, India ink on paper, 38 × 28 centimeters, in Tabacow, José, *Arte & Paisagem. Conferências Escolhidas*, São Paulo: Nobel, 1987, p. 85.

I am thinking, here, of our legislation that provides for the protection of a series of constituent elements of the landscape throughout the country, albeit in a very limited way: the protection of the edges of water formations, such as springs, beaches, and lakeshores. It also prohibits logging on area beyond a certain degree of slope or in cases where the soil would not be able to support a layer of vegetation. It provides for the maintenance of 10% of natural forest areas, or the replanting of native species in the event of reforestation. It prohibits hunting for profit. It protects historical or archaeological sites. The urban legislation is the code that governs how our cities are built and regulates their visual features. This list is not intended as comprehensive in terms of our legislation regarding the protection of the environment. I have cited but a few examples.

I am convinced that, if we applied them rigorously, these laws would benefit our territory on the whole, forming, in tandem with the creation and maintenance of special zones, a landscape *continuum* with a greater richness and variety.

The criteria for carrying out this type of landscape zoning (determining various zones governed by a special regime and defining certain rare elements that require protection, as well as applying landscape criteria, even in non-specific areas) demand detailed and multidisciplinary studies.

The first approach is physical. It involves a study of the geographical environment of the region. The geographical position, the orography, the hydrography, the climate, and the regional microclimates already establish some criteria

Figure 271. Royal poinciana, *Delonix regia* (Hook.) Raf., in the *Praça Casa Forte*, *Recife*, Brazil. The plants construct the urban limit and turn it into a landscape monument. Photograph: María A. Villalobos H., 2021.

Figure 272. *Delonix regia* (Hook.) Raf., known as the royal poinciana, in the *Parque do Flamengo*, designed by Roberto Burle Marx and collaborators, and opened to the public in 1965, *Rio de Janeiro*, Brazil. Photograph: María A. Villalobos H., 2021.

for the aforementioned zoning. This should be followed by biogeographic studies, studies of flora and fauna, and studies of the evolution of the landscape that also include human intervention, cultures, roads, constructions and works of art.

Given this data, and following a socioeconomic study of the region, we would be able to draw up a map of the area's potential or possible uses. At the regional level, this would establish which areas should be subject to a special regime, which ones should be allocated to agricultural uses, or forestry, which directions urban expansion should take, etc. From there, the zones for culture can be distributed in a balanced way, so that some representative areas of the native flora can be preserved, an important factor in identifying the different regions. Therefore, in the same way that our impression of a landscape is a synthesis of diverse elements, from scenic values to the socioeconomic level of the inhabitants, the transformation of landscapes is also processed through a synthesis of information, where the same criteria direct our actions. Our goal should be a sequence of landscapes, where the care we give encompasses both an apparently insignificant stretch of road and a landscape monument.

Until now we have only emphasized the sociocultural value of our landscape heritage as a guarantee of quality of life and as a means of ensuring forms of leisure worthy of the name.

Figure 273. *Vale do Rio Pancas, Espírito Santo,* Brazil. Photograph: Oscar Bressane, 2013.

Indirectly, leisure and tourism still generate wealth for the respective regions. It would only be fair, then, to extend those benefits not only to certain privileged areas in the country but to the community as a whole.

Because this global action would involve a lot of work and capital, it would be impossible to implement simultaneously throughout the country, given our current economic conditions.

As a concrete measure, however, we could envision the implementation of the measures outlined above in certain regions that stand out from the rest because of their location. The criterion of ease of access has two reasons behind it: on the one hand, it constitutes a weak point in our landscape structure, due to the possibilities opened by disorganized transformations along roadways. At the same time, accessibility is a way of ensuring that all the efforts put into a major project will benefit the community. In this sense, our national parks still don't live up to their true mission, since the difficulties of access for most people create a serious obstacle, which undercuts the parks' cultural and educational purpose.

Roads, however, in addition to providing a simple means of access, play an active role and contribute substantially to the understanding of a landscape, provided they are well planned.

During any journey, they offer continuous contact with different views, from different angles.

Figure 274. *Serra do Cipó, Minas Gerais*, Brazil. Photograph: Oscar Bressane, 2013.

Moving through the landscape will show the attentive traveler the particular rhythm of the formations, the interrelations between their various aspects. Forests, fields, farmhouses, plantations, mountains, rivers, waterways follow one another in their own sequences, characteristic of each region, since, as they are interdependent elements, their distribution obeys its own laws.

For these reasons, I believe that areas offering ease of access should be given priority in the work to be done. Despite all that I have stated above, I do not intend to make a list of our potential landscape resources. That is a task that requires extensive research and studies of all different kinds.

Instead, I will list some of the areas I have had the opportunity visit on my travels through Brazil and which, because of their accessibility, could be more easily subjected to this type of study and intervention. They are the following:

Figure 275. *Guaratiba*, on the coast of the state of *Rio de Janeiro*, Brazil. Photograph: Robert T. Wahlen, 2021.

Vale do Rio Pancas – Espírito Santo
Região de Lagoa Santa – Minas Gerais
Coastal areas in the state of Rio de Janeiro
Serra do Cipó / Chapada Diamantina – Minas Gerais
Morro do Chapéu and surrounding cities – Bahia
Lençóis, Andaraí and Mucugê – Serra do Sincorá – Bahia
Pedra Azul – Minas Gerais
Milagres – Bahia
Chapada dos Guimarães – Mato Grosso
Região das Dunas de Torres – Rio Grande do Sul
Vale do Imbé – Santa María Madalena – Rio de Janeiro

I must say that, in the ongoing contact I had over the years, each new trip revealed only the accelerated advance of the destruction. Perhaps that is the reason behind this list: the hope for some protective measures that will stop the process of their destruction.

Rio de Janeiro, March 1976

Figure 276. [Top] Buzios, on the coast of the state of *Rio de Janeiro*, Brazil. Photograph: María A. Villalobos H., 2021.
Figure 277. [Center] Buzios, on the coast of the state of *Rio de Janeiro*, Brazil. Photograph: Carla Urbina, 2020. **Figure 278.** [Bottom] *Angra dos Reis*, on the coast of the state of *Rio de Janeiro*, Brazil. Photograph: María A. Villalobos H., 2021.

Figure 279. [Top] Buzios, on the coast of the state of *Rio de Janeiro*, Brazil. Photograph: María A. Villalobos H., 2021.
Figure 280. [Center] Cabo Frio, on the coast of the state of *Rio de Janeiro*, Brazil. Photograph: María A. Villalobos H., 2021.
Figure 281. [Bottom] Arraial do Cabo, on the coast of the state of *Rio de Janeiro*, Brazil. Photograph: María A. Villalobos H., 2021.

Figure 282. [Top] *Milagres – Bahia*, Brazil. Photograph: María A. Villalobos H., 2020.

Figure 283. [Bottom] Landscape along route BR-116 on the way to *Milagres – Bahia*, Brazil. Photograph: María A. Villalobos H., 2020.

Figure 284. [Top] *Rio de Janeiro*, on the coast of the state of *Rio de Janeiro*, Brazil. Photograph: María A. Villalobos H., 2021. **Figure 285.** [Center] *Morro do Chapéu* and surrounding cities – *Bahia*, Brazil. Photograph: Oscar Bressane, 2019. **Figure 286.** [Bottom] *Chapada Diamantina, Minas Gerais*, Brazil. Photograph: Oscar Bressane, 2013.

Figure 287. Roberto Burle Marx giving instructions to one of his collection assistants in a *restinga* formation in the region of *Porto Seguro*, to the south of *Bahia*, Brazil. Photograph: Koiti Mori in Motta, Flavio Lichtenfels, Gautherot, Marcel. *Roberto Burle Marx e a nova visão da paisagem*. Brazil: Nobel, 1984, p. 171.

Figure 288. Landscapes created by Roberto Burle Marx and collaborators at the *Palácio Itamaraty*, on the way to the Federal Senate, *Brasília*, Brazil. Photograph: María A. Villalobos H., 2021.

STATEMENT TO THE FEDERAL SENATE 1976

From the explorers' first contacts with our territory, the opinion was unanimous: the land was endowed with exceptional natural wealth. This opinion, expressed for the first time by Pêro Vaz de Caminha,[86] persisted through centuries of occupation upheld by Nóbrega, Anchieta, Hans Staden and Gabriel Sores de Souza, among many others.

After that period, travelers, researchers, and scientists offered a new kind of content, showing not only their admiration for the wealth and beauty of the country, but also highlighting the problems they encountered – poverty, disorganization, poor exploration practices, gratuitous or needless attacks on heritage.

The works of Spix,[87] Martius,[88] Schott,[89] Gardner,[90] Lund,[91] the prince Wied-Neuwied,[92] Saint-Hilaire,[93] Langsdorff,[94] Sellow,[95] Loefgrsen,[96] and many others, whether in books, annotations, designs, or engravings, now constitute a true monument to the Brazilian landscape.

[86] Pêro Vaz de Caminha (c. 1451-1500). Portuguese notary and member of the Portuguese court, in charge of redirecting royal decrees presented to the courts. He was the official scribe for the fleet of Pedro Álvares Cabral. In his letter addressed to King Manuel I of Portugal, dated May 1, 1500, Pêro Vaz de Caminha recounts both the expedition and the events of April 22, with the arrival in the port, the new territory and its people. This letter is known as "Brazil's Birth Certificate". For more information, see: Itaú Cultural, 2017; Vaz de Caminha, 1500.

[87] Johann Baptist von Spix (1781-1826). German philosopher and doctor, who also studied the natural sciences. During his tenure as a zoologist at the Munich Zoological Museum, he was invited to join the scientific commission together with Karl Friedrich Philipp von Martius. His participation in the expedition was of great importance for his observations, records and descriptions of zoology and indigenous languages, and his illustrations of ethnological material (Heizer, 2018, pp. 29-33).

[88] Karl Friedrich Philipp von Martius (1794-1868) and Johann Baptist von Spix (1781-1826) led the expedition that took place with other scientists between 1817 and 1835 known as the Austrian Expedition to Brazil (*Missão austríaca*/Osterreichische *Brasilien-Expedition*). The expedition was associated with the trip made by the Austrian archduchess Maria Lepoldina of Habsburg (1797-1826) to marry the prince Dom Pedro (1798-1834), heir to the throne of Portugal. The explorers traveled 4,000 km from north to south and 6,500 from east to west across the vast Brazilian territory over the course of three years (1817-1820). As a result of these explorations in Brazil and the Upper Amazon, observations were recorded in a variety of areas of knowledge: botany, zoology, linguistics, anthropology. The German naturalist Karl Friedrich Philipp von Martius, who held a PhD in medicine and had an ongoing involvement with the natural sciences, was a student of Carl von Linné. Martius found his "spiritual homeland" in Brazil and took it upon himself to record the riches he encountered in extensive herbaria and rigorous publications incorporating studies of flora and fauna, history, geography and music, such as: *Flora brasiliensis* (1840-1906), *Historia naturalis palmarum* (1823-1850), *Reise in Brasilien* (1823-1831). For more information, see: Ormindo, 2018, pp. 11-13; Heizer, 2018, pp. 29-33; Brasiliana Iconográfica. Equipe Pinacoteca, 2017; Martius K. F., 1840-1906.

Figure 289. Representation of a mining operation, panning for gold. Johann Moritz Rugendas. *Lavage du Minerai d' Or, Pres de la Montagne Itacolumi*, 1835. Archive of the *Coleção Brasiliana Itaú* (Rugendas, 1835). Rugendas worked alongside Langsdorff during the expeditions to the interior of *Minas Gerais* between 1824 and 1825. Before and after that expedition, the artist Rugendas recorded the life, landscapes, fauna and flora of Brazil; he was the author of one of the largest collections of illustrations from the 1820s. His work *Voyage Pittoresque dans le Brésil* [*Viagem Pitoresca através do Brasil*] (1827-1835) published by the Engelmann publishing house, it was promoted upon its arrival in France by another great explorer: Alexander von Humboldt. For more information, see: Brasiliana Iconográfica, 2017.

[89] Heinrich Wilhelm Schott (1794-1865). Naturalist and researcher of the Araceae family. Together with the zoologist Spix and the botanist Martius, he was part of the Austrian Expedition (along with other naturalists). Schott's trip (from 1817 to 1821) made it possible to collect information on the natural history, agriculture, and ethnology of Brazil. During the expedition he worked with the botanist Mikan, the zoologist Natterer, and the mineralogist Pohl. He founded and directed a garden in *Rio de Janeiro* with the aim of acclimating living plants to temperate climates, preparing them to be transported to Europe. For more information, see: Riedl, 1965; Brasiliana Iconográfica. Equipe Pinacoteca, 2017.

[90] The Scottish botanist George Gardner (1812-1849) carried out expeditions between 1836 and 1841 in regions not visited by Marius and Spix, following itineraries that ran through the provinces of *Rio de Janeiro*, *Pernambuco*, *Bahia*, *Alagoas*, *Ceará*, *Piauí*, *Goias* and *Minas Gerais*. In the province of *Rio de Janeiro*, the intense expeditions through the *Serra dos Órgãos* are worth of note. Based on his travels through the province of *Ceará* and his observations on geological and botanical aspects, he published three works (see: Gardner, 1840-41; Gardner, 1841 and Gardner, 1843), in addition to the book *Viagens no Brasil* (Gardner, 1846). He was the first naturalist to study fish fossils found at the foot of the slope of the *Chapada de Araripe* in *Ceará*. Based on these expeditions he developed important collections and a description of species of flora and fauna (Pinto Palva, 1993, pp. 77-95). Gardner's Brazilian herbarium is divided between the collection of the British Museum of Natural History in London and the Fielding Herbarium at the University of Oxford. To access the digital herbaria, see: *Natural History Museum*, n.d.; Oxford University, 1985-2021.

[91] Peter Wilhelm Lund (1801-1880). Danish paleontologist known as the "father of paleontology and archeology in Brazil". He settled definitively in the *Minas Gerais* region of Brazil in 1833, where he excavated limestone caverns in the *Rio das Velhas* valley, describing mammals and environmental changes that had taken place since the Pleistocene. In Brazil, Lund discovered in traces of animals and hominids from ages prior to the arrival of man on the American continent. For more information, see: Peter Wilhelm Lund, *Pai da Paleontologia Brasileira*, 2020.

[92] Alexander Philipp Maximilian zu Wied-Neuwied (1782-1867). A German prince, naturalist, and ethnologist, he began his scientific expeditions in Brazil in 1808. Influenced by Alexander von Humboldt and Johann Friedrich Blumenbach, Neuwied recorded ethnographic material (drawings, notes) on native populations in the southern regions of *Bahia* and *Espírito Santo*, and in the northern mining regions. For more information, see: Brasiliana Iconográfica, 2017.

Figure 290. View of the village of *Porto Seguro*, three centuries after the arrival of the Portuguese fleet led by Pedro Álvares Cabral. Príncipe Maximilian von Wied. Engraving: Johann Carl Schleich II, *Vue de la ville de Porto Seguro, Bahia*, Brazil, 1822. (Id: PINA07291). *Fundação Estudar. Doação da Fundação Estudar, 2007/Acervo da Pinacoteca do Estado de São Paulo*, Brazil. *Coleção Brasiliana* (Wied, 1822).

[93] The French botanist Augustin François César Prouvençal de Saint-Hilaire (1779-1853) went on an expedition to Brazil between 1816 and 1822 as part of the Duke of Luxembourg's delegation. His travel itinerary included exploring the regions of *Rio de Janeiro*, *Minas Gerais*, *Espírito Santo*, *Goiás*, *São Paulo*, *Santa Catarina* and *Rio Grande do Sul*. He studied the province of *Goiás* in depth, like Johan Emmanuel Pohl, George Gardner and Francis Castelnau. His notable works include *Voyages dans l'intérieur du Brésil, 1779-1853*, *Flora Brasiliae Meridionalis*, 1824-1833 and *Viagem as Nascentes do Rio S. Francisco*, 1847. For more information, see: Santos Andrade & Bastiani, 2012, p. 172; Guimarães Ferri, 2004, p. 11-12; Damasceno, 2019; Saint-Hilaire, 1847.

[94] Georg Heinrich von Langsdorff (1774-1852) was a German naturalist physician, who became a Russian citizen. He moved to *Rio de Janeiro* in 1813 to serve as consul general. As a member of the Imperial Academy of Sciences of Saint Petersburg, he was part of the scientific expedition to explore the interior of Brazil, through *Minas Gerais*, *São Paulo*, *Mato Grosso*, and the Amazon. The artist Johann Moritz Rugendas, the botanist Ludwig Riedel, the astronomer Néster Rubtsov, and the zoologist and linguist Édouard Ménétries joined the group for the expeditions to the interior of *Minas Gerais* between 1824 and 1825. Two other artists accompanied him during the second phase (1825-1829): Hercule Florence and Aimé-Adrien Taunay. For more information, see: Brasiliana Iconográfica, 2017; Centro Cultural *Banco do Brasil*, 2010; Bernardino da Silva, 1997.

[95] Friedrich Sellow (1789-1831), German botanist and naturalist. He was the gardener for the royal castle of *Sans-Souci* and an assistant at the Berlin Botanical Garden. With the support of Alexander von Humboldt, he went to Paris and London to further his scientific education in botany and the natural sciences. He joined Langsdorff's expedition team to Brazil. He accompanied Maximiliano Wied-Neuwied on the expedition to *Bahia*. Friedrich Sellow was the great explorer of southern Brazil and Uruguay. For more information, see: Marchiori, Corrêa Pontes y Marchiori Neto, 2016.

[96] Johan Albert Constantin Lofgren (Alberto Loefgren) (1854-1918). Swedish botanist who relocated to Brazil in 1874. Sponsored by the Stockholm Academy of Natural Sciences, he studied the flora of the regions of *Minas Gerais* and *São Paulo*. He worked as an engineer for the railway company Compañia Paulista de Vías Férreas and as a natural sciences teacher for the Colegio Morton. As part of the Geographic and Geological Commission in *São Paulo*, he worked for the departments of meteorology and botany. In 1896, together with Orville Derby and Francisco Ramos de Azevedo, he founded the *Horto Botânico* (now the Parque Estadual Alberto Löfgren). He oversaw the Botany Section of the Rio de Janeiro Botanical Garden until 1918. For more information, see: Persiani, 2012, pp. 24-26.

Figure 291. View of *Ilhéus*. Prince Maximilian von Wied. Engraving: Johann Carl Schleich II, *Vue de la ville et du port d´Ilhéos*, Brazil, 1822. (Id: PINA07293). *Fundação Estudar. Doação da Fundação Estudar*, 2007/*Acervo da Pinacoteca do Estado de São Paulo*, Brazil. *Coleção Brasiliana* (Wied, 1822).

But, at the same time, they contain a bitter criticism and warnings about the administration of those assets on the part of the inhabitants.

Spix and Martius's travel diary show such respect for that heritage, for example, that the serious hardships, inconveniences, and troubles they suffered on their arduous journey disappear in the face of their delight at glimpsing one formation or another or by their horror at seeing the destruction and irrational treatment of nature. Along those lines, it is enough to look at the engraving from one of the *Tabulae Physiognomicae*, showing the burning of an area of *Cerrado*, or their observation on the irrational and ecologically criminal collection of turtle eggs, which the government sponsored for the manufacture of cooking oil.

For today's reader, the excerpt from Saint-Hilaire's travel notes is also bitterly ironic, when he writes that:

"It will take many years before any trace of culture can be seen from the top of the Brazilian Pyrenees, and it will be a long time before the São Francisco River can be navigated by boats larger than the fragile canoes that now glide across its waters."[97]

He would never have imagined that, today, even those fragile canoes would be unable to access certain stretches of the river, due to the excess of silt caused by clearcutting at its headwaters.

Despite the warnings of those imminent scientists, our behavior regarding nature has only worsened, to the point of making its destruction official, for example through article 19 of the Forest Code,[98] which reads:

"Taking into account the greater economic benefit, the owners of heterogeneous forests are allowed to transform them into homogeneous ones, knocking down, either all at once or successively, all the vegetation to be replaced, so long as they undertake, before the start of the works, before the competent authority, an obligation of replacement and 'tratos culturais.'"[99]

---

[97] Notes by Auguste de Saint-Hilaire (1779-1853) in *Viagem às nascentes do Rio São Francisco e à província de Goiás*, accounts of a trip he took to the northeastern basin of Brazil in 1819, during his stay in Brazil from 1816 to 1822 (Saint-Hilaire, 1847).

[98] Forest Code - Law 4771/65 | Law No. 4,771, dated September 15, 1965 (Federal Senate, 1965).

[99] *Tratos culturais* are the efforts necessary to maintain adequate soil quality and support proper conditions for the development and survival of crops (Embrapa, s.f.).

Figure 292. Burning in an area of the *Cerrado*. Martius, K. F., & Spix, J. B. *Campi aestate sicca ignibus adusti*. 1794-1868. Digital version available at: Martius, 1794-1868.

When I agreed to make this statement, I set as a priority the importance of clarifying once and for all the difference between economic reforestation and environmental conservation. In our country, the statistics and data that are published are analyzed carelessly. I frequently hear news about millions of trees being planted in reforestation projects. But this news never specifies that the species being planted – pine and eucalyptus – are misguided from an ecological point of view. By substituting heterogeneous native forests, they are removing any possibility of spontaneous regrowth and they do not offer fauna the conditions they need for their survival. It seems clear to me that, by way of article 19, our Forest Code promotes the devastation of our forests, which, according to article 1 of the same Code, are assets of interest to all the country's inhabitants. Note that I am highlighting a conceptual contradiction. I am not yet referring to the constant and unpunished disrespect for those assets. Thus, these statistics may impress someone who is not in the know, but we are aware that they offer no contribution to a possible counterbalancing of our actions in nature.

On my travels throughout the Brazilian territory, I have witnessed the efficiency of the IBDF[100] when it comes to economic reforestation. But I have also seen a complete disregard for our natural riches. If the IBDF has proven to be ineffectual when it comes to preservation, why not limit its actions solely to activities of an economic nature, where its performance is efficient? It would be ideal to entrust another body, the Special Secretariat of the Environment, directed so effectively by Paulo Nogueira Neto,[101]

Figure 293. Disruption of the natural landscape on highway BR-101, *Rio de Janeiro*, Brazil. Photograph: María A. Villalobos H., 2021.

with the protection and perpetuation of our natural wealth.

I want to clarify that I am not an expert in the legal or constitutional structures, and therefore I cannot suggest modifications to those structures. But I can, and I have the obligation to denounce the empiricism and the frivolity with which we have interfered with nature. For that duty I offer up for analysis, the idea of exploring the transfer to SEMA[102] of the responsibility and authority over all matters related to conservation.[103] Within that scope, I include the determination and administration of national parks, botanical gardens and other entities dedicated to conservation, which, under the direction of the IBDF, have been shown to be inoperative.

Obviously, for this to be possible, it will be necessary to provide SEMA with a structure and resources suited to the proposed responsibilities. I base my proposal on the need for an organ that exclusively supervises conservation and

[100] Instituto Brasileiro de Desarrollo Florestal (IBDF). The IBDF was divided into two: the IBAMA and the ICMBio (ICMBio, n.d.).

[101] Paulo Nogueira Neto (1922-2019) was a Brazilian naturalist, professor, and politician. Nogueira Neto was the first person to occupy the Special Secretariat for the Environment, which gave rise to the current Ministry of the Environment. For more information, see: Nogueira Neto, 1992.

[102] Municipal Secretariat of the Environment (SEMA).

[103] Conservation is a term that refers specifically to environmental conservation. According to Webster's dictionary, it refers to: "planned management of a natural resource to prevent exploitation, destruction, or neglect" (Merriam-Webster, 2022).

Figure 294. Disruption of the natural landscape linked to the construction of the *Pedra do Cavalo* dam, on the BR-101 highway, *Bahia*, Brazil. Photograph: María A. Villalobos H., 2020.

the scientific attitudes with which we must approach our environment, without making it an issue from the economic point of view. In short, the country needs wood as a raw material to feed its industries, which must be produced, according to the current reforestation models in areas that have already been devastated or compromised, and under the authority of the IDBF. But the other need that must be urgently attended to – that is, the preservation of our natural wealth, and we must activate, enhance, or create all possible mechanisms for that purpose. If we confirm the feasibility of strengthening SEMA as an organ for preservation, it is evident that it should not function as an isolated entity. On the contrary, it should work closely with the IBDF to make sure their actions are compatible, whether in determining the appropriate use for land in accordance with its purpose, or in the zoning of areas for economic exploration or permanent conservation.

It would be necessary to adopt criteria that could determine the use of available areas for economic reforestation or for conservation based on parameters such as access conditions, proximity to urban centers, water-related characteristics, soil conditions, morphology, and other features. From

Figure 295. *Rio-Petrópolis* road, from the *Mirante do Cristo*, Brazil, showing how the natural landscape is showcased in the construction of access roads. Photograph: María A. Villalobos H., 2021.

what I have observed, to date there have been no established criteria in this regard. Along the *Belo Horizonte - Brasíla* highway there are immense areas, in the middle of the *Cerrado*, covered with eucalyptus trees. It would be necessary to set regulations and extensions so that these reforestation efforts don't interfere with the ecological balance of an entire region. It is worth remembering that, for the purposes the native fauna, an area of pine trees and a desert are the same thing. When I was in the Ducke Reserve, near *Manaus*, I was shocked to observe experiments using *Pinus elliottii* Engelm., on the part of an institution whose task is the study and perpetuation of the Amazonian flora – not research for the introduction of exotic species with an economic interest. The south of *Bahia* and the north of *Espírito Santo* were completely devastated without, at least, having established an occupation strategy that would ensure a minimum preservation of the original forest. Nature is not defended even on the so-called tourist roads, if not for any other reason, at least to guarantee the maximum potential for recreation of the regions they pass through.

The *Rio-Santos* highway could be considered an example of how roads should not be built. Following the total destruction of the roadsides and surrounding, they plant agaves and Mexican yuccas, *Spathodea africana* or another entirely incompatible species, only exacerbating the disruption of the natural landscape. I am positive that the technical means at our disposal today for the opening of roads could, and should, work in defense of nature, instead of causing catastrophic effects.

A few decades ago, despite primitive resources, the old *Rio-Petrópolis* and *Teresópolis-Petrópolis* roads were built, both of which are beautiful, respecting the topography and the natural surroundings and, most importantly, treating nature as an element to be respected as opposed to an obstacle.

On the roads being torn into the Amazon, two gigantic tractors connected by a 100-meter-long chain, raze 50,000 m^2 of forest in 90 minutes, and all the vegetation from the area is piled up and burned, without any study of the use of the species, as street trees or in other urban configurations. And at the same time as this terrible waste, almost all the country's nurseries are busy growing what is conventionally used in gardens, in a flagrant reversal of roles. If the administrators of these nurseries were not so inept, they could make it understood that our flora deserves to be and should be used, instead of adding to the distortion of the landscape through the widespread use of exotic species.

Rose bushes are grown in the nurseries of *Manaus*, pines in *Maranhão*, pines, and African tulip trees in Fortaleza,[104] while the *cassias*, *tabebuias* and thousands of other trees from our natural environments are dismissed as scrub.

These examples are sufficient to portray the Brazilian situation as chaotic in terms of conservation. Its scope demands the establishment of an acceptable policy for conservation. In the opinion of Aziz Ab'Sáber,[105] a geographer of the highest scientific merit, the price that we have paid and that we are still paying for progress has compromised our natural heritage. Given the size of the territory we live in, significant areas should have been fully reserved as a guarantee to protect the balance of nature. They have not been respected, and today a large part of the territory has been robbed of its power.

We need to outline the areas where, due to socioeconomic contingencies, there has been a persistence of forests of this category. Ab'Sáber called them *"Biosphere Reserves"*. In regions where devastation has ruled out the possibility of creating *"Biosphere Reserves"*, he suggests the creation or maintenance of *"Biosphere Filters"*. Measurements taken in the vicinity of the *Serra do Cantareira* and on the slopes of the *Serra do Mar* proved that these formations act as true filters of pollution. It is true that the situation in *São Paulo* would be even worse without the contribution from these bands of vegetation.

---

[104] *Spathodea* is a genus of species native to the African tropical dry forest. The species *Spathodea* P. Beauv. also known as the African tulip tree, is often described as an invasive species. It can be found in agricultural areas and forests in tropical regions: Invasive Species Specialist Group (ISSG), 2010.

[105] Aziz Ab'Sáber (1924-2012) was a scholar of geography, geology, and ecology. He received the International Prize in Ecology and the UNESCO Prize for Science and the Environmental. His work focused on preserving the environment and preventing deforestation in the Amazon. For more information, see: Menezes & Ab'Sáber, 2007.

The formalization of measures to protect the *"Biosphere Filters"* that exist in our territory would depend on implementation throughout the country to determine their effectiveness in combating pollution. As a complementary measure, it would be appropriate to create them where necessary. The third type of proposal, called an *Integral Reserve*, corresponds to an area allocated for scientific purposes where human intervention is minimized.

Access is exclusively reserved for these activities. A large number of areas that could be included in this regimen – and which are familiar to field scientists and SUPREN (the IBGE's Superintendency of Natural Resources) – could be added to the category through the simple fulfillment of its purposes or functions. It is important to note that the sizes of some of these areas are quite manageable in terms of cost and the possibilities of expropriation. Should this official designation be impossible, Ab'Sáber even suggests the possibility of purchase through the constitution of a consortium of research entities interested in a particular formation. In the context of this proposal, *Nature Reserves* are fully protected zones with limited access, intended to a preserve scientific, historical, or aesthetic interest for the purposes of culture and recreation.

This typology, developed by Ab'Sáber, has some points of contact with other studies in the field, including the Brazilian Forest Code itself. The Code, however, does not address the problems related to *"Biosphere Reserves"*.

Figure 296. Disruption of the natural landscape linked to the construction of new roads, Amazon, Brazil. Photograph: José Tabacow, 1982.

If there are differences between the various studies by eminent researchers, why not set up a high-level commission with these scientists to define the types of areas to be preserved? Thus, a definitive preservation policy could be laid out for our country. On this point, I would like to draw Your Excellencies' attention to a fact that I consider of great importance: nature doesn't respond to bureaucratic solutions. It is of little use to determine, through laws, the preservation of this or that area, if those laws are not subsequently enforced. The *Chapada dos Veadeiros* National Park, created by Federal Decree No. 49,875 in 1961, is expected to shrink by some 170,000 hectares, due to extensive devastation, cattle ranches, and the erosion of the purpose behind its creation. A road was plowed through the Xingu Park. In the *Monte Pascoal National Park*, what is left of the *Pataxós* communities have little chance of survival, and a former Minister of Transportation ordered the areas bordering the forest to be cleared to provide visibility for tourists from the BR-101. These examples and the measures based on a complete failure to understand the situation support my opinion that what we have created are just green blotches on the map of Brazil. In order for those blotches to effectively become National Parks, we have to give them the resources suited with their objectives, and their management needs to be placed in proven capable hands.

The fact of maintaining certain exemplary areas of the environment does not ensure a valuable ecological habitat for people. It is of little use for 40% of the territory to be covered with native forests if that part is entirely concentrated in the Amazon and the rest of the country is made up of states with just 3%, as in the case of *Espírito Santo*, or 8% like in *São Paulo*. However, if we could rely on private initiative through the creation of incentives, we could come very close to the goal, or better yet, to reaching a point of equilibrium between man and nature, which will support a more humane way of life.

The tax legislation offers rebates to encourage economic reforestation. If, in the opinion of scientists, the preservation of the environment is the most urgent of our economic problems − since economic problems will only worsen with environmental degradation, why not give much larger incentives to individuals or companies that aim to engage in maintenance projects and ecological recovery? That would bring about an increase in conservation efforts and at the same time we would be making it financially interesting for the private sector to become involved in our search for balance. Given the marked increase in economic reforestation that followed

Figure 297. *Parque Estadual de Cantareira*, entrance through *Aguas Claras, Serra da Cantareira, São Paulo*, Brazil. Photograph: María A. Villalobos H., 2021.

the introduction of tax incentives, we can suppose the participation of taxpayers interested in ecological maintenance or recovery would be significant in the event of more interesting financial grounds. In this scheme, the maintenance aspect takes on outsized importance, to the extent that it effectively contributes to the automatic ennoblement and subsequent preservation of a large part of the significant ecological formations in the Brazilian environment, regardless of their size. Another advantage that I also consider to be meaningful is the fact that, with these incentives, there would be a need for taxpayers to engage in an analysis focused on the existing nature and its ownership, which means that owners would collaborate in raising awareness of the importance of the natural environment in its original state. It is easy to understand the importance of this awareness if we look at how the Forest Code is disrespected with impunity: in the Amazon, Volkswagen caused the largest fire in the entire history of the planet, detected by artificial satellites, a fact that caused concern even abroad. Charcoal is produced at distances of more than 300 km into the heart of the *Cerrado* and is then transported in trucks to the steel mills near *Belo Horizonte*, which, in keeping with the Code, are obliged to produce quantities of wood equivalent to what they consume (article 21). Thus, the Fauna Protection Law is frequently violated, and this disregard is even encouraged by article 6, which reads:

"The Public Power will stimulate the formation and operation of amateur hunting and shooting clubs and associations, aiming to promote the associative spirit through the practice of this sport."[106]

If the issue is the conservation of fauna and flora, I am categorically in disagreement with a law that promotes hunting, even for amateurs.

In the newspaper *O Estado de São Paulo*, dated February 13, 1976, the President of the Gaúcha Association for the Protection of the Natural Environment, José Lutzenberger, states:

"Demolitions in prohibited places and conditions are still going on; demolitions without permission are still going on; permits are still being granted for demolitions without prior inspection of the terrain, which leads to the authorization of illegal demolitions; burning and illegal hunting is still going on; there irrational exploitation of rare and endangered species and specimens of flora and fauna is still going on; the irreversible destruction of precious ecosystems and irreplaceable formations is still going on; speculative 'reforestation' continues, often at the cost of intact and previously unthreatened native forests".

[106] Fauna Protection Law Hunting Code - Law ° 5197/67 | Law No. 5,197, January 3, 1967 (*Presidência da Republica*, 1967).

Figure 298. Deforestation, mining, and extraction processes in the Canaima National Park, Bolivar, Venezuela. Photograph: Carla Urbina, 2010.

But it would be impossible to describe all the abuses that I have witnessed. It would take hours.

However, there is a monstrous abuse that is taking place in this country, and which is the greatest crime that can be committed against the economy, culture, and human life itself. As a Brazilian, I am ashamed to have been forced to condemn, as late as 1973, the use of Agent Orange in our country. As the first to file a complaint, I received the following telegram from the IBDF:

"Taking into account your interview with the state of *São Paulo*, on this date, I request more precise information on areas of the Amazon where they are using herbicides containing Agent Orange. Paulo Azevedo Berutti, President of the IBDF".

I received this telegram on February 4, 1976 – that is, three years after my initial complaint. My answer was as follows:

"In my absence from the country, as a special guest of the UN in Nairobi, I was made aware of your recent telegram. Only His Excellency has the possibility to gather local knowledge regarding the application of the chemical defoliant.[107] In addition to considering my statements, motivated by an interest in the defense of natural environments and, also, statements pertinent to the matter at hand issued in interviews by professors Amilcar Vianna of the University of Belo Horizonte and Warwik Kerr, president of the National Institute of Amazonian Research – SOPREN in Pará, many other scholars who work on the problems of nature conservation can also offer their opinions on the matter, although only Your Excellency has the power to do something about it. Roberto Burle Marx".

My sources are limited to what has been published in public media or the statements of those who have had the opportunity to confirm such use, in practice.

Based on this data, unfortunately, the situation is discouraging. In truth, the chemical leaf removers have already been used throughout the country, wherever a forest formation was hindering someone's immediate interests.

[107] A defoliant is any chemical product that is sprayed or sprinkled on plants to cause their leaves to fall off.

Figure 299. Page 6 of the newspaper *O Globo* dated November 18, 1973, which published the complaint about deforestation in *São Paulo*, *Mato Grosso* and *Pará*. For more information, see: *O Globo*, 1973

Assim ficam as árvores após ser usado o desfolhamento

A PESAR de não ter sido a mais mortífera arma usada na guerra do Vietnam, os desfolhantes agrícolas foram deixados de lado pelos inconvenientes que apresentam, em virtude do seu alto índice de toxidez. O líquido venenoso é capaz de destruir em poucas horas uma floresta, após uma aplicação aérea. Agora, ele vem sendo usado por fazendeiros no Brasil, que aproveitam as sobras da guerra.

As árvores perdem as folhas e os animais morrem intoxicados: é o fim desta floresta, em São Paulo.

Fazendeiros devastam as florestas com desfolhante usado no Vietnam

SÃO PAULO (O GLOBO). — Aproveitando as sobras da guerra, fazendeiros estão aplicando o desfolhante em São Paulo, Mato Grosso e no Pará. No noroeste paulista, percorrendo de avião uma área de 100 quilômetros, O GLOBO documentou o que era apenas uma denúncia há um ano: galhos secos das árvores atingidas pelos desfolhantes, a ausência dos animais nativos, as reclamações de trabalhadores e uma Polícia Florestal que só tem as condições de fiscalizar as fazendas quando consegue uma carona.

O veneno

— A aplicação dessa desfolhante, sei não, parece coisa do outro mundo. Desemprega os trabalhadores porque a gente poderia ganhar mais, derrubando as árvores, e é um veneno como eu nunca tinha visto. Num instante derruba estas folhas e a copa desaparece, fica tudo seco, como vocês estão vendo. Eu mesmo fiquei sujo do líquido quando o avião jogou, mas acho que a invenção essa conversa de que ele intoxica, os homens disseram que da mata bicho pequeno.

A explicação é de Antônio Siqueira, trabalhador, há 16 anos, da Fazenda Alcídia, no município de Teodoro Sampaio, a 723 quilômetros de São Paulo e às margens do rio Paraná.

— Talvez por pura falta de sorte; como afirmou o administrador Nelson Blazan, que já se acostumara a ver "os homens do Governo chegarem todo dia para olhar a derrubada", a Fazenda Alcídia foi a primeira a ser descoberta pelo que não se pode chamar de "intenção da Lei". É que o uso dos desfolhantes ainda não é ilegal no Brasil.

O começo

No Município de Presidente Venceslau, onde a presença do destacamento da Polícia Florestal tornou seguro o dia o uso dos desfolhantes, o sargento Dorival Madrid diz, com a pouca convicção de um homem que não tem carros para fazer a patrulhamento, com um jeep caindo aos pedaços e a privilégio da derrubada:

— Em 1972, a fazenda Guandu, vizinha da Alcídia, já usou o desfolhante mas só alguns me deixou ficar com consequências desculpáveis. Mesmo assim, a Secretaria de Agricultura só mandou os agrônomos para a área um ano depois. Agora, com o exemplo da Alcídia porque a Câmara Municipal de Teodoro Sampaio fez a denúncia, ineditamente me mandei saber em São Paulo como devia proceder e até agora não tive resposta. Não quiseram o lei porque ele não sabe, nem eu sei, o que há por trás disso. Eu sou responsável, é possível que o Governo tome uma providência ou purja a lei que eu vou fazer cumprir.

Os vendedores do Conselho de Vitrines, Interiores e Fachadas também receberão os prêmios na próxima semana.

50 por cento da fazenda como reserva florestal, mas como não são fiscalizados, em apenas um dia, de avião, conseguem destruir a mata que seria derrubada em oito dias, por um homem, desde que apanhadas em copiar de tempo brega e equivale a ser visto por algum dos 30 guardas responsáveis pela floresta da redondeza.

— Quando essa lei chegar, sem dúvida, vai o nome de "Lei Alcídia" comenta, no munícipio de Assis, um dos trabalhadores da família do deputado estadual Rui Silva, dono da fazenda.

Segundo ele, a "onda" surgiu, por simples questão política:

— Acontece que o presidente da Câmara Municipal de Teodoro Sampaio é inimigo político do Dr. Rui e fez a denúncia, mas o privilégio não foi da Alcídia que, inclusive, teve autorização da Secretaria de Agricultura para derrubar a mata de 1.220 hectares. Se o Governo for mais além vai encontrar uso muito maior no sul do Mato Grosso e no Estado do Pará, lugares que não têm Polícia Florestal.

Em São Paulo, o presidente da Associação de Defesa da Fauna e da Flora, Paulo Nogueira Neto, reconhece, por enquanto, a falta de motivos para iniciar uma campanha maior contra os desfolhantes.

— Eu enviei um telegrama ao Ministro da Agricultura solicitando a proibição dos desfolhantes porque li, na imprensa estrangeira que uma quantidade enorme dessas desfolhantes ficou estocada, após a guerra do Vietnam, e estaria sendo vendida aos países onde não é proibido o seu uso. Sai que, na Flórida, não é permitido o uso dos desfolhantes e deve haver uma razão para isso. No Brasil não temos condições imediatas de provar os seus efeitos nos animais e no homem, e o meu medo é que o veneno termine atingindo qualquer um. Com o DDT, e só venha a ser tomar perigoso depois a alguns anos.

Paulo Nogueira Ricarda já está preocupado se soubesse que, no interior do Estado de São Paulo, o desfolhante é aplicado perto de lagos e rios, caindo nos homens que ajudam aos pilotos. Alheia na Fazenda Alcídia, o lavrador Getúlio Alves fez um elogio ao puro veneno. Outra coisa que ele quer dizer é: Estes americanos trabalham com arte, sem não usam máscara. Esse veneno desemprega muita gente.

A venda

O Brasil não tem condições de fabricar os herbicidas, como afirma Paulo Nogueira Neto, há controle e grande parte dos produtos importados vem por meio de grandes empresas ou multinacionais.

Mas, da mesma forma afirmam que não têm conhecimento exato da quantidade de desfolhantes que entra no País, os técnicos da Secretaria de Agricultura não sabem informar por que o Ministério da Agricultura tão trouxe para os desfolhantes a mesma restrição do grande parte deles.

Agora, por exemplo, na Fazenda Alcídia, os agrônomos da Secretaria de Agricultura reconheceram, uma parte do "Pinatom" por examinar e não deram resposta. Concorda-se que a análise vai direto ao Ministério da Agricultura, ou até o 2º Escalão, que envia técnicos a Fazenda, para verificar o favor das componentes químicos. O "Pinatom" que, segundo a empresa "Planta Herbicidas", contém 51,48 por cento de ácidos $2,4$ e $2,4,5$, 2,45 por cento de triclorofenoxiacético e 25,54 por cento do ácido diclorofenoxiacético, é apenas um dos desfolhantes usados no Brasil. É conhecido de todos é o "Thordon" ou "agente laranja", difundido em todo o País.

Importados pelas multinacionais, os desfolhantes são entregues, depois, às empresas intermediárias que vendem a fazem aplicação. As críticas contra eles, no entanto, firmam com as algumas intermediárias desistiram do produto, antes que o Governo tome a iniciativa de proibí-lo.

Até o momento, as empresas de aviação foram as únicas que tiveram prejuízo com os desfolhantes. Quando aplicam cá o veneno, elas atingem as plantações vizinhas, a como aconteceu na cidade de Navirai, Mato Grosso, são processadas e pagam o prejuízo. A Fazenda Alcídia foi acusada por um lavrador de uma das linhas do rio Paraná mas, segundo a Polícia Florestal de Presidente Venceslau, "ninguém ainda procurou o desfolhante como prejudicial à lei colocada". Os guardas dizem que o veneno tiver chegado à flha, terá chegado, também, as águas do rio, levado pelo vento.

Os prejuízos

Não precisa mais que isso: uma semana. Nesse tempo, o veneno, aplicado por avião, começa a transformar em cinzas o que antes era verde floresta, habitada por aratas, onças e veados, como na Fazenda Alcídia.

Agora só os passarinhos passam nas árvores secas, para fazer um chamada, durante o dia. O resto à galho seco à espera do pasto.

Todos os fazendeiros após a derrubada do de mata está sendo feita para que se amplie a criação de gado. O partido do sudoeste paulista, no momento, contribui com 10 por cento do rebanho bovino nacional. O boi vai vencendo a floresta, apesar da lei que determina que 50 por cento da propriedade sejam conservados como reserva.

A Polícia Florestal tem que "os desfolhantes acabem atingindo até a reserva do IBDF, na área (16 mil alqueires)". Mas tem pouca esperança de solucionar o problema como o Sargento Dorival.

— Não vou cobrir os municípios, numa área de 144.687 quilômetros quadrados. Se temos condições do saber da derrubada quando aparece uma denúncia porque temos também que fiscalizar a pesca. Quanto à essa lei proibindo os desfolhantes, acho que vai ser igual ao que acontece, há muito anos: determinam que 50 por cento da casa fazenda daqui do pontal devem ser de mata nativa mas, quando a polícia Foi foi apontada, um dos proprietários mais importantes, o Calut, não tinha sequer 100 hectares de floresta.

Por enquanto, o grande número destes fazendeiros apenas para olunizar a morte dos animais atingidos pelos desfolhantes. Mais tem pouco sabor a esperança de que as folhas velhas venham lavrar também a jamais vão denunciar o vizinho, sabendo que estão impunes, no Brasil.

Comissão alertou, em junho, sobre os perigos do produto

Sensibilizada com a informação dada pelo Deputado Pacheco Chaves de que uma companhia norte-americana estaria fazendo gestões para vender no Brasil o Agente Laranja, a Comissão de Agricultura da Câmara enviou ao Ministro da Agricultura, em junho deste ano, ofício em que pedia cautela na aquisição do produto, já que seu uso estava proibido pelas autoridades sanitárias dos Estados Unidos.

No início deste ano, a Secretaria de Agricultura de São Paulo constatou a aquisição do produto e agricultores paulistas o reconhecia o perigo do seu uso. O Diretor da Divisão de Proteção de Coordenadoria de Pesquisa de Recursos Naturais, Roberto Melo Alvarenga, informou também que o Instituto de Botânica da Secretaria deveria concluir em dezembro uma pesquisa de laboratório para determinar exatamente as propriedades do produto. Na opinião do Sr. Roberto Melo Alvarenga, somente quando o laboratório encerrasse esses estudos é que teria "condições de solicitar ao Governo uma atitude rigorosa contra o herbicida".

Segundo a revista "Science", da Associação Americana para o Progresso da Ciência, desde o princípio deste ano o Governo dos Estados Unidos debate a questão de permitir ou não a venda dos estoques de Agente Laranja a empresas particulares interessadas em exportar o produto.

A Força Aérea dos EUA, segundo a revista, tem um estoque de 2.335.900 galões do produto, no valor de US$ 16.540.000. Parte desse estoque contém 28 vezes o máximo aceitável, dentro dos limites de segurança, de dioxin, um dos mais poderosos agentes teratogênicos.

Duas empresas norte-americanas estariam interessadas em abastecer o mercado latino-americano como o herbicida, apesar da declaração feita pelo Dr. Samuel Epstein, toxicologista da Case Western Reserve University

"A idéia de vender o produto para países da América Latina é simplesmente grotesca".

Em janeiro deste ano — afirma a revista Science —, o representante da Força Aérea para Suprimento e Manutenção, Lloyd Moseman, recebeu de Arnold Livingston, da Blue Spruce International, de New Jersey, uma proposta para que a Força Aérea cedesse o estoque de Agente Laranja para sua firma, que se propunha distribui-lo na América Latina. Como Moseman respondesse que a Força Aérea não poderia tratar esses estoques como se fossem propriedade privada, Livingston procurou uma associação com o IRI, Instituto de pesquisas tem lucrativos e que se dedica a programas de pesquisas agrícolas na América Latina.

Jerome Harrington, presidente do IRI, afirma que o Agente Laranja pode ser diluído e vendido a fazendeiros por preços inferiores a 5 dólares por galão — um terço do preço atual.

Antes de aceitar a proposta das duas instituições Moseman decidiu consultar o Departamento de Estado, que se recusou a liberar a exportação do produto antes que a EPA — Environmental Protection Agency — regulamentasse seu uso interno.

Abre segundo o informe, no número de abril deste ano, a EPA estudava uma fórmula do Agente Laranja na qual Dioxin participa se com 0,1 por milhão, já as concentrações de dioxin permitidos atualmente são de 0,1 por milhão para novos herbicidas e 0,5 para estoques já manufaturados.

O Agente Laranja é um composto de 2, 4, 5-T (50%) e de 2, 4-T (50%). O primeiro contém o dioxin, uma terceiro altamente teratogênica, isto é, produz malformações no feto, além de ser teratogênico de próprio. Seu aplicando, proibida pela EPA em plantações, só é permitida em pastagens. Quanto ao 2, 4-T, há também indicações de que seja teratogênico

---

TERMINA HOJE X SEMANA DA TIJUCA

Termina hoje a X Semana da Tijuca, promoção da VIII Região Administrativa e da Associação Comercial e Industrial da Tijuca, com o encerramento marcado para as 20 horas, na Rua Conde de Bonfim, 472, local onde os montado o Salão de Arte e Artesanato e a Mostra da Exposição Infantil. A Banda de Música da Polícia Militar estará presente à solenidade. Durante o dia serão disputadas as finalíssimas da Olimpíada da Juventude, abrangendo diversas competições desportivas dos clubes e colégios da Tijuca e terá também na Praça Xavier de Brito. As medalhas serão entregues aos vencedores no decorrer da próxima semana, em local e hora a serem divulgados. Hoje, ainda, às 20 horas, a Casa da Juventude Tijucana, na Casa da Vila da Feira e Terras de Santa Marta, será franqueado aos sócios dos clubes tijucanos e aos estudantes, mediante a apresentação da carteira escolar.

O Jornal, dated June 17, 1973, reported the intention of the United States – which has a reserve of 2.3 million gallons of Agent Orange – to send the product to Brazil.

According to *O Globo*, from November 18, 1973, the Secretary of Agriculture of the State of *São Paulo* confirmed the acquisition of *"agent orange"* on the part of *São Paulo* farmers. On the same day, the same newspaper reported the use of the orange herbicide in *São Paulo*, *Mato Grosso* and *Pará*. The note complements reports that the plant physiologist Dantas Machado, from the National Research Council, was being contacted in *Brasília* by companies that commercialized defoliants, intending to set up their businesses in the Amazon. *O Estado de Minas*, on February 14, 1976, reported the same news.

The scientist Warwick Kerr, president of the National Research Institute of the Amazon, warns about the use of chemical agents that represent serious dangers for the fauna, flora, and the biological environment. In the *Jornal de Santa Catarina* from February 3, 1976, he denounces the companies that supply these defoliants, which offer their products to farmers and agricultural companies in southern Brazil. If I, as an individual, was able to gather documentation on the matter, all the more reason the IBDF, which has a structure created to detect and monitor these abuses, should be able to offer a response to my telegram.

I understand that the task of controlling taxation our territory is arduous. The possibility of assistance from the army, meant to defend the integrity of the national territory, should be considered, due to the ease of putting an efficient inspection operation into effect because Army units are already stationed throughout the national territory. If such a measure were adopted, beyond the immediate practical action, it would have the convenience or advantage of raising awareness on the part of all the Army personnel and young men of an age to serve in the military. In the same way that the engineering battalions collaborate so efficiently in the construction of roads, this suggestion could open another area of action that would surely be viewed with respect and sympathy on the part of the population.

At the end of this statement, I would like to make it clear that these complaints and suggestions were made by someone who understands and loves nature. Environmental protection measures are difficult to put into practice, and expensive in the short term. And yet, contempt or abandonment would be much more burdensome. That is why I wanted to emphasize the awareness that, in my opinion, is an indispensable condition for the coexistence of so-called "civilized" man with so-called "savage" nature.

June 1976

Figure 300. The aerial observations for the construction of the Maracaibo Botanical Garden in Maracaibo, Venezuela, were carried out in collaboration with the Venezuelan army. Photograph: José Tabacow in the early 1980s.

Figure 301. *Mata Atlântica* in *Rio de Janeiro*, Brazil. Photograph: María A. Villalobos H., 2018.

PROBLEMS WITH NATURE CONSERVATION 1976

Lately, there has been talk of ecological balance, preserving the environment, the fight against pollution, etc. The media are responsible for keeping these issues in the public eye. It seems to me that this fact alone justifies an effort to promote a conservation program at the national level. A few laws, some isolated actions, the closure of certain factories, or an educational campaign don't constitute a program. They are isolated events.

The development of a conservation program in our country is highly complex. Brazil has a large number of landscape domains (corresponding to the botanical provinces defined by Martius). Each of these provinces has its own structure and its own balance. Within each of them, it is possible to distinguish a series of smaller units, local variations, or enclaves of other units.

The macrocommunities have been sufficiently described in theoretical terms. However, we lack detailed studies of each of their constituent parts, the survey of their characteristics at the level of landscape, geology, vegetation, and fauna.

Preservation, in its correct sense, does not imply the arbitrary selection of a particular natural environment to be preserved. Nor can this conscious action be confused with the accidental *"preservation"* of certain territories, usually due to lack of economic interest at a certain moment in time. Conservation does not exclude a rational use of the land. On the contrary, it advocates it. But, unless we want to see the quantity and quality of our natural environments diminished, it will have to be developed as a global system that works for the entire national system.

The reality stands in radical contrast to those principles. More and more rapidly, as human occupation advances, we are destroying entire entities, leaving no trace. Each new economic cycle attacks a different formation, with renewed voracity. The semi-deciduous forests of the state of *São Paulo* will disappear completely. The *Mata Atlântica* is subject to a double attack from deforesters: tourism incentive programs and real estate exploitation. The most recent front of destruction is the Amazon, with its gigantic fires wiping out thousands of hectares.

There is a generalization we can make: the disrespect and waste with which we treat our natural resources have been a constant in our history, and they have tended to worsen as technological power increases. As an example, it is sufficient to that recall how the *Rio-Santos* highway was built. It is a fairly recent example of the misappropriation of technology to commit atrocities.

It is also bitterly irony that, along with these sophisticated forms of destruction (napalm, bulldozers, etc.), we also use indigenous techniques, such as the *coivara*. With the difference that, while the indigenous peoples destroyed only small portions of land, which the surrounding bushes were able to regenerate, today's burning destroys an irreplaceable tree material, subjecting the bare soil to the processes of erosion and leaching, so widespread today in tropical regions. That level of destruction is irreparable. It is the case of the transformation of very large, forested areas of the Amazon into pastureland.

Nor are there any possibilities of recovery for an infinite number of small areas with an incalculable landscape value – subjected to so many other anachronistic processes. In those cases, the driving forces are misery and ignorance. It happens over and over, as people try to cultivate an area that is impossible to cultivate, due to the poor quality of the soil, the presence of rocks or the uneven and infertile terrain. A landscape of incalculable scenic value, or a floristic formation of rare beauty, is destroyed for a negligible material yield.

In the *Morro do Chapéu*, *Ferro Doido*, people used to raise pigs. I don't know whether they still do. In Torres, *Rio Grande do Sur*, the very small tree formations that once supported the dunes were deforested, leading to serious disturbances in the very fragile balance of those formations. In an impersonal analysis of this data, it is almost inevitable to reach the conclusion that our relationship with nature is basically characterized by violence and contempt.

It seems to me, therefore, that this is a partial truth. Considered as a collective, we are undoubtedly the most insensitive and irresponsible predators imaginable. But man, the individual, patiently and on daily basis, remakes the fragile ties that connect our society to nature. He raises livestock. He plants flowers. He looks to the woods to relax from tiring work. He loves the sea, the mountains, the rivers. These attitudes are obviously miniscule, crude and even vulgar in the face of the overwhelming level of destruction. But there is one difference between them, which is radical: while individual and conscious action is the result of a profound understanding of the man-nature connection, destruction is impersonal. Destruction is dictated by the economic interests of groups, regions and, sometimes, the entire country.

Destruction is always anonymous. The responsibility cannot be attributed to anyone in particular. It is diluted among thousands, not only horizontally, but also vertically (that is: in the sense of the chain of causes and effects, of needs, of orders and their execution). Therein lies the difficulty when it comes to conservation. The change that needs to be implemented is not on an individual level: the collective mentality regarding the management of natural resources needs to be

reimagined. I will try to explain this better, with some examples:

a) The inhabitants of the interior were once familiar with the plants from their region. They knew the specific utility of many types of wood, and they knew the uses and dangers of many plants. They distinguished the blooms and had knowledge of the regional fauna. Very beautiful passages in our literature, by Euclides da Cunha or Guimarães Rosa, attest to this fact. It is clear that this knowledge was pragmatic and limited in its specific field of interest. But no more can be demanded of a culturally isolated population without regular education. If the form of agricultural exploration was economically unviable for the population there, certainly guidance and adequate technical assistance could correct the situation. But, as man disassociates himself from his land, and the population from the northeast is transferred to the Amazon, when waves and waves of *retirantes*[108] migrate to other regions, fleeing misery, we cannot expect that awareness from them.

The foundations of their knowledge fade away. From that moment on, they become amorphous elements when it comes to nature – whose actions are regulated by the demands of the market – or their bosses. Or a multinational corporation, who knows? (We cannot forget that part of this current urban population is made up of men in these conditions).

b) In recent decades, logging has desertified entire regions. Although the agents may be

Figure 302. Postcard from the Agronomic Institute of Campinas. Collection of the Museu Paulista da USP (Anonymous, n.d.).

people from the region, the destination for the raw materials are the urban centers. A fleeting vision of progress, derived from that exploration, drives entire populations – living in a stagnant economic regime – to destroy their own natural heritage. Let us repeat that the model of progress is imposed from outside and that the request for raw material is not local, or even regional.

c) Who is paying the unscrupulous hunters of crocodiles, monkeys, birds, and butterflies? Who is the intended target of crocodile skin wallets and tourist souvenirs? Urban buyers, therefore, feel relieved of the responsibility for the slaughter of thousands of animals.

I think I have managed to demonstrate what I referred to as the dilution of responsibility. I believe that in the face of these circumstances, campaigns, warnings, popular education are all worthless. Education will only achieve its results when today's students begin to occupy positions of responsibility.

I am convinced that only protective governmental measures, specific legislation, supervision, and the execution of projects directed at conservation will be able to reach significant measures.

[108] *Retirantes* is a term that refers to migrants from the Brazilian *Sertão* driven from their homes by drought and misery (Massaud, 1999).

Figure 303. Aerial view of the botanical garden at the Agronomic Institute of Campinas, *São Paulo*, Brazil, which was created in 1960, thanks to the work of Hermes Moreira de Souza, who continued his work there until his retirement. Photograph: Botanical Garden of the Agronomic Institute of Campinas, in the Central Experimental Center (Hacienda Santa Elisa), *São Paulo*, Brazil, 2013. For more information on the current situation, see: Instituto Agronómico, n.d.

I have dedicated myself to denouncing, proposing, suggesting, and contributing so that we can coexist with nature and achieve progress without sacrificing it. More often than not, my pronouncements are somber. However, I don't want my attitude to appear biased or one-sided. I also care about positive examples. For this reason, I cannot fail to mention the formidable work that the botanist and agronomist Hermes Moreira de Souza[109] has been carrying out at the Agronomic Institute of Campinas. The institute has a collection of approximately 1,500 species of trees, most of them native, and that fact by itself justifies the mention.

If there were more people who, like him, are dedicated to preserving our flora, we would one step farther along in that immense climb, which is the defense of nature, on which our survival depends.

I hope to gain more supporters in this fight, which, I repeat, requires a veritable army. We will never be able to show measurable results if we continue to rely on isolated efforts.

October 1976

[109] Hermes Moreira de Souza (1918-2011) was an agricultural engineer recognized for his work in environmental preservation, to the point of being known as the *semeador de floresta* or "planter of forests". To learn more about his work, see: Lorenzi & Souza, 2001.

Figure 304. *Myrcia tomentosa* (Aubl.) DC., collector H. M. de Souza 21309, *Bosque dos Jaquitibás, Campinas, São Paulo*, Brazil. Available at the New York Botanical Garden, No. 616632, ID 09c5966f-25b2-42cb-944e-227eed421129.

Myrtaceae

INSTITUTO AGRONÔMICO

HERBÁRIO I.A.C. Nº

Nome científico *Myrcia tomentosa* Berg.
Det. J. Mattos.
Proc. Campinas-SP-Bosque dos Jequitibás.

Obs. Árvore.

Figure 305. *Dyckia burle-marxii* Smith & Read at the *Sítio Burle Marx, Santo Antônio da Bica,* Brazil. Photograph: María A. Villalobos H., 2021.

THE INVOLVEMENT OF BOTANISTS IN MY PROFESSIONAL TRAINING   1983

My nomination as an honorary member of the Brazilian Botanical Society moves me and fills me with pride. Although I am not a botanist, throughout my activity as a landscape architect, I have always sought out the support of botanical scientists who could help me use vegetation in a conscious and, above all, more coherent way. But my ongoing contact with botanists taught me much more than that. Going beyond the confines of landscape design – that is, of the simple aesthetic composition of a garden – I began to understand the importance of valuing our flora, the environmental needs of each plant, the plant associations that constitute balanced aesthetic and ecological ensembles.

During all this time, I had the pleasure of working with Mello Barreto, who helped me understand the importance of learning about plants in their native habitat; with Aparício Pereira, a record holder in the collection of specimens for the herbarium of the Rio de Janeiro Botanical Garden; with Graziella Barroso, whose kindness and gentle demeanor contrasts with her extraordinary knowledge, and with the confidence and scientific rigor of her work; with Nanuza Menezes and João Semir, who have both shown a contagious enthusiasm in our travels together; with Adolpho Ducke, who had such a profound knowledge of the Amazon, which he loved so much; with José Correia Gómes, a great connoisseur of Bignoniaceae, who died prematurely and tragically in a car accident; with Luiz Emygdio de Mello Filho, whom I always my admired for the objectivity and power of synthesis he brought to the work we did together; with Kullman, whose intuitive perception made it possible for him to classify many plants by simply examining their seeds; with Pacheco Leão, whose dedication to preserving the integrity of the Rio de Janeiro Botanical Garden led him into an exhausting, thankless battle; with Hoehne, whose capacity for observation and documentation is beyond dispute; and, with many others, in what was always a fertile relationship.

Figure 306. [Top] Henrique Lahmeyer de Mello Barreto (in the white vest) leading visitors through the Rio de Janeiro Zoological Garden, Brazil. Photograph: Family archive. Published in: Santos Silva, 2018, p. 29. **Figure 307.** [Center left]: João Geraldo Kuhlmann (1882-1958) was a specialist in angiosperms and a great collector material for herbaria. He was director of the Botanical Garden of Rio de Janeiro, Brazil, between 1944 and 1951. Photograph published in: Reitz, 1972. **Figure 308.** [Center] Adolpho Ducke (1876-1959) (L029_N0458). Photograph: Archive of *Museu do Meio Ambiente*/JBRJ. **Figure 309.** [Center right] João Semir (1937-2018). He worked for more than 50 years as a dedicated botanist at the Laboratory of Plant Systematics in Campinas, São Paulo, Brazil. Photograph: Antoninho Perri, 2018 (Perri & Cavalheri, 2018). **Figure 310.** [Bottom left]: Pacheco Leão (1914- 1993) on the left with Albert Einstein at the Rio de Janeiro Botanical Garden, Brazil (AB001_P06_0384.1925). Photograph: Archive of *Museu do Meio Ambiente*/JBRJ. **Figure 311.** [Bottom right]: Frederico Carlos Hoehne (1882-1959) was a botanist, defender of nature, and the first director of the botanical garden of the Institute of Botany in São Paulo, Brazil. Photograph published in: Aniversario Frederico Carlos Hoehne, n.d.

Figure 312. Superintendent Aparício Pereira Duarte (1910-1984) on the left, during a tree planting ceremony with General Rondon. (P053_E10_F002.JPG). Photograph: Archive of *Museu do Meio Ambiente*/JBRJ. **Figure 313.** [Opposite page, top] Graziela Barroso (1912-2003) and Roberto Burle Marx (on the right). Walter Burle Marx, wearing glasses, on the right. Photograph: Collection of Nanuza Menezes, 1974. **Figure 314.** [Center]: José Correia Gómez (1919-1965), expert

in Bignoniaceae. José Correia Gomes, Graziela Maciel Barroso, Paulo Campos Porto and Ambassador Manuel Farrajota Rocheta next to the "Palma Mater" (imperial palm), Rio de Janeiro Botanical Garden (CLP_P01_F130). Photograph: Archive of *Museu do Meio Ambiente*/JBRJ. **Figure 315.** [Bottom] Roberto Burle Marx, Nanuza Luiza de Menezes, and Koiti Mori (1934), *Palácio da Alvorada, Brasília*, Brazil. Photograph: Collection of Nanuza Menezes, n.d.

Figure 316. Luiz Emygdio de Mello Filho during research in the restinga in the north of *Rio de Janeiro*. Rio de Janeiro, Brazil. Photograph: Unknown author and date. Collection of Lúcia Maria Sá Antunes Costa.

Figure 317. *Heliconia adeliana* Emygdio & E. Santos, a species described by Luiz Emygdio de Mello Filho, named in honor of Adélio da Rocha, who was an employee at the *Sítio Roberto Burle Marx* and a driver for various expeditions. For more information, see: Iphan, 2019, pp. 173-174. Illustration: Margaret Mee. Available in: Mee, 1981.

Figure 318. [Top] *Philodendron grazielae* G. S. Bunting, named in honor of Graziela Barroso. Archive of the *Sítio Burle Marx, Santo Antônio da Bica*, Brazil. Photograph: Carla Urbina, 2014. **Figure 319.** [Center left] *Alcantarea glaziouana* (Lem.) Leme, *Sítio Roberto Burle Marx, Santo Antônio da Bica*, Brazil. Photograph: María A. Villalobos H., 2021. **Figure 320.** [Center right] *Merianthera burle-marxii* Wurdack, *Sítio Roberto Burle Marx, Santo Antônio da Bica*, Brazil. Photograph: Carla Urbina, 2009. **Figure 321.** [Bottom] The *Philodendron mello-barretoanum* Burle Marx & G.

M. Barroso, was named in honor of the botanist Mello Barreto. Collection of the *Sítio Burle Marx, Santo Antônio da Bica*, Brazil. Photograph: Carla Urbina, 2014. **Figure 322.** *Philodendron acutatum* Schott. Det.: Thomas Croat (2015). Origin: Caracas, Venezuela. Surroundings of Caracas. Collected by Burle Marx (1960). RB00474578. *Herbário do Jardim botânico do Rio de Janeiro* (RB) (Reflora, 2020) (JBRJ - Instituto de Pesquisas Jardim Botânico do Rio de Janeiro, n.d.).

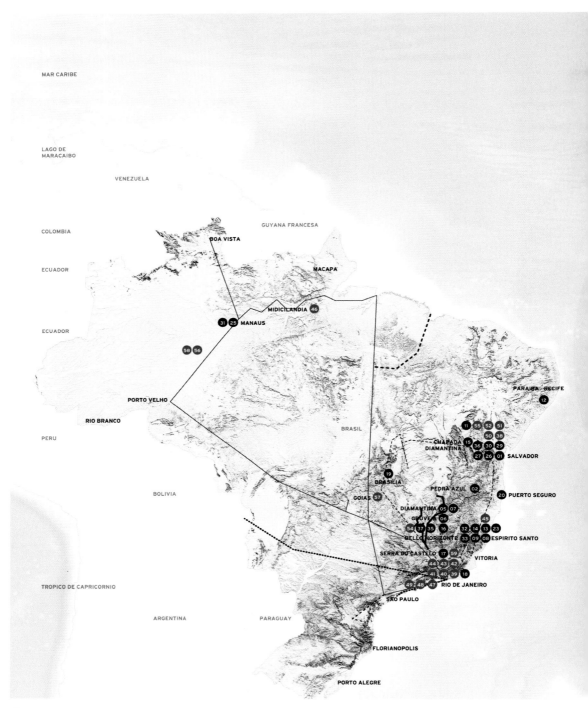

Figure 323. Map and cladogram of the plant universe associated with Burle Marx, based on the lists published in (Rizzo, G., 2009), developed by María A. Villalobos H. and Benjamin Jensen, in 2021. This research will be the focus of the publication *BurleMarxii* by María A. Villalobos H., which will track the habitats these botanical and cultural treasures live in and keep alive.

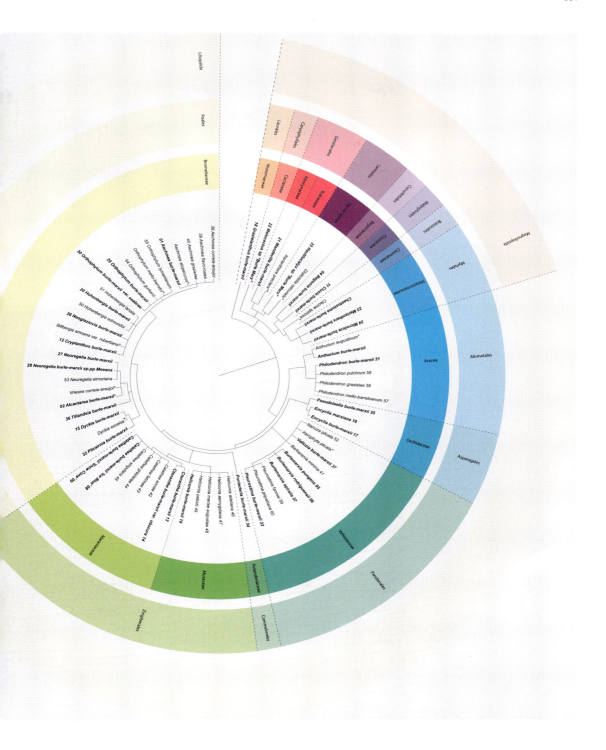

The role played by botanists was essential to my becoming known as a great defender of nature. In my talks, interviews, reports, and lectures, I have sought to base my criticisms on the information collected with my botanist friends, to give them consistency and solidity, avoiding flimsy conclusions or empty declarations.

It seems clear to me that the relationship is healthy because our goals are the same. I trust the information from botanists, and I present it to the public whenever I have access to the media; always with the awareness that, without the support of botanists, I would have done less than I did.

Our fight continues. A large dam wiped out the *São Simão* canal, a geographical feature that was one-of-a-kind in the world, and which had an extraordinary flora. Another pharaonic dam caused the disappearance of *Sete Quedas*. Nuclear power plants have destroyed and continue to destroy the flora and the tourist potential of the most valuable areas, not to mention their associated dangers, which are well known. Because of these facts, and a thousand others, less important individually but extremely harmful as a whole, we must stand together in our fight against *dendroclastic*[110] madness and the push for immediate gain.

I view my nomination as an honorary member of the Brazilian Botanical Society as a strengthening of my relations with botanists, which is exciting, and as an opportunity for an even closer collaboration, which fills me with pride.

Thank you very much.

January 1983

[110] *In Portuguese, dendroclasta refers to someone who does not respect trees (Dicionario Online de Português, 2009-2021).*

Figure 324. Marlon da Costa Souza, director of the Technical Division of the *Sítio Burle Marx, Santo Antônio da Bica*, Brazil. Photograph: Carla Urbina, 2009.

Figure 325. *Parque de Ibirapuera, São Paulo*, Brazil. Photograph: María A. Villalobos H., 2012.

LANDSCAPE DESIGN IN THE URBAN STRUCTURE 1983

In the transition from the craftsmanship to mass production, man brought about radical transformations in his way of life and in his environment. In the great metropolises, these transformations became cemented, and we were forced to experience them daily, emphatically.

Ancient cities were built in harmony with their surroundings, and there was more of a balance between people and the urban environment.

Several reasons contributed to this: the careful selection of the sites where cities would be built, in relation to topography, climate, natural geographic formations, etc.; the public squares were meeting places, and the streets, where people could walk freely, were the object of careful study; the houses were related to one another spatially, forming groups for common living; in the fields, nature was close at hand.

The change that occurred in the character of the cities, as a result of the transformation of the production processes, was violent. The rural exodus, sparked by the concentration of the means of production, and the demographic explosion, took on enormous proportions. The technological means employed to solve the problems resulting from population growth (housing and transportation) warped the essence of urban life and distorted the collective character of cities.

We are crowds of anonymous people who aren't coexisting but contending with one another every day, with increasing aggressivity, to occupy a fraction of space for our lives, our movement, our leisure. And to get just a little peace, silence, we try to ignore our neighbors, we shut ourselves away. We don't enjoy urban life. There is less and less to enjoy.

The sheer amount of stone, cement, accumulated metals, the impermeabilization of the ground due to construction, asphalt, and the removal of vegetation, are changing the climate. The temperatures are rising and changing the moisture content in the air. There is noise pollution, air pollution, water pollution..., and attacks on the landscape. The arbitrariness, the abuses are endless. Respect for public assets disappears.

In a city like *Rio de Janeiro*, there is an increasingly rapid destruction of the landscape. The beaches are dirty, and the original vegetation has been spoiled: real estate speculation devours the hills, eliminating their perspectives.

According to the scientists' opinion, it would take the *Guaíba* River more than in 400 years to recover from the ravages caused by the paper industry.

Figure 326. Water garden in the *Largo da Carioca*, Centro, *Rio de Janeiro*, Brazil. Photograph: María A. Villalobos H., 2014.

In *Belo Horizonte*, the *Serra do Curral* is being destroyed by the mining industry and the explosions are causing nearby houses to collapse. In *São Paulo*, a steel company has invaded the grounds of the Botanical Garden and is contaminating the headwaters of the *Ipiranga* River. We could cite hundreds of similar examples.

There has been a failure to reign in abuses of public heritage. Governments aren't dealing with this. They're also contributing to the destruction of cities, occupying or allowing the occupation of the few remaining open spaces, parks, and squares, with the most varied of constructions, without realizing that some of the most beautiful landscapes in the world are being destroyed.

Exceptions are made in urban legislation on behalf of the tourism industry because of its fashionable status, (for example, the changes in regulations for hotels along the *Copacabana*).

The infrastructure does not and cannot support this vertiginous growth in extension and height. The number of vehicles circulating cities is larger than what the roads can handle, which causes congestion. Drivers invade the sidewalks to park their cars. Pedestrians, for their part, having been pushed off the sidewalks, mix with vehicles on the streets, risking their lives and causing accidents. The problems of growth, of expansion, are increasing with incredible speed in these areas. New land is taken and areas suitable for agriculture

Figure 327. Panoramic view of *Copacabana, Rio de Janeiro*, Brazil. Photograph: Maria A. Villalobos H., 2021.

are occupied by houses or industry, many times without any consideration for the quality of the soil. There is a lack of infrastructure planning. Waste accumulates, the waters are polluted. What remains of the vegetation is depleted.

Balanced growth needs to be based on studies with a vision for the future. Conscious zoning must preserve the city's heritage, analyze the direction of expansion based on the geography, the economy, the relationship with the streets and with the surrounding nature, and to maintain the forests around the urban periphery (in the footsteps of Houver), the natural fields, where birds and animals can thrive, planning agricultural and industrial activities so, they don't conflict, cause mutual damage or harm the population. In this context of organization, it would even be necessary to find a balance between heterogeneous forests and homogeneous reforestation for wood production. Let's not be naive.

Both are productive. Going back to urban problems, we have seen a widespread practice in our cities: green areas, and vegetation in general, are constantly being sacrificed for a wide variety of reasons. Although, in the short term, it may seem like a fitting solution to eliminate a plaza for the construction of a public building, or to fell trees for the expansion of roads, over time, both those trees and the open space of

the plazas will be sorely needed. And replanting trees and rebuilding squares will take dozens of years – and that's only if there is the political will to rebuild them. In most cases, there is merely demolition without replanting, and cities become increasingly arid, with no peaceful spaces, with no shade.

This false conception of urban renewal or progress has sacrificed not only the existing vegetation, but also the very history of cities. Important works of art and architecture are disappearing daily, giving in to this attitude of denying the past. We forget that the coexistence of different time periods, embodied in the work of many generations, is one of the main charms of cities.

However, let's get back to the topic at hand. I'd like to talk a little about the roles that gardens have played at different moments in their history. In ancient times, they were born to protect medicinal plants and fruit-bearing trees. There were few places where trees and herbs were planted just for the beauty of their flowers and foliage. In the Middle Ages, gardens were places for religious and philosophical meditation. In the reign of Louis XIV, Versailles played an important political role: it was created for people to gather around the king and for the French nobility, which had been spread out across the country up to that point.

Today, the most general opinion is that a park is a place for contemplation. I have nothing against that idea if we understand that parks also need to fulfill a series of other functions, have other attributes.

Figure 328. University of Padua Botanical Garden, Padua, Italy. Photograph: María A. Villalobos H., 2013.

Residential yards and gardens are getting smaller and smaller. The leisure areas they provide will have to be offered in public gardens. With our sedentary lifestyles, sports have taken on an important role, and parks will need to offer possibilities for playing sports and for children's playgrounds. And we should create educational parks, botanical gardens, and zoos to teach people about plant life. And spaces for picnics, where people can take breaks from their work.

The design of the vast majority of our squares and parks is not suited to those purposes. They are like islands in a river of urban traffic, they are difficult to access, and their quality is compromised by noise. The squares of the interior, where these problems are not so accentuated, fare somewhat better but they are not peaceful places either: the paths cut through them become mere circulation areas. They are sacrificed for the erection of monuments, often in questionable taste. The benches (engraved with the names of donors) are arranged indiscriminately, and they aren't inviting for people to sit on. The plants are all distributed in innumerable pots, as though they were obstacles that the network of paths has to avoid. The analysis of the species of trees, shrubs and grasses used is melancholic. They are always species from other regions – when they don't come from other countries or even other continents. In short, it doesn't support our education at all, which already so limited that it doesn't even include knowledge of the native flora.

Education, targeted mainly at young people, may be the only viable measure to save our country

Figure 329. Montpellier Botanical Garden, Montpellier, France. Photograph: María A. Villalobos H., 2012.

Figure 330. Trees as a play area, *Parque do Flamengo, Rio de Janeiro*, Brazil. Photograph: María A. Villalobos H., 2021.

Figure 331. [All] Maracaibo Botanical Garden, Venezuela during the early years of its operations. Photographs: Archive of the Maracaibo Botanical Garden Foundation, c. 1983. **Figure 332.** [Opposite page] Press release for the inauguration of the Maracaibo Botanical Garden, Venezuela. Diario Panorama, Venezuela. It is considered the first

El Dr. Luis Jiménez Segura, directivo de la Fundación Jardín Botánico de Maracaibo, declara al periodista Angel Alberto Briceño. (Foto Colina)

Escuela Nacional de Horticultura es la primera en su tipo instalada en los países de América Latina

La Escuela Nacional de Horticultura del Jardín Botánico de Maracaibo, cuyas actividades inició ayer el Presidente de la República doctor Luis Herrera Campins, con la clase magisterial inaugural es la primera escuela de este género que se organiza en América Latina.

La información la suministró el doctor Luis Jiménez Segura, concejal maracaibero y directivo de la Fundación Jardín Botánico de Maracaibo, quien señaló que dicha institución ha nacido bajo los auspicios del Gobierno Nacional a través del Ministerio de Educación.

Dijo que el acto de inauguración de la Escuela Nacional de Horticultura tiene una extraordinaria trascendencia para la colectividad zuliana, para el país y para Suramérica.

–Para Maracaibo y el Zulia –explicó el doctor Jiménez Segura– porque viene a convertirse en sede de una nueva enseñanza que no la hay en Venezuela ni la hay en Latinoamérica.

school of its kind, dedicated to the education of horticulturists as they simultaneously build the botanical garden themselves. In an innovative gesture, it combines landscape design and education by celebrating the combination of education and action. Photograph: Archive of the Maracaibo Botanical Garden Foundation, c. 1983.

from total desertification and ensure a more balanced nature for future generations. Its survival depends on the measures we take in the face of the barbaric destruction processes we are witnessing today.

We must ensure that our children have contact with nature, that they understand the heritage within their reach. We should teach them to plant trees, to understand how important trees are, teach them not to harm them. Show them the importance of plant associations, of ecology. Teach them to collect seeds, to sow them, to plant the little seedlings, to show love for them, so that they can prosper. They should see plants as living beings with the right to grow, flourish and bear fruit, instilling in them the importance of perpetuation, the wonder of waiting for buds to flower, opening into bloom. We should teach them to observe the richness of the phenomenon of fertilization, sometimes carried out by bees, other times by birds, or by the wind and the water. They should understand the complexity of nature, where the most amazing associations stir aesthetic emotions, awakened by shapes, by rhythms, by the exuberance of color. All that richness is within our reach. But we need to really understand and interiorize the importance of parks. Every city, every municipality, should have enough parkland to serve its population. And each State should have its own nurseries, where species that are valuable to the region can be grown intensively to make it possible to distribute them to the different districts and to individuals, so that they can be used in gardens, as street trees, in squares, and in parks. These nurseries should also support experiments in the field of applied botany, selecting species, studying the possible unique functions of trees, shrubs, and understory vegetation.

There is an unexplored world in front of us. Of the 5,000 native tree species, very few are grown in gardens. There are more than 50,000 species of plants in extremely rich associations, characterizing our phytogeographical regions, including nebular flora, rainforests, savannahs, the *Caatinga*, the vegetation that grows in brackish freshwater, in sand, humid fields, the saxicolous flora that grows on granite, on limestone formations, in iron-rich systems, on sandy quartzite, on basalt rock, etc. This is the fabulous heritage that nature offers us and that we must defend, preserve, and pass on knowledge about by every means possible.

June 1983.

Figure 333. Artistic and scientific traces of the *Primavera de Oro* in the tropical forest of the Maracaibo Botanical Garden, Maracaibo, Venezuela. Photograph: María A. Villalobos H., 2014. **Figure 334.** [Opposite page] Meeting José Tabacow, *Florianópolis*, Brazil, 2021. Photograph: Carla Urbina, 2012.

NATURE AS A SOURCE
JOSÉ TABACOW[111]

The Vegetation of Brazilian Landscapes

Because of its size, Brazil contains a broad diversity of landscapes, depending on the nature of the soil (e.g., *Cerrados*), or depending on the weather (e.g., *Mata Atlântica*, Amazon). These determining factors are directly reflected in the plant life, which reveals the peculiarities among the phytophysionomies (vegetation of the landscapes) that form the territory. These aspects end up identifying Brazilian landscapes through the presence of vegetation with a structure, shape and density that are reflected in the architecture of the plants and, more generally, in the overall appearance. Thus, nature can produce landscapes with dense, forested vegetation that is highly dependent on rainfall; they may show characteristics that appear with a strong seasonality, in which elements like color, foliage (or absence thereof), flowers and many other features announce the dry or rainy seasons. In regions where water is a scarce element in the landscape, it shows through in the forms of the vegetation, in how the flora, fauna – and human beings – adapt to the unfavorable living conditions.

The individualization of landscapes takes place mainly through vegetation and geomorphology, but also through geology and soil. Examples of flora from these formations – especially the ones that contributed the most plants introduced or used by the landscape architect Burle Marx in his projects – are present in gardens designed under his influence all over the world.

Collecting plants in their natural environments, taking tropical nature as a source, was not the only activity that the landscaper used for his compositions. A keen observation and perception of natural examples allowed him to reinterpret – or transpose, as he liked to say – ensembles and associations between plants, rocks, soils, water, and other components of the landscape that offered him inspiration and models that he drew from to re-work and rearrange those components according to his own objectives. *"Creating gardens does not mean subserviently imitating nature!"* he often said. Or even: *"Gardens are nature organized by man for man!"*, another common saying, which unquestionably reinforces his idea of gardens as a form of artistic expression.

[111] **José Tabacow** earned a degree in Architecture and Urbanism from the Federal University of Rio de Janeiro (UFRJ) in 1968. Tabacow earned a degree in Ecology and Natural Resources from the Universidade Federal do Espírito Santo (UFES) in 1991, and he received a Ph.D. in Geography from UFRJ in 2002. He was an intern, collaborator, collaborating architect and associate architect for Burle Marx & Cia. Ltda. for 17 years. As part of Burle Marx's team, he worked on the design and execution of various landscape projects such as the *Praça do Ministério do exército, Brasília*; the *Parque das Magabeiras, Belo Horizonte*; and the Avenida *Atlântica, Rio de Janeiro*, among many others. The Maracaibo Botanical Garden in Venezuela was the last work that Tabacow carried out with Burle Marx & Cia. Ltda., and he describes it as his most important job with the firm. *José Tabacow - Arquitetura da Paisagem e Consultoria Ambiental Ltda.* executes landscape design projects and provides consulting in the environmental sector. Tabacow is a consultant for Portal Vitruvius and Universidade Mackenzie. As a consultant for the IPHAN –*Instituto do Patrimônio Histórico e Artístico Nacional*, Tabacow was part of the team that prepared the UNESCO World Heritage candidacy dossier for the *Sítio Roberto Burle Marx*, which led to the classification of the *Sítio* as World Heritage on July 27, 2021.

What it means is that, although Roberto Burle Marx sought to elevate Brazilian flora and, later, its ecological associations, he never advocated a restriction to autochthonism as a compositional principle in his work with vegetation. In one of his lectures, he says that, if a plant that comes from Paraguay or Ecuador displays formal convergences and can be grown with Brazilian species, there is no reason not to use it.

In any case, Brazilian nature was a permanent source of new plants and new ideas for him, because the artist tried to maintain contact with this nature, which provided him with inexhaustible material in his search for a new approach to landscape design.

The Collection of Plants and the *Sítio*

Roberto Burle Marx was a compulsive collector not only of plants but many other things that sparked his interest, including traditional pottery, baroque imagery, seashells, glass from northern Europe, ancient earthenware, pre-Columbian ceramics, books, and records. Beyond the monetary or symbolic value that his collections might have, what motivated him were his collections' deeper ties with the arts in general. As an abstract artist, he was not concerned with meanings or values, but rather with forms, colors, textures, sizes, and relationships.

Just as passionately as he sought out new inks for his paintings, new materials for sculpting, or new printing techniques to use on paper, canvas, or cloth, Burle Marx also searched for surprising new plants that he could use to update the possibilities for expression in landscape design.

It has often been said that his search for plants revealed an enormous concern for nature. That isn't true, however. His actions in defense of the environment came much later. They began when he became aware of the environmental harm that was taking place arbitrarily and destructively, with no foundation in understanding, irresponsibly and without any concern for the future. He learned of these processes of destruction because he was present as they were happening, not because of the news on TV or second-hand information. He witnessed the destruction of environments as he was observing them, studying, and aiming to understand the potential of tropical flora and tropical environments for use in his designs.

As a plant collector, Burle Marx never limited himself to just Brazilian vegetation. As we said before, he was interested in new possibilities for expression. In that sense, he was looking for any plants that were not in his collection, regardless of their origin or nationality.

He had no problem including *"oddities"* in his collection, in the form of rare plants, isolated from their native habitats, or that might be difficult to adapt to cultivation, for the simple reason that he was a collector, driven by an insatiable desire to expand his botanical legacy. Thus, many plants were incorporated even they did not have the possibility of landscape use.

Although, over time, his concern with the ecological coherence of his gardens gained in importance, that fact never diminished his interest in the plant novelties that he sought out from other collectors, at botanical gardens or in commercial establishments. It is worth mentioning a certain behavior, by virtue of which his searches were concentrated on a particular family or genus at certain times. Significant examples that confirm this statement are palm trees (Arecaceae), Velloziaceae, and Philodendrons (from the Araceae family, which includes some 300 species), collections that he made a focused effort to augment during certain periods of his life. Based on a chronology of his collecting excursions, it is possible to identify those periods, analyzing the routes and the information from botanists that he used to determine the sites for his searches.

All these collections were kept at the *Sítio* in Guaratiba. Aware of the maintenance difficulties and the complexity, size, and necessary know-how on tropical environments, he donated everything to the IPHAN – the Institute of National Historical and Artistic Heritage, a body then linked to the now extinct Ministry of Culture (today, the Ministry of Tourism) under the Brazilian federal government, which has maintained the institution in a dedicated and impeccable manner, under the name *Sítio Roberto Burle Marx*. After more than a quarter of a century, all the collections that make up this formidable holding are recorded, cataloged and subject to continuous care.

Meanwhile, and referring exclusively to the collections of living plants, the complex organization of such a vast collection requires an enormous effort in the scientific and physical knowledge of some 3,000 different species of plants that grow, compete with one another, die and are reborn in a dynamic that evolves over time and across space. Added to all this effort is the need for a constant updating of the scientific-botanical information, which, in turn, is also governed by its own intense dynamics.

Perhaps because he never had time and opportunity, Roberto Burle Marx did not pay special attention to the physical space allocated to the plants he collected in natural environments, which were discoveries for botanical science. There were almost 100 plants hitherto unknown to science. Many plants were given his name to differentiate the species: some examples include *Philodendron burlemarxii*, *Anthurium burlemarxii*, *Heliconia burlemarxii* and *Merianthera burlemarxii*. In this regard, a project is under development, called the *Memorial Botánico Roberto Burle Marx* (Roberto Burle Marx Botanical Memorial) dedicated to the documentation and public exhibition of living plants and the information on the special trips he made to collect them in natural environments. The aim is to showcase a fundamental part of the work of a landscape architect who was never satisfied with the limited supply of *"ornamental"* plants. To begin with, for him, in his own words, *"All plants are ornamental!"*

The knowledge revealed by him is spread across the *Sítio*, preserved according to the conditions and criteria that the landscape architect determined for the conservation of his botanical collections. The proposal for the Botanical Memorial Roberto Burle Marx is a reorganization intended to make the size and quality of his scientific contribution accessible to researchers and the visiting public.

SUGGESTED BIBLIOGRAPHY AND CHRONOLOGY OF URBAN LANDSCAPE DESIGNS BY ROBERTO BURLE MARX AND COLLABORATORS INCLUDED IN THIS BOOK

Brazil
Recife

1935	*Praça Casa Forte*
1935	*Praça Euclides da Cunha*, Pernambuco Ecological Garden
1936	*Praça do Derby* [remodel]
1936	*Praça do Entroncamento* [remodel]
1936/37	*Praça da República* [remodel]
1936/37	*Praça Pinto Damaso*
1937	*Praça Dezessete* [remodel]

Carneiro, A. R., Alcántara Onofre, S., & Veras, L. M. (2021). *Mexico-Brazil: Paisagem e Jardim como Patrimônio Cultural*. Ukraine: Aprris.

Cavalcanti, M., Sá Carneiro, A. R., & Veras, L. M. (2019). *Burle Marx e o Recife: Um passeio pelos jardins da cidade*. Brazil: Cepe.

Minas Gerais

1942	*Casa de Baile*
1980	*Parque das Mangabeiras*

Hoffmann, J., & Nahson, C. J. (2016). *Roberto Burle Marx: Brazilian Modernist*. United Kingdom: Jewish Museum.

Macedo, S. S., & Sakata, F. G. (2002). *Brazilian Urban Parks*. Brazil: EDUSP.

Cavalcanti, L. (org.) (2009). *Roberto Burle Marx 100 anos: a permanência do instável*. Brazil: Rocco.

Brasília

1961	*Parque Zoobotânico*
1962*	*Superquadra 308 Sul*
1970*	*Praça dos Cristais*
1970*	*Ministério da Justicia e Cidadania*
1970	*Parque da Cidade*

Bardi, P. M., Burle Marx, R., & Gautherot, M. (1964). *The Tropical Gardens of Burle Marx*. Brazil: Reinhold.

Montero, M.I. (2001): *Burle Marx: The Lyrical Landscape*. California: University of California Press.

Burle Marx, R., & Finotti, L. (2011). *Roberto Burle Marx: The Modernity of Landscape*. Italy: Actar Brikhäuser.

Rio de Janeiro

1949/94	*Sítio Roberto Burle Marx*
1961	*Aterro do Flamengo*
1970	*Copacabana*
1981	*Largo da Carioca*

Costa, L. M. (1992). *Popular Values for Urban Parks: A Case Study of the Changing Meanings do Parque do Flamengo in Rio de Janeiro*. London: N.P.: University College.

Gautherot, M., & Motta, F. L. (1984). *Roberto Burle Marx e a nova visão da paisagem*. Brazil: Nobel.

Rizzo, G. G., & Burle Marx, R. (1992). *Roberto Burle Marx: il giardino del Novecento*. Italy: Cantini.

Rizzo, G. G. (2009). *Il giardino privato di Roberto Burle Marx: il sítio: sessant'anni dalla fondazione cent'anni dalla nascita di Roberto Burle Marx*. Italy: Gangemi.

Venezuela
Caracas

1956/61	*Parque del Este General Francisco de Miranda*

Maracaibo

1981	*Jardín Botánico de Maracaibo Leandro Aristeguieta*

Berrisbetia, A. (2005): *Roberto Burle Marx in Caracas: Parque Del Este, 1956 - 1961*. United States: University of Pennsylvania Press.

Urbina, C., & Villalobos H., M. A. (2014). "Botanical Garden, Jardin botanique, système paysager et paysage urban durable. Réflexion à partir du jardin botanique de Roberto Burle Marx à Maracaibo (Venezuela)". In C. Chomarat-Ruiz, *L'utopie d'une ville sustenable* (pp. 88-111). Paris: Editopics.

Villalobos H., M. A. (2015). *El jardín botánico de Roberto Burle Marx en Maracaibo como proceso creativo hacia un paisaje urbano botánico*. Paris: Universite Agroparis-Tech, Ecole Dotorale ABIES, Laboratorio de investigación de la ENSP-Versalles.

Note: This list reflects the dates as they are presented in Motta, Flávio Lichtenfels, Gautherot, Marcel. *Roberto Burle Marx e a nova visão da paisagem*. Brazil: Nobel, 1984.

(*) Official confirmation required.

Figure 335. Roberto Burle Marx during one of his lectures in which he presented essential principles and values in the defense and protection of the landscape and living things, *American Society of Landscape Architects* (ASLA), Cincinnati, Ohio, United States, 1985. Photograph: *Instituto Burle Marx*.

BIBLIOGRAPHY

Ab'Saber, A. (2003). *Os domínios de Natureza no Brasil. Potencialidades paisagísticas*. São Paulo: Ateliê Editorial.

Acervo da biblioteca pública de Santa Catarina (1958). Edições do Livro de Arte. Sonetos da Noite. *Boi de Mamão*. Florianópolis, Brazil. Retrieved March 31, 2021, from http://hemeroteca.ciasc.sc.gov.br/jornais/boidemam%C3%A3o/BOI1980cruzesouza.pdf

Alvarenga Zavatin, D. (2017). *Mandacaru (Cereus jamacaru)*. iNaturalist. Retrieved April 23, 2021, from https://www.inaturalist.org/photos/13494922

Alves Pereira Penha, J. (2002). *Filólogos Brasileiros*. Editora Ribeirão Gráfica.

American Orchid Society (2019). American Orchid Society. Retrieved August 11, 2020, from https://www.aos.org

_____ (2019). *Sophronitis*. Retrieved August 11, 2020, from American Orchid Society: https://www.aos.org/orchids/orchids-a-to-z/letter-s/sophronitis.aspx

Andresen, T. (2003). Do Estádio Nacional ao Jardim Gulbenkian. *Francisco Caldeira Cabral e a primeira geração de arquitectos paisagistas (1940-1970). Catálogo de exposición en la Fundação Calouste Gulbenkian*. Lisbon: FCG.

Araujo, M. (n.d.). *Escultura em madeira*. Museu Afro Brasil. Retrieved March 31, 2021, from https://www.flickr.com/photos/artexplorer/2716691545/in/photostream/

Archer, W. A. (1962, October). *Adolpho Ducke, Botanist of the Brazilian Amazon (1876 - 1959)*. 11(8), p. 233. doi: https://doi.org/10.2307/1217031

Arzberger, A. (2018). *Cereus jamacaru DC*. Encyclopedias of living forms. Retrieved January, 25, 2021, from https://llifle.com/plant_album/6995/30312

Ávila, e. a. (1996). *Barroco Mineiro. Glossário de Arquitetura e Ornamentação*. Brazil: Fundação João Pinheiro.

Bardi, P. M., Burle Marx, R., & Gautherot, M. (1964). *The Tropical Gardens of Burle Marx*. Brazil: Reinhold.

Barleus, C. (1974). *História dos feitos recentemente praticados durante oito anos no Brasil*. (Brandão, Cláudio -Trad.) Belo Horizonte: Livraria Itatiaia editora Ltda.

Batista Falda, G. (1643-1678). *Planta de los Jardines de la Villa Medici*. Italia. Retrieved January 29, 2021, from https://www.rijksmuseum.nl/nl/collectie/RP-P-1909-1386

Beltrá, D. (2019). *Foco de incêndio na Floresta Amazônia em São Félix do Xingu, no Pará, registrado pelo Greenpeace*. Retrieved January 25, 2021, from https://noticias.uol.com.br/ultimas-noticias/afp/2019/08/21/desmatamento-e-principal-causa-de-incendios-na-amazonia-afirma-paulo-moutinho.htm

Bernardino da Silva, D. G. (1997). *Os diários de Langsdorff. Rio de Janeiro e Minas Gerais (Vol. 1)*. Campinas: Editora Fiocruz. Retrieved May 4, 2021, from https://static.scielo.org/scielobooks/q5cc4/pdf/silva-9788575412442.pdf

Berrisbetia, A. (2005). *Roberto Burle Marx in Caracas: Parque Del Este, 1956-1961*. United States: University of Pennsylvania Press.

_____ (2008, October 02). Defensa del Parque del Este. Minha Cidade. *Vitruvius, año 09*. Retrieved March 02, 2014, from https://vitruvius.com.br/revistas/read/minhacidade/ 09.099/1873

Bertoni, E. (2011, March 12). Fernando Chacel (1931-2011) - Paisagista sucessor de Burle Marx. *Folha de São Paulo*. Retrieved March 31, 2021, from https://www1.folha.uol.com.br/cotidiano/887670-fernando-chacel-1931-2011---paisagista-sucessor-de-burle-marx.shtml

Bethell, L. (1999). *Historia da América Latina: América Latina Colonial*. EdUSP, II, p. 686.

Biblioteca Nacional de Brasil (1979). *A. Saint-Hilaire [Livro: 1779-1853: catálogo da exposição comemorativa do bicentenário de nascimento]*. Rio de Janeiro: A Biblioteca. Retrieved April 26, 2021, from http://bdlb.bn.gov.br

Biblioteca Nacional (2020, June 15). *Peter Wilhelm Lund - o Pai da Paleontologia Brasileira*. Retrieved May 04, 2021, from https://www.bn.gov.br/acontece/noticias/2020/06/peter-wilhelm-lund-pai-paleontologia-brasileira

Bin, É. (1870). *The Hamadryad / Le Bûcheron et l'Hamadryade Aigeiros*. Musee d'Art Thomas Henry, Cherbourg, France. Retrieved December 11, 2020, from https://pt.m.wikipedia.org/wiki/Ficheiro:The_Hamadryad_by_%C3%89mile_Bin.jpg

Bisilliat, M. (1974). *A João Guimarães Rosa* (2nd ed.). Gráficos Brunner.

_____ (1982). *Sertões: luz & trevas*. Raízes Artes Gráficas.

Blackmore, L. (2010, April 13). *Pronunciamiento del CAV ante la situación actual del Leander en el Parque del Este. 04/08/2010*. Colegio de Arquitectos de Venezuela. Retrieved October 13, 2012, from http://lisablackmore.net/?p=2208

Botanischer Garten und Botanisches Museum Berlin (n.d.). *Gartenplan*. Retrieved February 08, 2021, from https://www.bgbm.org/de/node/1079

Botticelli, S. (1480). *El nacimiento de Venus*. Gallerie degli Uffizi, Florence, Italy. Retrieved January 29, 2021, from https://www.florenceartmuseums.com/uffizi-gallery

Bouguereau, A.-W. (1902). *Les Oréades*. Musée d'Orsay, dist. RMN-Grand Palais / Patrice Schmidt. Retrieved May 01, 2021, from http://www.musee-orsay.fr/fr/collections/oeuvres-commentees/peinture/commentaire_id/les-oreades-21296.html?tx_commentaire_pi1%5BpidLi%5D=509&tx_commentaire_pi1%5Bfrom%5D=841&cHash=d0621a55f2

Braga, T., Vieira, D., & Coelho, A. (1871). *Grande diccionario portuguez ou Thesouro da lingua portugueza*. Portugal: E. Chadron e B. H. de Moraes.

Brasiliana Iconográfica (2017). *A Expedição Langsdorff e a vinda de Rugendas ao Brasil*. Retrieved May 04, 2021, from https://www.brasilianaiconografica.art.br/artigos/20193/a-expedicao-langsdorff-e-a-vinda-de-rugendas-ao-brasil

_____ (2017). *Botocudos: de Wied-Neuwied à tragédia no Vale do Rio Doce*. Retrieved May 04, 2021, from https://www.brasilianaiconografica.art.br/artigos/20219/botocudos-de-wied-neuwied-a-tragedia-no-vale-do-rio-doce

Brasiliana Iconográfica. Equipe Pinacoteca (2017). *A Missão Austríaca*. Retrieved May 04, 2021, from Itaú Cultural: https://www.brasilianaiconografica.art.br/artigos/15636/a-missao-austriaca

Britannica, T. E. (n.d.). *Encyclopaedia Britannica*. Retrieved December 11, 2020, from Nymph. Greek mythology: https://www.britannica.com/topic/Naiad-Greek-mythology

Buarque de Holanda, A., & Rosa, L. (2007). *Melhores contos. Aurélio Buarque de Holanda*. (E. V. Steen, Ed.) Brazil: Global Editora.

Burle Marx, R. (1984). *Expedição Burle Marx a Amazônia – 1983*. Rio de Janeiro: Cnpq.

Burle Marx, R., & Tabacow, J. (org.) (1987). *Arte e paisagem. Conferências escolhidas*. São Paulo: Livraria Nobel S.A.

_____ (2004). *Arte e Paisagem, Conferências escolhidas*. São Paulo: Editorial Livros Studio Nobel Ltda.

Burle Marx, R., & Finotti, L. (2011). *Roberto Burle Marx: The modernity of Landscape*. Italia: Actar Brikhäuser.

Caldas Aulete, F. J., Nascentes, A., & Garcia, H. d. (1968). *Dicionário contemporâneo da língua portuguesa*. Brazil: Editôra Delta.

Caldas, G. M. (2006). *Acrocomia aculeata (Jacq.) Lodd. ex Mart. - Aracaceae: Bases para o Extrativismo Sustentável, Science Phd. Thesis*. Curitiba: Universidad Federal de Paraná.

Carauta J. P. P. & Diaz, B. E. (2002). *Figueiras no Brasil*. Rio de Janeiro: UFRJ.

Carneiro, A. R., Alcántara Onofre, S., & Veras, L. M. (2021). *México-Brasil: Paisagem e Jardim como Patrimonio Cultural*. Ucrania: Aprris.

Carvalho, B. d. (1961). *Igrejas Barrocas do Rio de Janeiro*. Rio de Janeiro: Editora Civilização Brasileira S.A.

Catalog of life (2020). *Catalog of life*. Retrieved April 26, 2021, from https://www.catalogueoflife.org/data/browse?taxonKey=7F2ZP

Cavalcanti, L. (2009). *Roberto Burle Marx 100 anos: a permanência do instável*. Brazil: Rocco.

Cavalcanti, M., Sá Carneiro, A. R., & Veras, L. M. (2019). *Burle Marx e o Recife: Um passeio pelos jardins da cidade*. Brazil: Cepe.

Centro de Referência em Informação Ambiental, CRIA (2005). Retrieved April 28, 2021, from http://florabrasiliensis.cria.org.br/opus

Cross, H.-E. (1908). *Napéias.* Retrieved May 01, 2021, from https://fantasia.fandom.com/pt/wiki/Nap%C3%A9ias

Costa, L. M. (1992). *Popular Values for Urban Parks: A Case Study of the Changing Meanings do Parque do Flamengo in Rio de Janeiro.* London: N.P.: University College.

Da Vinci, L. (1472). *La Anunciación.* Gallerie degli Uffizi, Florence, Italy. Retrieved January 29, 2021, from https://www.florenceartmuseums.com/uffizi-gallery/

Damasceno, C. (2019). *As viagens de Auguste de Saint-Hilaire.* Retrieved May 04, 2021, from https://heritage.bnf.fr/france-bresil/pt-br/viagens-auguste-st-hilaire-artigo#viagens-auguste-st-hilaire

De Morgan, E. (1884-1885). *The Dryad/Die Dryade.* De Morgan Foundation. Retrieved May 01, 2021, from https://www.meisterdrucke.uk/fine-art-prints/Evelyn-De-Morgan/284746/The-Dryad,-1884-85-.html

Diario Oficial (2016, March). *Decreto No 29.537. Disposiciones sobre la clasificación como históricos Jardines Burle Marx de los espacios públicos vegetados de Recife, que especifica, integrándolos al sistema municipal de estados unidos protegidos. Ley Municipal de 18.014.* Retrieved January 29, 2021, from https://bit.ly/2QGSWwE

Diario Oficial Prefeitura do Recife (2016). *Decreto Nº 29.537 march 23, 2016.* Prefeitura do Recife, Recife. Retrieved April 01, 2021, from https://licenciamento.recife.pe.gov.br/sites/default/files/Decreto%20nº%20 29.537.16-burle%20max.pdf

Dicionário Online de Português (2009-2021). Retrieved March, 2020, from https://www.dicio.com.br/

Dourado, G. O. (2000). *Modernidade verde: jardins de Burle Marx. Lecture of Master in architecture and urbanism.* São Carlos: Universidade de São Paulo.

Dream exotic rentals (n.d.). *Torre Berardesca.* Retrieved March 31, 2021, from https://www.dreamexoticrentals.com/properties/Europe/italy/vacation-italy-TorreBerardesca.htm

Eckhout, A. (1641-1643). *Still-life of citrus fruit and bananas.* Nationalmuseet, Copenhagen, Denmark. Retrieved April 29, 2021, from https://rkd.nl/en/explore/images/259758

Edwards, M. (2020). WWF, Brasil. rom https://www.wwf.org.br/natureza_brasileira/areas_prioritarias/amazonia1/amazonia__desmatamento_e_queimadas__uma_nova_tragedia_em_2020/

Embrapa (n.d.). *Tratos culturais.* Retrieved May 02, 2021, from Embrapa hortaliças: https://www.embrapa.br/hortalicas/batata-doce/tratos-culturais

_____ **(n.d.).** *Vellozia.* Retrieved April 26, 2021, from https://www.vellozia.cnptia.embrapa.br/

Engler, A. (1844-1930). *Die Natürlichen Pflanzenfamilien nebst ihren Gattungen und wichtigeren Arten, insbesondere den Nutzpflanzen, unter Mitwirkung zahlreicher hervorragender Fachgelehrten begründet.* doi: https://doi.org/10.5962/bhl.title.4635

Escala H (Producer) (2009). *IFLA 2009 RIO. Parque del Este de Caracas.* [Film]. Retrieved February 03, 2014, from https://www.youtube.com/watch?v=gmZfg38jcHg

Escandell, M. (2014). *Cañón del rio Sil.* Galicia, España. Retrieved March 31, 2021, from https://magazine.trivago.es/de-ruta-por-la-espana-verde-galicia/

Equipe Brasil Escola (n.d.). *"João Cruz e Sousa".* Retrieved March 31, 2021, from Brasil Escola: https://brasilescola.uol.com.br/biografia/joao-cruz-sousa.htm

Fatumbi Verger, P. (2002). *Orixás.* São Paulo: Corrupio.

Ferrez, M. (c. 1882). *Indivíduos escravizados em terreiro de uma fazenda de café na região do Vale do Paraíba.* Instituto Moreira Salles, Brazil, Vale do Paraíba. Retrieved December, 11, 2021, from https://acervos.ims.com.br/portals/#/detailpage/7069

_____ **(c. 1891).** *Escola Nacional de Belas Artes.* Instituto Moreira Salles, Rio de Janeiro. Retrieved March 11, 2020, from https://acervos.ims.com.br/portals/#/detailpage/77576

_____ **(n.d.).** *Campo Santa Ana.* Fundação Casa de Rui Barbosa. Retrieved January 26, 2021, from http://www.casaruibarbosa.gov.br/glaziou/img/campo/09_hi.jpg

Field Museum of Natural History (n.d.). Desmoncus orthacanthos Mart. Specimen: T. S. Dos Santos 2914. Retrieved February 08, 2021, from https://plantidtools.fieldmuseum.org/en/rrc/catalogue/313827

Floyd, S. K., Lerner, V. T., & Friedman, W. E. (1999, November 01). A developmental and evolutionary analysis of embryology in Platanus (platanaceae), abasal eudicot. *American Journal of Botany,* 86(11), pp. 1523-1537.doi: https://doi.org/10.2307/2656790

Forzza, R. C. (2010). *Lista de espécies Flora do Brasil.* Retrieved January 26, 2021, from Jardim Botânico do Rio de Janeiro: https://web.archive.org/web/20150906080403/

Franca, R. (1977). *Monumentos do Recife.* Recife: Secretaria de Educação e Cultura.

Funatura (n.d.). *PN Grande Sertão Veredas. Morro Três Irmãos ou fundo.* Funatura. Retrieved March, 31 2021, from https://funatura.org.br/uma-visita-ao-parque-nacional-grande-sertao-veredas-natureza-e-cultura/

Fundação Carlos Chagas Filho de Amparo. (2004). *Pesquisa do Estado do Rio de Janeiro.* Rio de Janeiro. Retrieved January 26, 2021, from http://www.faperj.br/?id=308.3.2

Gambarini, A. (2020). WWF Brasil, Brazil. Retrieved April 27, 2021, from https://www.wwf.org.br/natureza_brasileira/areas_prioritarias/amazonia1/amazonia__desmatamento_e_queimadas__uma_nova_tragedia_em_2020/

Gardner, G. (1840-1841). *On the Geology and Fossil Fishes of North Brazil. Report for 1840.* London: Trans. British Assoc. Adv. Sci.

_____ **(1841).** *Geological Notes made during a Journey from the Coast into the Interior of the Province of Ceará, in the North of Brazil, embracing an Account of a Deposit od Fossil Fishes* (Vol. LIX). (XXX, Ed.) New Edin. Phil. Jour.

Gautherot, M. (c. 1957). *Roberto Burle Marx.* Instituto Moreira Salles, Barra de Guaratiba. Retrieved April 27, 2021, from https://acervos.ims.com.br/portals/#/detailpage/51264

_____ **(c. 1961).** *Célio, Burle Marx e Flamarion Soares da Gama, no Sítio Burle Marx.* Instituto Moreira Salles, Rio de Janeiro, Barra de Guaratiba, Brazil. Retrieved April 28, 2021, from https://acervos.ims.com.br/portals/#/detailpage/51406

_____ **(c. 1966).** *Aterro do Flamengo - Passarela com Outeiro da Glória.* Instituto Moreira Salles, Rio de Janeiro.

_____ **(c. 1966).** *Aterro do Flamengo - vista aérea - destaque para o Monumento aos Pracinhas, ao centro.* Instituto Moreira Salles, Rio de Janeiro. Retrieved April 30, 2021, from https://acervos.ims.com.br/portals/#/detailpage/51678

Gautherot, M., & Motta, F. L. (1984). *Roberto Burle Marx e a nova visão da paisagem.* Brazil: Nobel.

Global Invasive Species Database (2021). *Species profile: Terminalia catappa.* Retrieved September 06, 2021, from http://www.iucngisd.org/gisd/species.php?sc=1581

Govaerts R. (ed.). Digital resource at www.catalogueoflife.org. Species 2000: Naturalis, L. (2021). *WCSP: World Checklist of Selected Plant Families* (version Aug. 2017). Retrieved April 28, 2021, from Catalogue of Life, et al. (2021). Species 2000 & ITIS Catalogue of Life: www.catalogueoflife.org

_____ **(2021).** *Euphorbia phosphorea Mart.* (Catalogue of Life, et al. (2021). Species 2000 & ITIS Catalogue of Life, 2021-04-05) Retrieved April 28, 2021, from WCSP: World Checklist of Selected Plant Families (version Aug. 2017): https://www.catalogueoflife.org/data/taxon/3CQ8M

_____ **(2021, May 04).** *Ligustrum.* Retrieved April 26, 2021, from WCSP: World Checklist of Selected Plant Families (version August 2017): https://www.catalogueoflife.org/data/taxon/62X65

_____ **(2021, May 04).** *Vellozia.* (W. W. 2017), Editor) Retrieved April 26, 2021, from Catalogue of Life, et al. (2021). Species 2000 & ITIS Catalogue of Life: https://www.catalogueoflife.org/data/taxon/8678

_____ **(2021).** *WCSP: World Checklist of Selected Plant Families* (version august 2017). Retrieved April 26, 2021, from Catalogue of Life, et al. (2021). Species 2000 & ITIS Catalogue of Life: https://www.catalogueoflife.org/data/dataset/1024

356 BIBLIOGRAPHY

Guia das Artes. (2015). *Maurino de Araujo*. Retrieved March 31, 2021, from https://www.guiadasartes.com.br/maurino-de-araujo/obras-e-biografia

Guimarães Ferri, M. (2004). Prefácio. In A. d. Saint-Hilaire, *Viagem às nascentes do Rio São Francisco* (R. Regis Junqueira, Translator., 2 ed.). Belo Horizonte: Editora Itatiaia.

_____ **(1985).** A Botânica no Brasil: considerações históricas. *História da ciência. Fisiologia Vegetal, I.*

_____ **(1974).** A Botânica no Brasil: considerações históricas. *História da ciência, 46.*

Guimarães Rosa, J. (2001). *Grande sertão: veredas* (19 ed.). Rio de Janeiro: Nova Fronteira.

Haeckel, E. 1.-1. (1866). *Generelle morphologie der organismen. Allgemeine grundzuge der naturlichen formen-wissenschaft, mechanisch begründet durch die von Charles Darwin reformirte descendenztheorie.* Berlin: G. Reimer. Retrieved April 22, 2021, from https://www.biodiversitylibrary.org/page/15099620

Hassler, M. (2021, March 14). *Bougainvillea Comm. ex Juss.* Retrieved April 28, 2021, from *World Plants. Synonymic Checklist and Distribution of the World Flora:* https://www.worldplants.de/world-plants-complete-list/complete-plant-list/?name=Bougainvillea

_____ **(2021, March 14).** *Gloxinia L'Hér.* Retrieved April 28, 2021, from *World Plants. Synonymic Checklist and Distribution of the World Flora:* https://www.worldplants.de/world-plants-complete-list/complete-plant-list/?name=Gloxinia

_____ **(2021, March 14).** *Platanus L.*, 12.1. (World plants) Retrieved April 28, 2021, from Synonymic Checklist and Distribution of the World Flora: https://www.catalogueoflife.org/data/taxon/6RKR

_____ **(2021, March 14).** *Prunus dulcis.* Retrieved April 22, 2021, from http://www.worldplants.de/?deeplink=Prunus-dulcis

_____ **(2021, March 14).** *Pseudobombax ellipticum (Kunth) Dugand.* Retrieved April 28, 2021, from *World Plants. Synonymic Checklist and Distribution of the World Flora.* Version 12.1 (2004 - 2021): https://www.worldplants.de/world-plants-complete-list/complete-plant-list/?name=Pseudobombax-ellipticum#plantUid-241911

_____ **(2021, March 14).** *Sipolisia Glaz. ex Oliv.* 12.1. Retrieved April 26, 2021, from *World Plants. Synonymic Checklist and Distribution of the World Flora:* https://www.worldplants.de/world-plants-complete-list/complete-plant-list/?name=Heterocoma-lanuginosa#plantUid369602

_____ **(2004-2021).** World Plants. Synonymic Checklist and Distribution of the World Flora, 12.1. Retrieved April 26, 2021, from www.worldplants.de

_____ **(2021, March 14).** *Wunderlichia Riedel ex Benth. & Hook. fil.*, 12.1. Retrieved April 26, 2021, from World Plants. Synonymic Checklist and Distribution of the World Flora: www.worldplants.de

Henríquez, D., Bacci, M. E., & Genatios, M. (2009, May). Parque del Este, Caracas, Venezuela: patrimonio en riesgo.

Hoffmann, J., & Nahson, C. J. (2016). *Roberto Burle Marx: Brazilian Modernist.* Reino Unido: Jewish Museum.

ICMBio (n.d.). *Nossa história.* Retrieved May 22, 2021, from https://www.icmbio.gov.br/ran/quem-somos/nossa-historia.html

Imagem e Memoria Candangolandia (1958). Viveiro de cobras no Zoológico de Brasília. *Flickr.* Brasilia: Fundo: Arquivo Público do Distrito Federal. Retrieved September 22, 2021, from https://www.flickr.com/photos/imagemememoriacandanga/48915091028/in/album-72157711252964158/

Instituto agronómico (n.d.). Retrieved April 25, 2021, from http://www.iac.sp.gov.br/

Instituto Chico Mendes de Conservação da biodiversidade (2016). *Sumário Executivo do Livro Vermelho da Fauna Brasileira Ameaçada de Extinção.* Brasília: ICMBio.

Instituto de Botânica (n.d.). *Aniversário Frederico Carlos Hoehne.* Instituto de Botânica. Retrieved May 01, 2021, from https://www.infraestruturameioambiente.sp.gov.br/institutodebotanica/2020/02/aniversariofrederico-carlos-hoehne/

Instituto Moreira Salles (n.d.). Obtained from https://acervos.ims.com.br/

Instituto Parque do Flamengo (2017). *Grandes Nomes, Grandes Feitos.* Obtained from http://institutoparquedoflamengo.org/grandes-nomes-grandes-feitos/

Iphan (2019). *Nomination of Sítio Roberto Burle Marx for Inscription on the World Heritage List.* Rio de Janeiro: Iphan.

Itaú Cultural (2017, February 23). *Pero Vaz de Caminha.* Retrieved May 01, 2021, from Enciclopédia Itaú Cultural. Verbete da Enciclopédia: https://enciclopedia.itaucultural.org.br/pessoa7833/pero-vaz-de-caminha

IUCN (2021). *The IUCN Red List of Threatened Species*, 2021-1. Retrieved April 28, 2021, from IUCN: https://www.iucnredlist.org

Jansen, R. (2019, October 22). Palmeiras plantadas na decada de 1960 no Rio dão flores pela primeira vez. *Estadão.* Obtained from: https://noticias.uol.com.br/ultimas-noticias/agencia-estado/2019/10/22/palmeirasplantadas-na-decada-de-1960-no-rio-dao-flores-pela-primeira-vez.htm

Jardim Botânico de Brasília (n.d.). *História.* Retrieved September 23, 2021, from https://www.jardimbotanico.df.gov.br/institucional_01/historia/

Jardim Botânico do Rio de Janeiro (n.d.). Retrieved May 25, 2020, from http://www.jbrj.gov.br/jardim/plantas?page=6

_____ Instituto de Pesquisas Jardim Botânico do Rio de Janeiro (n.d.). *Jabot - Banco de Dados da Flora Brasileira.* Retrieved February 29, 2020, de http://jabot.jbrj.gov.br/

Jones, H. (1970). Orchidaceae Americanae. Caldasia. 10(50), pp. 491-495. Retrieved January 26, 2021, from http://www.jstor.org/stable/23641426

Kew Science (n.d.). *Orthophytum mello-barretoi L.B.Sm.* Retrieved February 08, 2021, from http://powo.science.kew.org/taxon/urn:lsid:ipni.org:names:176844-2

Kircheri, A., Lairesse, G. d., Munnichuysen, I., Decker, C., & Cruyl, L. (1679). *Turris Babel.* Amsterdam: Janssonius van Waesberge. Retrieved October 20, 2021, from https://archive.org/details/A087234174/page/n91/mode/2up

Kirk, P. (2021, May 04). *Usnea* (Catalogue of Life, Editor. Retrieved April 28, 2021, from Species Fungorum Plus: Species Fungorum for CoL (version february 2020): https://www.catalogueoflife.org/data/taxon/85FL

Knapp, S. (2013). *Solanum lycocarpum.* Minas Gerais, Brazil. Retrieved February 08, 2021, from http://solanaceaesource.org/file-colorboxed/1058

Leenhardt, J. (1994). *Dans les jardins de Roberto Burle Marx.* Crestet: Actes Sud.

_____ **(2016).** *Nos jardins de Burle Marx.* São Paulo: Editora Perspectiva.

Leighton, F. (c. 1892). *The Garden of the Hesperides.* The Bridgeman Art Library. Retrieved October 03, 2021, from https://commons.wikimedia.org/wiki/File:Frederic_Leighton_-_The_Garden_of_the_Hesperides.jpg

Leiva, L. (2021). *Chrysocyon brachyurus.* Santa Fé, Argentina. Retrieved February 25, 2021, from https://www.argentinat.org/observations/69388407

Lemos, R. (2014, September 14). *Curiosidades em torno da amendoeira, presente em todos os bairros do Rio.* Retrieved September 06, 2021, from https://oglobo.globo.com/rio/curiosidades-em-torno-da-amendoeira-presente-em-todos-os-bairros-do-rio-13918544

Lomba, S. (2019). *Vellozia hemisphaerica.* iNaturalist, Andaraí, Bahia, Brazil. Retrieved May 02, 2021, from https://www.inaturalist.org/photos/52977575

Lorenzi, H., & Souza, H. M. (2001). *Plantas ornamentais no Brasil: arbustivas, herbáceas e trepadeiras.* Brazil: Instituto Plantarum de Estudos da Flora.

Luna, Y. (2016). *Segundo andar. Sala onde realizam-se aulas de música, em Casa Mário de Andrade.* São Paulo, Brazil. Retrieved March 31, 2021, from https://upload.wikimedia.org/wikipedia/commons/e/e7/Casa_M%C3%A1rio_de_Andrade_16.jpg

Luze, B. D. (1820-1840). *Fazenda Pombal, Colônia Leopoldina, Bahia.* Brasiliana Iconográfica, América - Brasil - Bahia. Retrieved December 11, 2020, from https://www.brasilianaiconografica.art.br/obras/19833/fazenda-pombal-colonia-leopoldina-bahia

Macedo, S. S., & Sakata, F. G. (2002). *Brazilian Urban Parks.* Brazil: EDUSP.

Marcelo Alvarenga Braga, J., & Joffily, A. (2014). Validation of the name Heliconia ×rauliniana (Heliconiaceae). Phytotaxa. 161. 173. 10.11646/phytotaxa.161.2.10. (161), 173-176. Retrieved April 26, 2021, from https://

www.researchgate.net/figure/Holotype-of-Heliconia-rauliniana-R-Burle-Marx-sn-RB-159909_fig1_292182327

Marcgrave, G., & Piso, W. (1648). *Historia Naturalis Brasiliae... in qua non tantum.* Retrieved April 29, 2021, from http://biblio.wdfiles.com/local--files/marcgrave-1648-historia/marcgrave_1648_historia.pdf

Marchiori, J. N., Corrêa Pontes, R., & Marchiori Neto, D. L. (2016). Textos inéditos de Friedrich Sellow. 1 – Viagem às missões jesuíticas da Província de São Pedro do Sul. *Balduinia,* pp. 12-24. Retrieved May 04, 2021, from https://doi.org/10.5902/2358198021422

Martins, J. (1939). Apontamentos para a bibliografia referente a Antônio Francisco Lisboa. *Revista do Patrimônio Histórico e Artístico Nacional* (3), p. 179.

Martius, K. F. (1794-1868). Campi aestate sicca ignibus adusti. *Brasiliensis, enumeratio plantarum in Brasilia hactenus detectarum: quas suis aliorumque botanicorum studiis descriptas et methodo naturali digestas partim icone illustratas. Vol. I.* Retrieved May 02, 2021, from https://www.biodiversitylibrary.org/page/309567

_____ (1794-1868). Tabela Geográfica Brasiliae. En K. F. Martius, *Flora Brasiliensis, enumeratio plantarum in Brasilia hactenus detectarum: quas suis aliorumque botanicorum studiis descriptas et methodo naturali digestas partim icone illustratas.* Retrieved December 11, 2021, from https://www.biodiversitylibrary.org/page/309609

_____ (1794-1868). Tabula geografica brasiliae et terrarum adjacentium exhibens itinera botanicorum [et florae brasiliensis quinque provincias]. Provinciae florae brasiliensis. En K. F. Martius, & C. F. Martius (Ed.), *Flora Brasiliensis, enumeratio plantarum in Brasilia hactenus detectarum: quas suis aliorumque botanicorum studiis descriptas et methodo naturali digestas partim icone illustratas.* Retrieved December 11, 2021, from https://www.biodiversitylibrary.org/page/309609

_____ (1794-1868). Sylva aestu aphylla, quam dicunt caa-tinga. *Flora Brasiliensis, enumeratio plantarum in Brasilia hactenus detectarum: quas suis aliorumque botanicorum studiis descriptas et methodo naturali digestas partim icone illustratas. Vol. I.* Retrieved May 01, 2021, from https://www.biodiversitylibrary.org/page/309556

_____ (1823-1853). Desmoncus orthacanthos Mart. *Historia Naturalis Palmarum. Vol. 2 (1839).* Missouri Botanical Garden, St. Louis, U.S.A. Retrieved February 18, 2021, from http://www.plantillustrations.org/illustration.php?id_illustration=47445

_____ (c. 1842). Silva Caesa, Cum Ficu Grandaeva, ad S. Joannen Marcum, Prov. Rio de Janeiro. *Flora Brasiliensis - Volume I, parte I.* Acervo de Iconografia / Instituto Moreira Salles, Região Sudeste - Rio de Janeiro. Retrieved December 11, 2020, from https://www.brasilianaiconografica.art.br/obras/19110/silva-caesa-cum-ficu-grandaeva-ad-s-joannen-marcum-prov-rio-de-janeiro

Martius, K. F., & Spix, J. B. (1794-1868). Cataracta rivi, qui dicitur Riberão do Palmital. Prope Sabará in Prov. Minarum. *Flora Brasiliensis, enumeratio plantarum in Brasilia hactenus detectarum: quas suis aliorumque botanicorum studiis descriptas et methodo naturali digestas partim icone illustratas. Vol. I.* Martius, Karl Friedrich Philipp von; Spix, Johann Baptist von. Cataracta rivi, qui dicitur Riberão do Palmital. Prope Sabará in Prov. Minarum. Retrieved May 01, 2021, from https://www.biodiversitylibrary.org/page/309568

_____ (1794-1868). Lucus Araucariae Brasilianae. *Flora Brasiliensis, enumeratio plantarum in Brasilia hactenus detectarum: quas suis aliorumque botanicorum studiis descriptas et methodo naturali digestas partim icone illustratas. Vol. I.* Retrieved May 01, 2021, from https://www.biodiversitylibrary.org/page/309586

_____ (1794-1868). Silva Montium Serra dos Órgãos declivia obumbrans. Rio de Janeiro. *Flora Brasiliensis, enumeratio plantarum in Brasilia hactenus detectarum: quas suis aliorumque botanicorum studiis descriptas et methodo naturali digestas partim icone illustratas. Vol. I.* Rio de Janeiro. Retrieved May 01, 2021, from https://www.biodiversitylibrary.org/page/309606

_____ (1817-1820). *Viagem pelo Brasil – Spix e Martius.* Obtenido de https://www.oscarbressane.com/portfolio-item/revivendo-a-expedicao-de-spix-e-martius-excursoes/

_____ (1829). *Iter Brasiliense. Pisces icones.*

_____ (n.d.). Extração e Preparo dos Ovos de Tartaruga, no Rio Amazonas, Estado do Amazonas, Brasil (Ausgrabung und Zubereitung der Schildkroteneier, am Amazonenstrome). *Atlas zur Reise in Brasilien.* Retrieved December 11, 2020, from https://ribeiraopretoculturaljaf.blogspot.com/2019/08/extracao-e-preparo-dos-ovos-de.html

Massaud, M. (1999). *Pequeno dicionário de literatura brasileira* (5ta ed.). Brazil: Cultrix.

Matias, L. (2020). *Alismataceae.* (Jardim Botânico do Rio de Janeiro). Retrieved April 28, 2021, from Flora do Brasil 2020: http://reflora.jbrj.gov.br/reflora/floradobrasil/FB102842

_____ (2020). *Hydrocleys Rich.* (Jardim Botânico do Rio de Janeiro). Retrieved April 28, 2021, from Flora do Brasil 2020: http://reflora.jbrj.gov.br/reflora/floradobrasil/FB102842

Mattos dos Santos, J., & Rodriguez Salgado, A. A. (2010). Genese da Superfície Erosiva em Ambienbiente Semi-Árido - Milagres/Ba: Considerações Preliminares. *Revista de Geografia, especial VIII SINAGEO*(1). Retrieved April 27, 2021, from https://www.researchgate.net/publication/305282236_GENESE_DA_SUPERFICIE_EROSIVA_EM_AMBIENTE_SEMI-ARIDO_-_MILAGRESBA_CONSI DERACOES_PRELIMINARES

Mee, M. (1957). *Stanhopea graveolens.* Instituto de Botánica, Santa Caterina, Brazil. Retrieved January 26, 2021, from https://www.doaks.org/resources/online-exhibits/margaret-mee-portra its-of-plants/plant-portraits/18

_____ (1968). *Flowers of the Brazilian Forests.* London: Tyron Gallery.

_____ (1981). Heliconia adeliana. Lam. 20. *The Flowering Amazon, The Oppenheimer Kew Gardens Edition.* Oppenheimer Editions and Royal Botanic Gardens. Retrieved April 26, 2021, from https://www.audubonart.com/shop/product/okme-020-mee-pl-20-heliconia-adeliana-2930

Menezes, C., & Ab'Sáber, A. N. (2007). *O que é ser geógrafo: memórias profissionais de Aziz Nacib Ab'Saber.* Brazil: Editora Record.

Merian, M. S. (1702-03). Heliconia acuminata with Southern Armyworm Moth 1702-03. *Insect life of tropical south america with gorgeous butterflies flying around luxuriant flowering fruit or plants.* Royal Collection. Retrieved April 22, 2021, from https://www.rct.uk/collection/search#/39/collection/921211/heliconia-acuminata-with-southern-armyworm-moth

Miho Museum (2015). Nyūyōkā ga miserareta bi no sekai: Jon shī Uebā korekushon. *A New Yor-ker's View of the World: The John C.,* 54-55. Weber Collection.

Miller, J. (1804). *Canna indica. Illustatio systematis sexuales Linnaei.* Retrieved January 26, 2021, from https://www.nybg.org/poetic-botany/canna/

Montero, M. I. (2001). *Burle Marx: The Lyrical Landscape.* California: University of California Press.

Moritz Rugendas, J. G. (1827-1835). *Serra Ouro-Branco dans la province de Minas Geraes.* Obtained from https://www.brasilianaiconografica.art.br/obras/20017/serra-ouro-branco-dans-la-province-de-minas-geraes

Moritz Rugendas, J. G.-L. (1827-1835). Defrichement d'une forêt. *Voyage Pittoresque dans le Brésil.* Acervo da Pinacoteca do Estado de São Paulo, Brazil. Coleção Brasiliana. Retrieved December 11, 2021, from https://www.brasilianaiconografica.art.br/obras/19495/defrichement-dune-foret

Museu Casa Kubitschek (2018). *Conhecer e Reconhecer: Patrimônio Cultural.* Belo Horizonte: Fundação Municipal de Cultura.

Nascimento Jr, J., & Alencar, A. (2020). *Clusia in Flora do Brasil 2020.* (Jardim Botânico do Rio de Janeiro) Retrieved April 28, 2021, from http://reflora.jbrj.gov.br/reflora/floradobrasil/FB6830

Nervi, L. (1942). *A fürdő csarnokának kupolája.* Retrieved December 01, 2021, from https://epiteszforum.hu/a-logika-esztetikuma-40-eve-hunyt-el-pier-luigi-nervi

Nilsen, F. (n.d.). *Prometheus de José Clemente Orozco.* Retrieved January 25, 2021, from https://artsandculture.google.com/asset/_/8AHkK7oQDYy05w

Nogueira Neto, P. (1992). *Ecological Stations: A Saga of Ecology and Environmental Policy.* Brazil: Empresa das Artes.

O Globo (1973). *Fazenderos devastam as florestas com desfolhante usado no Vietnam.* Retrieved April 25, 2021, from https://acervo.oglobo.globo.com/consulta-ao-acervo/?navegacaoPorData=197019731118

Oliveira, A. R. (2014, February). Ordem e representação. Paisagens de Brasília. *Vitruvius* (166.05). Retrieved September 23, 2021, from https://vitruvius.com.br/revistas/read/arquitextos/14.165/5067

Ono, I. (2019, October 21). Palmeiras plantadas por Burle Marx ha meio século finalmente dão flores no Rio. *Bom dia RJ.* Rio de Janeiro.

Ormindo, P. (2018). Natureza, ciência e arte na viagem pelo Brasil de Spix e Martius. 1817-1820. En A. Hetzer, & P. Ormindo, *Natureza, ciência e arte na viagem pelo Brasil de Spix e Martius. 1817-1820* (pp. 11-12). Rio de Janeiro: Jakobson Estúdio.

358 BIBLIOGRAPHY

Oxford University (1985 - 2021). *Oxford University Herbaria.* (Department of Plant Sciences, University of Oxford) Retrieved May 04, 2021, from https://herbaria.plants.ox.ac.uk/bol/oxford/Herbaria

Orto Botánico Universitá di Padova (2014). The University of Padua Botanical Garden. Retrieved April 30, 2021, from https://www.ortobotanicopd.it/en/lorto-botanico-di-padova

Pabst, G. F. (1967). *Alexandre (sic) Curt Brade. Taxon.* (Vol. 16).

Padilla, F., & Pugnaire, F. (2006). The role of nurse plants in the restoration of degraded environments. *Frontiers in Ecology and the Environment,* 4(4), pp. 196-202. Retrieved January 26, 2021, from http://www.seb-ecologia.org.br/revistas/indexar/anais/2009/resumos_ixceb/106.pdf

Pellegrini, M. (2020). *Nymphaea L.* (Jardim Botânico do Rio de Janeiro) Retrieved April 28, 2021, from Flora do Brasil 2020: http://reflora.jbrj.gov.br/reflora/floradobrasil/FB10936

Pereira, S. G. (2008). A Escola Real de Ciência, Artes e Ofícios e a Academia Imperial de Belas Artes do Rio de Janeiro. In. Ipanema, Rogéria Moreira. D. João e a cidade do Rio de Janeiro. Rio de Janeiro. In R. M. Ipanema, *D. João e a cidade do Rio de Janeiro* (pp. 383-370). Rio de Janeiro: Instituto Histórico e Geográfico do Rio de Janeiro.

Perioto, N. W., Lara, R. I., & Macedo, A. C. (2020, October 28). Gasteruptiidae (Hymenoptera, Evanioidea) of three savannah phytophysiognomies of the Estação Ecológica do Jataí, in southeastern Brazil, under three sampling methods and a new record for Gasteruption helenae Macedo, 2011. *Anais da Academia Brasileira de Ciências,* 92(2). doi: https://doi.org/10.1590/0001-3765202020181073

Perri, A., & Cavalheri, P. (2018). *João Semir morre aos 81 anos de idade.* Unicamp. Retrieved April 25, 2021, from https://www.unicamp.br/unicamp/noticias/2018/11/09/joao-semir-morre-aos-81-anos-de-idade

Persiani, A. (2012). *Albert Löfgren: resgate, sistematização e atualidade do pensamento de um pioneiro nos campos da climatologia, fitogeografia e conservação da natureza no Brasil. Master's Dissertation.* São Paulo: Universidade de São Paulo. Facultade de filosofia, letras e ciências humanas. Departamento de geografia. Retrieved May 04, 2021, from https://teses.usp.br/teses/disponiveis/8/8135/tde-14032013-120725/publico/2012_AdrianaPersiani.pdf

Peterson, A. P. (November 29). *Furnarius rufus (Gmelin, 1788).* (ITIS: The Integrated Taxonomic Information System) Retrieved May 25, 2020, from ITIS: https://www.itis.gov/servlet/SingleRpt/SingleRpt?search_topic=TSN&search_value=560127

_____ **(November 29, 2006).** *Procnias nudicollis (Vieillot, 1817).* Retrieved April 28, 2021, from ITIS: The Integrated Taxonomic Information System: https://www.itis.gov/servlet/SingleRpt/SingleRpt?search_topic=TSN&search_value=562473

Peterson, A. P., & Banks, R. C. (2011, September 22). *Ardea Linnaeus, 1758.* (ITIS: The Integrated Taxonomic Information System). Retrieved May 26, 2020, from https://www.itis.gov

Phaf-Rheinberge, I. L. (2011, June). Precisão do olhar e canibalismo: Georg Marcgrave e a história do Atlântico Sul,. *Projeto História. Viagens, Viajantes e Deslocamentos*(42), pp. 233-250. Retrieved January 29, 2021, from https://revistas.pucsp.br/index.php/revph/article/viewFile/7989/5862

Picton, B. (2013). *Actinothoe sphyrodeta.* iNaturalist United Kingdom. Retrieved April 23, 2021, de https://www.inaturalist.org/photos/6881557

Pignal M., R.-N. S. (2013). *Saint-Hilaire virtual herbarium, a new upgradeable tool to study Brazilian botany.* Adansonia, sér. 3, 35 (1): 7-18. doi:http://dx.doi.org/10.5252/a2013n1a1

Pinto Palva, M. (1993). Os naturalistas e o Ceará> II - George Gardner (1812-1849). *Revista do Instituto do Ceará,* pp. 77-95. Retrieved May 04, 2021, from https://www.institutodoceara.org.br/revista/Rev-apresentaca/RevPorAno/1993/1993-OsNaturalistaseoCearaIIGeorgeGardner-1812-1849.pdf

PNUD (2020). *Fauna.* (COPPETEC-UFRJ, Ed.) Retrieved June 26, 2021, from Catálogo Taxonômico da Fauna do Brasil (CTFB): http://fauna.jbrj.gov.br/fauna/listaBrasil/ConsultaPublicaUC/ResultadoDaConsultaNovaConsulta.do

Poiesis (n.d.). Morada do coração perdido. Retrieved March 31, 2021, from http://casamariodeandrade.org.br/morada-coracao-perdido/

Poitou, R. (2013). *Towers of Chartres Cathedral; Flamboyant Gothic on left, early Gothic on the right.* Retrieved March 31, 2021, from https://commons.wikimedia.org/wiki/File:Facade_cathedral.jpg#/media/File:Facade_cathedral.jpg

Portal Amazonia (2020, September 21). *Buriti.* Retrieved April 28, 2021, from https://portalamazonia.com/amazonia-az/letra-b/buriti

_____ **(2020, September 21).** *Inajá.* Retrieved April 28, 2021, from https://portalamazonia.com/amazonia-az/letra-i/inaja

_____ **(2020, September 23).** *Pupunha.* Retrieved April 28, 2021, from https://portalamazonia.com/amazonia-az/letra-p/pupunha

_____ **(2021, April 27).** *Tucumã.* Retrieved April 28, 2021, from https://portalamazonia.com/amazonia/amazonia-de-a-a-z-saiba-tudo-sobre-o-tucuma-a-fruta-que-e-a-cara-da-regiao

Portal do Museu Villa-Lobos (n.d.). *Acervo do Museu Villa-Lobos.* Retrieved March 31, 2021, from Acervo do Museu Villa-Lobos

Post, F. (S. XVII). *Recife visto desde la isla de Santo Antônio.* Retrieved January 29, 2021, from https://upload.wikimedia.org/wikipedia/commons/4/41/Recife_sto_antonio

Prefeitura Belo Horizonte (2021, April). *Parque Municipal das Mangabeiras.* Retrieved April 13, 2021, from https://prefeitura.pbh.gov.br/fundacao-de-parques-e-zoobotanica/informacoes/parques/parque-das-mangabeiras

Prefeitura de Rio de Janeiro (2016, November 07). *Decreto Rio No 42557. Declara Patrimônio Cultural de Natureza Imaterial a Umbanda e cria o cadastro dos terreiros de umbanda.* Rio de Janeiro. Retrieved March 31, 2021, from http://www.rio.rj.gov.br/dlstatic/10112/4368015/4176955/40DECRETO42557CadastrodosTerreirosdeUmbanda08112016.pdf

Presidência da Republica (1967). *Código de Caça - Lei ° 5197/67 | Lei N° 5.197, january 03, 1967.* Retrieved August 11, 2020, from https://presrepublica.jusbrasil.com.br/legislacao/91706/codigo-de-caca-lei-5197-67

Rae, H. (1910). *Hylas and the Water Nymphs.* London Royal Academy. Retrieved May 01, 2021, from https://commons.wikimedia.org/wiki/File:Rae_-_Water_Nymphs_(color).png#/media/File:Hylas_and_the_Water_Nymphs.jpg

Real Academia Española (2020, August 11). *Conservacionismo.* Retrieved May 02, 2020, from Diccionario panhispánico del español jurídico: https://dej.rae.es/lema/conservacionismo

Reflora. Jardím Botânico do Rio de Janeiro (2020, February 29). *Herbário Virtual.* Obtained from http://reflora.jbrj.gov.br/reflora/herbarioVirtual/

_____ **(2020).** *Mandevilla.* (Jardim Botânico do Rio de Janeiro) Retrieved April 28, 2021, from Mandevilla: http://reflora.jbrj.gov.br/reflora/floradobrasil/FB4652

_____ **(2020).** *Flora do Brasil 2020.* Retrieved May 25, 2020, from Flora do Brasil 2020: http://reflora.jbrj.gov.br/listaBrasil/ConsultaPublicaUC/ResultadoDaConsultaNovaConsulta.do#CondicaoTaxonCP

_____ **(2020).** *Lychnophora.* (J. B. Janeiro, Editor) Retrieved May 25, 2020, from Flora do Brasil 2020: http://reflora.jbrj.gov.br/reflora/floradobrasil/FB16171

Rego, T. (2018). Bombeiros controlam incêndio no Museu Nacional, mas dano 'é irreparável' (A. Brasil, Ed.) *Poder 360.* Retrieved January 29, 2021, from https://www.poder360.com.br/brasil/bombeiros-controlam-incendio-no-museu-nacional-mas-dano-e-irreparavel/

Reitz, C. R. (1972, June). Museu Botanico Kuhlmann. *Blumenau em cadernos,* Tomo XIII(6), p. 103. Retrieved April 25, 2021, from http://hemeroteca.ciasc.sc.gov.br/blumenau%20em%20cadernos/1972/BLU1972006.pdf

Resende Porto, D. (2005). *O Barreiro de Araxá. Proyectos para una estancia hidromineral en Minas Gerais. Master's Dissertation.* São Carlos: Universidade de São Paulo.

Ribeiro da Silva Bevilacqua, J. (2015). Beyond the revealed unconscious: Agnaldo Manoel dos Santos as the protagonist of his own art. *Critical Interventions. Journal of African Art History and Visual Culture,* 9(2), pp. 107-122.

Ribeiro, R., Marquet, N., & Loiola, M. (2020). *Combretaceae in Flora do Brasil 2020.* Retrieved September 06, 2021, from Jardim Botânico do Rio de Janeiro: http://reflora.jbrj.gov.br/reflora/floradobrasil/FB22511

Rizzo, G. G. (1992). *Roberto Burle Marx: il giardino del Novecento.* Italy: Cantini.

_____ **(2009).** *Il giardino privato di Roberto Burle Marx: il sítio: sessant'anni dalla fondazione cent'anni dalla nascita di Roberto Burle Marx.* Italy: Gangemi.

Romeiro Chuva, M. R. (2017, September-December). Parque do Flamengo: projetar a cidade, desenhando patrimônio. *Estudos de cultura material/dossiê, An. mus. paul,* 25(3). doi:https://doi.org/10.1590/1982-02672017v25n0305

Roskov Y., B. F. (2021). *Bauhinia blakeana Dunn.* (Catalogue of Life, *et al.* (2021). Species 2000 & ITIS Catalogue of Life, 2021). Retrieved April 28, 2021, from ILDIS: World Database of Legumes (May 12, 2014): https://www.catalogueoflife.org/data/taxon/L3TS

Rubens, P. P., & Brueghel The Elder, J. (1615). *El huerto del Edén con la caída del hombre.* Geheugen can Nederland. Retrieved January 28, 2021, from www.geheugenvannederland.nl

Saint-Hilaire, A. (1847). *Voyage aux Sources du Rio S. Francisco.* Paris: Arthus Bertrand, Librarie - Éditeur.

_____ (1887). *Mapa Voyage à Rio-Grande do Sul (Brasil).* Retrieved April 28, 2021, from https://books.openedition.org/mnhn/docanne xe/image/3201/img-1.jpg

Sanctuaria.art (n.d.). *Histórias, fotografías e significados das igrejas mais bonitas do Brasil.* Retrieved January 29, 2021, from Igreja do Divino Espiritu Santo - Recife, Pernambuco: https://sanctuaria.art/2016/05/06/igreja-do-divino-espirito-santo-recife-pernambuco/

Santana, R. M. (2006, December). *O movimento Modernista Verde,* de Cataguases – MG. Thesis, 10, pp. 172-177.

Santos Silva, G. (2018). *O botânico Henrique Lahmeyer de Mello Barreto e sua contribuição para o conhecimento da flora de Minas Gerais. Master's Dissertation.* (U. F. Gerais, Ed.) Retrieved April 25, 2021, from http://hdl.handle.net/1843/35314

Seavitt Nordenson, C. (2018). *Depositions: Roberto Burle Marx and Public Landscapes Under Dictatorships.* Estados Unidos: University of Texas Press.

Senado Federal (1965). Lei N. 4.771, september 15, 1965. Retrieved May 02, 2021, from https://legis.senado.leg.br/norma/546624/publicacao/15635836

Schnessel, S. (2019). Irak celebra el nombramiento de Babilonia como Patrimonio de la Humanidad por la UNESCO. Retrieved April 30, 2021, from Enlace Judío: https://www.enlacejudio.com/2019/07/06/irak-nombramiento--babilonia-patrimonio-humanidad-unesco/

Silva, G. S. (2018). *O botânico Henrique Lahmeyer de Mello Barreto e sua contribuição para o conhecimento da flora de Minas Gerais [manuscript] (Master degree in Vegetal Biology).* Belo Horizonte: Universidade Federal de Minas Gerais. Mestrado em Biologia Vegetal.

Smith, K. G. (1987). Darwin's insects: Charles Darwin's entomological notes, with an introduction and comments by Kenneth G. V. Smith. (e. 2. John van Wyhe, Ed.) *Bulletin of the British Museum (Natural History) Historical Series,* 14(1), pp. 1-143. Retrieved December 02, 2020, from http://darwin-online.uk/content/frameset?pageseq=94&itemID=F1830&viewtype=side

Sousa, D. (2020). *Eichhornia Kunth.* Retrieved April 28, 2021, from Flora do Brasil 2020: http://reflora.jbrj.gov.br/reflora/floradobrasil/FB13740

_____ (2020). *Pontederiaceae.* Retrieved April 28, 2021, from Flora do Brasil 2020: http://reflora.jbrj.gov.br/reflora/floradobrasil/FB13740

Špindler, P. (2012). *Templo de Kalasasaya a socha Monolito Ponce - Tiwanaku.* Retrieved March 31, 2021, from https://es.wikipedia.org/wiki/Tiahuanaco#/media/Archivo:Templo_de_Kalasasaya_a_socha_Monolito_Ponce_-_Tiwanaku_-_panoramio_(1).jpg

Tabacow, J. (1987). Prefácio. En R. Burle Marx, & Tabacow, J. *Arte e Paisagem, Conferências escolhidas* (pp. 7-9). São Paulo: Livraria Nobel S.A.

Tábora, F. (2007). *Dos parques, un equipo: Parque del Este, Caracas, Venezuela y Aterro do Flamengo, Río de Janeiro, Brasil.* Caracas: Embajada de Brasil en Venezuela, Norberto Odebrecht Constructora S.A.

Teixeira, L. (2017). *Cyrtopodium flavum.* iNaturalist, Arraial do Cabo, Brazil. Retrieved April 01, 2021, from https://www.inaturalist.org/photos/45962538

The Cornell Lab of Ornithology (2021). *Birds of the World.* Retrieved April 30, 2021, from https://birdsoftheworld.org/bow/home

Tissiani, A. S.-d.-M.-J. (2017). Dung beetles of Brazilian pastures and key to genera identification (Coleoptera: Scarabaeidae). *Pesquisa Agropecuária Brasileira,* 52(6), pp. 401-418. doi: https://doi.org/10.1590/S0100-204X2017000600004

Toledo Rizzini, C., & de Mattos Filho, A. (1984). Nota sobre a floração e frutificação de Corypha umbraculifera L. *Rodriguésia.*

Torres, C. (2014). *Grand Hotel - Caiaque.* Retrieved February 09, 2021, from http://www.colecionandoimas.com.br/wp-content/uploads/2014/10/grand_hotel_caiaque.jpg

Urbina, C., & Villalobos H., M. A. (2014). Botanical Garden, Jardin botanique, système paysager et paysage urban durable. Réflexion à partir du jardin botanique de Roberto Burle Marx à Maracaibo (Venezuela). In C. Chomarat-Ruiz, *L'utopie d'une ville sustenable* (pp. 88-111). Paris: Editopics.

University of Zurich (n.d.). Paisagens americanas. Land Art, arte ambiental e estéticas territoriais na América Latina e nos Estados Unidos. *Estudios Latinoamericanos. Estudios Luso-Brasileiros.* Retrieved February 08, 2021, from https://files.cercomp.ufg.br/weby/up/459/o/Jens_Andermann_slide1.pdf

Valladares, C. d. (1974). *Roberto Burle Marx.* São Paulo: MAM.

Vargas, J. (Direction) (2013). *Coleccionador. Serie documental Expedições Burle Marx* [Film].

Vaz de Caminha, P. (1500). *A carta de Pero Vaz de Caminha. Ministerio da Cultura. Fundação Biblioteca Nacional.* Retrieved May 01, 2021, from http://objdigital.bn.br/Acervo_Digital/Livros_eletronicos/carta.pdf

Vecelli, T. (1556-1559). *Diana y Callisto.* National Gallery, London. Retrieved January 29, 2021, from https://www.nationalgallery.org.uk/paintings/titian-diana-and-callisto

Venezuela tuya (2017-2021). *Venezuela tuya.* Retrieved March 02, 2021, from https://www.venezuelatuya.com/caracas/parquedeleste.htm

Vieira de Carvalho, R. (2017). *Buritizal.* "Jalapão" State Park, Tocantins, Brasil. Retrieved April 01, 2021, from https://www.flickr.com/photos/149673510@N03/34121218305/in/photostream

Villalobos H., M. A. (2015). *El jardín botánico de Roberto Burle Marx en Maracaibo como proceso creativo hacia un paisaje urbano Botánico.* Paris: Universite Agroparis-Tech, Ecole Doctorale ABIES, Laboratory of Research ENSP-Versailles.

Werneck, F. (2018). *Illegal logging on Pirititi indigenous amazon lands with a repository of round logs.* IBAMA, Amazonas. Retrieved April 27, 2021, from https://www.flickr.com/photos/hinkelstone/48610743566/in/photostream/

Wolf, T. (2017). *Cologne Cathedral towers (begun 13th century, completed 20th century).* Retrieved March 31, 2021, from https://commons.wikimedia.org/wiki/File:Kölner_Dom_von_Osten.jpg

Wright, S. (1992). *VillaLobos.* Oxford/New York, Venezuela: Oxford University Press.

WWF (n.d.). *Cerrado.* Retrieved February 18, 2021, from https://www.wwf.org.br/natureza_brasileira/questoes_ambientais/biomas/bioma_cerrado/

_____ (n.d.). *Guará: o grande lobo do cerrado.* Retrieved February 18, 2021, from https://www.wwf.org.br/natureza_brasileira/especiais/biodiversidade/especie_do_mes/dezembro_lobo_guara/

Intangible Heritage was designed and developed in Venezuela, Brazil, Argentina, Mexico, France, Italy, Spain, Germany, and the United States. Printing was finished on the Asia Pacific Offset presses, in China, in February 2023. The papers used for the inside pages are 128 g Kinmari Matt DULL EX and 70 g Enso Classic 2.0. The fonts used are from the Interstate typeface family designed by Tobias Frere-Jones and Fira Sans designed by the German studio Carrois Apostrophe. The print run is 1,000 copies.